GREED AND GLORY

THE RISE AND FALL OF DOC GOODEN, LAWRENCE TAYLOR, ED KOCH, RUDY GIULIANI, DONALD TRUMP, AND THE MAFIA IN 1980s NEW YORK

SEAN DEVENEY

Skyhorse Publishing

Skyhorse Publishing books may be purchased in bulk at special discounts for sales promotion, corporate gifts, fund-raising, or educational purposes. Special editions can also be created to specifications. For details, contact the Special Sales Department, Skyhorse Publishing, 307 West 36th Street, 11th Floor, New York, NY 10018 or info@skyhorsepublishing.com.

Skyhorse® and Skyhorse Publishing® is are registered trademarks of Skyhorse Publishing, Inc.®, a Delaware corporation.

Visit our website at www.skyhorsepublishing.com.

10 9 8 7 6 5 4 3 2 1

Library of Congress Cataloging-in-Publication Data is available on file.

Cover design by Tom Lau
Cover photos courtesy of Associated Press
All photos in insert courtesy of Associated Press
Print ISBN: 978-1-5107-3063-2
Ebook ISBN: 978-1-5107-3064-9

Printed in the United States of America

CONTENTS

Preface

IN 2012, A STUDY BY Northwestern Medicine appeared to support a neurological theory about the inconsistencies of memory. The authors of the study compared the brain's ability to remember specific events to the playing of a game of telephone, where one participant whispers a sentence to the next participant until, by the time the game is over, the sentence becomes twisted and unrecognizable. Your memories, the theory went, undergo some twist each time they are recalled, and the twists add up until you remember something falsely altogether. For example, a 2003 study showed that 73 percent of 569 college students polled about 9/11 said they remembered watching the first plane fly into the north tower of the World Trade Center on the day itself, almost as it happened. But that footage did not reach news desks until the following day. Only two years after the tragedy, their brains had reordered things, tricked them into remembering something that hadn't happened.

For any one of us, an individual memory of an event changes over time in the same way. Each time the brain recalls the memory, some detail, minuscule perhaps, is omitted or added or changed. When the memory comes back again, the change is still there, only this time, some additional detail may be altered, too, which is then included in the next recollection of the memory. The more the human brain returns to a memory, then, the more alterations it makes and the less accurate it becomes as the modifications are absorbed. Just as the sentence gets more mangled as the number of participants in the game of telephone increases, the more times the human brain returns to a specific memory, the more mangled that memory gets over time. The consequence of this can be jarring: The more you remember something, the more you are forgetting it.

This was a useful lesson to keep in mind as I was researching and conducting interviews into this book, and struck me especially when considering the varying accounts of the 1986 World Series, won by the Mets over the Red Sox, put out by members of the losing side over the years. I spent much of my free time with three-decades-old periodicals and books, trying to dig into the contemporaneous documentation of the era (with help from the patience of my partner, Carrie Russell, and our newborn daughter, Maisie) to better understand what the mood was as major events were unfolding. That sort of dry and straightforward documentation, of course, serves as the framework of any reconstruction of a particular place and time—in this case, New York in the middle of the decade, when the city and the 1980s were at their height. It is through that methodical research that the foundation of the story emerges, without the vagaries of memories that have been yellowed and distorted by the passage of years.

But what stands out from the research into this project is the details, the small things that are indelibly etched into the memories—neurology be damned—of people who lived and worked in New York, and were at the center of the events described here. Journalist Margot Roosevelt, then known as Margot Hornblower and covering New York for the Washington Post, had trouble recalling some of the specific stories she'd written at the time. But she remembered vividly some details, memories she'd not tapped into in a long time, like when powerful city lawyer Roy Cohn answered the door to his office townhouse at Saxe, Bacon and Bolan wearing nothing but a thin blue robe, obviously naked underneath, or the snide and contemptuous letter she'd received from Ed Koch days after having interviewed the mayor in 1987. I sat across a conference table from Michael Chertoff, who was a thirty-two-year-old assistant US attorney in Rudy Giuliani's Southern District of New

York office before, twenty years later, becoming the Secretary of the Department of Homeland Security. In 1986, Chertoff had conducted the biggest Mafia-busting prosecution in the nation's history, just the beginning of an illustrious career. But what stood out from our conversation was the way his face broke into a smile when he remembered his mentors, US Circuit Court judge Murray Gurfein and prosecutor Barbara Jordan, and the excitement he still conjured up when he told me the story of the New York police finding a palm print in a car—at his suggestion—that helped lock in his prosecution of the murder of Carmine Galante.

Giants star linebacker Harry Carson, who helped the team to its first championship of the modern era, has a photo to solidify one of his most vivid memories, of him at midfield at the Rose Bowl in Pasadena, alone for the coin toss and standing across from five Broncos captains just ahead of Super Bowl XXI. But again, it's the little things he remembers that stand out to the interviewer, like his affinity for cheap-steak chain restaurant Beefsteak Charlie's, where he liked to hang out while teammates frequented bars and clubs. Likewise, former Brooklyn prosecutor Ed McDonald has been involved in some of the most high-profile cases around New York's underworld—he handled Mafia informant and *Goodfellas* subject Henry Hill—but his low-voiced impersonation of foul-mouthed former Brooklyn Democratic boss Meade Esposito, whom he convicted in 1987, is uncanny and funny, the kind of detail that can't be culled from magazines or newspapers. Neurologists are surely right to say memories can be frayed with time and use, and that some element of truth is stripped away as memories are revisited. But for an interviewer and researcher, there is nothing quite as satisfying as one of those intensely remembered details, one kernel of truth that emerges from the rubble and sheds a different light on the narrative, one bit of proof that memory does matter.

. . . . .

From a distance of decades, what we think of as the high-living 1980s encapsulates only about five years or so, and centers on one place: New

York City. The economic boom that followed the fiscal crisis of the mid-1970s, when the city had to be rescued from bankruptcy, did not kick in until late 1982, after the stock market dove to a low of 776 points and new federal orders on deregulation under president Ronald Reagan took hold. That boom can be traced alongside the success of the market, to a high of 2,746 in August 1987 and ultimately, to its crash two months later, when the entire world economy deflated and the Dow Jones average lost a record 22.6 percent. In that brief time, fortunes were amassed by corporate raiders, money pumped through the financial sector of New York and propped up the city coffers, an entire class of *nouveau riche* New Yorkers was minted and celebrated, and greed (heretofore the third on the list of the seven deadly sins) was extolled as a virtue—or, as Ivan Boesky said in a speech, "greed is all right."

This story is told against that backdrop, but as the focus tightens, the picture changes. The glimmering rebuilt city was infested with rot, and by the end of the decade, that rot crippled New York. Two of the city icons of the 1980s—Donald Trump, the nation's first celebrity real estate developer, and Ed Koch, the most famous mayor in the country at the time—were headed for disgrace, Koch done in by the greed-driven scandals of his associates, Trump nearly bankrupted by his own delusion, pathological lying, and greed. The rings of organized crime that dominated the city and profited off its people for years were undone by their own greed, especially by one violent and overambitious Queens-based capo named John Gotti. And as those at the top of the 1980s New York boom feted themselves with lavish parties and magazine spreads, the rest of the city foundered, beset by crises of poverty, racial division, the rise of addiction to crack cocaine and the crime that went with it, the rapid and mostly ignored spread of AIDS and the spike in homelessness that seemed to highlight the heartlessness of a nation and city that had put greed on such a pedestal.

Fittingly, New York was buoyed through its political scandals and social crises by two championship-winning teams that rank among the all-time greats in their respective sports, but were anchored by inherently flawed star players. The 1986 Mets were a juggernaut of a team that managed to prevail through the most exciting postseason in baseball history, even as their ace pitcher, Dwight Gooden, battled a cocaine addiction that would ultimately doom a career that had shaped up to be among the greatest ever. The Giants of the same year were the greatest team in franchise history, going 14–2 and steamrolling through the postseason with an average margin of victory of 27 points. But their best player, Lawrence Taylor, had already been to drug rehab the previous offseason, and would be suspended by the league on drug violations in 1988. Taylor has spent much of his post-playing career in substance-related legal trouble.

New York at the height of the 1980s was driven by a motley cast of characters, from shady dealers like Cohn and his protégé Trump, to fallen sports stars Taylor and Gooden, to crusading prosecutor Rudy Giuliani and his rival lawyer Tom Puccio, to savvy coaches Bill Parcells and Davey Johnson. There are brazen Mafia hits, a fatal and tragic racial attack, a headline-grabbing political suicide, a fallen Miss America, a mayor's rumored homosexual lover, courtroom drama, a shameless municipal bribery scheme, a failed football league, and drugs, lots of drugs. It was the era of greed in Wall Street boardrooms and swank Midtown restaurants, and it was an era of glory on the fields for the Mets and Giants. But it was, too, an era of downfall.

PART I

In the Dark

1

DONALD TRUMP NEEDED A TAX break. In 1981 he was in the process of building his second major New York City project, the Trump Tower on Fifth Avenue. As part of putting up the new skyscraper, he had applied to the city for an abatement of $20 million, which was intended to be a gift from the taxpayers given to developers for their willingness to build middle- or lower-class housing in areas defined as "underutilized." But anyone who had ever strolled New York's streets over the past five or six decades knew Fifth Avenue was hardly an underutilized area. It was as well-trafficked and upscale a slab of real estate as you could find anywhere in the country, let alone New York. On that basis, Mayor Ed Koch had instructed his administration to turn down Trump's abatement application. Enraged, Trump called Koch's housing commissioner, Tony Gliedman, and told him, "I am a very rich and powerful person in this town and there is a reason I got that way. I will never forget what you did." When Trump called Koch to complain about Gliedman's decision, Koch told him, "There is nothing I can do for you."

Trump did what he best knew how to do: He sued. By his side was shark-lawyer Roy Cohn, who had made his reputation decades earlier as the top aide to Red-baiting Senator Joseph McCarthy but had since settled into a multitude of city roles: New York gadabout, manipulator of a wide swath of media sources, political kingmaker, and shoulder-rubber with the well known and well to do ranging from publisher Si Newhouse and conservative icon William F. Buckley to Barbara Walters and Norman Mailer. But he was still, mostly, a lawyer, and Trump had grown to appreciate the value of having a guy who could grease city wheels like Cohn on his side. While Cohn was the big name, his law partner at the firm of Saxe, Bacon and Bolan was Bronx Democratic leader Stanley Friedman, and Friedman had the connections—as a boss of a borough political machine, he was heavily involved in the naming of judges across the city—that facilitated Cohn's manipulations. Friedman found out Trump's abatement case would start out in what was called Special Term 1 with Judge Frank Blangiardo, a twenty-two-year veteran of the bench who was an old hand at New York's political gamesmanship. (Blangiardo would later be reprimanded for slapping the hand of a female attorney and saying, "I like to hit girls because they are soft.") This was good news for Cohn, Friedman, and their client. Blangiardo was pliable. He knew Friedman's power. "You didn't have to bribe Blangiardo," *New York Post* court reporter Hal Davis said. "He was a hack. He was more than happy to do the bidding of the political bosses. When Cohn and Friedman saw that Blangiardo was getting the case, it was tailor-made for them."

That did not mean Friedman or Cohn would be sitting before Blangiardo. They were the pullers of strings in the city, but they were not big on actual courtroom litigation. Cohn was not known to proffer eloquent legal arguments—you hired him because he was a blunt object with which to bludgeon your opponent. Trump had a real estate lawyer who was to present the case, and during the opening session of the case, she handed Blangiardo two folders for consideration. One contained the usual legal documents. Inside the other was a statement from Friedman, at the bottom of which were two words and a signature that registered immediately with Blangiardo: "No adjournment. —Stanley Friedman." When the lawyer for the city told Blangiardo she would need an adjournment to have time to put together a response to the filing, Blangiardo's initial response was to parrot Friedman's note:

"No adjournment." He eventually acquiesced and granted a three-week adjournment, but only with the caveat that, in three weeks, he would be keeping the case for himself, a highly unusual step considering he was not scheduled to be in session at that time. Despite the adjournment, the message from Friedman had been received—Trump was to get his abatement—and Blangiardo obliged. On July 21, the judge ruled in Trump's favor. That was the power Friedman had, pulling strings with judges. Cohn's power was a little different, but was evident the next day. Trump filed an absurd, $138 million lawsuit against the city and Tony Gliedman. Trump had no chance of winning, and the lawsuit was quickly tossed. But Cohn got the suit in all the papers, and in addition to Blangiardo's abatement, he earned Trump, the hero builder and victim of an unjust city bureaucracy by Cohn's account, a day of free PR.

This was not the first time the trio of Cohn, Friedman, and Trump had worked together to bilk New York taxpayers out of tens of millions of dollars for Trump's benefit. As detailed by *Village Voice* writer Wayne Barrett, Cohn had taken on Friedman as a partner in his firm after Friedman's tenure as former mayor Abe Beame's deputy was up in 1977, and as one of his final acts in Beame's office, Friedman pushed through spools of bureaucratic red tape to secure another tax abatement for Trump, this one for $160 million and covering his development of the Grand Hyatt at Grand Central Station. Once, at a lunch at 21 with a journalist, Friedman admitted, "Roy could fix anyone in the city. He's a genius." To which Trump added, "He's a lousy lawyer, but he's a genius."

. . . . .

It was August 1980, and Ed Koch was conceding. The mayor, having engaged Queens borough president Donald Manes in a wager over who could lose five pounds in the space of a week, had to acknowledge that Manes had gotten the better of him, though Koch, typically, would not go without getting the last word. He bore a significant paunch and weighed in at about 200 pounds, while Manes was much heftier, around 220 pounds or more. Thus, Koch reasoned, Manes's five pounds came off easier. "Tubby wins because he had more to lose," Koch said. "Dinner in Queens is being planned."

The smiling wager masked a brewing squabble between Manes and Koch, two of the city's most powerful men. In just a little more than a week, New York City would be hosting the Democratic National Convention, and the party was being splintered by dissatisfaction with the incumbent, President Jimmy Carter, who was beating back calls for an open convention and an insurrection led by liberal Massachusetts senator Ted Kennedy. Carter had been forced to fight off primary challenges from Kennedy, who had won in New York and California. For those officials who controlled the levers of party government at the local level, this was a big problem. It was their duty to hold the party together and pull their voters into line with the mainstream, and Carter was the mainstream. In New York, that challenge was made even more difficult by the defection of Governor Hugh Carey, who was on his way out of office and had little to lose. He backed the Kennedy open-convention camp. For an operative like Manes, keeping his people in line behind Carter—with whom Manes would walk, arm in arm, down Queens Boulevard in an attempt to drum up the borough's Jewish vote—was imperative. Because he held a dual role, as both county leader of the party and Queens borough president, Manes was among the most powerful local politicians in the nation. He wielded an inordinate influence in doling out city jobs in Queens, from judicial appointments to summer work for kids. He would be paying attention to those who stuck with Carter and those who bolted for Kennedy. "The smart ones," Manes said, "know there is a tomorrow."

Stanley Friedman was hard at work, too, on Carter's behalf in the Bronx. He was not borough president like Manes, but as the Democratic boss in the Bronx, he controlled the borough president. Democrats had a stranglehold on New York City politics, steeped in patronage and quid pro quo deal-making, that had kept the city firmly in the column for the Ds for most of the century—only twice since 1917 had New York elected Republican mayors, and the most recent one, John Lindsay, was a liberal who switched parties and joined the Democrats in his second term. Friedman was very much a creature of this patronage system. He had never run for office, never had to face the electorate, but he had an outsize influence on the lives of that electorate nonetheless. He carried himself like a guy who need not worry about how he appeared to voters, a fast talker who wore a goatee that recalled Mephistopheles, dressed in designer suits with silk pocket squares, and had an ever-present, high-grade, unlit Te Amo Toro cigar dangling from his mouth. Friedman cut the figure of a young Mafia capo more than a political lifer. His partnership with Roy Cohn amplified his appearance of power. "He's got the title, he controls judgeships, but that's about it," one Democratic legislator said. "Mainly he is, however, a very bright and strong and tenacious personality, and that together with the illusion of power sometimes creates a power base all of its own."

In Brooklyn, Meade Esposito was asked about possibly joining Hugh Carey's revolt against Carter and backing an open convention in New York. "No way," Esposito said. "I'm standing fast." That was little surprise, because Esposito was the grizzled old head among county leaders. He had been running the Democrats in Brooklyn for years. Where Manes carried an air of political ambition and Friedman was a city slickster, Esposito had a certain unperturbed wisdom, a face that was all olive-toned jowls, a voice like eighty-grit sandpaper and a head adorned with waves of gray hair. He had no pretense toward power—he simply *had* power. He was described by a cohort as "a Damon Runyon capitalist . . . the last of the great old-timers," and "all-powerful, not only in Brooklyn, the city, but the state." Esposito acted the part, too. He would set up most days at a table near a window at Foffe, an Italian restaurant on Montague Street in Brooklyn, and would never get through a meal without being approached by a succession of judges who owed their benches to his benevolence. A Brooklyn prosecutor recalled seeing Esposito at Foffe once, and was shocked by the parade of judges approaching him. "It was like they had to go pay their respects," he said. When Carter was running for president in 1976, he made a stop to meet with Esposito, and in the early hours after his victory on election night (knowing how important the forty-one electoral votes from New York had been) Carter called Esposito personally to thank him. His long-game political philosophy was summed up by a parable he liked to tell about a papa bull and his son on a hill watching cows in a meadow below. The son tells the papa bull, "Let's run down there and screw a cow!" But, as Esposito told it, the more patient papa responded, "No, son, let's *walk* down there and screw 'em all."

For Carter, having the backing of county bosses Manes, Friedman, and Esposito meant he would almost certainly win New York City in a primary. Koch, though, was no fan of Carter. He had been an early endorser of the president, but the move was purely political, and even while he was backing Carter, Koch had developed a rapport with Republican challenger Ronald Reagan and said publicly as far back as April that he thought Reagan would win the state. The Koch-Carter disdain was mutual. As former Carter speechwriter Hendrik Hertzberg noted, "For Carter, Koch was a royal pain in the ass, the kind of friend that makes enemies superfluous." Ostensibly, the source of the friction was Koch's staunch pro-Israel stance, and his feeling that Carter was far too favorable toward Palestinians, an offense Koch never forgave. There was sincerity in that feeling—Koch once penned an editorial in which he called Carter "a miserable human being," and, later, when Koch was asked to name the person whom he most despised, he named Carter. Carter later said of Koch, "I felt that he was kind of stabbing me in the back. I felt like he was my friend, but never acted as though he was supporting me." When it came to endorsing Carter, Koch did his party duty, but would not campaign with Carter, and while the support of county leaders was vital at the Democratic convention, Carter understood that not having Koch's enthusiastic backing would be costly in a general election. As much of a windbag as Koch could be, Carter knew the mayor had overseen a resuscitation of the city, after it had been on the edge of bankruptcy in the mid-1970s. By tightening budgets and encouraging investments in the city, particularly among real estate developers, Koch had done the unthinkable: While balancing the city's books, he had also imbued New York with some hope and excitement about its future. For Carter to have a chance to hold onto the presidency, he would need to borrow some of the mayor's gift for inspiring enthusiasm.

Carter did survive the Kennedy challenge at the convention. But he still had a Koch problem. The mayor did all he could to publicly undermine the president. In October, with nineteen days to go before the election, Koch again criticized Carter on his Middle East policy, and announced his refusal to appear with Carter during a trip to New York. Worse, the day after that criticism, Koch invited Reagan to visit with him at Gracie Mansion, the mayor's residence, amid reports that Reagan's polling looked so bad in New York, he was preparing to write off the state altogether. But Koch was popular, and he had ulterior motives. He wanted to bolster support for his 1981 reelection campaign, and as part of that plan, he sought Republican support by welcoming Reagan wholeheartedly to the city. Koch could not endorse Reagan outright, but he could do even more damage to Carter from his perch as a poisonous endorser. Cohn, a conservative Democrat who had become a fierce backer of Reagan, claimed to have been part of the arrangement. "Koch could say he was supporting Carter and then sabotage him," Cohn told his biographer, Sidney Zion. "And that's just what he did."

Reagan won the 1980 election, of course, and trounced Carter in the Electoral College, taking forty-five states and 489 of 538 electoral votes. To the chagrin of Esposito, Friedman, and Manes, Reagan won New York, getting 46.7 percent of the vote to Carter's 43.9 percent. The party machine heads had tremendous power within their fiefdoms in the city, but Koch—with his self-interested ulterior motive—had wielded his own influence and had an impact on the national election. Koch would later brag that Carter had told him he had done more harm to him than any other person. Cohn, however, would describe it in much more vivid terms, telling NBC's Gabe Pressman on the Sunday-morning program *NewsForum* that Koch "slit Carter's throat from ear to ear."

2

BY THE LATE 1970S, COCAINE was still a minor phenomenon in the forbidden world of American drug use, but for the doctors and scientists at the National Institute of Drug Abuse, it required further investigation. In the spring of 1977, research was compiled into a 223-page paperback book called *Cocaine: 1977*, which described the romantic past of the drug, a staple among some South American cultures before it was isolated in Europe and the United States, hyped as a miracle drug that could be used in dozens of applications. It was an anesthetic for surgery, a cure for melancholy, a remedy for nerve pain favored by Sigmund Freud, a staple for a coca wine brain tonic endorsed by Henrik Ibsen and Thomas Edison, an ingredient in early versions of Coca-Cola and, for literature's Sherlock Holmes, an escape from the "dull routine of existence." And, in its own way, cocaine remained romanticized in the late 1970s—it was exotic and expensive, a drug of the elites that did not require users to suffer the debasement of smoking the drug or injecting it hypodermically. "At least part of its appeal is its rarity, high price and use by celebrities, musicians and other folk heroes," the book's editors wrote. "Users also believe that cocaine is relatively free from markedly undesirable side effects and is generally safe."

Two San Francisco doctors, Dr. David Smith (known as Dr. Dave among the drug-addicted patients he knew so well) and Dr. Donald Wesson, who ran the Haight-Ashbury Free Clinic and had been observing cocaine users there, noted with frustration that even medical experts espoused the safety of cocaine, without having done real testing. One article in the *San Francisco Chronicle* from 1976, they noted, quoted an expert in the drug field saying, "Most of the evidence is that there aren't any adverse effects to normal cocaine use. It looks to be much safer than barbiturates and amphetamines, and there's no evidence it has the body effects of cigarettes or alcohol." But from their observations of patients, Wesson and Smith found the only thing that truly made cocaine safe was its cost and how difficult it was to come by, which had the practical effect of limiting how much cocaine a typical user could take. They found very real consequences for heavy users of the drug, and not enough doctors were acknowledging that. "Unfortunately, the difference between current abuse versus abuse potential is a concept not well understood by many laboratory scientists, drug experts who do not see cocaine abuse in their treatment programs, or by the general public," the doctors concluded. "However, if the drug were more readily available at a substantially lower cost, or if certain socio-cultural rituals endorsed and supported the higher dose patterns, more destructive patterns of abuse could develop."

Within a few years, that was changing. In 1980 a Colombian judge who was working on a major narcotics prosecution, Ana Cecilia Cartajena Hernandez, was murdered in Medellin by what was known as an *asesinos de moto*, killers who would hunt their victims on the roadways and murder them while passing by on a motorcycle, then disappear into traffic. After Cartajena was killed, the second judge murdered within a span of ten days, 182 judges resigned en masse in Medellin, bringing international attention to a problem citizens of Medellin had tried to shrug off—increasingly, their proud industrial city in the center of the country was being hijacked by a sophisticated and violent cartel that was processing coca plants bought from poor farmers in nearby Bolivia and Peru and running the finished cocaine product up to Miami, to be distributed in the United States. The violence in Medellin moved to Miami, too. By the summer of 1981, there were so many murders in the city (621 for the year, a record and the highest rate in the nation) that the coroner had to rent out a refrigerated truck because the city morgue was overcrowded. In March 1982, American officials got a sense of the increased brazenness of the Colombian cocaine export business when they seized a Tampa International Airlines Boeing 707 at Miami's airport carrying twenty-one boxes labeled "clothing." Inside those clothing boxes: thirty-nine hundred pounds of pure cocaine, with an estimated street value of nearly $1 billion. It was the largest cocaine interception in the nation's history, by an astronomical margin—the previous biggest had been 826 pounds, and this one shipment brought in more seized cocaine than all of 1981's busts combined. It was after that bust President Ronald Reagan acknowledged that the United States had a cocaine trafficking problem and created the South Florida Drug Task Force, headed by Vice President George Bush, a precursor to the wider War on Drugs that Reagan announced in October, which would include an outlay of as much as $200 million in federal money.

Considering the resources the drug bosses had amassed, that financial outlay was comparatively unimpressive. "Their commitment is minuscule in terms of dollars," Senator Joe Biden said. "Illegal drug traffic in this country was estimated to exceed $80 billion, but we spend less than $3 billion for the entire criminal justice effort, for all crimes on the Federal level, and the states can't do anything about it." In other words, as Drs. Wesson and Smith feared, cocaine was now, "more readily available at a substantially lower cost," and there was not much being done to stop it. The barriers they had seen in the late '70s to widespread cocaine abuse in the United States were gone.

. . . . .

Late 1985 was one of the most difficult periods of Mets first baseman Keith Hernandez's life. He had been coping privately with a divorce while very publicly enduring the most humiliating experience of his professional career. On September 6, Hernandez sat in a US district court in Pittsburgh and faced questions from defense attorney Adam Renfroe, who pried eagerly into a particularly dark personal period. Hernandez had been implicated in the drug-trafficking trial of a former catering employee with the Philadelphia Phillies, Curtis Strong, who had compiled a long list of ballplayer clients. Several of those players had been granted immunity to get their testimony against Strong, but the trial devolved into a soap opera, aimed less at the dismantling of a drug ring than at the juicy details provided by coke-snorting players and the teammates they would be willing to name as snorters, too. The trial came on the heels of the jailing of four members of the Kansas City Royals in late 1983 for cocaine use, and a striking *New York Times* story in which a convicted drug dealer named thirteen American

League players with whom he had done cocaine. "It's all over baseball," the dealer told the paper.

Hernandez was an outstanding first baseman, arguably the best fielder ever at his position, and among baseball's best hitters in his time. He had batted a league-best .344 for the St. Louis Cardinals in 1979, earning an All-Star spot and winning the National League's MVP award. But, as he explained to the packed courtroom, in 1980, he was introduced to cocaine by veteran teammate Bernie Carbo and grew an immediate attachment. He recalled using the drug so much that, by November of 1980, he had lost ten pounds and had woken up bleeding from his nose, spurring an attempt to kick his habit. When Renfroe (who, ironically, was later disbarred and confessed to being a drug addict himself) pushed Hernandez to admit he was an addict, Hernandez demurred and said, "It's the drug itself. It's the devil on this earth. It has a strong emotional lure to it. It took me two and a half years after 1980 to get off it." It was just after he had finally gotten off it, in 1983, that the Cardinals traded him to the Mets, for the bargain price of flameout reliever Neil Allen. Herzog would later claim he did not know for sure Hernandez had dabbled with cocaine at the time of the trade. "Unless you spot a guy snorting coke or smoking marijuana, or unless some reliable witness comes to you or it blows up in the press, you never know for sure," Herzog wrote in his autobiography, *The White Rat*. "There were things about him that made me suspicious, but I can live with suspicions. What I couldn't live with was his attitude." Attitude and all, Hernandez thrived in New York, not only as a hitter and fielder, but as a leader and a calming influence on a talented but youthful team.

For the entire winter of 1985, Hernandez was held in limbo by first-year commissioner Peter Ueberroth, who interviewed twenty-four players implicated in the scandal with the intention of doling out some form of as-yet unknown punishment. The reaction to the players who testified in the trial was intense, but split—general support from fans but almost universal derision from the media. When Hernandez returned to Shea Stadium four days after his appearance in Pittsburgh, he was given a thirty-second standing ovation and was seen wiping away a tear. Broadcaster Howard Cosell lambasted the Mets rooters for the welcome, telling late-night host David Letterman, "You've got to wonder about a country when, in this great city, a man can be rendered a standing ovation after, under immunity, admitting he played the game of baseball after snorting cocaine." Longtime *Philadelphia Daily News* columnist Bill Conlin was similarly outraged, saying of Hernandez, "This is the man who was accorded a hero's ovation by the Shea Stadium rabble after he spilled his guts in Pittsburgh last summer, helping put a couple of male groupies . . . into the federal slammer. What a guy." (Conlin, it should be noted, later died in disgrace after his career was ended by child molestation accusations.) Bernie Carbo, having been outed by Hernandez, was so angry, he would later claim, that he contacted some friends with Mafia connections to have Hernandez's arms broken, though he said he was talked out of it when it was pointed out that he would be a prime suspect in any physical assault on his former teammate. Former White Sox owner Bill Veeck wrote in *The Sporting News*, calling the week of the Pittsburgh trial "rat-fink week," taking players to task for fingering teammates as a condition of their immunity from prosecution, drawing a harsh distinction between the players and Hollywood writers who refused to name names during the anti-Communist McCarthy trials of the 1950s. "They spilled their guts with the dedication and abandon of endangered sea cucumbers, the only other animals which at the first sign of trouble spill forth all their internal organs before collapsing like burst balloons—alive but empty."

But Hernandez—and baseball in general—was not alone. The NFL had long been said to have a serious cocaine issue. In 1982, former Saints running back Michael Strachan was arrested on charges of selling cocaine, which led to a federal investigation of the entire New Orleans team (twelve admitted to buying cocaine from him). Days later, former Saints and Dolphins defensive end Don Reese, who was sent to prison (with teammate Randy Crowder) for selling cocaine in 1977, wrote an article for *Sports Illustrated* in which he claimed that a "cocaine cloud" loomed over the league and that the drug "now controls and corrupts the game because so many players are on it." This came amid a spate of stories of NFL players checking into rehab facilities to deal with cocaine abuse problems, including Cowboys star Thomas "Hollywood" Henderson, who claimed to have had a $1,200-per-day habit that was sending him into bankruptcy, and 1981 number one draft pick George Rogers, who had been selected one spot above the Giants' Lawrence Taylor. In the NBA, the league had become the first to agree with its union about a testing policy, though that policy was too weak to be effective, and big-name players kept getting wrapped up in scandal. Most prominent was Nets star Micheal Ray Richardson, who disappeared from the team in late 1985 and eventually turned up, seeking an assignment in drug rehab. Richardson would later be suspended for life from the NBA. The Phoenix Suns coped with a scandal, too, which included star guard Walter Davis, who had sought help and was admitted to a treatment center in December 1985. Five players would eventually get caught up in the Suns scandal.

But Davis pointed out that athletes who were caught using drugs were being treated with some hypocrisy. As availability of the drug became more democratic, much of America was experimenting with cocaine. From 1983 to 1985, while drug use in general in the United States slipped, cocaine use spiked. According to an FDA study, those who admitted using cocaine once a month or more jumped 38 percent over three years, to an estimated 5.8 million by late 1985. "It was just prevalent," Davis said. "Cocaine was prevalent in society, at all levels, from the homeless to the richest people in the country. It should not have been a surprise that so many players were using it. The rest of the country was using it, too."

. . . . .

Desiderata was written by Max Ehrmann, the poet/lawyer from Terre Haute, Indiana, in 1927, a largely unknown piece of work in its time. But in the late 1960s and into the '70s, the poem had enjoyed a resurgence, its themes of soulful serenity and humility before the universe bridging the free-love wantonism of one decade with the spiritual transcendentalism of the next. In 1965, the *New York Times* reported that upon the death of Adlai Stevenson, a copy of the poem was found next to his bed, apparently to be used in his Christmas cards that year. Three years later, the actor Leonard Nimoy read the poem for a track called "Spock Thoughts," on his album, *The Two Sides of Leonard Nimoy*. In 1972, broadcaster Les Crane had a hit record with his spoken-word version of *Desiderata*. The obscure poem had a strong second act.

Giants linebacker Harry Carson, a student at South Carolina State in the heart of the '70s, had always taken the poem to heart. He had first encountered *Desiderata* in college, but it was as a professional linebacker in New York that Carson really put it to use. What stood out most to him was the line, "If you compare yourself with others, you may become vain and bitter; for always there will be greater and lesser persons than yourself." Carson had repeated those words to himself frequently in recent years, especially after the Giants had drafted outside linebacker Lawrence Taylor in 1981. Carson had built an excellent career in the middle of the Giants defense since his arrival in the league as a fourth-round pick in 1976—he had been to the Pro Bowl in every season he had been healthy since 1978. But where Carson had to put forth such labor to maintain his level of play, Taylor was a natural at his position, built for football the way sharks are built to kill. Taylor did not train; he did not lift weights. "He was gifted," Carson said. "I did all the things I should have done when he first came into the league—we became friends, I would take him to Beefsteak Charlie's for lunch. But I had to fight against jealousy with Lawrence. I would become vain and bitter if I let myself."

The bitterness had gotten to him in the summer of 1984. It was not just Taylor, though the local media quickly concluded his motivations were rooted in his contract, compared to Taylor's. There was good reason for that. Carson had been the anchor of the Giants defense for eight years, but Taylor was now making $750,000 per season, two-and-a-half times Carson's $300,000 contract. Worse, rookie Carl Banks was making $600,000. For Carson, it was not just money, though. There was the grind of constant losing. Carson's Giants had been to the play-offs just once in eight years, and finished in last place in the NFC East five times—including the previous season, a woebegone year in which the team went 3–12–1. Late in that season, Carson had publicly requested to be traded. Instead, that offseason, the Giants traded away Carson's longest-tenured teammates and linebacking brethren, Brad Van Pelt and Brian Kelley, his close friends who had been with the team three years longer than Carson. So Carson, the defensive captain (he had voluntarily given up the title of captain the previous few years) and a favorite of coach Bill Parcells, decided to leave training camp to go back to South Carolina. He did not tell anyone of his plan because he knew whomever he told would try to talk him out of it. He did not want to be talked out of it. When Parcells addressed Carson's absence, he told reporters it was "despicable." That did not bother Carson. What he wanted more than anything was a voice in the organization—management never truly considered his trade request, nor did the franchise higher-ups consult him on personnel moves, at the very least to let him know the thinking behind the team's transactions, if not to seek his actual input. Carson felt he was being taken for granted. Team president George Young did ease Carson's concerns, giving him a raise, assuring him of his importance and talking him out of his trade demand.

This took on special importance the following season, when the Giants began to cope with their own drug problem in the locker room and a veteran leader like Carson was needed. It had been kept from the media, but in May that year, Taylor failed a spot-check drug test, prompting the team to begin monitoring him closely—Parcells, in fact, drove Taylor himself to a recovery facility in New York just three weeks before the start of 1985's training camp. Still, Taylor began to behave more and more erratically. One day at practice, he was found sleeping on a sofa near the locker room. Another time, he was in the parking lot of the Giants' practice facility in his gold Mercedes, zipping in and out of a line of steel barrels that had been placed to mark off the players' parking area, at about 40 mph. There was the time that, after lackluster showings in back-to-back games, Taylor came alive in a win over

Washington, registering two sacks and 11 tackles. He had not spoken to the media during the season, but consented to be interviewed after that performance, saying, "I prepared well for this game, got some sleep and didn't go to the bars as much as usual." He was not joking. Taylor later confessed to using cocaine and crack as much as three times a week during the 1985 season, and beating the Giants' drug screens by having teammates urinate into an aspirin bottle, and hiding the bottle in his jock strap before the test. When the Giants got suspicious and began having a team representative stand behind Taylor during his tests, he switched to an eye-drop bottle, which he could squeeze into the cup to give the impression he was urinating on the spot.

Of additional concern was Taylor's association with Vincent Ravo, a convicted felon with ties to the Genovese Mafia clan, and owner of The Bench, a strip bar a stone's throw from Giants Stadium. Ravo had bragged that he was tight enough with Taylor that they had gone on vacations together, and that Taylor had been to his house for Christmas. "We're very close," Ravo said at the time, and back in 1983, when Ravo was being sentenced for having received stolen goods, Taylor (and two other Giants) wrote a character reference to the sentencing judge, calling Ravo "sincere" and "devoted," and adding, "It would be a tragedy to have this man go to jail." But there was reason to keep a distance from The Bench. Giants defensive end Leonard Marshall said, "The Bench has all the possibility of becoming a bad joint, the type of joint where a drug guy would hang out." George Young felt there was not much to be done about Taylor's association with Ravo. "What can we do," Young said, "tell them who their friends can be?"

Worse for Giants coaches was that they had seen on the field that Taylor was off his game. When the Giants graded out defensive players for the 1985 season, Taylor had been third, and eighth overall—unacceptable for a guy who should not just be the best defensive player on the team, but should be the best in the entire league. Television analyst John Madden said of Taylor's play after the 1985 season, "I thought Lawrence was the best defensive player in the league in 1984, and last

year, I didn't feel that way. . . . I think Lawrence Taylor slipped in great-
ness last year."

．．．．．

"Is it still up there?" Dwight Gooden wanted to know.

It was April 1985, and Gooden was preparing for the Mets' opener
against St. Louis. Someone mentioned to him the 102-foot mural that
had gone up in Midtown, on the side of the Holland Hotel facing
New Jersey. In it, Gooden was in mid-windup, his back foot driving
forward, his chin properly tucked into his left shoulder, his right arm
cocked in an upside-down L, looking ready to fling a fastball clear to
Newark. It was a Nike advertisement, and greeted those newly arrived
in Manhattan from the Holland Tunnel. He did not know it then, but
it would stand for a decade in the spot. Gooden himself was newly
arrived and still very unfamiliar with the intricacies of stardom in New
York. He had been a sterling rookie in 1984, going 17–9 with a 2.60
ERA, leading the league in strikeouts and averaging just 1.073 walks
and hits per nine innings, the best ratio in baseball. He had done that
at just nineteen years old. Gooden had been the fifth overall pick by the
Mets in the 1982 draft after starring at Hillsborough High in Tampa,
and spent just one-and-a-half seasons in the minor leagues before the
Mets inserted him into the starting rotation as part of an overall youth
movement led by manager Davey Johnson. He needed time to adjust to
major-league talent, but late in the 1984 season, he hit his stride. In his
final nine starts, Gooden had registered eight wins, a 1.07 ERA, and
just 13 walks allowed against 105 strikeouts.

The Mets were cautious with Gooden as a rookie, using him in the
fourth starter's role and allowing him to succeed by using just two basic
pitches: his whirring, uphill fastball and standard-issue curveball. But
he had spent five weeks in the offseason developing a changeup that
mimicked his fastball motion, a pitch that would prove devastating to
opposing batters. His success in 1984 left no doubt that he would be the
team's ace, and its Opening Day starter, in 1985. Gooden came through
with one of the best seasons in modern baseball history, following up

that strong rookie year with a 24–4 record. He struck out 268 batters in 276.2 innings pitched, he posted an ERA of 1.53, he lost just once in his last 25 starts and, with the Mets battling for first place down the stretch, he plowed through a streak of 49 innings without allowing an earned run spread over seven starts. Against division-rival Chicago, Gooden had gone 5–0 and thrown a complete game in each outing, allowing a total of six runs and a .227 batting average. During the 1985 season, the Cubs had released infielder Larry Bowa, who hitched on with the Mets later in the summer. Bowa had a chat with Gooden, and told him that Chicago had figured out he was tipping his pitches based on where he was placing his finger on his glove. Bowa was trying to get Gooden to stop tipping his pitches, but revealed a pretty amazing fact in the process: The Cubs knew what pitches Gooden was about to throw them, and *still* Gooden dominated them.

Gooden did more than dominate opponents, though. He had overwhelmed the city's sports scene, sending all of Queens rollicking whenever he took the mound, and giving life to a Mets franchise that had not been to the postseason since 1973. They won 98 games in the 1985 season, finishing three behind the rival Cardinals in their division. A joke had gone around the team: "If only Doc hadn't lost those four games, we'd have had 'em!" *New Yorker* writer Roger Angell noted that one fellow journalist had declared, with only two seasons under his belt, "Dwight Gooden is the greatest pitcher who ever lived." A nook in Shea Stadium became known as K Corner, where a K sign would be hung every time Gooden registered a strikeout, which was often, seeing as he had 11 double-digit strikeout games in 1985. A two-strike count with Gooden on the mound would get the stadium rattling to its bushings, and get Gooden's adrenaline jackhammering through his veins. Pitching coach Mel Stottlemyre repeatedly advised Gooden not to let the crowd get him caught up in trying to strike out all comers. But he had the ability to place whichever pitch he wanted wherever he wanted, with dartboard accuracy. If he wanted to, it seemed, he *could* strike out every batter.

The thrill of that performance proved to be a difficult high from which to come down for Gooden. When the Mets' season ended in October, the routine of taking the mound every five days and electrifying thousands was suddenly gone. He simply went back home to Tampa, to stay with his parents and idle away hours with the same guys he had been around for years. He did not have hobbies. He did not have friends around baseball. Back home, Gooden was not much different than the mildly employed young men who had long floated around his neighborhood. Tampa was an entertainment desert for Gooden, and he had been finding it increasingly difficult to shake his agitation as the winter after the 1985 season wore on. His friends had gotten older and now, in his words, "had been polishing off their screwing-off skills." That meant beer, and lots of it, and some dabbling with marijuana. It was around the end of 1985 that he was just barely able to dodge trouble. Driving with his friend, Herman Cousin, Gooden had been pulled over by Hillsborough police going to an isolated spot in Tampa's Ybor City, an area known for its easy access to illicit substances. In the car with Gooden and Cousin: $4,000, a gun, and a bag of baking soda, commonly used to mix with cocaine. Gooden was not arrested. Cousin would later offer explanations for the gun (it was, "protection because a lot of guys are crazy around here") and the money (Gooden earned a lot of money, and thus, carried a lot of money), but the baking soda was hard to explain. When he was asked why they were carrying baking soda, the only reply Cousin could muster was, "Good question."

But, while Gooden had been around cocaine plenty of times in Tampa, it was not until the following month, he would later admit, that he finally tried it himself. Gooden was at his cousin Bo's house, killing time. Bo was a low-level pimp and drug dealer, but Gooden at the time did not think of him that way. He was just the same cousin he had known all his life. There were two women in a bedroom nearby, and Gooden could see inside the room, but did not quite know why they were giggling so much. Gooden was having beers with Bo and wanted some marijuana. Bo had to leave to get some, and told Gooden to just ignore whatever was going on in the room. Once Bo left, Gooden—not the superstar Gooden but the shy, young, idle, out-of-place Gooden—joined the women in the room anyway. They offered him cocaine. He had certainly heard plenty about it, but had never tried it. He resisted at first, but the women were beautiful and Gooden was curious and bored. So he leaned over and breathed in deep through his nose. The rush shook him, jolting away his bashfulness. Nothing would be the same for Gooden after that. As he put it: "It was love at first sniff."

3

IT STARTED WITH TOILETS. MAYBE not entirely—for Jets owner and powerful oil magnate Leon Hess, the indignities he and his franchise had suffered over the years had been cumulative, and went beyond unkempt urinals. His tormentors, as he saw it, were the City of New York's Parks Department and the entity that department empowered to run Shea Stadium, Major League Baseball's Mets. Shea had been built for the expansion Mets in 1964, the team and stadium acting as a salve for the wounds still being nursed by fans who had watched baseball's Giants and Dodgers bolt for the West Coast in 1958. The Jets had moved into Shea from the rickety old Polo Grounds at the same time, as a shoestring operation in the fledgling American Football League, spending the early '60s simply trying to survive against the behemoth NFL. But they had survived, and in the intervening years, the NFL had overtaken baseball as the juggernaut of American sports. Not at Shea, though, and Hess resented the way Mets honcho M. Donald Grant flaunted his power over the stadium. The Jets were not allowed, unless the Mets agreed, to play a home game until after the baseball season ended, and in 1976, for example, that forced the Jets on the road for their first four games. Financially, the Mets reaped any rewards the Jets generated. Hess could collect no revenues on any stadium extras, from luxury boxes to parking fees to popcorn. That money went to the Mets. He could live with the loss of income, but he couldn't live with the filthy toilets for which Shea was known. For Hess, the state of disrepair in the stadium bathrooms represented that second-citizen status, a perpetual lavatorial slap in the face of his franchise.

Hess might have thought he would get a chance to change his fortunes in 1977, when New York elected his friend and political ally Ed Koch to be its mayor. Hess had donated $10,000 to Koch's mayoral campaign, and in Koch's unsuccessful bid for governor in 1982, Hess ponied up $50,000. Koch had promised to make improvements to Shea Stadium for Hess, or to even build a new football-only home for the Jets. But New York was still wary of excessive spending as it emerged from the fiscal crisis of the 1970s, and was coping with a slew of municipal pressures. Koch well understood the poor visuals attached to a massive public investment in a football stadium while thousands of New Yorkers suffered homelessness, and while New York kids lagged in public education. Besides, despite Hess's patronage, Koch had little patience for sports. Only once in his first five years in office did he attend a Jets game, and he bolted from that one early. During Jets training camp in the summer of 1983, Hess shared with the media a letter he had sent to Koch stating that Shea had become "run-down" and "neglected," and that the Jets would be leaving to play in more favorable conditions at Giants Stadium in the Meadowlands of New Jersey. The puddles of standing water fans braved to get to the toilets were his chief complaint.

Koch did not take Hess's criticism kindly and insisted the owner was being overly finicky about the bathroom conditions to gain leverage. But that was not a wise strategy—the millions who had attended games at Shea Stadium knew well that Hess was right. As Russell Baker wrote in the *Times*, "In suggesting that Mr. Hess was obsessed with toilets, the Mayor seemed to be trying to belittle him. What kind of man would whine about filthy toilets when his company has the honor of performing in the greatest city on earth? My sentiments here lie entirely with Mr. Hess. What he is saying is that he doesn't want to do business in a tenement." Koch claimed Hess was bluffing on his

Meadowlands move. He was not. In October 1983, Hess announced he was giving up on Shea Stadium and accepting a new lease in New Jersey, leaving New York City without a football team.

But he offered the city one last chance. If New York could show him a plan for a new stadium—a "proper football facility" in Hess's words—that would allow for the Jets to return to the city by the 1989 season, he would move the Jets back to New York. He gave the city more than two years to put together that plan. He left open a two-week period, from February 1 to February 15, 1986, to finalize a stadium and bring New York's sports landscape back into balance.

.....

Ira Berkow had a bag of grapes on his lap as he sat on the twenty-sixth floor of the newly opened Trump Tower on Fifth Avenue in Midtown. When Berkow was growing up on the West Side of Chicago, his mother had taught him never to show up for a meal without offering a gift to the host. He was slated to meet with the building's namesake, Donald Trump, in late 1983 to discuss the prospects for Trump's latest venture, his purchase of the New Jersey Generals of the United States Football League, for an article in the *New York Times*. Before leaving for the interview, he had checked in with Trump, and Trump told Berkow he would order them some lunch—Berkow resisted at first, then said he would take a pastrami on rye and a Coke. But the lesson from his mother kicked in on the way to the interview, and Berkow stopped at a fruit stand. He paid $1 for the grapes. Dessert, he figured. That would be his offering to Trump.

Before being ushered into the office, Berkow—then forty-three and a relative newcomer to his *Times* column—was shown an eight-minute slide show, extolling both the virtues of living in the Tower and of Trump himself. "This is Manhattan through a golden eye," according to the show's narrator, "and only for a select few." Condos in the building ranged from $600,000 to $12 million. Sports columnists are almost never considered among "the select few." Berkow asked Trump's secretary if he could skip the slides and see Trump. "Mr. Trump would like you to see it," Berkow was told, in a tone that brooked no further protestation.

When he was finally inside, Berkow and Trump discussed his plans for the Generals. The USFL had gotten underway in 1982, with modest budgets and a chicken-wire-and-bubble-gum operating structure. The league derived its stability from its small-time aspirations. It played a spring schedule, offering ABC a safe run of television football programming away from the competition of the NFL and college football monoliths in the fall, and it was dedicated to bringing in low-dollar talent without sparking a salary war it could not win against the NFL. Its major attraction was running back Herschel Walker, signed to a three-year, $5 million contract by the Generals, before Trump's arrival, as a junior out of Georgia. But in just two-and-a-half months, Trump had blown away the USFL's cautious model. Two days earlier, he held a press conference to announce the signing of former Browns quarterback Brian Sipe to a two-year, $1.9 million deal. He had, back in October, gone through a delicate dance with Dolphins coaching legend Don Shula, who was said to be unhappy in Miami and had engaged in discussions about the Generals job. Word of the talks leaked to the papers, with Trump said to be offering $5 million for five years. That leak—Shula was certain it had come from Trump—was the first blow to Shula's potential signing. The second blow was another leak, a story claiming that Shula would only take the Generals job if he would be given a condo in Trump Tower. Shula had made no such claim and, irate, he backed away from any further Generals negotiations. "I can assure you," Shula said, "that my price is not a condominium." Trump instead made a more modest, but still competent hire, signing former Jets coach Walt Michaels. Truth was, he was never going to hire Shula, but he was interested in the illusion that he might hire him and the attention it brought him. After the botched Shula negotiation, a USFL executive contacted Trump to tell him how upset Shula had been about the Trump Tower story, and that it caused Shula to walk away altogether.

Expecting contrition or at least frustration, the official instead got Trump smugness. "Hey," Trump said, "is that great publicity for Trump Tower?"

Trump had done much the same with Giants star linebacker Lawrence Taylor, who had not been particularly happy with his contract in New York but had little recourse to change it. Taylor had an option in his deal, but it was not slated to come until 1988. So Trump did something unusual—he signed Taylor to a future deal, promising to pay him $2.7 million over four years once his NFL contract was up. But Trump also left an option for Taylor to renegotiate with the Giants if he so chose, as long as Trump's end of the contract was bought out. The move was all three-card monte, of course. The option year was still far off, and there was no doubt the Giants would renegotiate with Taylor rather than risk losing him. There was virtually no chance Taylor would play for the Generals. But Trump got what he wanted: attention. Berkow asked him about the rumors of him signing Taylor. "No one knows if we signed him," Trump said. "Actually, only three people know, that's Lawrence, his agent and me." The Generals, at the very least, served that purpose for Trump. They got him some headlines. For Trump, fame and power were interchangeable, and the Generals brought him fame. "I hire a general manager to help run a billion-dollar business and there's a squib in the papers," Trump told Berkow. "I hire a coach for a football team and there are 60 or 70 reporters calling to interview me."

When they finished their lunch, Berkow put his bag of grapes on Trump's desk. He told him what he had paid for the dessert, and knowing he might be mistaken for a cheapskate, Berkow said, "You know, Donald, this lunch has had a bigger relative impact on my bank account than yours." Berkow thought his joke might draw a laugh or at least a chuckle from Trump. It barely drew a smile. Later, Berkow said that in twenty-plus years of interactions with Trump, "I don't think he ever laughed once."

.....

For weeks and months (eventually, years), Ira Silverman was sending off letters to Donald Trump at Trump Tower on Fifth Avenue, and to attorney Roy Cohn at the townhouse office of Saxe, Bacon and Bolan on 68th Street. In October 1984, Silverman had begun his own fledgling sports public relations company and had landed a high-profile gig: He was to arrange a press conference for Cohn and Trump at Cohn's office. The announcement was a big deal. Cohn and Trump, who had been a USFL owner for just about a year, were filing an antitrust lawsuit against the NFL on behalf of the USFL, claiming the NFL had created a monopoly over pro football and its broadcasting. They were seeking $1.3 billion in damages. It had been one of the most bizarre events Silverman would have to set up, because although he was informed in advance what the subject matter was, he was told that he could not call the press conference until he got the word from Cohn. Once he was given the OK, Silverman would have just four hours to contact the media and get them to Cohn's office. "Not an easy thing to do in the middle of a week in New York," Silverman said. "But Cohn had a very forceful way of saying how he wanted things done, and that was what he wanted. And I did it."

The previous day, the USFL owners had agreed to file the suit in a conference call ahead of league meetings that were scheduled for Florida. Trump and Cohn waited until most of those owners were en route to the meetings before telling Silverman to call the press conference. That ensured Trump would be the sole spokesman for the league, which was his right according to Cohn, because the suit was being filed in New York and Trump was the owner of the New York-area team. Once there, seated on the tan couches of his office lounge next to Trump, Cohn was in his element, employing all the tactics he had taught Trump when making public statements over the years—put out brash but vague accusations, express outrage over all injustices, and never sue small. The NFL had a monopoly on television contracts, the lawsuit claimed, preventing all three major networks from televising USFL games as it transitioned from a spring to a fall schedule (a transition Trump himself had engineered and forced through), and Cohn ominously stated there was a "secret cabal" within the NFL that had plotted the demise of the USFL, a statement that greatly exaggerated the facts. "They just put every roadblock in your way, which they can do," Cohn said in his staccato Bronx cadence, "by virtue of the economic muscle. And that is exactly what the Sherman and Clayton antitrust act say if you do it, you pay treble damages to the people who suffer as a result of your doing it."

At the USFL owners meetings in Florida the next day, the reviews of Trump's press conference were generally positive. But not for Silverman. His contract with Cohn and Trump called for him to be paid $2,000, with $1,000 coming up front. At the end of the press conference, Silverman presented the two with a bill for the remaining $1,000. By the end of the year, Trump, the thirty-eight-year-old billionaire, still had not paid Silverman, who was left with no recourse but to keep firing off letters. To no avail—Trump never paid the remainder of the bill. Silverman, looking back, said he should have known. In the 1960s, his father, Leo Silverman, was a state auditor who helped reveal that Trump's father, Fred Trump, had bilked the state out of millions in fees by inflating construction costs on projects in Brooklyn and Queens.

· · · · ·

In late 1985, Trump held the fate of football in New York in his hands. The dots appeared easy to connect. Trump was to present plans for a new stadium in Queens, the city and state would offer those plans to Leon Hess, and the Jets would move back to the city. New York, which had been suffering the embarrassment of having two teams bearing its name playing in New Jersey, would be an NFL town again. That was how it was supposed to work. But Trump had other plans. Trump and his attorney, Allen Schwartz, were meeting with representatives of New York City and the State of New York at the Times Square offices of the state-run Urban Development Corporation. For much of the past year, the groups had ambled through a slow dance around plans to build the stadium, as Trump had positioned himself to beat out other bidders and win the deal, and to finish by building a spectacular domed project at Willets Point, just across from Shea Stadium at the tip of Flushing Bay. While there were few other bidders in the process, Trump had done all he could to move the odds in his favor, particularly by bringing in Schwartz, who had been a partner at Ed Koch's old law firm, helping to ensure city cooperation and smooth what was a sometimes contentious Koch-Trump relationship.

Schwartz was just one political advantage Trump pressed to help along his stadium idea. He had Stanley Friedman, who as the Bronx county leader was a member of the powerful Board of Estimate, on his side, but more important, he had Queens Democratic boss Donald Manes. The two had old ties going back to Manes's political start at Brooklyn's Madison Democratic Club, a sort of factory specializing in the world of city patronage. Trump's father had been heavily involved in the club for decades and actively courted club members as he sought approvals for his buildings in Queens and Brooklyn. Manes had known Trump long enough that they knew each other as "Donny," which put him in select company—few were friendly enough to call Donald Trump "Donny." Trump could count on Manes to help push the dome to approval. Manes had proven adept at bringing home pork-barrel projects, which included a law school and a medical school for the City University in his borough. Now, Manes badly wanted to see the dome built. When *Times* writer George Vecsey, back in April, had written that there was little chance of Trump actually building a new stadium, Manes wrote a letter to the *Times* chiding Vecsey and saying that a new stadium could be built if left to "people with ideas and proven track records . . . people with faith, imagination and vision." There was little doubt Manes meant Trump.

With so much at stake—for the city and state, for Queens, for the Jets and the NFL—officials were stunned to find that Trump was stubbornly holding onto one aspect of the planned dome that seemed almost irrelevant, yet could scotch the whole deal. He wanted his name on the stadium. After all those months going through the motions of bidding out the new, eighty-two-thousand-seat stadium project, which would cost about $286 million to build, Trump was not budging on the name.

Trumpdome, it had to be called. Koch and Governor Mario Cuomo had insisted that the place would be privately funded, and Trump had come up with a plan for that, and thus wanted it to have his name. Of course, there were some seriously objectionable details within that funding plan, which fit a pattern that helped fuel Trump's rise as arguably the first celebrity real estate developer: He would use other people's private money. Trump wanted to follow the model of NFL owner Joe Robbie, who was building a new stadium outside of Miami for the Dolphins, funded with down payments on the right to buy tickets for arena events. The situations were different. Robbie had zero help from local political forces, and an already established team with a solid fan base, while Trump was selling licenses for a team that did not exist in a building that was nothing more than a drawing. Trump's plan would charge an average of $12,000 for presale of some seats, $2,400 for year-to-year leases on other seats, and an average of $60,000 up front for 221 luxury boxes. Fans who bought those licenses would still have to buy tickets. In selling the leases, Trump was asking fans to also foot the bill for the building on which he wanted his name, and from which he would suck all profits. The city and state would pay $75 million each for the acquisition of the land, and would grant Trump a twenty-five-year tax abatement. The presale of seats was expected to generate $276 million, meaning the cost to Trump himself to build the stadium would be just $10 million.

It was a sweetheart deal, but the insistence on Trump's name being on the stadium had the whole thing on the brink of collapse. As late December 4 turned to early December 5, a compromise was reached. There would be no name attached to the dome just yet, and when it came time to officially put a name on it, that name would have to be approved unanimously by the city, state, and Trump. All the haggling had caused the parties to blow past the scheduled time for the press conference, which had been 10:30 a.m. It was not until 2:30 that the announcement was finally made. Trump was cleared to build a stadium in Queens, and the project would move forward once an NFL team could be found to be the primary tenant. That meant three possibilities: first, a Jets return; second, attracting an outside NFL franchise (the Patriots, Steelers, and Cardinals were all, at one point, rumored to be possibilities, though the Jets and Giants would forcefully object to a third team in the New York market); third, Trump's Generals. A Jets return would be a coup for New York and for Queens, but it was not necessarily ideal for Trump at that time, not as long as he held control of a USFL team that was a potential Trump bonanza if it were to be absorbed by the NFL and play in the new dome. And if presented a choice between civic good and self-interest, Trump would always choose Trump.

That is how it looked to Hess when he finally saw the plans. His promise to New York was that if a credible plan was in place by February 1986, he would agree to move back. He looked at Trump's plan and told reporters, "There is no way this can be ready by February." Besides, he felt the notion of leasing seats was absurd, because Trump would be asking to build the Jets' stadium "on the backs of our fans." Asked about Hess and the Jets at the press conference to announce the stadium agreement, Trump surprised the gathered media by all but ruling out a Jets return. "Leon Hess is a friend of mine," Trump said, stretching the truth. "He's a very, very fine gentleman. I would say the Jets are perhaps not a very likely candidate to leave where they are. I personally don't put great credence to the fact that they may come back." At the press conference, though, Vincent Tese, the head of the Urban Development Corporation, contradicted Trump. He called the Jets "the most likely suspect" for the new building, and chalked up Trump's negativity on that prospect as part of the "mating dance" of negotiations.

Newsday columnist Stan Isaacs saw through the smoke that Trump was screening. He called the deal a "boondoggle" for Trump. There was little chance Trump could persuade an NFL owner to come to Queens and fill his new stadium, especially not while he was suing the league, and Hess seemed bent on staying in New Jersey. What Tese called a mating dance, Isaacs called a lie. "If we discount Trump's words on that not-so-piddling matter," Isaacs wrote, "who's to say on which items he can be believed?"

4

"Keep shooting," the cop said, under his breath, leaning over toward Tom Monaster as his Nikon snapped and whirred, capturing the flash of the red lights from the 17th Precinct police car parked at an angle to blockade the scene. It was December 16, 1985, and Monaster had been sent out for photos of a bizarre scene: two well-dressed men, shot dead while exiting their car, by a quartet of assassins all dressed in beige trench coats and dark Cossack-style fur hats. In the background, an uncertain dusk in Manhattan blinked and pulsed up toward Times Square. The officer was known to Monaster from the Manhattan South precinct, and had figured that Monaster did not yet know what he was photographing. For sure, there were two dead bodies on the ground outside the opened doors of a Lincoln Town Car near a normally busy sidewalk outside Sparks Steakhouse on 46th Street near Third Avenue. But these were nameless victims of a stunningly audacious homicide. One of the bodies was just a pair of tailored pants leading to highly polished shoes poking out from the bottom of a sheet, and the other, still uncovered, was a stout middle-aged man on his back, lying still with his face pointed upward like a sunbather on an asphalt beach. "It's big," the cop told Monaster, knowingly. Snap. Whir.

About three miles downtown, at New York University Law School, a reception was being held for Notre Dame professor Robert Blakey, a former Justice Department official and now a consultant on the practice and history of organized crime. Blakey had been the architect of the Federal Racketeer Influenced and Corrupt Organizations Act, known as RICO, designed in the late 1960s as a tool for prosecutors to take down organized crime families. Blakey had made it his life's mission to educate law enforcement on the use of RICO to go after high-ranking Mafia figures, and that is what he had been doing in New York. Just before 6:00 p.m., while crowds milled around the protected scene outside of Sparks in Midtown, all manner of cops and lawyers were mingling outside the reception room for Blakey, downing cheap cocktails and beer, dragging on cigarettes and cigars. But Blakey soon was relegated to second billing when a familiar burst of digital noise came forth—a beeper. Then another. And more. Slowly at first, then building to a cacophonous crescendo, the sound of beepers filled the room, blinking and wailing. There was a rush to nearby phones (there were only two on hand), and out to the officers' car radios. The news spread quickly. There had been a double homicide. It was big. "I think I lost the bulk of my audience in a hurry," Blakey said.

Just about a half-hour before that beeper storm, and minutes before Monaster came upon the scene, a black Lincoln pulled up outside of Sparks. Emerging from the passenger side was seventy-year-old "Big Paul" Castellano, the head of the Gambino crime family since 1976, and arguably the most powerful mobster in the country. Dignified and circumspect, nicknamed, "The Pope," with a square jaw and a 6-foot-3, 270-pound frame, Castellano had mostly avoided the limelight, taking careful pains to find ways to legitimize himself by investing his criminal earnings into upstanding businesses. His approach had divided the Gambinos into two factions, so that about half of his crews were the street thugs and head-knockers who hustled to collect loansharking and gambling debts, and the other half—the half he preferred—was a white-collar group that had control of the market for construction labor and concrete in a booming city, as well as a hand in the garment industry and food distribution. His chicken business, Dial Poultry, got national attention in 1986 when Frank Perdue ("It takes a tough man to make a tender chicken") testified before Congress that he had done business with Castellano and even sought his help in suppressing efforts to unionize at his factories. Castellano lived in a mansion in Staten Island, but was in the city to meet with some of his top underlings, including Frank DeCicco, a trusted protégé and labor manipulator who was one of Castellano's white-collar heavies. Though Castellano, a butcher himself with a shop in Queens, preferred the ornate wooden carvings, burgundy interior, and high quality of Sparks's steaks, he complained to two associates, "You know who is making a fortune?

Fucking Sparks. What those guys do is good for 100 grand a week. Me, I don't get five cents when I go in there. They don't even buy you a fucking drink."

This time, though, Castellano would not make it into Sparks, for a drink or for anything. As he hoisted himself out of the Town Car, he did not give much notice to the four men in Cossack-style fur hats who had approached the car. They pulled their .32 and .380-caliber semiautomatics from their coats as they drew near. Two of them fired a total of six rounds into Castellano's head and torso, not breaking stride as they moved east on 46th, toward three rented getaway Lincolns with New Jersey plates on Second Avenue. Two others did the same to Castellano's driver and top deputy, Tommy Bilotti, who was left sprawled on the street as Castellano, one of the top rulers of the American underground, bled near the gutter. The bodies would remain there for more than an hour.

Nearby, in a black Lincoln sedan with tinted windows pointed east on 46th Street on the northwest corner of Third Avenue, Gambino capo John Gotti and his deputy, Sammy Gravano, watched the slaughter. They pulled across Third, slowing down in front of Sparks to inspect the carnage. Bilotti and Castellano were dead. There was no doubt. Satisfied, Gotti's car picked up speed and turned south on Second Avenue, heading downtown to the Brooklyn-Battery Tunnel and safely out of Manhattan.

Monaster's photo of Bilotti lying lifeless next to his opened car door was splayed across the front of the *Daily News* the next morning, under the headline RUBOUT. Inside the paper was a diagram of the top of the Gambino family, with Castellano at the head. Beneath him was Neil Dellacroce, the Gambino underboss and a mentor to Gotti, who had died of cancer a month earlier. Beneath Dellacroce was Bilotti. Next to Bilotti was Gotti. After that night at Sparks, everyone on the chart was dead but Gotti. As the state's top organized crime fighter put it, the old-world mobsters were dying off and "the yuppie generation" was taking over. Citing anonymous investigators, the *News* speculated that it may have been the relatively unknown Gotti—"the handsome, dapper Gotti" the paper noted—who orchestrated the Castellano hit.

. . . . .

Back in July 1983, Sal Avellino was behind the wheel of a black 1982 Jaguar XJ-6, driving through New York and talking with his boss, the head of the Lucchese crime family of New York, Antonio "Tony Ducks" Corallo. At seventy, Corallo was a gangster of the old school, and enjoyed the company of Avellino, who was respectful but had a natural intelligence and some ambition. That made him inquisitive, and Corallo enjoyed explaining to Avellino the ins and outs of his day, the capos and bosses he would meet with, the problems he would have to iron out, the arbitration of disputes that arose. Corallo trusted Avellino enough to have him serve as a go-between in the Jaguar, delivering messages to Lucchese underboss Tom "Mix" Santoro—first Corallo would ride with Avellino, let him know what he wanted passed along to Santoro, then Avellino would drive Santoro and explain in detail Corallo's instructions or opinions. Corallo had long been of interest to law enforcement, and had a rap sheet that dated back to his youth in East Harlem. In 1929, at sixteen, he was charged with grand larceny, but he avoided conviction, and would dodge punishment on twelve of the fourteen occasions on which he was arrested in the three decades that followed. His knack for wriggling out of charges earned him the nickname "Tony Ducks," and it stuck. He was a natty dresser, preferring French cuff shirts, and held fast to the old-world code of silence around all Mafia-related activities, known in Italian as *omerta*. When he was hauled before Congress as part of the Senate's Select Committee on Improper Activities in the Labor Management Field in 1957, Corallo annoyed his questioners by invoking the Fifth Amendment 120 times. He was a Lucchese underboss, and that level of steadfast, stiff-lipped stonewalling ensured he was the type to eventually take over as head of the family in 1970.

Around this time, Corallo had taken special interest in the arrival of a new US attorney who would be heading up the Southern District of New York office, thirty-nine-year-old Rudy Giuliani, the youngest prosecutor in the SDNY's history. Giuliani had been the number three man in the Justice Department under William French Smith in Washington, but had volunteered to take the job in his home city of New York. In interviews after his June swearing-in, Giuliani listed organized crime as one of his primary targets in the coming years. Giuliani linked the city's heroin scourge to the Mafia, and said he was in the process of adding eight new assistant attorneys to beef up his staff and begin the process of systematically dismantling the Mafia. Given his long history with organized crime, and his deftness at avoiding penalty, Corallo was naturally skeptical.

"The Italians are traditional gangsters, ah, and they feel that within the next 10 to 20 years they can completely eliminate it," Avellino told Corallo as he drove the Jaguar. "Because they've been getting more and more information on them."

Corallo scoffed. "They'll eliminate themselves," he said.

Avellino was not impressed by Giuliani's push for new attorneys. He noted that six new Mafia members had only recently been inducted. "That was the day [Giuliani] says, ahm, we have to hire more prosecutors because if we hire more we can now win," Avellino said. "So I says to myself, well ya better go and hire six right away because we just added six last night."

Corallo indicated that he and other heads of New York's families had at least considered a way to scale back operations should investigators get too close. "They were talking about breaking this thing up," Corallo said, "that each boss take a certain amount of their key men, their main men. The ones that don't talk, all that shit you understand, and the rest they leave along the side."

Corallo and Avellino did not know that as part of a widespread offensive against the Mob undertaken four months earlier, the state's Organized Crime Task Force had managed to pull off a major coup in electronic surveillance—they had bugged the dashboard of Corallo's beloved car, three agents conducting a daring operation in the pouring rain in which they pulled out the Jaguar's dashboard and fitted a small microphone and transmitter, before replacing the dashboard and tidying up the car to remove any signs of entry, in the span of just ten minutes.

Their discussion about Giuliani was being listened to and recorded by a nearby FBI agent, part of a massive swarm of bugs targeting all five of New York's Mafia families, particularly the family heads. For too long, the government had been focusing its efforts on the small-time criminals who populate Mafia families, but the FBI was now taking Robert Blakey's advice and homing in on ways to build bigger cases on the Mob bosses, a strategy that started even before Giuliani's arrival at SDNY. They would attack both the brains and the funding of these criminal organizations.

The bugs were just about everywhere agents could access, and they managed to get at least one device close on four of five family heads. Corallo's was in the car. They bugged a lamp in the well-guarded home of the Gambinos' Paul Castellano. They had the Palma Boys Social Club, headquarters for Genovese acting boss Tony Salerno, bugged. They bugged Casa Storta, a Brooklyn restaurant where Colombo family head Gerry Langella frequently did business. There was no bug on Bonanno head Rusty Rastelli, but the Bonannos were in shambles and Rastelli's position within the group of Mob leaders was uncertain. The bugs would prove to be a goldmine for city crime fighters, and a death knell for the old Mafia of Chianti, pomade, and musty back rooms. All of law enforcement figured to benefit, but none more than the especially ambitious new prosecutor, Giuliani.

. . . . .

Ten months before he was shot dead at Sparks, in February 1985, Castellano was seated downtown with handcuffs on his wrists while two FBI agents who had been surveilling him for years, Andris Kurins and Joe O'Brien, stood guard. Across the street, at the Federal Building at 26 Federal Plaza, Giuliani was holding forth with the media, conducting a well-scripted press conference to laud the landmark indictment of ten high-ranking Mafia figures, including the heads of all five families in New York. The fifteen-count indictment charged that the families had exercised illegal control over illicit activities ranging from Mob classics like loansharking and gambling, to price-fixing in the concrete

industry and labor racketeering, and even murder. Giuliani was bringing the case under the RICO statute, and was charging that the heads
of the Mafia families operated under the guidance of a so-called Commission of bosses who made decisions and fashioned orders directing
their illegal activities. He would be the first prosecutor to execute a
RICO case against a multi-family Mafia arrangement like New York's
Commission. "It is a great day for law enforcement, probably the worst
day for the Mafia," Giuliani stated triumphantly. Castellano, held on
$2 million bail, looked out and saw the horde of press around Giuliani
on the courthouse stairs. He shook his head and said, serenely, "Well, if
you're gonna get fucked, it may as well be by a paisan."

But in the end, it was not Giuliani who did in Castellano. It was
Gotti. Though the mystery of who killed Castellano played out in the
press over weeks, the FBI knew immediately that he had been the victim of a Gotti power grab. There were plenty of Mafioso across the
families who had issues with Castellano for a variety of reasons: He
had become the most powerful of the bosses, his moves to bring the
Gambinos into legitimate businesses engendered some jealousy, he was
notoriously tightfisted, he had been perceived to be too close to some
members of law enforcement which could make him susceptible to
turning informant, and he had been indicted as the head of a murderous car-theft ring, which could be another source of government pressure on Castellano. But only Gotti had the kind of axe to grind against
Castellano, whom he called, "that rat motherfucker," that would lead to
a cold-blooded hit. His mentor, underboss Neil Dellacroce, had long
detested Castellano, and Gotti followed suit. When Dellacroce died,
Castellano failed to even show up for his own underboss's funeral, a
sin Gotti could not forgive. Word had gone out that Castellano would
replace Dellacroce not with Gotti but with Thomas Bilotti, Castellano's sycophantic and vastly underqualified driver, another negative
mark against Castellano. Most significant may have been government
tapes that had emerged which made it clear that two of Gotti's men—
Angelo Ruggiero and Gotti's brother, Gene—had been running a heroin trafficking ring. While some families tolerated drug dealing, the

official Cosa Nostra position was to stay away from drugs, and Castellano remained staunchly opposed to narcotics in the Gambino clan. If Castellano had heard the tapes, Gotti reasoned, Castellano would have little choice but to order a hit on some members of Gotti's crew, or on Gotti himself. To Gotti, it was kill or be killed. There was no more sacrosanct dictum among Mafioso than the one that protected family bosses from being killed without consent from the ruling Commission. But the problem was, Gotti was not interested in the old rules.

Law enforcement officials feared a Mafia war in the absence of Castellano. "That was one of the problems with the removal of the older, more powerful bosses," Blakey said. "Those who rose to the top generally did so because they were smart, they knew how to avoid exposure, they were diplomatic and not just violent. There was some wisdom. But once there was that vacuum, you did not know who was going to fill it. It was going to be someone younger. And maybe more violent. That's what you got with Gotti. Someone a lot more violent."

5

DONALD MANES STOOD BEFORE A small gathered crowd at Borough Hall in Queens giving the annual State of the County address, his portly frame tucked into a dark suit, reading glasses perched on his nose, a large posterboard marked 1986—AN ACTION PLAN resting next to his podium, featuring a spate of the usual goals of a local politician (improved services for senior citizens, creating and retaining jobs, waterfront development). Always affable, Manes was as engaging as a public speaker as he was guffawing and glad-handing with fellow politicians and constituents. Once, during an especially rambunctious Board of Estimate meeting, Manes immediately lightened the mood by taking off his shoe and pounding the table before him as though he were Nikita Khrushchev at the United Nations. Manes harkened back to his 1984 speech, when he had bubbled with pride at the success of Queens locals Mario Cuomo, the state's high-profile governor, and former congresswoman Geraldine Ferraro, who was plucked by Democratic presidential candidate Walter Mondale to be the first woman on a major-party ticket. He also beamed over the Mets, just as he had done the previous year. The team had nearly won 1984's exciting divisional title chase, which they ultimately lost to the Cubs despite winning 90 games, and came back even stronger in 1985, with 98 wins and drawing 2.7 million fans to Shea Stadium, an astonishing 50 percent increase over the 1984 season and a half-million ahead of the more-celebrated Yankees. "In the hearts and minds of 200 million Americans," Manes said, "Queens was finally on the map."

The previous month, as Ed Koch won his third term as mayor, Manes had won for the fourth time as president of Queens. When he first won the borough presidency, Manes was just thirty-seven, making him the youngest to hold that office in any borough in the city's history, just as he had been the youngest assistant DA in the Queens office (at age twenty-seven) and the youngest elected to the City Council (he was thirty-one). In 1985, well ahead of that year's election, Manes had been asked by David Johnson of CBS News whether he would have a primary challenge. He laughed and said, "What are you, nuts? Primaries are for *goyim*." His Republican opponent, Barbara LeGoff, had no expectation of challenging Manes, and he won 85 percent of the vote. That put Manes only slightly below Koch on the totem pole of municipal power. The two had established a close relationship over the decades, serving on the City Council together in the 1960s and moving through the Democratic political ranks in the '70s. Their bond got tighter when Koch was elected mayor in 1977, even as Koch ran as a reformer who denounced the dominance of clubhouse politics in the city, of which Manes was an undisputed member. But Koch was a political manipulator, and even before he was elected he solicited behind-the-scenes support from established outer borough political chiefs. Once in office, he cozied up to them freely. In 1982, when Koch lost the gubernatorial primary to Cuomo, Manes was able to push the borough into Koch's column—despite Cuomo's roots in Queens, and the fact that he still lived there. "Ed Koch is as close to me as a brother," Manes said.

Koch's loss in the race for governor, combined with his personal popularity as mayor, were political roadblocks for Manes, who had bigger plans than borough president. He had been a presumed mayor-in-waiting for years now, mentioned by Koch himself as his eventual successor to the job. But with Koch ensconced, Manes had begun to cast for his political future elsewhere—speculation had him considering a run for governor, if Cuomo ran for president in 1988, or for the Senate seat of Republican Al D'Amato. That fall, despite minimal electoral challenge, Manes ran a series of up-with-Queens ads, forty-seven in all, at a cost of $75,000 each, offering such chamber-of-commerce platitudes as "something is happening in Queens," and "the future is Queens." This was ambition, and Manes did not hide it. Manes's campaign manager, Michael Nussbaum, conceded that the ads were designed to help Manes raise his profile statewide, and Manes told the *Daily News*, "I represent two million people. . . . There's no reason I couldn't represent more."

But on this day, Manes was firming up his Queens base. "This year, I want people everywhere to recognize what we in Queens have known for some time," Manes said. "Queens is a place where the American dream is still alive."

. . . . .

Bernie Sandow made a small fortune off the misery of his fellow citizens. He was forty-nine years old, porky and balding, and ran a company called Systematic Recovery Service he had founded in 1970. Its function was to locate and hunt down municipal-bill scofflaws. If you had an unpaid parking ticket in New York, it could be Sandow who was coming after you. Missed your water payment in Chicago? Beware of Bernie. His business was booming, with one hundred employees and a $500,000 salary for the boss. Three times divorced, Sandow was fond of high living, with a $3,400-a-month apartment on West 57th, a choice of chauffeured cars (one gray Mercedes, one black Mercedes, each with a car phone), a luxury apartment in Miami and, according to friends, a taste for jewelry and "big, brassy blonde" women. He had been working the political fundraiser scene in New York City since the early '70s and eventually fell in with the head of the Parking Violations Bureau, a bureaucrat named Lester Shafran. Sandow got his first contract with the PVB through Shafran in 1976, and had built up his business with the agency over time—from 1983 to 1985, SRS took in $7 million from the city contract. Sandow was an aggressive fast-talker, and won allies in the political realm by using the fairer sex. As one report delicately put it, "If the occasion arose, Sandow would provide women as dates for business friends."

On December 19, Sandow was enjoying a boozy lunch with Shafran at one of his favorite spots, Joanna, just a four-minute walk down Broadway from his office. His success in parking-ticket collection had come thanks in large part to lunches like this one. During the meal, Sandow reached under the table and offered an envelope to Shafran. In it was $3,000. This, Sandow had accepted, was just part of the cost of doing business with the PVB. Sandow estimated he paid $10,000 to $13,000 per month to Shafran or (more often) his PVB deputy, Geoffrey Lindenauer, as a kickback for the SRS contract to collect on city tickets. And it was not just Sandow. There were eleven collection agencies contracted to bring in parking violators by the city, and all were slipping envelopes to Shafran and Lindenauer at meetings like this.

But neither Sandow nor Shafran knew that three weeks earlier at Hisae's, an Asian restaurant in Cooper Square, one of Sandow's employees had been fitted with a wire by the FBI. The employee was a career criminal and murderer with an alias of Michael Burnett, who had conned his way into a job with Sandow's company and was cooperating with the FBI to wriggle out of a gun charge. Burnett had captured Sandow admitting to paying bribes to Lindenauer. Burnett, described as a "marketing director" for SRS, had drummed up much of Sandow's Chicago business and made similar tapes with city officials there, setting into motion a scandal in the municipal bureaucracy of the Second City that would hit the newspapers on December 20. But once word in New York got out that Sandow and Burnett were in trouble in Chicago, it would be obvious to anyone involved that the next step was to link those troubles to the payments SRS had been making to Lindenauer and Shafran for the parking ticket contracts. Relatively speaking, Lindenauer was not a big fish in the government, and Shafran was planning to retire early in 1986. But Lindenauer's close ties to good friend and political patron Donald Manes—around City Hall, Manes and Lindenauer were known as "Fat Boy One" and "Fat Boy Two"—sparked more interest on the part of the FBI and federal prosecutors.

The following day, Sandow had another lunch, this time with Lindenauer, and returned to his office in the early afternoon. Around 2:30, he was visited by two men he had not met before: FBI agents, one from New York and one from Chicago. They were terse with Sandow. They knew about his PVB payments, and about similar payments (totaling about $300,000 over the years) to Chicago officials. "This is the most important day of your life," the New York agent told him. They were not looking to bust Sandow, but wanted his cooperation going after bribe-taking elected officials higher up in the chain. Sandow was taken aback. He wanted a lawyer and some time to think it over. The agents granted him that. But while the agents coolly told him that everything would change for him from here on out, Sandow's eyes were darting nervously toward the safe in his office, which contained a stack of records detailing his bribes to city officials, records that would have offered an instant road map to some of New York's most insidious municipal graft. Most of it led to a much bigger target than Lindenauer or Shafran. It led to Donald Manes.

. . . . .

When the first stories about Michael Burnett and Bernie Sandow showed up in the papers at the tail end of 1985, Manes knew there would be trouble, and that only a stroke of luck would keep law enforcement and the New York media from tying together the entirety of his involvement with kickbacks at the Parking Violations Bureau. Sandow had agreed to make an immunity deal just after Christmas, and it would be only a matter of time before he pointed to Manes's top accomplice, Lindenauer. Manes had lifestyle perks that certainly would raise suspicions—the $20,000 gold BMW leased for him by the Queens party apparatus, the cushy hospital job he had gotten for his wife, Marlene, the $625,000 estate he had built up, oversized for a borough president's bank account. All that was in mind when Manes sat with Lindenauer in his living room in the ritzy Jamaica section of Queens, two days before New Year's Eve. By this time, Manes was not doing well, debilitated by the stress of the spreading Sandow stories. His thoughts turned dark. In addition to their friendship, Manes and Lindenauer shared a tragic bond: Both men had lost their fathers to suicide at a young age, and both had vowed never to consider that path themselves. But now, with Lindenauer in the sights of the federal prosecutor, Manes was having a change of heart. He knew Lindenauer could be manipulated. Manes asked whether Lindenauer was considering leaving town.

"Where would I go?" Lindenauer asked. "I don't have any money." Manes then said to Lindenauer that, if another associate of his had been caught in this situation, "He would have gone like this," holding two fingers to his head and popping the imaginary trigger. Manes was suggesting Lindenauer kill himself. Lindenauer was taken aback. "Donald, nothing has happened yet," he said. "God forbid, if something should happen, I wouldn't turn you in."

Manes and Lindenauer agreed to meet the next day, first outside the office of Bronx borough president Stanley Friedman on 68th Street, then—when an increasingly paranoid Manes got spooked into thinking he was being tailed by the FBI—outside of the office of a mutual friend, psychologist Dr. Jerome Driesen. Lindenauer had gone to see Driesen earlier in the day with a bizarre question: He had inquired about methods of suicide that would mask the ugliness of the act and leave the impression that the death was by natural causes. Dreisen was alarmed and would not help Lindenauer on that, but it showed Lindenauer had taken Manes's suggestion about suicide seriously. Lindenauer explained the trouble he was facing to Driesen, who advised Lindenauer to leave the country and told him to pressure Manes to pay him $400,000 to do so. Outside Driesen's office, Lindenauer made the cash request. Manes responded, "What are you, nuts?" The following day, though, Manes did collect $58,000 to support an escape for Lindenauer. But Manes was becoming unhinged by the pressure of the situation, and seemed to worsen by the day. "He was nervous, he was erratic," Lindenauer said. "I had not seen Donald like that before." All Manes wanted to know was whether Lindenauer was going to skip town. Yes, Lindenauer said, that was still the plan. But Lindenauer would never get that chance.

·····

Ed McDonald was ahead of his time. In the spring of 1982, at age thirty-five, he had already reached a lofty post, the head of the federal Organized Crime Strike Force in Brooklyn, the youngest Strike Force chief in the country, by far. He had been the deputy of Tom Puccio at the Strike Force beginning in 1977 before taking over the office, and was alongside Puccio during the sensational takedown of congressmen and other politicians in the Abscam sting of the late '70s and early '80s. Most of McDonald's job centered on bringing down Mafia figures, but over the past two months in the fall of 1985, as his office had been tracking Genovese family mobster Fritzy Giovanelli, something stood out: Giovanelli was in frequent contact with Meade Esposito, ex-Democratic boss of Brooklyn, who had retired from that post with some fanfare earlier in the year. Though nominally out of politics, it was clear Esposito was still pulling strings, discussing with Giovanelli the selling of judicial nominations and the fixing of court cases in Brooklyn. This was not necessarily a surprise. Throughout his history, Esposito had been known to associate with Mob figures, especially Lucchese family capo Paul Vario (one of the main subjects in the movie *Goodfellas*), with whom he had had regular meetings. In 1972, when federal agents bugged Vario's trailer/office in Canarsie over a six-month period, Esposito's name came up repeatedly, though he was not implicated in any crimes. There was even speculation Esposito was so entrenched with Mafia figures that he had been "made" into the Mob, which would be an alarming distinction for a powerful party boss.

It stood to reason that Mafia-types would seek out Esposito, and not—as he would often say—simply because they hailed from the same neighborhoods and had grown up together. Esposito was a skilled fixer, particularly when it came to the legal system, and one FBI agent said of him, "Esposito was responsible for the election of all the New York State judges seated in Kings County, as well as all local, state and Federal elected officials from Kings County. Esposito also controlled hundreds of political patronage jobs given out after each election." In 1977, when Ed Koch was running for mayor against Mario Cuomo, he drove out to meet Esposito in Brooklyn at his mother's house, despite the anti-machine-politics rhetoric Koch had been using on the campaign trail. Koch was seeking Esposito's support, but it was expected Esposito would back fellow Italian Cuomo, and Koch feared he would have to make specific promises to Esposito to get his backing. But Koch was shocked to find that Esposito agreed, with no arm-twisting or promises, to support him. Esposito simply pulled Koch aside and told him, "Make a good mayor, and be honest with me." Then, Esposito's sister made meatballs, and they sealed their future partnership over the meal. Esposito backed Koch, and he won Brooklyn, 49 percent to 42 percent.

For all his old-school, street-smart charm, it could easily be deduced that Esposito had been lining his own pockets over the years as the leader of the Brooklyn Democrats. Like Donald Manes, his lifestyle was suspicious for is lavishness. Esposito owned four homes, including one in Brooklyn and a million-dollar estate on Long Island, plus vacation houses at a spa in Fort Lauderdale, Florida, and a villa on the Caribbean island of St. Maarten. He had been a frequent target of investigators from all levels of government and law enforcement. However, he made it through his tenure with plenty of investigatory smoke, but never any legal fire. Upon his retirement, he told of a run-in with an FBI agent in Greenwich Village, who asked if he was Meade Esposito. Suspicious, Esposito asked if the agent had a subpoena. The agent laughed and said, "We have 50 or 60 letters on you. We don't even open them anymore. Let's have a drink." At his retirement party, Esposito repeated a favorite phrase of his: "Hey, I've been dancing on a charlotte russe for 16 years and I never dented the cherry."

But retirement had not meant Esposito would be granted a free pass. McDonald found there was significant enough information being passed between Giovanelli and Esposito to warrant an application for a wire on Esposito to be placed in his third-floor office at Serres, Visone and Rice Insurance on Greenwich Street, where Esposito worked. In December, the agents listening in overheard a message being left by Esposito that raised some alarms. He was calling Bronx congressman Mario Biaggi, in Washington. For the past six months, at the behest of Esposito, Biaggi had been pushing for local and federal help for an SVR client called Coastal Drydock, a company specializing in the repair and conversion of large naval ships, located on the Brooklyn Navy Yard. As far back as 1984, Biaggi had sent letters to Mayor Koch's office, seeking to have the rates Coastal paid for utilities at the Navy Yard—which were priced above market and ran the company as much as $500,000 per year—reduced. At about 10:30, Biaggi returned Esposito's call, and to the surprise of those listening in on the wiretap, the first order of business was to arrange a vacation for Biaggi, something Esposito had done twice before, once in March 1984, when he paid all expenses for Biaggi to spend time at his villa in St. Maarten, and again the previous December, when he paid for a visit to the Bonaventure Spa and Hotel in Ft. Lauderdale. Biaggi was looking for a repeat of the Bonaventure trip, on which he had taken his forty-four-year-old mistress, the model and fashion executive Barbara Barlow. Biaggi, who was sixty-eight, was married with four children, and his wife, Marie, was hospitalized as she got treatment for Hodgkin's disease.

"Give me the name of that young lady," Esposito began.

"Barlow," Biaggi replied.

After working out the details of the trip—Barlow would be at the spa from December 22 through January 3, with Biaggi joining her five days into the stay—Esposito segued. "What else is doin'?" Biaggi understood what Esposito wanted to know. "By the way, we've been doin' wonders for [Coastal president Charles] Montanti," he said, reporting, "on the city side, we've been workin' very hard with them and on the . . . federal side, uh . . . we've been getting them money. I've been bird-dogging it right along." Esposito grunted his approval: "OK, that's all I want to know."

Esposito's next phone call was to attorney James LaRossa to ensure that Biaggi and Barlow would be taken care of at the Bonaventure. He called Montanti and told him, "Mario's doin' his best." Three days later, Esposito would have a phone conversation with his partner at SVR, Joseph Martuscello, and inform him of the impending vacation Biaggi would be taking on their dime. "That's good money invested," Esposito said. Martuscello agreed, and Esposito added, "Yeah, I did it last year, too." And it was, indeed, good money invested—Biaggi would spend more than $3,000 at the Bonaventure each of the two years he visited the spa, and he would be Coastal's biggest supporter, both in the House of Representatives and the office of the mayor, with whom he was close. For Esposito and Martuscello, that was critical. Coastal was one of SVR's biggest clients, and brought in as much as $200,000 in commissions per year.

For the agents listening in on the wiretap that had been set up in Esposito's office, the string of events seemed pretty straightforward: Esposito was setting up and paying for vacations for Biaggi and his mistress in exchange for Biaggi's influence in the House on behalf of Coastal. Esposito may have been retired as the Brooklyn Democratic boss, but his phone calls showed he remained an active political manipulator.

·····

The cover of *New York* magazine in November 1985 featured two hands, not quite touching, as the hands of God and Adam in Michelangelo's Sistine Chapel painting, in front of a bright, blue New York skyline. In what would be God's hand, however, a roll of $20 bills was tucked between the index and middle fingers. THE NEW CORRUPTION was the headline, a lament over the wave of small-time bribery that had overtaken the quotidian operation of New York City. Nick Pileggi's story laid out some staggering numbers. More than half the city's sewer inspectors, Pileggi found, had been arrested for taking bribes—nearly half of the electrical inspectors, too, and one-fourth of all housing superintendents. These were not big-time sacks of money exchanging hands. Some water inspectors were found to be willing to rubber-stamp a contractor's plumbing work without so much as a look at the pipes for a mere $5. A running joke in the city went, "What's the Civil Service test for inspectors?" The punchline: an extended open palm. "Even coming from New York and being fairly cynical," Rudy Giuliani said of the pervasiveness of the graft, "I was surprised." Among the many tasks he took on when he returned to New York from his time in Washington as the assistant attorney general, Giuliani was helping the city root out petty corruption, and agreed to charge even small cases of graft in federal court, where the sentences could be stiffer than in state courts. But that ploy had not quite worked. Judges were reluctant to harshly penalize crooked inspectors taking penny-ante bribes with jail time, especially those with no prior record who were supporting families at home. Two crackdown operations, one called "Ampscam" for electrical inspectors, a play on the congressional Abscam sting, and the other called "Norton" after Art Carney's character on *The Honeymooners* for sewer inspectors (Norton's vocation on the show), brought in twenty-four bribe-takers who faced maximum sentences of anywhere from five years to 360 years. Of the twenty-four, though, only five received prison sentences, the harshest of those sentences running just six months. Giuliani expressed his disappointment. Mayor Koch expressed his outrage: "When you violate the public trust, you should have the book thrown at you."

Pileggi's story indicated that the wave of small-time money-changing was a new phenomenon, that traditionally, bribery scandals reached into higher tiers of government. "In the past," Pileggi wrote, "a satchel of cash quietly delivered to a crooked county leader might have brought a zoning variance or a fat city contract, but most of the loot stayed at the top. . . . Today, the municipal graft being scooped up in town is largely sticking to the fingers of low- and middle-level bureaucrats and inspectors who actually collect it. At a time when fewer top officials seem to be on the take, the rank and file have their hands out as never before."

It would not take long to show that Pileggi was only half right. Sure, there were low-level city employees collecting bribes. But why should that stop satchels of cash from being quietly delivered to county leaders, too?

6

IN JUNE 1985, INVESTOR IVAN Boesky, hailed as "Wall Street's best-known independent arbitrageur" for his impeccable ability to buy up the stock of a company that was about to be the target of a takeover, then cash in by selling the stock when the takeover happened, spoke to the *Washington Post* in an interview. He was an "aggressive and feared" investor, according to the *New York Times*, and he was also becoming absurdly wealthy. Nine months after he spoke to the *Post*, in 1986, Boesky would have a fortune worth nearly $1 billion, all with the aim of doing nothing more than conducting more corporate takeovers, selling more stock, making more money. Boesky, a dour and almost paranoid man who drove employees hard, was asked an existential question by the *Post*: "What are you chasing?" He was at a loss. He could not quite explain why he was doing all this. "I was given the God-given gift of being a horse that's kind of good at running around a track," he said. "I don't know any other way. I don't know how to be a milk-horse, and I don't know how to go to pasture, so I just keep doing what I was allowed to have the good fortune to do well and to try to do it better and better and better."

Boesky shared another insight, too, when it came to his outlook for the future of the corporate takeover business: "The most ebullient merger and acquisition environment and deconglomeratization, all at the same time, in the history of America, for the next five years."

He had good reason for his optimism. The country was on the upswing. Shortly after he was inaugurated in 1981, President Ronald

Reagan went on national television and gave a stark assessment of the US economy: "I regret to say that we're in the worst economic mess since the Great Depression." From there, with the Dow Jones Industrial Average at a high of just over 1,000 points, market malaise set in. In March 1982, *Forbes* magazine ran an article under the headline WAITING FOR THE BLOODBATH. But the bloodbath was more of a slow bleeding. In late August 1982, the US economy, trying to pull itself out of the muck of the 1970s and a deepening recession, saw the stock market fall to 776 points, the lowest it had been in two years. From there, though, came the rebound. A tinkering with interest rates, a tax cut from the Reagan White House, and some changes to financial rules got investors perked up. The market was back over 1,000 by the end of October, and reached a record high of 1,070 by the end of 1982. By the time the market wrapped up in 1985, it was over 1,500 points, doubling itself in just a little more than three years. Along the way, the economy was performing a feat not seen since the industrialists of the Gilded Age: It was creating financial-sector celebrities. Wall Street's arbitrageurs, headed by Boesky and joined by the likes of corporate raiders Carl Icahn, Ron Perelman, and Asher Edelman, provided the ethos of the decade, the idea that one need not make money for any particular purpose, that making money itself was an end—or, as Boesky put it, to be a horse that keeps running around the track because it does not know how to do anything else. There were no products, only profits. In June of 1984, for example, Boesky bought 1.7 million shares of the Carnation company, playing a hunch that it would be a takeover target. When Nestle conducted a hostile takeover of Carnation in September, it bought those stocks off Boesky at a $28.3 million profit. All Boesky had to do was buy and hold the stock for three months. By 1987, this kind of merger activity was worth $300 billion annually.

This blossoming of the superwealthy was supported and encouraged by the neoliberal policies and rhetoric of Reagan, who presented the pursuit of wealth as a matter of individual morality—good, driven, intelligent people got ahead in the world, and if you were not ahead, you were not good, driven, or intelligent enough. Following the righteousness and violence of the 1960s and the grime and haze of the 1970s, most Americans held the glowing optimism of Reagan in high regard even as the many shortcomings of his policies played out in their lives. Reagan pulled government out of the way of business interests wherever he could, deregulating trucking, railroads, airlines, cable TV, phone companies, the labor market, the oil and gas industry, and more, while also providing generous tax cuts and a boost in military spending. Most significant to the investor class, Reagan's government created a laissez-faire climate for financial institutions, ignoring antitrust statutes to allow for big-money corporate mergers, blurring the line between commercial and savings banks, gouging consumer protections, and injecting a stream of easy cash into the market. This cash was the fuel for the likes of Boesky and an army of young emulators who made rapid fortunes on Wall Street. Reagan was given several rounds of standing ovations in March 1985 when he became the first sitting president to visit the stock market floor in 1985. Brokers went into chants of "Ron-nie! Ron-nie!" as he rifled through platitudes about the health of the market, saying, "Our economy will be free to expand to its full potential, driving the bears back into permanent hibernation. That's our economic program for the next four years—we're going to turn the bull loose."

The loosening of the bull, while good for the market, left poorer Americans behind. It was with the inauguration of Reagan that a split began to show, according to the Congressional Budget Office, between the incomes of the top 1 percent of wealth-holders in the United States and the rest of the population. For decades, going back to the Great Depression, the concentration of wealth in the hands of the top 1 percent of households shrank steadily, as middle-class incomes strengthened. Beginning in 1980 that trend reversed, and the reversal accelerated quickly. By 1986, the income of the top 1 percent had grown by 100 percent since 1979, while for the bottom 20 percent, income actually declined over the same period. In New York, with the rise of the Yuppies—the Young Urban Professionals—driven by stock-market gains amid the grinding poverty and homelessness being caused by a burgeoning drug issue and spikes in real estate prices, those of vastly unequal incomes were elbow-to-elbow. Raymond Horton, a Columbia University business professor who ran the Citizens Budget Commission, cautioned about the potential for class warfare. "This city is a densely conglomerated group of people living on top of each other. If 25 percent are poor and X percent are rich and getting richer, that's potentially a very bad thing."

Boesky had not started as a member of the 1 percent. He was a legal clerk and a tax accountant after he graduated law school in Michigan. But to be vaulted into America's top financial echelon, he had to be very, very good at picking companies that were ripe for takeover. He would call this "pre-arbitrage." Some (and eventually this group would include government lawyers) would call it "insider trading." But for the beginning of the decade, the alarm bells that should have been sounded by the actions of investors like Boesky were mostly ignored. In 1985, in fact, Boesky was invited to the University of California–Berkeley to give the commencement address, and delivered a speech that captured the tenor and tone of the decade. "I urge you, as part of your mission, seek wealth," he told the graduating students, to cheers and laughter. "It's all right. . . . Greed is all right."

PART II

Shocked

7

THIS WAS ED KOCH AT his zenith, standing before a frigid crowd of three thousand on a clear New Year's Day afternoon in 1986 outside at City Hall plaza, the cheap "I LOVE NEW YORK" scarf of which he was so fond draped around his overcoat, a batch of the city and state's most powerful citizens on hand to fete him for his inauguration. He had won reelection in November for a third term with an overwhelming margin, taking 78 percent of the vote, such that even the most hardened anti-Kochites had to acknowledge he had ascended to the kind of executive power the city had not seen since his hero, Fiorello La Guardia, had been mayor five decades earlier. There were anti-Koch folks on hand, for sure. Newly elected Manhattan borough president David Dinkins had become the first black man in eight years to have a seat on the Board of Estimate, and vowed to use that perch to direct the attention of Koch, who had been a racially divisive figure in his first two terms, away from the glittering developments of Midtown and toward neglected neighborhoods like Harlem and the Lower East Side. City councilwoman Carol Bellamy was there, after running as Koch's hopeless but acerbic Democratic challenger the previous year. City controller Jay Goldin was on hand, too. Goldin was one of the few capable of holding his own in a verbal joust with Koch, and the pair once had to temper their mutual and very public disdain for each other by agreeing that, in describing each other's feelings toward the other, "despise is too strong a word." Well, barely. But this was Koch's moment, and the mayor drew cheers from the gathering. His good friend, Cardinal John O'Connor, was on hand, and Koch invited him to the microphone. "He is the only man I know," the Cardinal said of Koch, "who speaks to God as an associate." The crowd responded with a wave of laughter.

Koch's speech, which spanned twenty minutes, was an exercise in triumphalism, an ode to the achievements and strides made by the city during his eight years at the helm. It was a classic Koch speech, sprinkling credit to "the commissioners and to the staffs and to every single Civil Servant who gave this glorious city their all," while hammering home the message that they could not have done it without Koch in charge. He acknowledged the shortcomings New York was still facing, particularly with its crisis in homelessness, but he did not miss the opportunity to tout his role in the city's journey from the treacherous fiscal crisis of the mid-'70s to the boom of the early 1980s. "I think we have earned the right to face the next four years," Koch said, "not as defenders of a damaged city but as defending champions."

It was an especially sweet line for Koch. Two decades running for office had transformed him into a politician who stood for very little beyond winning elections, and doing so with impressive margins, a far cry from the reforming crusader he had been when he was earning his elective stripes in Greenwich Village in the 1960s. Like the nation as a whole, Koch's postwar radicalism drifted to the right through the 1970s and into the '80s. For much of his early life, he had been a man who had difficulty finding his place. He was tall and gangly, almost certainly a closeted homosexual (something Koch never publicly acknowledged) willing to put aside personal principles in favor of his ambition. He described himself as "a liberal with sanity," but it was easy to blur sanity and political expediency. He favored the death penalty, for example, even though no mayor in the nation's history had a job description that required a position on capital punishment. But it played well with crime-weary New Yorkers, so it became Koch's position. When he tacitly helped defeat Jimmy Carter in favor of Ronald Reagan in 1980, currying favor with the Gipper along the way, he did so knowing that

Carter would have been much more generous with federal aid to cities, and that Reagan's election would mean federal budget cuts that would directly damage New York. By helping Reagan, he was making his own job harder. But it did not matter. America was moving in Reagan's direction, and Koch had to do likewise. Despite Koch's own personal life, he kept up his friendship with Cardinal O'Connor, who was staunchly anti-gay. After all, it helped with the Catholic vote.

Mostly, Koch just wanted to be liked, and he had managed to accomplish that. Part of the brilliance of his strategy was his ability to control his media coverage, which he achieved through utter saturation. With past mayors, the media at City Hall would be thankful to have a press conference per day—Abe Beame, Koch's predecessor, typically had two per week and took few questions. Koch would have four or five on a typical day, and as many as seven. He would have what were known as "radiator press conferences," conducted as he stood next to the radiator outside the press's designated headquarters, Room 9. One reporter joked that Koch was "unavoidable for comment." His nonstop availability was a problem in some cases, especially for wire services that would put out stories based on one Koch press conference, then would have to change the story entirely after he had another. It got to the point where reporters would approach Koch's press secretaries and beg them to cut back on the press conferences. But to little avail. "Ed was his own press secretary," said George Arzt, who covered Koch for the *Post*, and later became his press secretary. "He just felt he needed to respond to everything. He would say something in the morning, go to lunch, come back in the afternoon and decide he had something else to say, so he would have another session with reporters." Joyce Purnick, who was the City Hall chief for the *New York Times* during Koch's administration, said that Koch's aim with the press was to "manipulate with access . . . to overwhelm with access, to overwhelm with news." Purnick, frustrated by Koch's ability to be newsworthy at even the most mundane event outside City Hall, once suggested to him, "Why don't you just get an implant, and we'll put our tape recorders and plug into you? Then we don't have to cover you everywhere."

Not only was Koch racking up big margins in the city, but he was the best-known mayor in the country, a regular on national talk shows and magazine covers, whose book, *Mayor*, had been a bestseller when it was released in 1984 (the follow-up, *Politics*, released just before his inauguration, did not fare so well). The shtick for which he was best known was his willingness to approach strangers on a street corner or ask attendees at banquets or speeches, "How'm I doing?," nearly begging the locals to tell him just how great he was. On the flip side, though, for those whom Koch perceived as enemies—most notably, the media—he could be merciless and vicious. Consultant David Garth, who had masterminded Koch's first victory, in 1977, as a tremendous longshot in a crowded field, understood Koch's psyche best, and later explained:

> Koch's problem was that Koch was a guy who had his nose against the glass for years and years. When he first came in, he was the guy at camp whose underwear showed beneath his shorts. You remember that kid at camp—no matter what he did, his underwear showed? That was Ed Koch. He would swing the softball bat and hit himself in the back of the head and miss by a mile. OK? He wasn't soigné, and he wasn't wealthy. He had nothing going for him but just his own determination and guts. All the people whose ass he had to kiss for 20 years were now kissing his ass. . . . Ed Koch is now mayor of New York, OK? All these guys from the press who like to be wise guys, he beat the living shit out of them for 10 years. . . . Koch would give them the back of his hand. So then he ran three times, and he gets bigger and bigger majorities. And as a result, every time he did it, instead of becoming a nicer guy, he said, "Fuck you."

Just before the inauguration ceremony, Koch had welcomed a small group of close dignitaries into his office for coffee and a quick chat, a group that included two of the city's most powerful men: Queens president Donald Manes, and Bronx leader Stanley Friedman. The previous night, Friedman had done one better—he was present at the mayor's private midnight swearing-in, held at the home of Koch's friend and informal adviser, David Margolis. Both Friedman and Manes were given honored spots at the Koch inauguration, on the dais facing the crowd. Out among that crowd was the thin, balding federal prosecutor Rudy Giuliani who, in just the past week, had become familiar for the first time with the names Friedman and Manes, and their connections to what appeared to be a major scheme to defraud the city's Parking Violations Bureau. Giuliani had been sketching out a case in his mind in which both Democratic bosses were guilty of a host of crimes against the city. Giuliani studied Friedman up on the stage—confident, slick, goateed, and bespectacled. Then he fixed his gaze on Manes, who was portly, rumpled, and unsmiling. He went back and forth between the two, thinking that maybe there was something to be uncovered here, that maybe he could, as he would later say, take all the pieces he'd been gathering and, "figure out whether it was all true or not."

. . . . .

Donald Manes was beginning to worry those around him. In the week or so after Koch was inaugurated, Manes had been gaunt and aloof, drifting in and out of conversations, his eyes darting and unable to stay focused. He was sweating. He had always had a perspiration problem, but lately it had gotten much worse, his shirts stained with large semi-circles under his armpits, his rugged brow pilled with moisture. He had undergone throat surgery to remove polyps around Thanksgiving, and the prevailing wisdom was that something worse had come out of the procedure. "Where once he had been gregarious, cunning, a bright light shining through the zigs and zags of city politics, now he often seemed preoccupied and strangely detached," former city councilman Peter Vallone recalled. "I was 99 percent sure he was dying of cancer. I felt terribly sorry for him." Another friend, predecessor as Queens party leader Matty Troy, remembered, "I noticed something. I thought it was just a physical thing. He had just had the throat operation and he was very hoarse. . . . He never brought it up to me." Manes had been on a diet, too, one of the long litany of weight-loss fads he had tried over the years. This time it was a liquid diet, and some chalked up his rattled state to the side effects that come with abstaining from solid food. On January 9, Manes had a busy day with work, and afterward, he was to host the Israeli consul, Moshe Yegar, at a reception at the Borough Hall in Queens, the kind of glad-handing event at which Manes typically would shine. But he had cut out early, and sent his driver home. Manes also was supposed to attend a party for Vallone, to celebrate his election as majority leader of the City Council. But he never showed. Instead, Manes sent home his city-appointed driver, got behind the wheel of a 1984 Ford LTD, one of the cars registered to his office, drove off and, for the remainder of the night, disappeared.

Two days earlier, the *Daily News* ran a front-page headline blaring, SLAY SUSPECT DEALS FOR FBI, with an ominous photo of Brooklyn-born grifter and con man Michael Burnett in dark glasses. Beginning with that story, fascination grew with the sordid history of Burnett, the Brooklyn-born FBI informant who was linked to three murders. Burnett, the paper reported, had been giving out bribes to government officials in Chicago on behalf of Bernie Sandow. Reporters had not yet pieced together the angle of the story that would tie Burnett and Sandow to the city's government, but it was an angle Manes knew all too well. The one hope he had had of avoiding implication, he had known, was that federal investigators would not find much and stories would not hit the newspapers. The stories about Burnett's history meant that hope was dashed. As Manes surely saw it, it became almost certain that a connection would soon be made to Geoffrey Lindenauer, who had not followed through on his promise to take the $58,000 Manes gave him and leave the country. From Lindenauer, it was a short leap to Manes, his best friend. For Manes, every story about Burnett was like the tightening of a noose.

Approaching 2:00 a.m., two patrol officers from the Queens Highway Unit 3 noticed a car abruptly swerving over four lanes on the Grand Central Parkway near LaGuardia Airport. It was Manes in the LTD. The officers turned on the car's siren, but Manes continued for two miles before exiting at 126th Street and Northern Boulevard, the mostly empty stretch near Shea Stadium where Manes had pushed to have Donald Trump's domed stadium built. When he finally pulled over and was approached by officers, Manes opened his door and began fumbling for his wallet. He had forgotten to put the car into park, so when he mindlessly lifted his foot off the brake, it lunged forward and crashed into a chain-link fence. When they got a look inside the car, the officers were disturbed—Manes's suit and trench coat were covered in blood. They would later find a four-inch paring knife and Manes's wristwatch on the floor in front of the passenger seat. A closer look showed that Manes had a large, Y-shaped gash on his left wrist. After a few minutes, one of the officers figured out just who the driver was. They were ordered to stop using radios and only discuss the situation on landline telephones. No one wanted Manes's name going out over the police scanner. But one disgruntled dispatcher was heard to say, "You know what it is, they're trying to cover this shit. You know, you and I, we would have been jammed up the ass. Do you believe this shit?"

Manes was taken to Booth Memorial Hospital, in shock and near death from massive blood loss. He underwent three hours of surgery, groggy as doctors had a difficult time getting an explanation from him on what, exactly, had happened. He had originally told the police he had been ambushed. In the hospital, he said he had been forced to cut his own wrist. The following day, the *Daily News* reported, citing a police source, that Manes's cut had been self-inflicted. Mayor Ed Koch, who showed up at the hospital shortly after Manes had undergone surgery, blamed Manes's ongoing battle with his weight. "You know those liquid diets," Koch told reporters. "They'll kill you." Manes was shielded from the media, and in the absence of firm explanations from him, speculation took hold. According to the *Village Voice*, Manes had been pulled over in what was known at the time as "a well-established cruising area for female and transvestite prostitutes," and the following day, citing a single source, NBC radio reported that, "a prostitute was definitely involved." The drama around Manes had delivered a shock all over New York political circles. Joyce Purnick recalled the reaction when speculation arose that Manes had been involved in corruption. "'Donny is too smart,'" she remembered associates saying. "Everyone called him Donny. 'Donny would *never* get involved in something illegal.' Not maybe because he wasn't capable of it, ethically, but because he was too smart to get caught up. 'Not Donny.' I remember that line: 'Not Donny.'"

.....

Two days after the news of Manes's suicide attempt hit the papers, the *New York Post*'s City Hall beat writer, George Arzt, was at the Water Club on the East River, having a meal and watching the conference championship football games on a Sunday afternoon, the Patriots and Dolphins in the AFC, and the Bears against the Rams in the NFC. Mario Biaggi came into the restaurant, and the two talked. The *Daily News* had a front-page headline that morning: FEDS PROBE CITY BRIBES, the attached story disclosing Rudy Giuliani's calling of a grand jury to investigate the matter, and detailing payments made by Bernie Sandow to unnamed officials in the PVB. That included what, for Manes, was an ominous reference by a US attorney who said that Sandow implicated "significant people who are in responsible political positions in the sense that they are among the decision-makers, and people higher up in the political hierarchy." The story came up in Biaggi's conversation with Arzt, who was shocked when Biaggi turned to him and said, "That's the reason Manes tried to kill himself." *The PVB? That's why Manes's wrist was slit?* Arzt immediately sensed a scoop—no one outside law enforcement had yet connected Manes to the PVB issue. He went back to his office and called an FBI source to ask about the investigation. The FBI source told him, "I will only tell you if you're wrong." So Arzt tried out Biaggi's speculation. He asked whether Lester Shafran, head of the PVB, was under investigation. "Silence," Arzt said. He asked if number two man Geoffrey Lindenauer was under investigation. Silence again. Arzt wrote the story, connecting the investigations of Shafran and Lindenauer to Manes's botched suicide. But when the *Post*'s lawyers got hold of the story, they refused to let Arzt publish it. "Manes will own the paper if you print this," they told him. The lawyers would only let Arzt write that one city official and two PVB officials were under investigation. If Arzt had been able to report that it was Manes who was under investigation, his odd ride two nights before, which Manes had still not explained, would have made much more sense.

When Manes did finally offer an explanation to the police, on January 13, he stretched the bounds of credulity. Chief of Detectives Richard Nicastro read out the Manes explanation to the public: He had intended to go home when he got into the car at the Borough Hall, but instead found two men in the backseat who hit him on the back of the neck and abducted him, forcing him to drive around Queens for hours. Manes could not provide physical descriptions of his captors, and could not explain why they would want to kidnap him only to have him drive around Queens for the evening. When Nicastro was asked if Manes's story was credible, he said, flatly, "Drawing on my years of police work, I always take at face value what is said by a complainant." No one believed him, and it was apparent that Nicastro did not truly believe himself, either. The Manes tale drew skepticism from across New York's political world, but he had the backing of Mayor Koch, who said Manes deserved support even if he had been "with a hooker," and added, "People who have any brains know that we're all—what's that Catholic term?—*weak vessels*. We're all weak. We all have infirmities. We're all humans. We're all sinners. I'm not going to pass judgment."

Days later, Giuliani was ready to make his move. Lindenauer was arrested, charged with taking a $5,000 bribe from Burnett and Sandow during their lunch at Hisae's in November, becoming the highest ranking official in New York's government to be charged with misconduct in nearly two decades. Lindenauer's boss, Lester Shafran, who was scheduled to give up his post at the end of January, was fired two weeks ahead of time. While Giuliani and others denied that there was a direct link between Manes's bizarre wrist-slashing disappearance and the government's PVB investigation, word also got out that Manes had pushed for Lindenauer to take over Shafran's job at the top of the PVB. In fact, weeks earlier, Manes had gotten into a full-throated falling-out with Koch at City Hall over Lindenauer's future, though that stayed out of the press. Manes did not want the bribery train that he had set up in the PVB to end, and Shafran's departure would open the way for a Koch appointment who probably would not be willing to keep the scam going. But Manes had Lindenauer in his pocket. When Manes told deputy mayor Stanley Brezenoff that Lindenauer was his choice to take over the Parking Violations Bureau, Brezenoff did some vetting and was told overwhelmingly that Lindenauer was not up to the job—not for ethical reasons, but for lack of qualifications and competence. "I told Manes no," Brezenoff said. "He really went nuts. I had never seen that, so apoplectic, and he went to Ed and had a major screaming match over this. From Ed's perspective, he was just defending me because he didn't know this. And then of course it turned out why Donald was so anxious to have [Lindenauer] in those spots."

On January 17, an entirely new track was opened on the PVB scandal, beyond the envelopes stuffed with cash being paid out in restaurants all over the city. This was a more systematic and lucrative defrauding of the agency, rooted in a bogus $22.7 million contract the PVB had given to a company called Citisource two years earlier, which had been pushed through the parking agency by Lindenauer. This was different from the low-level shakedowns of ticket-chasing companies. The city contract was the brainchild of Stanley Friedman, who had not disclosed to the city that he was the company's director and its primary shareholder. He was careful to ensure support of the contract from the PVB by including stock giveaways in Citisource for Lindenauer and Manes. The city contract had called for the company to develop and manufacture small hand-held computers that would allow ticket-writers to log their violations in real time. If the computers were in production, there might have been no wrongdoing. But Citisource was barely a real company, with only a handful of employees and no engineering staff. There were no computers, not even a prototype.

The city canceled the contract with Citisource when the charges came to light, but with so much focus on the spectacular and mysterious troubles of Manes, the problems that the PVB scandal might bring Friedman—who raked in about $1 million when the company went public shortly after receiving the city contract—were easily obscured. Just after the cancellation of the Citisource contract, Manes (who had been transferred from Queens to NYU Medical Center in Manhattan) finally came clean on his disappearance. Reading from a five-paragraph statement, he admitted that there were no assailants and there was no kidnapping, but that he had cut his own wrist. He apologized to his family and offered no further explanation. Koch remained steadfast in his support, visiting Manes's hospital bed, kissing him on the head and telling him, "Don't worry about anything Donny, we all love you."

. . . . .

In the late morning of Super Bowl Sunday, Ed Koch appeared on *NewsForum* with Gabe Pressman, fiery and determined. He knew exactly where the questions were going, and he had girded himself. That week, *Daily News* columnist Jimmy Breslin—a Koch nemesis and Queens guy who had based many of his quirky characters on friends and associates he knew in the borough—had broken open the whole of the Parking Violations Bureau scandal. Breslin had held long, confessional discussions with his old friend Michael Dowd, a Queens lawyer whose office was directly across from Manes's Queens Borough Hall throne. Dowd, to Breslin's horror, had a company that was one of the eleven with a contract to collect on delinquent tickets for the Parking Violations Bureau, and as such, he had paid bribes to Lindenauer over a period of eighteen months. Breslin, having digested Dowd's teary admission, convinced him to confess to Rudy Giuliani, turn informant, and save his own hide. In Breslin's column, the real power behind the PVB bribes was Manes, now accused of extortion. In a press conference after Breslin's column appeared, one day after kissing Manes and professing his love, Koch turned on Manes, three times announcing to the gathered media, "I am shocked." As the truth of the PVB scandal took root, *Newsday* columnist Murray Kempton suggested the city, which did not have a civic motto, adopt "I am shocked." The *New Yorker*'s Andy Logan took it a step further: *Ego Sane Stupeo*—"I am shocked" in Latin.

"I would have staked my life on the honesty of Donald Manes," Koch told Pressman. "But, nevertheless, even though he is someone whom I would have allowed to be the executor of my estate—I've known him for more than 20 years—I am convinced now that he engaged in being a crook."

Koch went from kissing Manes to suggesting that Manes was exaggerating his health problems so he could remain in the hospital and avoid facing the press or prosecution. This was a problematic stance for a public official like Koch, because Manes had not been convicted of a crime, let alone charged. Koch was already summoning the hangman. While he was at it, Koch used Pressman's soapbox to settle political scores and to outline what would become his standard defense against attempts to link the corruption in the parking agency to his administration: *If all you reporters did not know what was going on, how should I have known what was going on?* He railed against Breslin, noting, "Breslin was not a good enough reporter to know he was hanging around with crooks." Koch went on, too, to pronounce Dowd a crook, and said of he and Manes, "the two of them should ultimately go to jail." His battle with Breslin long had been ongoing and public, but his grudge against Dowd stretched back further, to his first campaign for mayor in 1977. Dowd had been the campaign manager for Mario Cuomo, and Koch accused Dowd of hiring a private detective to investigate rumors of Koch's homosexuality. Koch would later blame Dowd for vicious posters circulated by Cuomo backers that read "Vote for Cuomo, not the Homo." The scandal was picking at old Koch wounds.

Dowd, writing in his journal immediately after Koch's harangue, speculated how much he had been damaged by the mayor's comments. He wondered how much of a life would be left for him when the PVB scandal played out. "I watched Koch call me a villain, a criminal, and say I should go to jail," he wrote. "It hurts. Hasn't this hurt me? He misstated the facts. . . . I'm frightened for my daughter. I think the machine is trying to protect itself. Koch on the point. How much of a life is left to me?" Then Dowd collected himself and, like a record 92.5 million Americans, watched Super Bowl XX.

8

THE BEARS. BILL PARCELLS WAS having a hard time letting them go. His Giants had just finished what could only be called a successful season, racking up 10 wins, finishing with a 7–3 record in their last 10 games after a slow start, and pounding the 49ers in their playoff opener, 17–3. But then there were the Bears. After beating San Francisco, the Giants had gone to Chicago and been drubbed, 21–0, in the conference semifinal, the second straight year the Giants had made strides but still been forced out of the postseason in their second game. This one had a particular sting to it, though, as Parcells lamented what came next— another chance to watch a different NFC team in the Super Bowl, another offseason, another draft, another training camp, and another 16 games just for the off chance that New York might again find itself in this position, trying to break through against the NFL's elites. In the locker room after the Chicago loss, Parcells had withstood the barrage of well-wishers telling him it had been a good season, answering in grunts and terse thank yous. He had done his media interviews, high-lighted by a national writer asking him if, in light of the six sacks the Bears defense laid on quarterback Phil Simms, Parcells should have called more three-step drops. The steam was nearly visible shooting out of Parcells's ears. After a bulldozing like that, this guy wanted to talk about three-step drops? "You wouldn't know a three-step drop," Parcells said, "if it grew teeth and bit you on the ass."

Parcells spoke to virtually no one after the Bears game, remaining stone-faced on the dreary bus ride from Soldier Field to O'Hare Airport. He made exceptions for linebacker Harry Carson and defensive end George Martin, the two deans of the team, who had been through some of the worst of times the Giants had endured as a franchise—and for a team that, before the previous year, had been to the postseason just once since 1963. They were there in 1983, Parcells's first year as head coach after he was promoted when Ray Perkins took the Alabama job, when New York went 3–12–1. Parcells managed to hang onto his job that year, barely, and since then, he had his ups and downs with both Carson and Martin. But he respected them as players and men, and the pit that had formed in his stomach was just a manifestation of how badly he wanted those guys to be rewarded with a championship. He told them as much after the game, making a promise: "We're gonna get there."

Now, on the team plane, Parcells was still silent. Next to him was Mickey Corcoran, his old coach at River Dell High in New Jersey, who was still a source of calm, perspective, and wisdom for Parcells. Corcoran had his own connection to coaching greats, having been mentored by Packers legend Vince Lombardi at St. Cecilia High School in New Jersey in the late 1930s. Lombardi had been Corcoran's basketball coach, admiring the toughness Corcoran showed despite his diminutive size—Lombardi nicknamed him "Mickey Mouse." But Lombardi's approach inspired Corcoran to become a coach himself. In 1955, he was coaching basketball, too, when he got a big, talented scorer named Bill Parcells, one of the best basketball players in New Jersey state history, who needed to be pushed a bit to maximize his talent. Parcells would remember one game, when he was just fifteen. River Dell had built a 17-point lead, with Parcells leading the way in scoring. Parcells was hit with a technical foul, though, and Corcoran, in his anger, removed Parcells from the game and told him he would not be going back in. He kept his word. With Parcells benched, River Dell collapsed, blew the lead, and lost by one point. If Corcoran had put Parcells back in, he probably would have won the game. But Corcoran would have sacrificed principle and lost some standing with his star. Parcells said if Corcoran would have put him back in, "I would've had him—forever. . . . I learned something that day."

Corcoran knew enough to leave Parcells time to soothe himself after what had happened at Soldier Field. When Parcells closed his eyes, he could only replay the Bears game. What bothered him most was the game was not as lopsided as the score indicated, that there were opportunities that, had the Giants capitalized, might have taken the game down to a last-minute decision. There were also enormous mistakes. There was the botched punt by Sean Landeta, the young playboy punter who had barely made the team coming out of training camp over Dave Jennings, a Parcells favorite who, at age thirty-three, had just reached the end of his usefulness. Landeta had a good leg, but was a headache on a number of fronts for Parcells—ahead of the Giants' playoff opener against the 49ers the previous week, he had been nabbed scalping his players' tickets, offering an autographed photo of himself as part of the deal, and his teammates razzed him by setting up a faux ticket window in front of his locker the next day (TICKETS: $50, the sign read). But Landeta was at the center of one of the most important plays of the Bears loss. After a third-down sack at the 12 yard line, Landeta lined up at the edge of his own end zone. It was a frigid and windy day on the shore of Lake Michigan. When he dropped the ball toward his swinging foot, a gust of wind pushed through, moving the ball out of Landeta's kicking line. He whiffed, the ball just grazing the side of his foot for a punt that netted minus-seven yards. Bears defensive back Shaun Gayle took the ball and scurried in for a five-yard touchdown. On the road against a monstrous defense like Chicago's, the Giants could not afford to give away points.

There was a slew of other miscues. The Giants moved the ball on their first possession, until a fumble by running back Rob Carpenter cut the drive short. There was a dropped touchdown pass by receiver Bobby Johnson at the end of the first half, which would have tied the game, 7–7, and a missed field goal by kicker Eric Schubert after that. There were two big touchdown passes from quarterback Jim McMahon to receiver Dennis McKinnon, both of which came against defensive back Elvis Patterson, who had been nicknamed "Toast" by Parcells because he got burned so often. There were the big hits taken by 5-foot-7 running back Joe Morris, who ran into 300-pound Bears lineman William "The Refrigerator" Perry, a blow that knocked Morris out of the game for a stretch with a concussion. As one Chicago writer quipped, "Morris returned, but at 5-6." He finished with only 32 yards. Over the course of the game, especially as the clock wound down, Parcells watched as his best player, linebacker Lawrence Taylor, lost his composure. He called Bears running back Matt Suhey a baby for blocking him low, though Suhey would add that "baby" was his own euphemism, because Taylor added "a little perverse language in there." McKinnon hit Taylor with a crackback block late in the game, and on the next play, Taylor went after McKinnon, attempting to clip his legs. Even with two touchdown catches to his credit, McKinnon took special pride in that block: "You could see the feet in the air. I knocked him on his butt." Taylor even approached the Bears bench, got into a war of words with coach Mike Ditka and, according to tight end Emery Moorhead, "wanted to fight everybody on the sidelines." Only nose tackle Jim Burt had the presence of mind to try to calm Taylor, and Parcells pulled Taylor aside for a long discussion as the clock ticked away. This was a poor ending to what had been an unimpressive year from Taylor.

On the plane, a beer cut Parcells's tensions a bit. After another, he was nearly ready to be returned to human company. Corcoran could sense it. But he was not about to offer Parcells platitudes about the accomplishments of the season. He had gotten enough of those already. Parcells needed to process what had just happened in Chicago. He did not need a pat on the back; he needed a productive target on which to focus his anger. Finally, Corcoran spoke. "You gotta figure out a way," he said, "to beat these fucking guys."

. . . . .

Howard Cosell, speaking during his show on ABC radio in mid-February 1986, began with a dramatic statement, which he dropped with relish. "Lawrence Taylor," he said, "is a sick man."

Taylor, Cosell was reporting, had checked himself into a rehab facility in Texas. There was no surprise among the Giants that Taylor had drug and alcohol problems—teammates and coaches had been aware of that throughout the 1985 season—but it was a surprise Taylor had been willing to get some help for himself. Somewhat skeptical, other media outlets scrambled to check Cosell's reporting. The *Daily News* cited a source confirming that Taylor was in rehab, but the Giants were denying the report outright. "If any player wants to check himself in and have the team pay for it, it has to cross my desk," general manager George Young said. "Nothing like that has happened. If a player wants to do it on his own and pay for it, he's free to go anywhere he chooses. But in any case, I'd know." Still the rumors circulated, and for two months after the Giants' season ended, no one heard much of anything from Taylor.

The timing was not great for the NFL. Any pretensions the league had toward cleaning up its drug problem had been crushed by what happened at the Super Bowl at the end of January. To little surprise on the part of Giants fans, the Bears tore apart the Patriots 46–10 in that game. With their rout of New York, followed by a 24–0 win over the Rams in the NFC Championship, Chicago had rolled through the postseason with three wins by a combined score of 91–10. It mattered little to Parcells, but the Giants had given them their toughest game in the playoffs.

Given the anticlimax of the game, the most important story coming out of Super Bowl XX did not get out until two days later, when the *Boston Globe* reported the AFC champion Patriots had a massive drug problem, and that coach Raymond Berry was aware of it but had told reporter Ron Borges he would not confirm the issue on the record until after the team's postseason run was over. Berry confronted the players with the problem at a team meeting the day after the Super Bowl, and it had been agreed that the team would submit to drug testing. The next day, the *Globe* ran the names of six players—which the team did not deny—who were allegedly using drugs. The outing of the players shook the NFL the way the Pittsburgh drug trials had shaken baseball, because now every player in the league knew teammates might sing to the media about drug issues in the locker room. And a team with a management group like that of the Patriots might sell out its players by allowing them to be identified in the papers without protection from the team. There was also the matter of the Patriots agreeing to drug testing. The NFL's players union was fighting testing measures at every turn and did not want the Patriots collectively submitting to them. A month earlier, a drug scandal had descended on the St. Louis Cardinals, and owner Bill Bidwill ordered the team to undergo postseason drug testing. That was not allowed under the collective bargaining agreement, and forty of Bidwill's Cardinals players refused the tests. They were each fined $1,000.

The day after their season ended in Chicago, one Giants player reported that management had not asked players to submit to a drug test. "Why have a witch hunt?" the player said. "I don't think we have a drug problem here." There were rumors that, in the depths of the miserable 1983 season, Giants management and coaches had suspected the team's poor play had been linked to drug and alcohol abuse, but the front office still only used "spot-checks" to keep an eye on its players. Speculation held that, during the 1985 season, as many as twelve players had been subject to spot-checks. One Giant told the *Village Voice* the maelstrom that followed the Patriots scandal had sent a chill through locker rooms everywhere, and was the product of media hysteria. "I know [the Patriots] and no bullshit, they're a clean team," he said. "I hear five of the six guys names, all they did was smoke a joint every once in a while on their day off. Listen, I don't do drugs, none at all, but I really can't see the harm in a couple of defensive backs smoking some reefer." The player requested anonymity, he said, because he feared the same kind of media drug-shaming in New York (particularly from conservative columnist Dick Young) that Patriots players were undergoing nationally. "You think," he said, "I want to end up in Dick Young's column every day for the rest of my life?"

Taylor did later admit he had gone to the facility at Houston Methodist Hospital, but to him, the space felt too much like a penitentiary.

Taylor checked out after just three days. He moved to a $1,500-per-day room at another Houston facility, but that did not suit him, either. Instead, he said, he mostly played golf in Texas ("my detox," he called it) and checked in with therapists from time to time. It was not until March 20, though, that Taylor and the Giants acknowledged his trip to rehab, when Giants PR man Tom Power called beat reporters and read a four-paragraph statement from the team's star linebacker. Taylor did not acknowledge where he was or what, exactly, his problems were, but said, "I have just completed the first phase of what I know will be a difficult and ongoing battle to overcome these problems."

9

DAVID GARTH KNEW A FEW things about the power of contrition. Garth had become a wunderkind in New York's political circles back in 1969, when he was hired as a media adviser to Mayor John Lindsay, who had been embattled by all manner of woes, from trouble plowing the streets during a blizzard to a racially divisive teachers strike. Lindsay was a tall, handsome Republican in a city that went more than 2-to-1 for Democrats, and disappointment in his first term had been so thorough that Lindsay was not picked by either party in their primaries that fall. He was forced to run in the general election on a Liberal ticket. But Garth had an idea for Lindsay: Say you're sorry. Admit your failures. And, as you're saying sorry, you can work in some of the things that had gone right. The plan was to have Lindsay sit in front of a camera for a series of ads and dolefully fess up to his own shortcomings. Lindsay hated the idea. "He didn't want to do it," Lindsay's campaign manager, Richard Aurelio, said. "He had to be talked into it. He didn't like the idea of going in front of millions of New Yorkers and eating crow." But Garth talked him into it, and the ads were effective. Lindsay won reelection.

Now, nearly two decades later, Garth had been giving much the same advice to Koch. At the beginning of February, Koch had summoned some of his top advisers, past and present, to the mayor's residence at Gracie Mansion for a counseling session. He was, he had publicly admitted, depressed and losing sleep over the Parking Violations Bureau scandal, which had begun to draw attention to corruption and graft in other parts of city government. Koch canceled the annual State of the City speech, which had been scheduled for February 3. He had been portraying himself as a victim. The Manes story had gotten out of control—the story was getting national play, the major New York papers were all jostling for scoops, Jimmy Breslin, having been provoked by Koch, was pummeling the mayor in the *Daily News*, and the crack team of investigative journalists at the *Village Voice*, led by Wayne Barrett and Jack Newfield, was uncovering new angles on unseemliness in the Koch government every week or two. (Barrett and Newfield, according to one-time Koch press secretary George Arzt, were the only reporters Koch refused to sit down with for an interview.) Just a little more than two weeks after Koch had announced the resignation of Transportation Department head Tony Ameruso, praising him as "honest" and "impeccable," the *Voice* ran an exposé about Ameruso's shady and lucrative real estate deal on a parking lot downtown. That was a direct blow to Koch's credibility—Ameruso had been kept on in the Koch administration back in 1977, at the request of Meade Esposito. One of Koch's defenses as the county leaders became embroiled in trouble was he had never taken nor given favors from them. Ameruso served as a reminder that he had, in fact, occasionally done the party bosses' bidding. As Esposito said, "I saved [Ameruso] by telling Koch that he's my guy, he's a good man, don't drop him."

With Rudy Giuliani (and with his affection for press conferences) leading the investigation into the growing corruption scandals, Koch had no way to reel in the story. There had been no evidence that Koch himself was involved in corruption, but, Garth warned Koch, even if he was not personally guilty, the public would judge him guilty of "schmuckism." That is, rather than carry the reputation of the savvy crook ripping off the government, Koch would be the schmuck blindly standing by while *other* crooks ripped off his government. Schmuckism would not put Koch into legal jeopardy, but it could torpedo the rest of his term as mayor, and possibly sink both his future and his legacy. So Garth retooled his Lindsay advice and, along with Koch's other advisers, convinced him the only way to get back ahead of the scandal would be to acknowledge his own responsibility for it. After weeks of jousting with the media over his lack of culpability for the Manes PVB bribery mess, and for the Stanley Friedman Citisource contract mess, and for the other messes (like Ameruso) that quickly followed, Koch was going to have to draw on his small well of humility and tell the city he was at fault, and he was sorry.

Koch's past ties to Esposito were brought back to light as the city scandal widened, as was his tight relationship with Friedman. Just the previous month, Friedman attended Koch's private inauguration party, and Koch had attended Friedman's wedding back in 1982. While Koch had gone after Manes by calling him a crook, he remained mostly silent on Friedman, who had been one of his most important political allies in his race for mayor in 1977, when Friedman had been Abe Beame's deputy and helped to arrange Koch's understanding with Esposito, a favor Koch returned by helping Friedman win the party chairmanship in the Bronx when Beame left office. Koch expressed his admiration for Friedman in his book, *Politics*. He told of a fundraising dinner he attended that had been arranged by Friedman for Bronx borough president Stanley Simon, which drew a thousand attendees. "I don't know how you did it," Koch recalled saying to Friedman. "I could not get a thousand people to attend one of my fund-raising dinners." To which Friedman replied, "If you give me a thousand jobs, I'll get them there for you." Koch noted Friedman was exaggerating, but added that Friedman pointed out to him how "each one of those who attended, whether they were working in government or were in the private sector, owed something to him or to Stanley Simon—not in a corrupt way, but just in terms of the regular glue of politics." In light of the scandals hitting the Koch regime, the mayor's understanding of the difference between corruption and the glue of politics came across as out of whack. An article in the *Voice* called Koch "Friedman's captive, a mouthy shill for an amoral shell."

Koch had little choice but to come around to Garth's idea of a Lindsay-style confessional. All around him, members of his administration were scuttling out of their offices with resignations, tinged with scandal either directly or tangentially. By the end of February, just two months into his second term, nineteen Koch officials had quit or been forced out. When Koch took the podium on February 24—which happened to be the day that Giuliani brought up an indictment on Geoffrey Lindenauer—at the Board of Estimate room in City Hall, he was somber and contrite. "I am embarrassed, I am chagrined, I am absolutely mortified that this kind of corruption could have existed and that I did not know of it," Koch said. Stubbornly, he did not issue a complete apology, and was quick to use the occasion to remind anyone listening that he had led the city out of its fiscal woes of the late '70s, and even leaned on that as a cause of his blindness to corruption. "As a result of having to work with the established political structure to resolve the fiscal crisis," Koch said, "my administration lost the distance and the controls I had hoped to maintain in order to avoid the undue influence of party leaders on the workings of government." For Ed Koch, eating crow in front of his fellow New Yorkers was painful, even more painful than it had been for Lindsay seventeen years earlier.

10

THROUGHOUT JANUARY, JETS OWNER LEON Hess had been sending letters to Mayor Koch and Governor Mario Cuomo, asserting his dissatisfaction with the outlines that had emerged for the new domed football stadium in Queens. The government had not secured the land, which Hess saw as a must if he were to agree to leave the Meadowlands in New Jersey and return to New York, and the plans had not undergone the needed vetting to ensure there would be no tie-ups. Most of all, Hess was opposed to the idea of financing the new dome by charging fans in advance for the right to lease seats—a plan calling for a family of four that would normally buy Jets season tickets at the 40 yard line for $480 to put down a whopping $48,000 on a lease, which would only buy them the right to continue to pay $480 for tickets. Hess wrote that fans of the Jets would be asked to pay $2 billion extra over the forty-year lease, and that was unacceptable. Trump, on the other hand, would offer little financial risk of his own, and in his lease agreement with the government, he would split all profits, 50-50 for the first twenty-five years, then take 75 percent after that. In Hess's view, then, if he agreed to come back and play in Trump's dome, he would be asking his fans to pay Trump more than $1 billion for the right to do so. "The result is a domed stadium built on the backs of our fans," Hess wrote to Koch and Cuomo. "And that is a burden which the Jets are not now prepared to impose on its loyal fans." Hess had just one meeting with city and state officials, at his headquarters in Manhattan on February 5. Trump was not invited.

The meeting lasted only ninety minutes, and Hess did not let go his insistence that the stadium be financed by the city and state, with the team repaying both through a lengthy lease—the same deal the Mets had gotten at Shea Stadium twenty-five years earlier. But the city and state had committed to Trump's plan. It would be the fans who paid, or nobody. Hess was not having it, and announced so publicly. Thus, the Jets' window to move out of the Meadowlands and back into New York closed, and it began to look as though Trump's pitch to bring an NFL team to Queens was withering. State officials held out hope for a new stadium. City officials pretty much gave up once Hess announced his team was remaining in New Jersey. Koch was opposed to giving Trump a tax abatement for the stadium in the first place, and the city's biggest political booster of the project, Trump's friend and Queens boss Donald Manes, faced extortion charges, was carrying a scar on his wrist from a botched suicide attempt, and subsequently resigned his post as president of the borough. The only hope for pro football in New York would be the USFL's Generals, who last played a game in July of 1985. With the USFL having pushed its schedule to the fall to compete with the NFL at Trump's insistence, it would be a while (late September 1986) before the upstart league was back on the field. That was a dodgy proposition. Its lawsuit against the NFL was slated to begin in a few months, and with the league having absorbed somewhere around $100–200 million in losses over four years, few USFL teams were bothering to renew their season tickets until they saw what the lawsuit held. That included the Generals. If the lawsuit failed, the USFL would likely go down with it, and Trump would have effectively killed any hope for pro football to return to the city.

.....

By March, Trump's mentor Roy Cohn was dying, just fifty-nine years old but undergoing waves of frail infirmity mixed with bursts of good health. Whenever asked about his affliction, he would say he was stricken by liver cancer, though it was known among a small group of friends and mumbled around New York society that Cohn was gay and had AIDS. As he was slipping toward his demise, Cohn was fending off a disbarment proceeding brought against him by the New York bar, which accused Cohn of fraud and professional misconduct. There was some irony as Cohn played the victim against a bullying government, having been the driving force behind Joseph McCarthy's persecution of suspected Communists in the 1950s. "What McCarthy was accused of practicing is actually being practiced against me," he said. In late February, Cohn had attended his birthday party at the home of former model Basha Szymanska, and on that occasion he was looking dapper and tanned in a white tuxedo and red bow tie, with Mike Wallace and a camera crew from *60 Minutes* on hand for a piece that would run later in the month. Trump, Stanley Friedman, and celebrities like Norman Mailer, Lee Iacocca, and Studio 54 owner Steve Rubell were there, too. On camera with Wallace, Cohn said his cancer was in remission and denied the talk of AIDS when Wallace broached the subject directly. "No," Cohn said. "That's easy to answer." Cohn paused and added, "Is there that much public curiosity as to whether I had AIDS?" When Wallace told Cohn the National Institutes of Health (where Cohn had been treated back in November) had him on its computers as an AIDS patient, Cohn said, "Well I shouldn't be, I am glad you told me that. I will get that taken care of very fast." For emphasis, Cohn added, "I ain't dying from nothing."

Cohn's close friends knew better. Trump likely had known about Cohn's illness since November 1984, when (it was later revealed) Cohn was given his diagnosis. That was just weeks after he and Cohn announced the USFL lawsuit against the NFL. While Cohn kept working through his AIDS treatment, Trump distanced himself, pulling the USFL suit away from Cohn a few months later and giving it to a colorful new lawyer, Harvey Myerson. That wasn't all. Trump stopped using Cohn for cases that would have been classic Cohn lawsuits in the past. In late summer 1985, when Trump sued the *Chicago Tribune* and its architecture critic for $500 million because of a negative review of a Trump plan, the kind of hopeless headline-grabber right out of Cohn's PR playbook, it was not Cohn who brought the case, but one of Trump's older lawyers, David Berger. When Cohn requested a favor of Trump—that he let a friend who was dying of AIDS stay at one of his hotels—Trump agreed. Then, to Cohn's shock, Trump sent him a bill for the room. Cohn should not have been surprised, though. Trump was notorious for being cheap. At one point, after Cohn had helped him through a tax issue, Trump sent him a pair of diamond cufflinks. The diamonds, it turned out, were fakes. According to notes taken by the switchboard operator at Cohn's office—who was said to have listened in on Cohn's calls—Cohn was bitter about the way Trump shunned him after finding out he had AIDS. "He pisses ice water!" Cohn supposedly said. Trump kept in close touch with Cohn as he was dying, but only by phone. The last time Trump saw Cohn was likely at his newly purchased Florida estate, Mar-a-Lago, on March 1. While Cohn's companion remembered the night as an intimate dinner among friends wishing to say their touching good-byes to Cohn, one of the guests reported that, in fact, it was more of a party, with about thirty people and no special commemoration of Cohn. Considering how Trump had kept Cohn at arm's length, the latter is more likely.

For Trump, this was an increasingly lonely time. Cohn and Friedman had always taken care of sticky situations for him. Now, Cohn was wilting under the force of AIDS, Friedman was facing an indictment, and Donny Manes was a wreck mentally and looking at jail time of his own. In some circles, Cohn's illness was blamed for the eruption of city scandals in the early part of 1986—if he had been healthy, the theory went, he would have used his media and political Rolodex to squelch the scandals before they became news. Cohn could not do that anymore. The usual allies, knaves, and fixers who guided Trump through New York's political morass were not to be counted on from here on.

11

FOR NEARLY THREE MONTHS AFTER prosecutors began moving in on the major players in the Parking Violations Bureau scandal, Geoffrey Lindenauer had held out against the entreaties, cajoling, and threats from Rudy Giuliani's office, pushing away offers to flip on the two bigger fish Giuliani was after in his city corruption prosecution: Stanley Friedman and Donald Manes. The negotiations had been complicated by Manhattan District Attorney Robert Morgenthau, who felt state charges against Lindenauer were warranted. This was frustrating for Giuliani. The Southern District of New York had the derisive nickname "the Sovereign District of New York" for the way its denizens tend to see themselves, and Giuliani acted the part of the sovereign among local prosecutors. With the PVB case and the Mafia Commission trial, Giuliani was attempting to gild a reputation as the city's crime-busting white knight, a contemporary Thomas Dewey, who nearly had ridden his New York anti-corruption credentials all the way to the White House in 1948. Morgenthau had been in the DA's job since 1975, however. He was not impressed. "He doesn't go by what Rudy Giuliani wants to do for Rudy Giuliani's career," one US attorney said of Morgenthau. Giuliani maintained the same adversarial posture. "I don't work for Bob Morgenthau or Mayor Koch," he said. "I work for the President of the United States." But by March 10, the egos had been tamed, and Lindenauer was brought into line. After a lengthy negotiation, it was decided that Morgenthau would focus on the case against Friedman, Giuliani would follow the other PVB leads, and Lindenauer would plead guilty to two federal counts against him and turn government witness.

That was it for Manes. Already, there were a number of pressures on him. The previous month, while still recovering from his suicide attempt—he had suffered a heart attack at the same time—Manes had resigned his roles as Queens president and county leader. Not only had he embarrassed his family and been stripped of his employment, power, and prestige, but Lindenauer was Manes's longtime friend and had kept all his secrets. Manes knew he was headed for further disgrace, and was struggling. On the morning of March 13, he visited his lawyer, Michael Armstrong, at his office at 26 Broadway in Queens, during which Armstrong characterized Manes's emotional state as "terrible." Those around Manes had been trying to nurse him out of his mental melancholy for weeks, and he had been on antidepressants since his troubles began on January 10. News about Lindenauer's cooperation with Giuliani only made things more difficult. Armstrong talked to Marlene Manes about getting her husband to a mental hospital, and talked to some doctors on her behalf.

Back home in Jamaica Estates that night, Marlene Manes was in a first-floor bedroom speaking with one of those doctors, Dr. Elliott Wineburg, who lived just five blocks away, while her husband listened in on a phone in the kitchen. She had assigned their twenty-five-year-old daughter, Lauren, to keep an eye on her father as plans were worked out to possibly take Donald to Mount Sinai Hospital in Manhattan. Lauren became nervous as her father paced back and forth, occasionally opening the drawer that contained the kitchen knives, then closing it. Worried, she began to leave the room to signal her mother to come into the kitchen. At the same time, Dr. Wineburg asked Donald and Marlene Manes to please hold on, he had someone at the door. In that instant, with Lauren leaving the room and his doctor off the line, Manes reached into the knife drawer and pulled out a fourteen-inch

Ecko Flint knife. He plunged the blade into his heart. Lauren, still in the room, looked over to see her father slumping to the floor, a red ring of blood spreading across his white shirt. Lauren screamed. At 9:52 p.m., Marlene called 911. Dr. Wineburg, when he returned to the phone and heard what had happened, bolted his house and ran to the Manes residence.

Medics arrived at the Manes home just two minutes later. Donald Manes had no pulse. He was not breathing. For the second time in two months, he had attempted suicide. By 11:00 p.m., he was officially pronounced dead.

.....

Manes had only been dead a little more than a half-day when, just three miles from his house, the Queens Chamber of Commerce kicked off its annual St. Patrick's Day lunch at Antun's banquet hall. Manes had been a fixture at just about every Antun's event remotely related to politics—even his birthday parties were held at Antun's. His suicide was fresh enough that some who were attending the event had only just heard the news, and certainly fresh enough to keep the Chamber from changing its plans out of respect for the guy who had been the borough president for more than three terms. So the room was done up with the usual ham-handed St. Pat's excesses: There was a band playing "Danny Boy" and "When Irish Eyes Are Smiling," the Lender's bagels were dyed green, the melon served was honeydew, the ice cream was pistachio, and, in a nod to the Chamber's large Jewish contingent, Citibank had donated green yarmulkes. Koch was scheduled to attend, part of a packed day on his schedule. He had a press conference in the morning, at which he suggested New Yorkers "remember the good things" about Manes and then, bizarrely, wondered aloud to reporters whether he would attend Manes's funeral, uncertain he would be welcomed by Marlene Manes after having lashed out at her husband as a "crook" on television. When he arrived in Queens, as guests were having dessert, the mayor was oddly ebullient, carrying himself as though the death of Manes had somehow absolved him, as though the rot within his administration, which had come to the fore beginning with Manes, was now safely submerged again.

At the podium in Antun's, Koch broke into his usual shtick, pronouncing himself "Edward O'Koch" for the week, and joking, "Haven't you heard of the 10 tribes of Israel that ended up in Ireland?" He asked the crowd, "How'm I doing?" and requested a show of hands from those who would vote for him, "if you were to have an election tomorrow?" When the yes votes vastly outnumbered the no votes, Koch exclaimed to the nays, "You lose!" He told the crowd he not only planned to run for a fourth term, but a fifth and a sixth, too. When a question was raised from the crowd about the Trumpdome plans near Shea Stadium, Koch said as long as an NFL team could be attracted, he would remain in favor of the stadium. "I mean, you're talking to a *jock*," he said with a smile and a heavy dose of sarcasm. Little was offered to honor Manes in any way.

The following day, at Manes's funeral, six hundred mourners attended, and Koch was among them. By some counts, there were as many as two thousand more outside who were not able to squeeze in, Manes's Queens constituents. There was bitterness that a turncoat like Koch could be granted a spot ahead of those loyal to Manes. One secretary who worked for the borough government complained that, "We can't get in to pray for his soul, and we worked with the man. And Koch gets in, and he was his worst enemy." When the service was done, Koch compounded the bitterness by stepping out onto Queens Boulevard, among hundreds of solemn mourners just blocks away from Borough Hall, and reading a prepared statement to the gathered media, beginning with, "God will be his ultimate judge, and I hope that on those scales that God will be merciful and will give him his rightful place in heaven." The mayor's flaks had even brought a microphone for him, creating a spectacle he would later acknowledge as "a foolish mistake." In the *New York Post* the following day, the headline was, GOD WILL BE MANES' FINAL JUDGE: KOCH.

But there was no question that the mayor was taking Manes's death as the end of the scandal story—Manes was both its culprit and victim, and the city could now move on. The unburdening penetrated Koch's entire team, which seemed incapable of recognizing Manes's suicide as a tragedy or as emblematic of deeper corruption. For Koch, it was only a positive mark on the political scoreboard. After Manes's funeral, David Garth giddily—and rather coldly—told a reporter: "I tell you, the guy's back. I spent three hours with him the other day, at lunch walking the streets, and I've never seen him in better shape. He was down for a while, no doubt about it, but he's back in form. A lot of hysteria was built up around Manes. Now, with Manes out of it, there will be a dampening effect. The press has been whipping people up over the scandal, but they're going to have a harder time carrying on with Manes out of it. Somehow, for the press, I think the fun will go out of the whole thing."

. . . . .

In a *New York Times* feature on Stanley Friedman from back in 1974, just after the election of Abe Beame as mayor and just before Friedman would ascend to the role of Beame's deputy, Friedman told an uncharacteristically schlocky tale of his young self, at age nine. He had written an autobiographical essay for school, he said, and in it, he declared he wanted to become a lawyer when he grew up. His reason: "to help people." He did become a lawyer. However, once he was ensconced in Beame's City Hall, Friedman mostly sought to help himself. He hung a sign in his office that might have disappointed his younger self. CRIME DOESN'T PAY—AS WELL AS POLITICS, it read.

While Koch's camp was buoyant over Manes's suicide, Friedman recognized there might be a problem for him: the Empty Chair. For more than two months, the media had been in a frenzy around the bribery scandal at the Parking Violations Bureau, and they had been whipped up, in part, by an ambitious prosecutor, Rudy Giuliani, who was eager to use the PVB to make his name as a city corruption-buster. Manes had been the perfect target. He was a powerful but flawed person, a wretched and pitiable figure whose guilt was confirmed from his failed suicide try. His story was easy to understand—there's nothing complicated about envelopes stuffed with cash passed under tables at restaurants. But his death took away the Manes focus, and left Geoffrey Lindenauer as the only indicted conspirator in the PVB bribe ring, which was not much of a ring with one criminal who had already been given a plea deal. Giuliani and the media (not, as Garth had hoped, bored with the topic) needed a new target. Someone had to fill the empty chair. It would be Friedman, whose crime was more sophisticated than the ham-handed Manes bribery scheme. He had sold the city a ticket-writing device that did not work, failing to disclose his financial interest in the company making those devices, and pocketing the stock profits.

According to Giuliani's deal with Robert Morgenthau, the state would get first crack at Friedman. But, eventually, with Manes dead, Giuliani and Morgenthau would amend their arrangement to allow both the state and federal government to try Friedman on separate charges without risking double jeopardy. On one morning in late March, Friedman arrived at Morgenthau's office at 1 Hogan Place, showing up before 8:00 a.m. with his lawyer, the former federal prosecutor-turned-defense attorney Tom Puccio. Friedman was handcuffed and taken for booking on State of New York charges at 1 Police Plaza. Cognizant of Friedman's long-standing influence over judges in the city, Governor Mario Cuomo appointed (at Morgenthau's request) an upstate judge with a sterling reputation—David S. Ritter, who had presided in 1983 over the sensational Brink's robbery and murder trial—to handle Friedman's trial. After Friedman was arraigned, he issued a statement professing his innocence and saying he would achieve "vindication in a court of law." Puccio declared the whole thing "a con game in how to make a little into a lot. Whether it's one count, 34 counts or 3,400 counts, the issue is quite plainly, did Stanley Friedman improperly influence contracts or act outside the law? We say he did not." After the proceedings, Morgenthau held a press conference, and Giuliani, naturally, was next to him at the podium. "These are difficult days for New York City," Giuliani said, gravely. "There is no doubt that, with our revelations, people have become more cynical about their government. But we must go ahead." Less than two weeks later, Friedman went through it all over again, arraigned by Giuliani and the federal government.

Koch, so close, he had believed, to being extricated from the mess of city scandal just ten days earlier, was right back in the quagmire. While Friedman was being indicted, a special agent from the FBI's New York office told reporters the Bureau had doubled the number of investigators working on corruption in the city to fifty-two, and that the process of sorting out city corruption might take two years—meaning more than half of Koch's second term could be overshadowed by scandal talk. That set Koch back into his bitter, angry public posture. The conciliatory, contrite mea culpa speech of the previous month might just as well not have happened. He had contentious sessions with the media on back-to-back days, and had returned to some of his old positions, portraying himself as the victim of the scandal, deceived by his friends and employees alike. When a reporter asked him if he should have known about the corruption going on in his administration, he fired back: "Did you know? The fact of the matter is there are five D.A.s in this city, two U.S. Attorneys, one Department of Investigation, two Comptrollers, city and state, and not one of them found corruption at the PVB, and no reporter." Koch bristled at reporters' continued use of the word *burgeoning* to describe the scandal, the implication being that something burgeoning was still growing. Koch was sure it was not. He could not have been pleased when the Associated Press, whose story would be picked up all over the country, led its story on Friedman's indictment with, "In a burgeoning city corruption scandal. . . ."

12

DWIGHT GOODEN WAS ON THE mound on March 18 at the Tigers' green bandbox, Joker Marchant Stadium in Lakeland, Florida, dealing with an unfamiliar problem. One of the hallmarks of his standout 1985 season had been his ability to locate his pitches with precision, putting his late-exploding fastball just above a hitter's belt or dropping his curveball just off a corner of the strike zone, and just out of a batter's reach. But, in his third start of the spring's exhibition season, the curve was being stubborn. It had not been great in his first two starts, but against Detroit, he went just four innings and gave up three runs on five hits. For much of spring training, the talk around Doc had been his retooled off-speed pitch, a changeup pitching coach Mel Stottlemyre had gotten him to hold deeper in his palm. He was still sorting out that pitch, but the mechanics of his curveball were not completely right. In all, he had pitched 10 spring innings, yielding four runs with only seven strikeouts but zero walks. Gooden took the usual what-me-worry posture about the pitch. "My fastball is O.K.," he said. "But I had trouble with my curveball in the first two games, and I had trouble getting it over today when I was warming up in the bullpen. So, I said to myself: Today's the day to work on it."

Expectations were high for Gooden, and his spring struggles did not garner much concern, even as he had been granted a new, one-year $1.32 million contract by the team, making him the youngest millionaire in baseball history. The notion of Gooden adding a changeup that could be as effective as his fastball and curve was daunting. There was talk that he could be the first pitcher to win 30 games since Denny McLain had done so in 1968, and Expos manager Buck Rodgers said, "A pitcher like him only comes around about once every 30 years." In its annual Top 10 major-league player ratings, *The Sporting News* picked Gooden as the top pitcher, despite only two years of experience. The magazine was also picking the Mets to win the NL East, citing its potential for four MVP candidates: Gooden, catcher Gary Carter, outfielder Darryl Strawberry, and first baseman Keith Hernandez, who was booed all over Florida in March for his involvement in the Pittsburgh drug trials the previous September. *Sports Illustrated* pegged the Mets as a first-place, 100-win team after having won 90 and 98 games the previous two seasons, but unable to get past the Cubs in 1984 or the Cardinals in 1985. Statisticians John Thorn and Pete Palmer put together their annual numbers-based projections, and picked the Dodgers and Mets in the NL, and the Yankees and Royals in the AL. (They would prove to be only one-quarter right, with the Mets.) In the *Village Voice*, writer Billy Altman pointed out that the previous year's Mets had played under the franchise slogan, "Catch the Rising Stars," but that in 1986, "the Mets are merely 'rising' no more."

For the first time in more than a decade, this was a team poised to—and expected to—win. Manager Davey Johnson had put pressure on himself and the team by saying, before the start of spring training, that the Mets had "a good chance not only of winning our division, but of winning it handily." He offered no retreat from that on the first day of spring training, when he said, "We intend to win this year, and if we don't, there will really be no excuses." If there were anything that could hold back the Mets this season, it would be their ability to handle the stresses, after two years in the role of up-and-comers, of being the favorites.

.....

The start of the 1986 season had been marred, for Gooden, by a relatively harmless incident back in January, one that highlighted the difficulty he was having handling his newfound fame. He had been playing catch with his cousin back in Tampa, and suffered a run-of-the-mill twisted ankle. The injury was minor, just a couple of days on crutches, to be safe, but nothing more. He had not even thought to tell the Mets about it, so when word of the injury got to the team, and subsequently to the New York papers, there was a whirl of speculation and innuendo. Because Gooden had not provided details, reports on the ankle conflicted. It was his right ankle; no, it was his left. He had hurt it stepping on a sprinkler head at his old high school; no, there were no sprinkler heads at his old high school. He had been playing basketball; no, it was just catch in the outfield. "The Mets and everybody else captivated by this now 21-year-old phenomenon," Dave Anderson wrote in the *Times*, "are holding their breath until his sprained right ankle is examined Monday by Dr. James Parkes, the club physician." That holding of the breath was heightened when, in mid-January, Gooden skipped the annual Baseball Writers' dinner in Manhattan, where he was to receive the 1985 Cy Young Award. He had to be hiding something.

Gooden finally showed up in New York on January 23, without crutches and with the explanation that he had missed the dinner because of the death of his grandmother, whose funeral was in Georgia. Mets vice president Al Harazin sat Gooden down and explained to him that anything he did, "up to and including sneering," was going to cause a wave of reports in New York, and he should be in constant contact with the club. For his first two years in the big leagues, the Mets had tried to shield Gooden from the press, which was not a problem for him because he was not one for talking much, anyway. As a rookie in 1984, Gooden struggled during long media sessions, finding himself talking too fast out of nervousness and losing track of what he was saying. The organization's PR people cut back on his one-on-one interviews, and kept his media obligations limited to days he was pitching. With the Mets, he was surrounded by an outgoing, flamboyant group of ruffians in the locker room and on the field, but that was not Gooden. "He's sometimes described as aloof," one feature in *The Sporting News* described Gooden. "Perhaps shy is a better choice." But a star could not afford to be too shy when coping with New York media. Addressing reporters about the ankle, Gooden said, "Next time, if I get a cold, I'll call the Mets."

The ankle mystery was easy to shrug off. But, then there was his inability to locate his curveball in the 1986 exhibition season, and his struggle to add a better changeup, the combination of which seemed to have an effect on his overall command. At the tail of spring training, there was something else that raised concern: Gooden missed one of the Mets' final games, in Bradenton, Florida. He called manager Davey Johnson to explain why he missed the team bus, and told him there had been a car accident—Gooden was not hurt, he said, but he and a friend had been run off the road, with the friend seriously injured and Gooden shaken up. Johnson was sympathetic to his star and allowed him the day off. When it came to light that there had been no accident or injury,

Johnson fined Gooden $500 and sternly told reporters, "Dwight and I had a good talk." But the quirks that popped up early in 1986 did raise questions about just how grown up Gooden was at age twenty-one. "He is such a good kid, I didn't think he would lie or scheme, and it makes me worry about the future," *New York Post* columnist Dick Young wrote on the morning of the Mets' Opening Day in April. "Now that he is 21, a man, does he think he can get away with things? . . . The kid who would have made the trip to Bradenton becomes the man who ducks it. It makes you wonder, and worry just a bit."

Johnson was not too stern with Gooden. He could not afford to be. Not only was Gooden crucial to the success of Johnson's 1986 season, but Johnson still held some responsibility for the way Gooden carried himself in the big leagues. In 1984, when Gooden was nineteen, Johnson argued with general manager Frank Cashen, insisting that even at such a tender age, Gooden was ready to handle pitching in New York. Johnson felt he knew Gooden well enough, having been his manager briefly at Triple-A Tidewater. But Cashen wanted to let him mature more in the minors, not only physically, but mentally and emotionally. Through two years, Johnson sure appeared to be right. Gooden's pure talent outweighed concerns about his maturity level. Cashen was still wary, especially as Gooden began receiving his new paychecks and was plied with endorsement opportunities. "Our orders are to protect him, not exploit him," Cashen said. "I give those orders twice a week. All the money they're trying to heap upon him could be a curse. It could rob him of his youth. He hasn't yet had the opportunity to enjoy being Dwight Gooden. On the mound, you can see him but not touch him, and that's about the only place in the world where he's safe."

It was no surprise that Gooden was on the mound when the Mets opened the 1986 season in Pittsburgh, making his second straight Opening Day start, this time in the city where Hernandez had been so humiliated in front of a national audience and ridiculed by an unforgiving press seven months earlier. Making matters worse, commissioner Peter Ueberroth was on hand for the game, to dust away the cobwebs of the drug trial and help the Pirates break in their new ownership group and new manager (Jim Leyland), as well as some newfound respect from a fan base that had been ready to dump the team after the embarrassment of the drug trial and a 104-loss season in 1985. For the opener, forty-four thousand fans turned out, and Gooden called it "like a World Series." Hernandez was quickly able to turn the page when he stroked a double in the first inning that scored leadoff man Lenny Dykstra, then scored on a Gary Carter sacrifice fly. But Gooden's off-season difficulties looked as though they would follow him into the season, as he got ahead of outfielder R. J. Reynolds with two fastballs for strikes, then left what was supposed to be an inside fastball out over the plate. Gooden had not given up a home-run ball since August 1985, and Reynolds had seven career home runs in three years to his credit. But Reynolds yanked the ball over the right-field fence, sparking the concern in Gooden's mind that was shared by much of the Mets' brass: "I thought it might be a long day."

It wasn't. After the first inning, Gooden allowed only three batters past first base until the ninth, when he had to battle through a second-and-third situation with one out, and managed a strikeout and a ground-out to seal a 4–2 win. He was efficient, throwing just 108 pitches. He had struck out six, which would have been fine for most pitchers who get the win after going nine innings, but for Gooden, that was a moderator in his pitching line, only six strikeouts. Pitching coach Mel Stottlemyre had been pressing Gooden to stop worrying about strikeouts and just get outs. He had done as Stottlemyre asked, with good results. But after the game, the question did come in: *only* six strikeouts, Dwight? After gutting out a complete game and earning the win, the gathered media still wanted to know what was wrong with Doc. Gooden could not stop thinking that he had won the game, the strikeouts were not important. Yet it was the focus for some reporters. Gooden still could not figure out just how much New York wanted out of him.

. . . . .

Just a week after Opening Day, there was another insignificant incident-turned-headline, the kind of thing that would have gone unnoticed if it had happened to just about anyone else in the wide expanse of New York City. After opening the season with four games on the road, the Mets had returned to New York and the team had a "Welcome Home" dinner. Some of Gooden's family had gotten a rental car and, really, it should have been a simple transaction: Gooden, his fiancée Carlene Pearson, and his older sister returning the car to the counter at Hertz at LaGuardia Airport. But there was some uncertainty about the mileage, and the clerk asked that they check the number again, sending Gooden's girlfriend out into the rain to look. When she came back with the same mileage, the clerk, according to Gooden, accused her of lying. That's when Gooden turned, as one witness claimed, "abusive and nasty." Gooden admitted to calling the clerk a liar, and peppering in some foul language. Gooden's sister threw a drink at the clerk. It turned out that Gooden's party did report the correct mileage, but once the tempers started to flare, it didn't matter. He was held for an hour at the Port Authority police station, his sister was charged with harassment, the story would get out to the press, and just like that, Gooden had become the focus of another unpleasant national story.

When he met with reporters the next day, Gooden said he was "thinking of bringing all my furniture and moving into the clubhouse" to avoid future trouble, again struggling with the scrutiny of stardom in New York. He had developed a knack for stepping into minor messes. "The kid can't walk down the street anymore," Cashen said. "He's on the verge of becoming reclusive." The press corps covering the Mets tried to have things both ways, lamenting the difficulty that so much minute criticism can have on a young guy who has not really done all that much wrong (at least, not that the reporters in question knew about) while their employers unfairly heaped that criticism on him anyway. *Daily News* columnist Mike Lupica warned Gooden, as if with genuine concern, "He might as well understand that if he steps out of line even a little, the penalty will be a public strip search. Every time." The headline in the *Daily News* after the incident, quoting Gooden, went: "I'M NOT A VIOLENT PERSON." Every time, indeed.

Also of concern for the Mets was their start. Rain had soaked much of the East Coast in early April, and it made for an uneven schedule. The Mets had no rhythm out of the gate. They won their opener in Pittsburgh behind Gooden, but their next game was rained out, then they won in Philadelphia. They dropped back-to-back games against the Phillies, and returned home to play the rival Cardinals—the team that had won the division in 1985—at Shea Stadium for the home opener. The two teams had already made it clear they did not much like each other, as during the spring, when St. Louis's crew-cut grumbler of a manager, Whitey Herzog, said of his New York rivals, who took a little too much delight in finishing second the past two seasons, "The team to beat is still the Mets. They think they won the last two years, anyway." Gooden started, just before the rental car dust-up, and again yielded two runs with six strikeouts. The Mets had, dramatically, tied the game 2–2 in the bottom of the ninth on a single by Darryl Strawberry, but were unable to bring home a runner from third base with just one out, the key blow being a foul popout by slugger George Foster, who was the highest-paid player in the game, but went an unforgiveable 0-for-4 and was booed throughout. "It gets to the point where I don't want my family and friends coming to the game," Foster said afterward. The game went to the 13th, where reliever Bruce Berenyi gave up a walk, a bunt single, and a double (with a key error in that stretch) to allow the Cardinals to break things open, 6–2.

The Mets were 2–3, and the pitching staff, projected to be the envy of the league, was already bruised. Gooden had been solid, but Ron Darling was hit for two home runs and six runs without making it out of the fifth inning in his start, and Sid Fernandez had given up seven walks and four runs, also failing to make it out of the fifth. Number five starter Rick Aguilera did slightly better—he pitched six full innings—but still let up two home runs and four earned runs. Davey Johnson wanted to get his team back on the field quickly to erase the sour flavor of the team's three-game losing streak. But instead, the rain continued and the Mets went from playing on Monday afternoon to sitting around without a game until Friday night. But the break might have been the best thing that could have happened to them.

13

It HAD BEEN MORE THAN twenty months since Roy Cohn and Donald Trump first filed their lawsuit on behalf of the USFL, charging the NFL with violations of antitrust law. At long last, after two days of jury selection, the trial was ready to get underway in front of Judge Peter Leisure, in Room 318 at the US District Court at Foley Square downtown. The fate of the young league, which had lost, by some estimates, $200 million in just three years, hinged on a simple question: Did the USFL find itself pushed to the brink of financial insolvency because of its own ineptitude, or because of treachery and sabotage from the sixty-six-year-old powerhouse NFL? If the NFL had been bullying the USFL out of existence, the young league would be entitled to as much as $1.3 billion in damages, and would be given a lifeline to move forward with a new season, in competition with the NFL, beginning that fall. Few, though, expected that to be the result, even if the USFL did win. The likely outcome would be the absorbing of a small number of teams into the NFL as part of a merger, and the dissolution of the USFL thereafter. Lose the lawsuit, and the league was all but dead. As it stood, it was in a coma of sorts—still technically alive, but dormant in every visible way, with no schedule drawn up and several of its eight teams (down from fourteen in 1985) without full rosters, some even without coaches. "There is no question," commissioner Harry Usher said, "if this goes against us, our future is bleak."

The fate of the league was largely in the hands of the lawyer Trump had picked to execute the case as Cohn's health gave out—Harvey Myerson, a short, stocky, and fierce litigator for powerhouse New York firm Finley Kumble. Myerson, who described himself as a South Philadelphia street kid, was skilled at massaging juries and directing public opinion toward his clients' favor, and would make that a priority for the USFL, ideally portraying the league as an upstart against a behemoth, a David vs. Goliath. Writing in *The Art of the Deal*, Trump described Myerson as possessing "the sort of pugnacious, confrontational attitude you need when you're the underdog taking on the establishment." What Trump did not mention was that Myerson was much despised among his colleagues, and was nearing the brink of a personal unraveling. Myerson had long slathered himself in excesses and left behind a trail of overbilled clients and bilked law partners, who paid for his Rolls Royces, his rather absurd raccoon-skin coat, vacation homes, and the jewels and furs with which he adorned his mistresses (some of whom, it was alleged, Myerson lured by posing as a movie producer and offering "auditions" to young models seeking acting careers). Myerson could be obsessed with his looks. One former law partner recalled, "Harvey had a series of toupees, of different lengths, that looked like old Knute Rockne football helmets. He'd keep changing them and then at the end of the month announce that he needed a haircut." Trump may have liked Myerson's pugnaciousness, but the reality was there were few major attorneys willing to take on the NFL in a courtroom. Most experts did not believe the USFL had much of a shot to win the case, and any lawyer who took it up would risk alienating the powerful men who ran the NFL (many of whom had far-reaching business interests beyond football) as well as the three major TV networks, who had been brought into the trial because they would not televise USFL games. Myerson's lifestyle was outpacing his career, and there was dissatisfaction with him from others at Finley Kumble, which he had only recently joined. Taking on the USFL case offered Myerson a way to draw media attention and quell chatter among his partners about his poor performance, while giving himself a chance to play the hero with an unlikely win.

Myerson had flair, and if the USFL suit was to be the one that could make or break the remainder of his career, he was going to try to win every detail. When he took the floor for his opening statement on May 19, the courtroom was packed, with more than three hundred onlookers. That included Trump, who would be a mainstay at the trial, appearing nearly every day to observe and chat with reporters, hoping to guide their coverage of the proceedings. Myerson was in full throat for his opening presentation, which ran eighty-seven minutes and was much more colloquial and engaging than the NFL's more standard and starched presentation. Myerson played up the USFL's underdog status, calling it "an itty-bitty league," and said the group was "trying to stand on our own little square of turf." He called the NFL representatives "henchmen," and despite the length of his opening, he was riveting. "It was like going to a Broadway show, he was so theatrical," said Mike Janofsky, who covered the trial for the *New York Times*. "He was an actor in a lawyer's suit, he was great. He was so much fun to watch—everything was 'outrageous' or 'crazy.' He was a TV lawyer." Myerson said he would show "three smoking guns," one of which was of special interest to New Yorkers, and tailored that way by Myerson. That was the so-called "New York Conspiracy," the allegation that the NFL had plotted to keep the USFL out of New York City by dangling the possibility of the Jets' return as leverage against the New Jersey Generals moving in. It was a preposterous charge, because it was the city and state that had failed to come up with a plan in time to meet Leon Hess's deadline for a Jets return, and it was Trump who won the bid to build his domed stadium in Queens. In fact, Trump and the city had agreed the project would only go forward (with $150 million in state and city money) if an NFL tenant could be secured. But that was their rule, not the NFL's. No one was stopping Trump from building his dome for the Generals. The USFL was charging the NFL with a conspiracy in which one of the USFL owners had been complicit. But Myerson could be convincing, and he had as possible witnesses well-known New Yorkers Senator Al D'Amato and Governor Mario Cuomo. It would be easy, the thinking went, to persuade six New Yorkers that the big-and-bad NFL, having already sent two teams to New Jersey, wanted to persecute their city by keeping teams out.

Myerson got the USFL off to a good start. His opening was effective, and the first witness would be NFL commissioner Pete Rozelle, a lawyer himself and a man experienced with handling the public stage. Myerson had entered the trial bent on chipping away at Rozelle's credibility, because if he could show inconsistency and deception at the top of the league, it would make it easier to portray the rest of the league's witnesses as liars. Beginning on May 15, for five days, Rozelle was on the witness stand, and Myerson hammered him. At one point, as Rozelle was giving a lengthy explanation, Myerson strode toward the spectators in the room, rolled his eyes and, by one account, "looked to the heavens." Rozelle, surprisingly, bent at times, coming off as dismissive to Myerson's questions and struggling to maintain his air of truthfulness. Myerson entered into the record as evidence of the anti-USFL conspiracy a Harvard Business School study entitled "How to Conquer the USFL," which had been presented to sixty-five NFL executives without Rozelle's knowledge. Rozelle said that when he found out about the study, "I almost got physically ill, to my stomach." Myerson pounced: "To your stomach sir?" When Rozelle answered yes, Myerson pressed, "I see. How long did it take you to recover?" Rozelle, flustered, answered, "About half a day." Myerson was throwing body blows. They were landing. As one league official recounted, "You could see Pete aging. The USFL did a real attack."

Myerson's questioning of Rozelle (which totaled nearly fourteen hours) turned to Trump. For Rozelle, Trump had been little more than an annoyance over the years. He had been mentioned as a potential buyer for the Baltimore Colts in 1981 and again, according to Rozelle, in 1983, before the team finally moved to Indianapolis. His bid was never taken seriously. Trump, as Rozelle had likely figured, had an interest in an NFL team but lacked the willingness to put up the money required to buy into the league. Trump had admitted as much the previous year, telling an interviewer, "I would prefer going up against a monopoly like the NFL—and I've been given very little chance of succeeding—than going out and just buying an NFL team. I could have been one of them by spending a lot of money, but I'd rather spend a small amount of money and make this league work." Rozelle was able to regain some of his composure when asked about Trump, while Myerson was gradually losing his—at one point, NFL attorney Frank Rothman objected to Myerson's tactic of "yelling at the witness." Rozelle fought back when Myerson suggested he had offered Trump an NFL expansion franchise if he would keep the New Jersey Generals from moving into the city. Rozelle leaned forward and jabbed his finger at Myerson saying, "If anyone says that, they are lying, because I never said that to anyone."

14

THE METS STUMBLED IN THEIR first five games, but their woes faded quickly. After the 2–3 start, an extended break because of an East Coast rain soaking, and a Dwight Gooden rental-car run-in, the Mets started to look like the team they were expected to be. They won five straight to close their April homestand, which included dominating performances from Sid Fernandez, Gooden, and Ron Darling. That moved them into a tie for first place as they prepared for a major early-season test: a ten-game road trip that began with four games against St. Louis, the Mets' division rivals and chief antagonists. It was also a reckoning of sorts for Keith Hernandez, who had been derided by manager Whitey Herzog when he was traded to the Mets by the Cardinals in 1983 and had been a target for St. Louis fans since. Since his Pittsburgh testimony in September, fans at Shea had embraced Hernandez, and he got a minute-long standing ovation when he came to bat during the Mets' home opener. But in St. Louis, Hernandez was still a pariah, and was hounded relentlessly by the locals. An 0-for-5 day in the opening of the series did not help, but the Mets did not need him. Trailing 4–2 in the ninth inning, the Mets rallied with two runs on a Howard Johnson homer, then won in the 10th on an RBI single by George Foster.

The Mets did not stop there. Gooden threw a complete-game shut-out in the second game of the series, a 9–0 win, reliever Jesse Orosco staved off a Cardinal comeback attempt for a 4–3 win in the third game, and the sweep was completed behind another complete game, by pitcher Bobby Ojeda, aided by a home run from rotund rookie utility man Kevin Mitchell, who was filling in at shortstop, the fourth position he played in the season's first few weeks. In all, the Mets outhit the Cardinals, 41–26, over the four games and outscored them, 23–10. When it was over, St. Louis first baseman Jack Clark said, "This series is like a real slap in the face to us." Cardinals coach Red Schoendienst pointed out that just one week before, the Cardinals had been 7–1. But after the Mets were done with them, they were 7–8, and slipping into a tailspin—by May 30, they would be 16–27. The rest of the division seemed to be drubbed into submission, too, even in the early going. The 1984 NL East champion Cubs got off to a terrible start, and after just eight games, manager Jim Frey, according to one report, "exploded with pent-up anger on the Cubs charter flight." Frey explained that, "I've been terribly disappointed at some of the guys who are supposed to be professionals who don't do the right thing. They always try to take the shortcut and when things don't work out, they make statements that reflect on me and my coaching staff. And I resent that." In late May, Cubs general manager Dallas Green gave Frey a vote of confidence. On June 12, with the Cubs at 23–33, the team fired Frey.

But it was the road trip, on which the Mets went 9–1, that most established the pecking order, not just in the division but in all of baseball. The Mets were at the top, and they knew it. "This team," Hernandez said, "is the best team I have played for." The Mets were not afraid to let their opponents know their superiority, either. They talked trash. They bickered with umpires. They took curtain calls after every home run hit at Shea Stadium. One member of the Phillies told writer Peter Gammons that when the Mets play there are twenty-four other teams rooting against them: "They're the only team in baseball that high fives in BP." On the final day of their road trip, Darling overcame six walks and Darryl Strawberry knocked two home runs on May 4, a Sunday, against the Reds. It was a 7–2 win and already, the Mets had a five-and-a-half-game lead over the rest of their division. Dave Anderson wrote a column in the *New York Times* from Cincinnati, with the headline: BREAK UP THE METS!

. . . . .

Robby Thompson was a rookie second baseman for the Giants, and was camped—safely, he thought—under a pop fly off the bat of light-hitting Mets shortstop Rafael Santana at Shea Stadium at the end of May.

It had been raucous from the beginning, the Giants offense clubbing spot starter Bruce Berenyi for four runs in two-plus innings, with the Mets countering with five runs in their first three innings. Three times, the Mets blew leads. The game was tied at 6–6 after nine innings, but the Giants took the lead in the 10th when Thompson led off with a homer on a pitch from Jesse Orosco. The Giants had, frustratingly, allowed the Mets to tie the game in the bottom of the 10th with an unlikely rally credited to Davey Johnson's instincts. Keith Hernandez led off with a single, and after an out, Johnson lifted slugger Darryl Strawberry for what was, according to Strawberry, the first time he had ever been pulled for a pinch-hitter. Strawberry had been 2-for-2 with two walks on the night, but Johnson said he was dealing with a bruise on his thumb, denying that he had pulled Strawberry because he was batting only .100 against lefty pitchers. (The thumb reasoning lost some credibility when, after the game, Strawberry did not mention that he was hurt and said, "It's not an easy decision to take.") Johnson inserted rookie pinch-hitter Kevin Mitchell, who slapped a ground-ball single to left field. Howard Johnson drew a walk, and Ray Knight (batting .336 to that point) knocked a sacrifice fly. That's when Santana came to bat, and appeared to end the inning. Except that, to Thompson's right, shortstop Jose Uribe drifted closer, watching the ball. Uribe claimed he called for it three times. Thompson never heard him. They collided, and Santana's popup dropped safely for a game-winning error.

The Mets had won six straight and had the best record in baseball, 31–11. They were six games ahead of the Expos, the only other team in the NL East over .500.

PART III

Fireworks

15

FRANK DECICCO HAD JUST LEFT the modest stucco storefront of the Veterans and Friends Club on 86th Street in Bensonhurst on a cloudy Sunday afternoon after a meeting with Jimmy Brown Failla, a longtime captain in the Gambino family and one of DeCicco's mentors. Inside, he had been asked for a business card by Frank Bellino, a concrete union agent and Lucchese family member. DeCicco could be absentminded at times, and had a tendency to scatter important documents and notes throughout his car or in his pockets, so when Bellino told him he would go to the car and find the number himself, DeCicco waved him off and said he was the only one who would be able to find it. Together, the two walked across the street to the year-old Buick Electra that DeCicco had been driving and went around to the passenger door. DeCicco was seated on the passenger seat going through his glove compartment. What neither he nor Bellino knew was that a brick of C4 explosive was on the underside of the car, held in place by a magnet, wired to connect to a remote control that had been part of a car set bought at Toys 'R' Us. An explosives expert and former rogue cop, Herbie Pate, watched and approached in his own car, holding the remote control that could send an electric impulse to the C4. With DeCicco in the passenger seat and Bellino standing next to the car, Pate flipped the switch, and the C4 detonated. The car immediately burst into flames, its windows blown out as the body of the car quickly turned to a crisp black husk. A billowing black mushroom cloud shot into the sky. DeCicco was killed instantly. Bellino suffered serious injuries, but survived. A hole about two feet wide was left in the street. Around 86th Street, the strength of the bomb shook buildings and shattered windows.

The killing of DeCicco presented an immediate mystery, both to the law enforcement agents that had been closely tracking Mafia movements, and to the Gambino clan to which DeCicco belonged. DeCicco made sense as a potential target, because he had been close to Paul Castellano, part of his white-collar group, but turned on the Pope and became a John Gotti loyalist when he helped set up his murder at Sparks Steakhouse. In the wake of Castellano's killing, it had been DeCicco who formally nominated Gotti to ascend to the boss's role, and the prize for his betrayal of Castellano was that DeCicco became Gotti's underboss. They were not personally close, but DeCicco—intelligent, understated, and camera-shy—made a good complement to Gotti, who broke the mold of the silent and hidden Mafia boss by playing up his Dapper Don image for the media. He traded in his windbreakers for tailored, $1,000 suits, well-groomed hair, and mono-grammed socks, while also moving his primary headquarters from the Bergin Hunt and Fish Club in Brooklyn to the Ravenite Social Club in downtown Manhattan, where reporters could more easily catch him strolling through the streets of the Village or Little Italy. There were factions of the Gambino clan that would have targeted DeCicco for his treachery, but there was not much about the execution of his murder to suggest this was retaliation. It had been four months, after all, and if this was a revenge killing, it was being served especially cold. Besides, car bombs were mostly against Mafia protocol, more a tool of old-world Sicilian gangsters than modern Americans. They drew too much police attention, and there was risk that innocent civilians could be injured or killed. That seemed to rule out the other New York families, even the Genovese, whose head, Vincent "Chin" Gigante, had enjoyed a close relationship and several fruitful business enterprises with Castellano. In the days after DeCicco's murder, Gotti scrambled for answers. "I don't know what the fuck is going on," he told his right-hand man Sam Gravano, "but we've got problems."

Gotti was unaware at the time that he had been lucky on the day DeCicco was killed. The bomb had been intended for him, and Pate had set it off thinking Bellino, who had a similar build and the same slicked hair, was Gotti. The attempt on his life had not come at the whim of unhappy Gambino underlings, as had been speculated in the press. It had come from the five families' Commission itself, pushed by Gigante, who was afraid respect for Mafia traditions was waning and felt Gotti was too loose a cannon to be a family head. Gigante did not like Gotti's involvement in the narcotics trade, either, but none of that rose to the level of a cause to kill him. Gigante really wanted Gotti dead because he had to be accountable for having broken one of the most sacred tenets of Mafia rules: No one kills a boss. There may have been reasons to want Paul Castellano dead, but only the Commission could sanction a move as weighty as the murder of a family head. Gotti had broken the rule, and the punishment was death. Gigante had a particular distaste for Gotti, who was on trial in Brooklyn and spent far too much time, in Gigante's view, preening for news cameras. Gigante could not have been more different. He was so careful that the FBI had never been able to bug him, was not even aware (at the time) of how powerful he was, and he was so eager to throw off federal agents and stay out of jail that he had taken to the habit of strolling feebly through his neighborhood in a tattered bathrobe, feigning insanity. Gigante was willing to absorb the humiliation of that ruse if it meant protecting the secrets of the Commission and the Genoveses. The use of the bomb, masterminded by a brutal mobster of the Lucchese family named Gaspipe Casso, was deliberate on Gigante's part, because he rightly assumed no one would suspect a traditionalist like him of breaching Mob protocol on bombs.

But the Gotti hit failed, leaving him in power and leaving law enforcement and the local citizenry fearing for a widening mob war. "[Such killings] advertise the defiance of the mobs and endanger not only bystanders but all society," read one *Times* editorial in the wake of the DeCicco murder. "The mobs' summary executions are the most extreme expression of their arrogance and contempt for the communities on which they prey." Legal pressure was exacerbating the internal tension within the Mafia and fueling fears of a wider war. All over New York, high-level Mafia members were being hauled into court, even as the city waited on the opening of Giuliani's crucial Commission trial. There was a complicated ongoing Bonanno family trial known as the "Pizza Connection" case, an international heroin ring that sold the drugs out of pizza-place storefronts in New York. There were two shakedown cases against Genovese capo Matty "The Horse" Iannello, and the trial of a murderous Gambino auto-theft ring that had involved Castellano. There were three racketeering trials ongoing: eleven members of the Colombo family, led by Carmine "The Snake" Persico; thirteen members of the Bonannos including family head Rusty Rastelli; and Tony Salerno of the Genovese family, along with fourteen family members and associates. There was also a Brooklyn trial against Gotti. It was a weak case, though, without strong surveillance evidence and without the support of the FBI, which would have to expose two of its informants during the trial. Many felt that case should have been pulled, not only because Gotti was unlikely to be convicted (he was not, in part because he had bribed a juror), but because it gave him a chance to confidently stand in front of the courthouse, surrounded by bodyguards, and pick up PR points in the papers and on television news.

No one was particularly fond of Gotti. He had come up through the ranks with violence and with little regard for the established order. His growing media profile embarrassed law enforcement and worried his fellow bosses—not only would it bring more scrutiny to Mob activity, it would be harder to attempt another hit on him, surrounded as he was by news cameras and a growing throng of fans. But Robert Blakey saw the rise of a boss like Gotti as one of the natural outgrowths of the RICO prosecutions he had been pushing. Gotti was a thug and hothead, lacking the foresight and discipline to provide the Gambinos with steady, long-term leadership. If the wizened, diplomatic old heads at the top of the Mafia org chart were removed, they would inevitably be replaced by younger, less cautious bosses like Gotti, which would make them easier to take down. Just a few months after DeCicco's murder, Gotti would show how reckless he could be. With the Commission trial looming and Rudy Giuliani in a personal holy war against organized crime, Gotti felt it would be worthwhile to send a message to law enforcement. He went to the other family heads with an audacious plan: put out a hit on Giuliani. This was way beyond protocol. As Giuliani had said, when asked by an interviewer on C-SPAN in 1988 whether he ever feared for his life as he went after the Mafia, "If you look at the things that we do, obviously the danger, any danger people would assume comes from organized crime, drug-dealing, that sort of thing. They have followed a rule in the United States—it's the only rule of organized crime I agree with and I endorse and I encourage— they leave prosecutors and agents and police officers largely alone. They don't attack us." Gotti was out to change that. He got Carmine Persico on board with the idea, which meant he needed only one more "Yes" vote from the other families to put the murder into action. They could not get a third vote, though, and Giuliani was spared. Still, though prosecutors had organized crime under siege, under Gotti, the Mafia would get much more violent.

. . . . .

If one of Leon Hess's big problems that had driven him from Shea Stadium across the George Washington Bridge had been the rancid, puddle-flooded bathrooms, he might have brought attention to Arc Plumbing, the Queens contractor whose two principal owners, brothers Anthony and Caesar Gurino, had been indicted in June 1985 on obstruction of justice charges in connection with a racketeering case. Arc had been handling most of the oft-derided Shea Stadium plumbing for the bulk of the 1980s, had done more than $600,000 in business at the stadium the previous year and, here in February, was granted a new set of contracts for Shea for the 1986 season. Shea was hardly the only work Arc got from the city—a total of more than $20 million worth of city contracts, according to the *Village Voice*, had been rung up since 1980.

Of special note was a $25,000-a-year "salesman" who was one of Arc's few regular employees: John Gotti. Gurino had granted his old friend Gotti a job back in 1977, when Gotti was paroled on condition he hold down a job. So, he became an Arc salesman. As part of his employment, Gotti set up an office at 98-04 101st Avenue in Ozone Park, the Bergin Hunt and Fish Club, and had ridden around in a chauffeured gray Lincoln registered to Arc. The car had been upgraded in the month after Castellano's murder, to a black Mercedes SEL worth $60,000, registered to the company. When asked what Gotti did for the company, Gurino would later only admit, "John points out locations." Gotti's lawyers frequently described him as a hard-working plumbing salesman, and judging by the way he got around town and the bespoke suits he wore, he must have been very hard-working indeed. Most high-level mobsters seek out anonymity. Gotti sought limelight. "I've never seen them so bold," one law enforcement officer said. "It's practically out in the open."

It was a small world. Gurino's neighbor, just across Chevy Chase Street in Jamaica Estates, was Donald Manes. For Giuliani, the coincidence was rich. As he pursued both the Mafia and city corruption, he said, "There is a great similarity between the two, because the essential business of both is to use their power and influence to prey on other people."

. . . . .

The patch above the right pocket on Rudy Giuliani's black leather vest read "DEQUIALLO," which is earned by members of the Hell's Angels motorcycle gang through a fight against law enforcement. He also wore a "Dirty Thirty" patch and one saying "Filthy Few," which were Nazi-linked elements of the gang. Giuliani had slid the vest over a white button-up shirt with its sleeves rolled up, and tucked into charcoal slacks that were pinstriped and neatly held up by a thin black belt. He had donned sunglasses to add credence to his improbable get-up. Together with Sen. Al D'Amato, dressed in military drab olive with a hat and sunglasses, Giuliani had traveled up to Washington Heights with a Spanish-speaking cop from the Drug Enforcement Agency. They had pulled up, double-parked, in front of known drug dens around 160th Street, ran a finger across their noses to signal their desire to buy crack cocaine, and walked away with multiple vials each, spending a mere $60. The whole thing had been videotaped so it could be replayed for the press. And that was really the point—Giuliani and D'Amato (who was up for reelection) were making a public show about how easy it was to buy crack cocaine in New York City. On the front page of the *Daily News* the next day, July 10, Giuliani and D'Amato, still in their absurd "disguises," were smiling and holding up the drugs under the caption, "Would you sell a vial to these guys?"

It was a publicity stunt all the way, and in the neighborhood around the Giuliani-D'Amato visit, the two men were greeted with rolled eyes. Crack sellers already had a firm grip on the area, taking control of pay phones to arrange deals, co-opting local kids to transport their products, and dumping bullet-riddled bodies behind apartment houses. The stop-in from Giuliani and D'Amato was not going to change that. "It wouldn't make any difference if President Reagan came up here," one resident said. *Daily News* columnist Earl Caldwell pointed out that the pair had picked a poor neighborhood to strut their stunt, when they could have gone to Times Square or Greenwich Village or Bryant Park and just as easily found someone willing to sell the drugs. "They're playing games in neighborhoods with people who are the victims," Caldwell wrote. Manhattan District Attorney Robert Morgenthau, whose office took considerable criticism for its inability to keep small-time dealers off the streets, bristled at the escapade. To Morgenthau, New York's drug problem was an issue of federal incompetence, not an issue of arresting more low-level dealers. New York, he pointed out, had more citizens in prison than the other forty-nine states combined. "The coca plant does not grow in Central Park, nor does the opium poppy," he said. "There is a flood of cocaine coming into this city on every tide. It's their job to stop it." Giuliani shot back, "He leaves the impression that the drug problem is not his to deal with, too."

The one point on which everyone could agree was that the cocaine epidemic was spiraling out of control. The ease with which cocaine could be converted into crack—by mixing the powder with store-bought ingredients and heating them in the microwave—had caused the drug to crash into big cities like New York with sudden force, overwhelming the ability of city services to keep up, from drug abuse counseling to hospital care to law enforcement. Crack was far more addictive than snorted cocaine, because it delivered a more potent high faster, and because that high would last only ten to fifteen minutes, users needed a steady stream of the drug. On a national level, a study released in July showed cocaine-related deaths had tripled in just the previous five years. The impact in New York was especially troublesome. There had been seven cocaine-related deaths in the city in 1983, but in 1985, there were 137. Not only were more city dwellers using cocaine and crack, but the drugs were fueling more violent crimes, either between rival drug-sellers or citizens being mugged by those needing money to support their habits. In the first five months of 1986, police reported a spike in murders of 29.8 percent, and a 15.7 percent rise in robberies.

Crack was the chief culprit. From January through March of 1986, a survey of 576 emergency rooms found 14.5 percent of those admitted with cocaine-related ailments had smoked the drug. That was up from 10.1 percent in 1985 and just 4.2 percent in 1984. In 1985, there were fifty-five thousand drug-related arrests for a city with jail space for thirteen thousand, which meant only a fraction of offenders spent time behind bars. It was only in the summer of 1986 that New York finally came to grips with the emergency crack was creating. But the options were limited. Ed Koch, typically, staked out unorthodox and harsh positions on the problem, many of which he knew would never be enacted, but would, at least, bolster his law-and-order credentials in a city where crime was gaining. He did take some controversial, street-level actions, like having cops raid two hundred newsstands and candy stores that also sold pipes, and having police impound cars of any driver who was pulled over and found to be in possession of crack. Koch was, reasonably enough, critical of federal budget cuts that had forced New York to trim its police force. Less reasonably, he suggested even low-level drug dealers be rounded up and shipped to barbed-wire outdoor encampments in Arizona during the summer, Alaska during the winter, or floating prisons off New York City's piers. He advocated having even misdemeanor drug offenses be subject to harsh mandatory sentences. Earlier in the spring, he proposed the death penalty for traffickers. He had called for the outlawing of $100 bills because they were so commonly used in drug transactions. In the wake of the Giuliani and D'Amato staged crack buys, Koch said in a press conference he would like to assign drug-sniffing dogs to greet every airplane that landed in New York from abroad (there were more than six hundred such flights daily). If drugs were on board, the plane would be sealed and sent back to its country of origin.

It was pointed out to Koch that there could be long delays for such cases, and unwitting Americans could be on board such flights. His response: "It's called T.S. Tough shit."

16

ALREADY FOR JIMMY BRESLIN, 1986 had been a strange and thrilling and depressing year. He had had plenty of those types of years, but there was something more personal about this one. He had been instrumental in blowing open the Parking Violations Bureau story, having nudged old friend Michael Dowd into admitting the bribes he had given out to get and maintain ticket-collection contracts with the PVB in January, and breaking the story at the same time. The scoops he drew from the scandal that had claimed Donald Manes as a victim were both his triumph and his heartbreak—in Queens, it is said everybody knows everybody, and as a child of Queens, he knew everybody. He had given the eulogy at the funeral of a Queens bar owner and city marshal named Sheldon Chevlowe, who died of cancer in 1983 and was a frequently cited character in his columns named Shelly the Bail Bondsman. He was close to a Queens lawyer named Mel Lebetkin, who showed up in Breslin's writing with the alias Klein the Lawyer and was described as "a man who had trouble getting paid from the criminals he represented, and then he had trouble with the women in the bar downstairs from his office."

They had been lovable rogues, and popular among readers for their foibles, failures, and their habit of stumbling into wisdom. Their world was packed into just a few blocks that made the sprawl of Queens, the city's biggest borough, feel like a small town. Chevlowe's bar was called Forty Yards because that was how far it was from his bail bonds shop across the street from the Queens courthouse where he, Lebetkin, and Dowd, also a lawyer, did business, past the Pastrami King where coffee and a daily racing form made for a Breslin morning ritual, and to the bar itself where they would gather at night, in the shadow of the Borough Hall. But Breslin cringed at Dowd's tale of borough corruption, the kind of corruption about which Breslin often moralized in his column. And Chevlowe, it turned out, had been in charge of collecting PVB bribes for Manes until his death, a duty Manes ordered Geoffrey Lindenauer to take over on the very day of Chevlowe's funeral. (For Breslin that was a shocking and appalling detail, to learn Manes was so greedy and craven as to soil Chevlowe's funeral that way.) Lebetkin was not only involved with PVB kickbacks, he also set up, with Manes, a fraudulent secondary collections company to further bilk the city. When the *New York Times* ran a story on the scandal troubles of Queens Boulevard in March, Lebetkin called Breslin at 5:45 in the morning. He told the writer the *Times* was "ruining me." The nation's paper of record had, in reporting the scandal, just identified Lebetkin as the real-life Klein the Lawyer. Breslin was aghast. "My character got stolen!" he shouted.

In the early weeks of 1986, all Breslin's Queens characters got stolen. The scandals had chastened Breslin, and left him in a sort of mourning. Mayor Koch, defending himself against charges that he must have known something rotten was going on in his government, had railed against Breslin, noting many of his friends were Queens-based "crooks" and yet Breslin had not known anything was askew. A mayor pointing fingers at a columnist for not identifying graft and corruption within that mayor's own government made for a bizarre political subplot, but Koch and Breslin had long been in open warfare. Besides, Koch didn't need to flog Breslin publicly, because Breslin was flogging himself. The romance of the windmill-tilting Klein the Lawyer was gone, Breslin wrote, "and I was left with only a man, Lebetkin, who had to serve as a grubby news source. . . . I learned again that one of the great handicaps of being a news writer and having friends is that at key moments, everybody must be opposed to each other."

In April, though, Breslin was feeling particularly manic as he strode around Queens with a young reporter, Margot Hornblower, who would be able to give his tale of righteousness and heartbreak a national scope in the *Washington Post*. He was a product of Queens and still spoke with the cadence and affectation of a Queens boy, using liberally his "dese" and "dems" colored by some fits of well-placed foul language. It was pointed out to him that he had, in fact, moved out of Queens long before to live on the Upper West Side of Manhattan (Hornblower met Breslin at his well-appointed apartment for the journey out to Queens), which he only grudgingly conceded. "It's bad for my image," he said. It was an image he cultivated carefully. A friend once wrote of Breslin, "It would destroy him if his readers were to discover he is as smart as any pontificating pundit in Washington . . . who can quote Camus or Teilhard de Chardin without losing his stool at Kennedy's."

Talking with Hornblower, Breslin acknowledged the difficulty the scandal had caused him personally, even as it further elevated him professionally. Overweight and meticulous in his slovenliness, Breslin cut a familiar figure on Queens Boulevard, and was stopped for autographs as he walked—while hailing a cab, a slightly dilapidated Ford LTD pulled over, the driver offering Breslin and Hornblower a ride, which Breslin accepted despite not knowing the driver. The driver asked whether Breslin remembered him from afternoons at the racetrack, and Breslin, politely, said yes. Breslin pointed out the Queens Borough

Hall and remembered the guy who until just months earlier had been the unquestioned lord of that manor. "I knew Manes well," Breslin said. "Too well. Twenty-one, 22 years. I knew his wife and kids. He knew my wife and kids." Hornblower recalled to Breslin a column he had written about Manes after the scandal broke, which touched on what was, at that time, still a mostly unreported look at Manes's darker side. Breslin had spoken to a TWA flight attendant who lived with a group of fellow flight attendants in an apartment building nearby, and had described nights with Manes taking her around in a limousine, drinking to excess, and engaging in repeated drug use. She said of Queens Boulevard: "I thought it was about the craziest place I've ever been."

Hornblower, seated with Breslin at Pastrami King, asked if that conversation with the flight attendant had been real, or if the flight attendant was another Breslin-embellished Queens character. "You think I make things up?" Breslin said, agitated. He popped up, rushed to the pay phone and, moments later, put Michelle Walton on the line. She told Hornblower she was the flight attendant in Breslin's story, and she was scheduled to meet with the FBI the following day. Of her experience with Manes, she said, "It started out fun, but it didn't turn out that way." Breslin would agree. He felt pangs of guilt after Manes committed suicide the previous month. His columns had helped expose Manes's corruption, and he had reveled in doing so—until tragedy struck when Manes stuck a knife in his own chest. "I don't even remember the day after," he told Hornblower. "I was no good. Jesus Christ, no one bargained for this!"

. . . . .

On New York's political circuit, May is fundraising season, and in a city dominated by Democrats, that meant a series of formal events at the ballroom of the Sheraton Centre in Midtown, which had become the de facto party headquarters. Never in the history of the city had there been such a chill on the very notion of political fundraising than there was in the spring of 1986, with every guest list doubling as a potential roster of persons-of-interest for state and federal prosecutors. In fact, as the Bronx Democrats opened the fundraising slate with a May 7 event, they did so with the borough party boss, Stanley Friedman, coming fresh from a federal courthouse where US attorney Rudy Giuliani announced a new set of indictments against him. As comedian Joey Adams, the emcee of the Bronx event, joked to the crowd, "All I can say is, if you're indicted, you're invited." Friedman had tried to pin the indictments on Giuliani's political motivations, saying, "Republicans in Washington will do everything in their power to embarrass the Democratic Party in New York State." Curiously, Friedman had also decided on a style change, showing up at the fundraiser with the goatee he had worn for the past fifteen years shaved off, perhaps operating under the assumption facial hair makes one look guilty. Despite the deepening scandal troubles engulfing Friedman, he defiantly refused to give up his role in the Bronx organization, even as his very presence drove away donors. In 1985, the Bronx fundraiser drew fifteen hundred guests at $250 per plate, but that was down to about nine hundred a year later. Major local Democrats turned down invitations, including Koch and Governor Mario Cuomo, but the guest of honor was Bronx's own, Rep. Mario Biaggi. Another honored guest was Donald Trump, who had good reason to stick with Friedman. It was Friedman, after all, who had been instrumental in getting Trump the tax abatements on his first two major real estate developments, the Grand Hyatt Hotel and Trump Tower. "There is such a thing as loyalty," Trump said of his support for Friedman.

A week later, it was the Queens Democrats holding their annual party. Where there was feistiness from the Bronx contingent, there was a hangdog atmosphere from the Queens folks, who cut the price of the event from $250 per person to $150. Despite that steep discount, attendance dropped from nine hundred in 1985 to five hundred in 1986. Koch did go to the Queens dinner, though it remained populated with loyalists to Donald Manes, who were none too pleased with the way Koch had publicly turned on Manes as his life fell apart. The topic of Manes was widely avoided at the dinner (a report on the event in the *New York Post* was headlined No-Manes Land), and when Koch was asked, he said that if Manes had not killed himself and he were at the Queens event, "I would not be here." That was a bold sentiment from Koch, because one thing the past few weeks had shown was the corruption in his administration was rippling beyond the Manes-Friedman-Parking Violations connection. Taxi and Limousine Commission head Jay Turoff, accused of soliciting bribes and under grand jury investigation, had, Koch admitted, aided the mayor's 1985 campaign illegally by ordering taxis to give free rides to Koch voters seeking to get to the polls. And just after that, a report showed one of the mayor's closest aides, Victor Botnick, billed the city's Health and Hospitals Corporation more than $20,000 for eleven trips to California to meet with a consulting company, expenses that the state comptroller called "shocking." Even allegations that hardly rose to the level of a scandal—one official was forced out because he had asked an employee to help him install an air conditioner—would be treated as a scandal by the press, which had been embarrassingly in the dark on Manes and Friedman, and did not want to miss another scoop.

Koch himself was badly in need of funds, his campaign organization carrying a debt of more than $500,000 from the 1985 election. In the campaign, despite the fact that he only had to beat a pair of lightweights, he still spent $7.2 million to beat Carol Bellamy on the Liberal line and Republican Diane McGrath, candidates he could have beaten with a quarter of his final spending, and certainly without overspending the $6.7 million he'd raised. Such was Koch's mania for approval that he felt the need not just to win reelection, but to bask in an electoral blowout victory. He had won more than 70 percent of the vote in all five boroughs, making his financial blitz of the previous year a bit like hooking up a fire hose to put out a candle. On May 15, Koch held the third in the series of Democratic fundraisers, at the Sheraton, drawing about 550 people at $1,000 and $2,000 per seat, depending on the proximity to the dais. There was $700,000 raised, enough to pay the dinner expenses and cover Koch's debt, but a far cry from the windfall Koch had been granted less than a year and a half earlier, when his sixtieth birthday party drew $1.7 million worth of donations. Outside,

Republican protesters heckled attendees, holding signs reading KING EDWARD, ABDICATE. Inside, the mood was subdued, and the mayor who had so often lashed out at his opponents remained restrained and introspective. By the time he spoke, several of those in attendance had already headed for the exits. "Nobody promised me a rose garden," Koch said. "But neither did they say it would be a bed of nails."

.....

In December 1985, a reporter had gone to Roy Cohn's townhouse to discuss Cohn's ongoing battle with the New York Bar Association, which was attempting to have him disbarred for fraud and professional misconduct. (Cohn had called the bar watchdogs "a bunch of yo-yos" among other things.) A string of well-known and well-heeled friends—Barbara Walters, Donald Trump, William F. Buckley, Congressman Mario Biaggi—had offered character references on Cohn. At his office, which he shared with partners Thomas Bolan and Stanley Friedman, it would not be unusual to find the likes of Fat Tony Salerno, ostensible boss of the Genovese crime family, publisher and close friend Si Newhouse, or Trump on the premises, perhaps even at the same time. Still, Cohn answered the door in a baby-blue bathrobe, not caring whom might be calling. And, as was obvious during the interview, Cohn was entirely naked underneath the robe. This was reflective of the oscillation Cohn underwent during his final days. There he was, wan and housebound in a robe as Christmas approached, a sad figure dying of what he insisted was liver cancer. Months later, in the spring, he would appear revitalized, combative in his banter with Mike Wallace on *60 Minutes*. Then, in June, after the disbarment ruling had gone against Cohn in New York's highest court, he barely had the energy to muster a response. Reporters who contacted Cohn's office were told he had gone boating. Local NBC anchor Gabe Pressman called Cohn's home number, and after months of bitter combat against the New York Bar, all the typically garrulous and self-righteous Cohn could tell Pressman was, "I could care less."

In late July, the lie of Cohn's liver cancer was laid bare. Columnists Jack Anderson and Dale Van Atta, who were syndicated in as many as eight hundred American newspapers, had obtained records from the National Institutes of Health in Maryland and published the gritty details about Cohn's condition and regimen of treatment. They showed Cohn had gone to the NIH the previous November, for twenty days, and was readmitted in early June for three days to test his reaction to the experimental AIDS drug, AZT. The details in the column—the time Cohn was admitted, what building he entered, the identity of his doctor—showed that someone at the NIH had leaked a full report to Anderson and Van Atta. Cohn's suffering was on national display. In November, he was listed as alert but "not always oriented," and "mixes up details." He was also called a problem patient because he was "somewhat reluctant to become celibate." By June, Cohn had deteriorated. He was "not self-reliant," needed help in the shower, and was so easily confused that he "should be given ample time for processing information." In the following weeks, Anderson and Van Atta were sharply criticized for publishing such intimate medical details about Cohn. But Cohn was not likely coherent enough to understand the public humiliation he had suffered. On August 2, back at the NIH, Cohn finally died.

By the time of Cohn's death, AIDS in New York was an epidemic. The numbers were spiking. According to the Centers for Disease Control, in 1986, AIDS would kill 2,139 people in the city, up from 1,313 in 1985, representing the largest increase in deaths from the disease since it was first identified in New York in 1981. In all, by the end of 1986, New York would have 8,681 AIDS cases, nearly a third of all cases in the United States. San Francisco, second on the list in total cases, had 2,912. As with New York's drug crisis, Koch took the brunt of the blame for failing to take preventive action early on to stop the disease. His chief antagonist was gay rights activist and writer Larry Kramer, who had been trying to marshal the appropriate sense of emergency both among government officials and the gay community, highlighted by a 1983 article he wrote in the *New York Native*, a magazine for gay men. It was called "1,112 and Counting" for the number of "serious" AIDS cases reported at that point. Kramer's piece began with an alarm:

"If this article doesn't scare the shit out of you, we're in real trouble. If this article doesn't rouse you to anger, fury, rage, and action, gay men may have no future on this earth. Our continued existence depends on just how angry you can get." Kramer got plenty angry with Koch, accusing him of ignoring the crisis. "I sometimes think he doesn't know what's going on," Kramer wrote. "I sometimes think that, like some king who has been so long on his throne he's lost touch with his people, Koch is so protected and isolated by his staff that he is unaware of what fear and pain we're in. No human being could otherwise continue to be so useless to his suffering constituents." In Kramer's 1985 play, *The Normal Heart*, Koch is excoriated for his weak response to the rise of AIDS, and Kramer long suggested that the mayor was afraid to act because he is a closeted homosexual. ("That is such bullshit," Koch noted.)

Koch had a good record on gay rights, but he fell far short on making an outspoken stance on AIDS, or providing adequate public funding for education, housing, and treatment costs. Early on, he declined to meet with groups concerned about the spread of AIDS, including Kramer's group, Gay Men's Health Crisis, and failed to make adequate public-safety warnings that could have raised awareness and mitigated the devastation the disease was causing in the city. Memos from the time show that Koch was, indeed, concerned about the problem, but because of fiscal pressures, not because of his own sexual leanings. According to one tally, by January 1984, the Koch administration had spent a mere $24,500 to stem the growing AIDS crisis. He corrected that eventually, and the money New York spent on AIDS treatment matched that of other cities. Problem was, New York had so many more cases than anywhere else, it needed to be spending exponentially more. One aide wrote to Koch in 1985, looking for the best way to care for AIDS patients when hospitals were increasingly wary of admitting them: "I know that we were careful not to create a new entitlement program for home care since it would be very costly and we do not provide these services free of charge to any other group. However, the need for hospice services is unique to this group and would not be nearly as costly as home care since the number of patients are far fewer." New York did not add a home-care program.

In Koch's defense, his tepid response to AIDS was robust compared to plenty of other entities in the city and beyond. In the media, the *New York Times* was especially slow to report on the epidemic seriously, and the conservative *New York Post* was eager to stoke fear of the disease. On back-to-back days, the Post ran front-page headlines: L.I. GRANDMA DIED OF AIDS, followed by, JUNKIE AIDS VICTIM WAS HOUSEKEEPER AT BELLEVUE. The legal system had given the gay community a bad turn, too. Just a month before Cohn's death, the Supreme Court set back the gay rights movement two decades when it upheld Georgia's anti-sodomy law and ruled against a gay man who had been arrested in his own bedroom, asserting that the Constitution does not "confer on homosexuals a fundamental right to engage in sodomy." Locally, violence against gays spiked, and there had been tumult in Queens at the start of the previous school year when the Board of Education determined that a second-grader afflicted with AIDS should be allowed to attend school. An estimated eleven thousand kids were kept out of classes in Queens as part of a boycott protesting the student's presence in school. The heavy thinkers of the conservative movement were equally extreme in proposals to combat the spread of AIDS. Buckley, in his syndicated column, advanced the idea of tattooing anyone known to have AIDS, placing one on the forearm as a warning to those who would share syringes for drug use, and another on the backside for those considering anal sex. (Buckley modified that view after the death of his friend Cohn.) White House communications director Pat Buchanan warned Koch to cancel the city's Gay Pride parade, but Koch instead beefed up the city's police presence to protect marchers.

If Koch was slow in recognizing AIDS as a threat, President Ronald Reagan moved glacially on the issue. It was not until the thirtieth press conference of his presidency, in 1985, that the issue of AIDS was raised to him, and when Reagan gave a speech about the disease in 1987, he hinted that gay men were being punished for their amoral lifestyle: "When it comes to preventing AIDS, don't medicine and morality teach the same lessons?" Reagan was booed loudly for that. For Kramer, Reagan was the AIDS crisis's chief malefactor, and when Reagan died, Kramer called him, "Adolf Reagan," explaining, Reagan was "responsible for the death of more gay people than anybody in the world, than Hitler. I believe it, and I can't see why people challenge me when I say these things. He's that much a beloved asshole." But Kramer's scorn for Koch was more personal and equally visceral. Koch would later say he regretted not meeting with Kramer and other activists earlier in his tenure, but pointed out that, eventually, there were tens of millions of people infected with HIV. "I'm responsible?" Koch said. "I mean, people who know they shouldn't fuck without a rubber and nevertheless do—*I'm responsible for that?*" In Kramer's mind, yes. He recalled having once run into Koch in the lobby of his apartment building. Koch was friendly and reached down to pet Kramer's dog, Molly, and tell him she was beautiful. "I yanked her away so hard she yelped," Kramer said. "I said, 'Molly, you can't talk to him. That is the man who killed all of Daddy's friends.'"

17

MIKE JANOFSKY HAD JUST BEEN poking around at the Southern District federal court. The USFL's lawsuit against the NFL—Janofsky's beat for the past month—was not then in session. But Janofsky had come across some documents that had been filed with judge Peter Leisure and had been previously unknown to the public, not been officially admitted into evidence. The documents showed that as far back as early 1984, nine months before Trump and Roy Cohn filed the USFL's antitrust suit against the NFL, the USFL had already been plotting to move teams out of markets in which it was competing directly with the NFL, not because they were being bullied and run out of town by the senior league, but because going to non-NFL markets would facilitate a merger between the leagues. Thus, the very successful Philadelphia franchise was moved to Baltimore, where the Colts had just vacated for Indianapolis. The Washington franchise left Redskins country and moved to Orlando, and the New Orleans Breakers went to Portland. Michigan merged with Oakland (left vacant by the Raiders, now in Los Angeles), and franchises in Pittsburgh and Chicago folded. Important to the USFL's case was the assertion that those teams had been damaged by the muscle-flexing of the NFL franchises in those cities. But here were court documents, in hard print, showing that the USFL had orchestrated the scattering of its franchises itself, not because of pressure from the NFL, but for the purposes of a merger. "I just had some time and wanted to see what documents had been filed in the case," Janofsky said. "And there was this letter, and when I read it, the letter put the lie to the whole proposition that the NFL was doing all these things to hurt the USFL. What it showed was that they were angling for the merger."

The letter was from Donald Trump to his other USFL owners. Trump, in his short time as the USFL's chief impresario, had not been shy about expressing his opinions on what the league ought to do: abandon the spring schedule, play in the fall, compete with the NFL, force the leagues to merge (and put his Generals into his domed stadium in Queens, though he was smart enough to mostly keep that to himself). But the NFL had no solid evidence the USFL had been operating with that motivation all along. Once the letter, and other supporting materials, were discovered, they were allowed into evidence and provided a sharp contradiction to the testimony of several USFL witnesses, including commissioner Harry Usher, who had already testified that the USFL moved to smaller markets because the league had been "pushed and shoved by the NFL and by the networks into this situation by NFL pressure." Trump's letter, from January 17, 1984, pushed for a move to a fall schedule as the first step toward an NFL merger. "If we expect the networks to pay us a great deal of money for a period where there is a small television audience," Trump wrote, "then we are being foolish. The NFL knows this and are just waiting. Their only fear is a switch of our league to the winter—an event which will either lead to a merger, or, in the alternative, a common draft with a first-class, traditional league."

There was also an account of the minutes of a USFL meeting, in which Trump was explaining to his fellow owners how they ought to inflate expectations on television ratings, a tactic he frequently took with his buildings. "When I build something for somebody, I always add $50 million or $60 million into the price. My guys come in. They say it is going to cost $75 million, I say it's going to cost $125 million, and I build it for $100 million. Basically, I did a lousy job, but they think I did a great job. So you have to do the same thing with television." Also coming to light was an interview on a National Public Radio channel with Charles Givens, one of the minority owners of the Orlando Renegades, taped in November 1985. In it, Givens said, "The real thing going on in the USFL is the merger possibility with the NFL. For a few hundred thousand dollars of your own investment, not much money for any of the USFL owners, you can take a chance on an instant net worth of $70 million if you merge with the NFL." None of this made the USFL look good, nor did it make lawyer Harvey Myerson's "itty-bitty" characterization of the league believable. There was still doubt, though, as to whether the technicalities and politics of football (none of the members of the jury professed to be a sports fan at all, let alone a football fan) registered with the jury, or if they simply had been dazzled by Myerson's theatrics.

Boston Globe football columnist Will McDonough, from his read, figured that even with the contradictions and revelations that had damaged the USFL case from a purely legal standpoint, the upstart league was way ahead of the NFL when the trial reached its midpoint in June, thanks mostly to the comportment of Myerson. "The major problem for the NFL is dynamic Harvey Myerson," McDonough wrote, "who has shown in this trial that his reputation as one of the best lawyers in the country is well deserved. By almost all accounts, Myerson is winning the case on his own, simply overpowering his NFL counterparts." McDonough also quoted an unnamed "football source," who told him: "The USFL came into this thing big underdogs. Now, I consider them favorites. It's unbelievable how they have turned this thing around. Put it this way: It's about halftime, and they have such a big lead, I don't think the NFL can catch up." William Nack, covering the trial for *Sports Illustrated*, agreed. He quoted Browns owner Art Modell saying that the USFL was up "by a touchdown and a safety," in the first weeks of the trial. While the NFL lawyers simply addressed the jurors, Nack wrote, Myerson "entertained and wooed them." At one point, during a conference with Leisure, NFL attorney Frank Rothman complained that Myerson was "looking at the jury, smiling at the jury, making motions toward the jury. . . . It is distracting, it is improper." But Leisure turned back his complaints, saying, "I'm not going to impose a restriction on the style of counsel." What was more, the USFL still had not called what were expected to be their star witnesses: broadcaster Howard Cosell, Raiders owner Al Davis, and Trump. By the time Myerson played those cards, McDonough suggested, "the lead may be too great to overcome."

. . . . .

Trump was the first of Myerson's big witnesses to testify, on June 23, and his testimony was expected to seal what would be an earth-shaking USFL win. Myerson had built his argument that the NFL had conspired to shut down the USFL by forcing television networks to forgo broadcasting games of the new league, and that the NFL had pulled strings to keep a USFL team from entering the New York market. Trump, the hope was, would charm the jury and chip away at commissioner Pete Rozelle's credibility with claims that Rozelle had courted Trump as an owner before. Davis and Cosell were only tangentially involved in the USFL vs. NFL squabble, but they had two common traits Myerson hoped to exploit: They were both big, engaging personalities, and they both had a deep-seated hatred for Rozelle.

Trump recounted his view of past interactions with Rozelle, and was very specific in his recollections. He had been friends with Rozelle, he said, but the NFL's top man now treated Trump like he had "the plague." Trump described a meeting at the Pierre Hotel in New York, which Rozelle had called to set up in March 1984. In the meeting, according to Trump, Rozelle told him he could have an NFL team if the USFL remained a spring league and if the USFL did not file an antitrust suit against the NFL. Despite his own letter that showed a merger with the NFL had long been his goal, Trump testified that a television contract for the USFL in the fall was "my number one priority." He insisted Rozelle had tried to pull him into the NFL. "Rozelle told me I should be in the NFL, not the USFL," Trump said. "At some point, he said, I would be in the NFL. Then he would reiterate that the USFL was not going to make it." Problem was, very little of it was true, and when Rozelle later re-took the stand, he contradicted virtually everything Trump had said—and he had taken contemporaneous notes to back him up. He had not offered Trump an NFL franchise, and did not have the power to do so in his role as commissioner, because only other owners could OK a new franchise. As Rozelle remembered it, the roles were reversed. Trump offered to have the USFL suit dropped if Rozelle would grant him an NFL franchise. Rozelle asked him what he would do with the Generals in that case. "I'll get some stiff to buy it," Trump had said. Even on the issue of friendship, Rozelle said Trump had lied. They may have seen each other occasionally at large events, but they were never friends. "Rozelle was dry, but he was straightforward," Janofsky said. "Trump was more improvised, it seemed. If you're asking me who was more believable, even going back to 1986? It wasn't Donald Trump."

Myerson made one critical mistake, too, in calling Trump to the stand: He did not call any other USFL owner. The rest of the league owners were not the cocky mega-builders that Trump was, and the losses they suffered in the USFL stung them far more than Trump. They would have been sympathetic characters, because Myerson was presenting his client as an underdog. Trump was no underdog. The lasting impression Trump left of USFL owners was that they struggled with the truth and could get any old stiff to buy their teams if they wanted.

18

THE FEDERAL ORGANIZED CRIME STRIKE Force in Brooklyn had Meade Esposito's office at Seres, Visone and Rice Insurance on Greenwich Street in Manhattan bugged, originally stemming from his connection to mobster Fritzy Giovanelli and the possibility of an extortion conspiracy aimed at a small chemical company in New Jersey. But there had been more picked up on the Esposito wire. Of course, critical to the success of any surveillance effort was that he remain unaware of the bug. There had been some near-misses, particularly when Giovanelli had been arrested after a surveillance operation at a Queens restaurant in January went bad, and a city cop was left dead—there would be questions, it was feared in the Strike Force office, about the intercepted communications of Giovanelli, which might lead to Esposito figuring out he had been bugged. There was also the media, still interested in Esposito's fortunes, especially as the city was undergoing convulsions of scandal in its municipal offices and headline-grabbing strife within the organized crime world. Esposito, as the former head of the Brooklyn Democrats, straddled both worlds. In the May 5 issue of *New York* magazine, writer Nick Pileggi sent what probably should have been taken as a clear signal to Esposito that, despite having been retired from politics for two years, he was still very much a person of interest to law enforcement. In it, Esposito pointed out that he had known mobsters for years from having grown up with them, but added, "I never do a thing for them."

But Pileggi then brought up the Brooklyn Navy Yard where "Esposito long held the patronage key." That key was now being used to favor Coastal Dry Dock, the ship-repair company that was the source of hundreds of thousands of dollars in insurance business for Esposito's company. But Coastal was foundering, thanks to high rents and a lack of business. For the head of the Brooklyn Organized Crime Task Force, Ed McDonald, the fortunes of Coastal were of particular interest. His agents were listening in on Esposito's conversations, which showed that he was providing vacations for Congressman Mario Biaggi in exchange for Biaggi's help for Coastal in Congress. Biaggi, in response, had held several conversations with the mayor's office, trying to get Coastal's rents reduced, and would also contact the Commandant of the Coast Guard, an attempt to drum up more business for the company. On May 15, Biaggi filed an ethics report with congressional overseers for 1985 that failed to mention the Florida trip Esposito set up. The next day, Coastal Dry Dock declared Chapter 11 bankruptcy. Despite having taken in $350 million in contracts from 1981 to 1985, the company was $30 million in debt. That did not stop Biaggi from continuing to advocate for the company, hoping it could be pulled out of bankruptcy. But by late May, it did not much matter. McDonald and his team figured they had already had enough on Biaggi and Esposito to begin making their move. "We weren't going after Biaggi, we were listening to Esposito," McDonald said. "Then, lo and behold, Biaggi walked into the middle of the whole thing very unexpectedly."

There was something about Mario Biaggi, for all his successes, that gave him a forlorn air. He had been the son of Italian immigrants and had made his mark as a cop, winning the Medal of Honor, the highest citation the city can give, for his actions in killing what was termed "an armed thug," in an off-duty shootout in the Bronx in 1959. He was wounded eleven times in a twenty-three-year career, and won dozens of citations in his time with the police. Biaggi was called the most decorated policeman in the nation, and he translated that into a seat in Congress, winning a heavily Republican Bronx district as a Democrat by appealing to conservative Italians and also securing the Irish vote with outspoken stances on Northern Ireland and support for the Irish Republican Army. Biaggi could well have been elected mayor when he ran for the seat in 1973, but his bid had been sabotaged, according to his friend, Roy Cohn, by none other than Roy Cohn himself. As Cohn told the story, Biaggi had, in 1971, given sworn testimony to a grand jury, and had asked Cohn's advice. Cohn told him to answer all questions, he had done nothing wrong. But Biaggi got cold feet and called another lawyer, who advised him to plead the Fifth Amendment on certain questions. Grand jury testimony comes with sworn secrecy, so the lawyer figured Biaggi had nothing to lose by avoiding questions that might imperil him.

Cohn found out that Biaggi had taken the Fifth and when the 1973 election came around, the party bosses—Meade Esposito in

Brooklyn and Pat Cunningham, Stanley Friedman's predecessor, in the Bronx—wanted Abe Beame to be mayor, while Queens boss Matty Troy (Donald Manes's predecessor) was pulling for Biaggi, who established an early lead for the Democratic nomination. Cohn called Biaggi into a meeting and told him Esposito and Cunningham wanted him to drop out, and that if he didn't, the Fifth Amendment testimony would be leaked to the press. Cohn did not say how it would come out, and Biaggi did not believe him. Cohn remembered Biaggi's response: "Fuck 'em." But Cohn, too, wanted Beame, explaining that Beame (who had lost to John Lindsay in the 1965 mayoral race) had been a dues-paying product of the Democratic machine for a long time, and it was "his turn." The next day, the story about Biaggi taking the Fifth was on the front page of the *New York Times*. When asked, Biaggi lied about the testimony, and denied he had taken the Fifth, "which became the big issue," Cohn said, "the whole thing." When it was shown that Biaggi lied about what he said to the grand jury, his mayoral chances were ended.

When McDonald and the FBI were deciding how to approach the next steps on the Esposito-Biaggi bribery case, one of the initial decisions was picking the first target. The idea was to pick the weaker of the two men, because he would be more likely to either break quickly and confess to wrongdoing, or to do something foolish. They went with Biaggi. "He was the hero cop, the tough guy and all that stuff," said McDonald, who credits the FBI with the decision. "But Esposito was an old hand. We could tell from the phone conversations that Biaggi was the weaker of the two." The Strike Force would still have the wire for the remainder of the day, so if anything unexpected happened on Esposito's telephone line, it would be captured. At 9:00 a.m., FBI agents met Biaggi as he stepped out of his car and went toward his office. He agreed to be questioned inside. There, Biaggi was evasive. He would not say at first who had provided the accommodations for him and Barlow at the Bonaventure Spa in Florida. He dodged questions about his ethics forms and solicitations on behalf of Coastal Dry Dock. As the agents wound up their questioning, Biaggi finally cracked enough to admit it had been Meade Esposito who provided the trips. But the real drama was on Esposito's phone line—agents were monitoring it hopefully, waiting to see if Biaggi cracked and called Esposito. Finally, about forty-five minutes after the agents started questioning him, Esposito's phone rang. It was Biaggi.

What followed was both possible obstruction of justice and high comedy—Biaggi whining and trying to subtly coach Esposito to say he had given Biaggi trips to Florida to help with his health and out of friendship. In reality, the two were not close. Biaggi knew FBI agents would be heading to Esposito soon, and they had to get their stories straight. But he was explaining things so subtly that Esposito, who saw Biaggi as a paid-for politician he had co-opted for help on the Coastal Dry Dock problem, got increasingly confused and frustrated. "How long have you and I known each other?" Biaggi asked.

Esposito: Quite a long time.

Biaggi: Say 20, 25 years?

Esposito: At least.

Biaggi: At least. We're very dear friends.

Esposito: Oh yeah.

Biaggi: You try, you regard me as a son?

Esposito: No problem.

Biaggi: Okay?

Esposito: Whatta you want?

Biaggi: Uh, you're, you're concerned about my health?

Esposito: Absolutely (laughs).

Biaggi: You knew I had, you knew I had some trouble with my heart?

Esposito: When?

Biaggi: Now just listen to what I'm saying.

Esposito: Go ahead.

Biaggi: And uh, and I needed some relaxation.

Esposito: Yeah.

Biaggi: And, and . . .

Esposito: Well, what the fuck do ya want, pal?

As Biaggi was trying to coordinate with Esposito, he could not have known that he was being recorded, and everything he was telling Esposito was firming up the case for McDonald and jeopardizing his congressional career. For agents listening in on the call, the real gut-buster came when Biaggi began asking Esposito about Barbara Barlow. His questions were coming so quickly and urgently that Esposito paused and said, "This sounds like a fuckin' grand jury." Biaggi had just the right response: "That's, that's what I'm talking about!" Biaggi and Esposito, plotting how they would cover their tracks, spelled out the entire case against them. "One of the things we had to do was to show that there was something being obstructed, that a grand jury proceeding was being obstructed," McDonald said. "We had a grand jury just before the FBI went to visit Biaggi in the Bronx. We had the grand jury pending. So Esposito uttered the magic words, 'This sounds like a grand jury.'" By the end of the month, federal prosecutors acknowledged that there was, in fact, a grand jury, and Biaggi's records were being subpoenaed. It would be the beginning of his downfall.

19

THE USFL's FINAL TWO WITNESSES were Raiders owner Al Davis and broadcaster Howard Cosell. Neither had a direct involvement in the alleged financial strangulation of the USFL, which made them flashy and notable witnesses, but not compelling in terms of establishing suffering on the league's part. Both were testifying because they hated Rozelle. Like Trump, both witnesses came off as cocky. When Davis took the stand, he wore a Raider-black suit with a silver tie, and according to one columnist, "black shoes shiny enough to read a playbook by." Davis, who had successfully sued the NFL over his team's move from Oakland to Los Angeles, had both of the two Super Bowl rings he had won with the Raiders on his fingers. Even the recitation of his name was delivered with a bit too much swagger: "My name is Allen, A-L-L-E-N, Davis." Davis spoke about his belief that the NFL and the City of Oakland had conspired to "destroy" the Oakland Invaders franchise, though he was not personally involved in that destruction. His testimony angered his fellow NFL owners and employees on hand, even as its relevance remained uncertain. "All that stuff about the Invaders," Giants owner Wellington Mara told a reporter, "what's that got to do with the price of potatoes?"

The coup de grace belonged, though, to Cosell, who took the stand on June 26 with the goal of contradicting the assertions of two of his former ABC Sports bosses, head Roone Arledge and former vice president Jim Spence. Instead, Room 318 became the stage for the Howard Cosell Show. When asked to give his credentials and background, Cosell took the jury on a thirty-nine-minute tour of his life, times, and career. He spoke of the overwhelming power of the NFL and his belief that they had established an illegal monopoly. He pulled for the little guy, and advocated for a free and fair market. Then lunchtime hit, and a recess of about ninety minutes was given. When Cosell returned to the stand, post-lunch, he was changed—he hung his head a bit more, he was more flippant, he was less cogent. There was speculation that, wherever Cosell had gone for lunch, he had almost certainly downed a cocktail, and maybe two or three. When he was back on the stand, it showed. He was primed to spar with the NFL's Rothman. Rothman asked Cosell, who was once a client of his, "Mr. Cosell, if I ask you a question you don't understand, you stop me, OK?" Cosell's retort: "If you ask a question that I don't understand, you'll have the biggest story of the century." Rothman mentioned that Cosell often put himself in the company of Johnny Carson and Walter Cronkite, as "the three great men of American television journalism." Cosell nodded and said, "Words spoken with an obvious jocularity sometimes contain total truth, sir, and that happens to be so in this case."

And there was the exchange between the two that grabbed the most attention.

Rothman: Let me see if I understand that, Mr. Cosell.

Cosell: I can't understand your inability to understand.

Rothman: I am not as smart as you are, sir.

Cosell: Well, we have learned that long ago.

Rothman: Are you through?

Cosell: Apparently you are groping for thought.

Rothman: I have a degree of civility and I am going to use it.

Cosell: Frank, you used to be my lawyer and I am sure you will use it.

Rothman: And I had trouble with you then, too.

When he was finished, Cosell climbed off the stand and, as he exited, said to a reporter, "What a performance!" But Jerry Izenberg, then a columnist for the *New York Post*, remembered almost pitying Cosell as his four hours of testimony wore on. "He was arrogant and it was obvious the jury thought so," Izenberg said. "He was not on TV anymore, he was just doing radio then. He wanted a platform, that was his platform. It didn't have a lot to do with the USFL. It was just about Howard Cosell."

With that, the USFL rested its case.

20

RICK RHODEN HAD BEEN THROUGH this wringer before. The veteran Pirates righty had come up to the big leagues with the Dodgers in the 1970s as a power pitcher, but suffered a shoulder injury in 1979 and, when he returned, had to figure out how to win games with finesse and guile. Baseball wisdom suggested that those pitchers who won with finesse and guile were very often those who figured out how to bend the rules. In the mid-'80s, that meant scuffing the baseball with a small bit of emery board tucked out of sight in the pitcher's glove. The scuff added extreme movement, and for a pitcher with great control like Rhoden, it meant he could be an All-Star at age thirty-three, posting one of the best seasons of his career for an otherwise terrible Pirates team. Rhoden never copped to it, but it had been said that he learned the fine art of scuffing from a master, Don Sutton, who finessed and guiled his way through baseball past his forty-third birthday. Rhoden's reputation ticked off the Mets, and when they faced him before a scant crowd of 15,113 in the first game of a Friday doubleheader in June at Three Rivers Stadium, they were on high alert for funny business. Rhoden had been knocked for a run in the second inning, with the Mets stranding a runner on third. He had allowed the bases to be loaded with one out in the fourth, but struck out number eight hitter Rafael Santana and pitcher Ron Darling to escape the jam. While Rhoden was delivering his pitches, Mets first base coach Bill Robinson—a former teammate of Rhoden with the Pirates—was continually complaining to umpire Billy Williams that Rhoden was scuffing. The calls were coming from the Mets' dugout, too. Mets manager Davey Johnson would later explain that Rhoden's doctoring of the ball was blatant: "He just flaunts it. That's what makes it so aggravating. To see it done right in front of your eyes."

In the fifth inning, Gary Carter came to bat with a runner on first and two out. Carter had been in what, for him, qualified as a groove: He had hit in ten of his last eleven games, boosting his batting average from .225 to .244. While Carter was at the plate, Robinson implored Williams to check Rhoden's ball for scuffs. Carter, who had also frequently complained about Rhoden to umpires, picked up one of Rhoden's pitched balls, which was otherwise new, and showed Williams a suspicious mark. Williams investigated Rhoden's glove but found nothing illegal and simply tossed the used ball out of the game. But Rhoden's next pitch was a big breaker of a curveball, and Carter swung and missed to end the Mets half of the inning. The Mets were angry again. Robinson was returning to the dugout and passed Rhoden, calling him a cheater as he passed. Rhoden turned to curse at his old teammate. Robinson shoved Rhoden, sparking a bench-clearing melee that lasted five minutes.

It was the second brawl of the past two weeks for the Mets. Back in late May, it was Ray Knight whose dander was raised. It had already been a tense night at Shea Stadium, with LA's Steve Sax and Greg Brock getting into a pregame intrasquad dugout fight that required several teammates to quell. But by the sixth inning, the animus turned toward the Mets, especially after George Foster unloaded a grand slam off reliever Tom Niedenfuer. Knight was the next to bat. Niedenfuer threw at him, and hit him. Knight charged the mound, setting off a full-scale team brawl. Dodgers manager Tommy Lasorda, who had recently put out a book, ran onto the field, his jowly face red with anger, demanding Knight be ejected (he wasn't). "I felt sure he was trying to throw at me," Knight said. "He did what he had to do. And I did what I had to do. I read Tommy Lasorda's book. I know how he plays the game."

It was also becoming clear how the Mets would play the game in 1986. They had, by early June, established a division lead of eight games, and looked like the best team in baseball. But this was not to be a team that would win with grace and class. They would poke, prod, and rile their foes as they beat them, and they would be a bunch that would themselves have a short fuse, unafraid of leaping off the bench en masse for fisticuffs. That only made their opponents despise them more. "There are too many tough guys over there," Reds star Dave Parker said. "I think they ought to be shown there are tough guys everywhere. All this gung-ho Mets mania that's going on, I've seen better teams than the Mets. I've played for better teams than the Mets." The Mets were good, maybe the best in baseball. They loved letting other teams in the league know about it. "Not too many teams I played against would rub your face in it like they did," former Astro Phil Garner later recalled. "New York teams can get on your nerves once in a while. They're always on TV, they get a lot of coverage in the media. But those guys took it to a different level. There were some good guys over there, but as a group they could get under your skin."

. . . . .

Times sports columnist Ira Berkow once sat at an eating and drinking establishment in Houston with another New York writer at about ten in the morning, seeking breakfast. Nearby at the bar, they were approached with the question few East Coast reporters want to hear when in Texas: "You aren't from around here, are you?" Well, no. But the intrepid reporters knew they were in for an earful when the fellow approaching them explained that, at this place, typically, the drinking would begin at about eight (yes, in the morning) before moving over to the Dark Horse a few hours later. For now, though, there would be a lecture on the many differences between life in Houston and life in New York. Berkow had already stocked up on topics for safe discussion when in town, among them: "the Challenger tragedy, sagging oil prices, the demise of the urban cowboy." But the local interloper had some other, more clichéd issues to cover, like the pushiness of folks from the Northeast when compared with the laid-back nature of the Southwest, and the tales of rampant muggings that apparently went down on every street corner in New York. "It's the difference in lifestyles," the reporters were told.

Differing lifestyles were a big part of what went down on July 19, and in its aftermath. In their first series after the All-Star break, the Mets were visiting Houston. Keith Hernandez, Gary Carter, Darryl Strawberry, Dwight Gooden, and Sid Fernandez were already in Houston for the All-Star Game, played at the Astrodome. Having lost to the Astros on a Friday night, 3–0, the Mets were now 60–26, still twelve and a half games better than any other National League team. The Astros were locked in a battle with the Giants, Padres, and Reds in the NL West, and the Mets' dominance in the East meant that, even with two and a half months to go in the season, the only question was which of those four teams would face the Mets for the right to go to the World Series. After the game, the Mets got back to their hotel, the Marriott Astrodome, around 11:15 p.m. Eight players went to a nearby nightclub, Cooter's, a yuppie dance bar with two dance floors, three bars, and a DJ. By 2:00 a.m., there were four Mets still at the place: pitchers Bob Ojeda, Rick Aguilera, and Ron Darling, and infielder Tim Teufel, who had just returned to the team following the birth of his first child, a boy, and was celebrating.

According to police, closing time had come and the players were asked to leave, but Teufel caused an incident (he was "loudly abusive"), which was compounded when he insisted on taking a drink outside with him, even after being told by an off-duty officer that was prohibited. Once outside (again, this was the police account), the officer went to arrest Teufel, with help from another off-duty cop. Teufel fought back and "during a struggle, blows were passed." Teufel supposedly kneed an officer in the groin. That was when Darling stepped in to pull Teufel away, but was instead slammed into a glass door by one of the officers, who claimed Darling had gotten him into "a choke hold." Aguilera and Ojeda came into the scuffle, and found themselves arrested, too. One cab driver who witnessed the incident said there were seven officers who descended on Teufel, a 175-pound second baseman. All four Mets were rounded up and thrown into a holding cell for eleven hours, released when team VP Joe McIlvaine arrived to bail them out, just a few hours before the team dropped a 5–4 game to the Astros. Their Mets teammates, always supportive, decorated the four players' lockers with vertical strands of black tape to represent prison bars, as well as an empty Budweiser can, an empty plastic cup marked "Tequila," and a lone cigarette with matches. The joke only slightly lifted the scofflaws' moods.

It was in the aftermath of the Cooter's fracas that the differing lifestyles came into play. The next day in the *Houston Chronicle*, Mets manager Davey Johnson was quoted saying, "I'm somewhat amazed that something like this didn't happen in Chicago or New York or L.A. We deal with all sorts of people in New York." Johnson meant that he had figured his team would find such a run-in when playing in a bigger, more rough-and-tumble city. Many among the New York sports press harkened back to 1957, when Billy Martin and six other Yankees got into a tussle with other club-goers at the Copacabana, and one deli owner threatened to sue Yankee slugger Hank Bauer. The players had not needed to leave the city to find trouble in that instance. But Judge Doug Shaver took Johnson's words differently. At a preliminary hearing for Teufel and Darling on July 20, Shaver took a moment to comment on Johnson's statement: "I take that as a blanket indictment of this city and this police department. It is as absurd as saying this wouldn't have occurred if this had been the Atlanta Braves or the San Diego Padres in town." The players' high-profile attorney, Dick DeGuerin, took exception to the judge's remark, calling it "gratuitous." He added that Teufel had been roughed up by the police unnecessarily, and though DeGuerin was a lifelong Texan, added, "I don't think it would have happened anywhere but Houston. I may be cynical about some Houston police officers, but they certainly don't teach common courtesy at the Houston Police Department." That, of course, drew a strong condemnation from Houston chief of police Lee C. Brown, who said, "I personally resent the statement. [It is an] unfortunate, blanket, unjustified indictment of our department and our city."

Just like that, a handful of drunk Mets at a bar near the Astrodome had set the city of Houston, economically depressed at the time thanks to a downturn in the oil industry, into a quagmire of self-reflection. There was some fun had with the incident—T-shirts reading "Houston Police 4 – New York Mets 0" popped up around the city. But there was concern about the way folks from the outside saw Houston. The *Houston Chronicle* even reached out to Bill Barclift in Washington, where he served as spokesman for the American Society of Association Executives, asking if the roughed-up Mets had hurt Houston's image as a convention city. "If it were a chronic problem and you read stories on such incidents on a weekly basis, you'd wonder, are [the police] going to overreact to your organization?" Barclift said before delivering the townsfolk some self-assurance. "I think Houston has a very good image."

Johnson did not see much need to come down on the Cooter's quartet. They were not, usually, a troublesome group, so Johnson merely fined them for missing curfew, a rule that was not much enforced. That had been Johnson's approach with the Mets since he was made manager in 1984, when he was just forty-one years old and five years removed from being a player himself. That was a young team, and where many managers would micromanage young players, Johnson was different. General manager Frank Cashen would typically press for a more orderly, disciplined locker room, but Johnson did his best to allow his players to be their own men. The Mets did cough up three out of four games to the Astros in the series, pulling Houston into a tie for first in the NL West. The quartet of players involved did not seem to suffer much, either. Teufel had been struggling, with a .223 batting average, before his Cooter's arrest, but hit .317 with a .407 on-base percentage in his next 34 games. Darling went 3–1 with a 2.88 ERA in his next seven starts. Ojeda was 7–3 with a 3.13 ERA through the end of the year, and Aguilera had the best post-Cooter's bounce, going 8–4 with a 2.76 ERA to close the year—he had been 2–3 with a 5.40 ERA before that.

.....

There were plenty of reasons for Ray Knight to be irritated, again. It had been a bizarre night in late July for the Mets, in what was an increasingly bizarre month for the team. Just days removed from Houston and the Cooter's-inspired culture war with the Southwest, they were now in Cincinnati, a team littered with well-worn veterans but with enough young talent to stay in the chase for their divisional crown. Knight knew the plight of the Reds all too well—he had been a Red up until 1981. Knight had played with franchise mainstays like Dave Concepción, Pete Rose, and Tony Pérez, holdovers from the Big Red Machine days of the mid-'70s who were still clinging to baseball life in 1986. He had spent two and a half years in Houston before landing with the Mets, and in his first full season in New York—1985—it looked as though Knight might be finished for good. He was thirty-two, had shoulder surgery the previous spring, batted just .218 for the season, and could not get himself to feel much like a productive member of the team. For the first time in his career, he platooned at third base, with switch-hitting Howard Johnson. It had not helped his batting average very much, and his struggles were amply noticed by the Shea Stadium fans. "The fans booed me," Knight said. "It hurt. I took it hard. I don't blame them. I didn't do much to cheer about."

In the offseason after 1985, Knight's wife—the professional golfer Nancy Lopez—was pregnant with the couple's second child. That pulled Lopez off the LPGA tour and Knight's usual winter activity, following Nancy to various winter tournaments, was put on hold. Instead, Lopez, pregnant, soft-tossed pitches to Knight so he could keep his swing in shape. Mets general manager Frank Cashen had been trying to trade Knight, but to no avail, which meant he would be sticking with the Mets for at least one more year. Knight consulted with coach Bill Robinson, who helped Knight remake his batting stance to take better advantage of his strong hands. For much of the early season, the added work paid off, as Knight came out of April with the league lead in home runs (six) and was batting .339 as late as June 13. But July had been much harsher for Knight. He was batting .136 on the month, dropping his average to a mundane .286. So he was not quite in high spirits when, in the bottom of the 10th inning against his old team at Riverfront Stadium, after the Mets had tied the game in the ninth with two runs on a dropped pop fly by Dave Parker, Reds speedster Eric Davis stole second, then attempted to steal third. Davis slid in easily with a large cloud of dust, but when he popped up out of his slide, Knight gave Davis a bump, hoping to force him off the bag. Davis turned and shoved into Knight as Knight stepped into Davis. There was a tangle. Finally, Knight snapped and simply unloaded a right fist to Davis's jaw. Knight would claim he and Davis had a verbal back-and-forth, that Davis swore at him and that he had felt threatened, all in a matter of seconds. To that, Davis said sarcastically, "That's a good one. If he had time to hear me curse, for me to elbow him and for him to see a look in my eye, recognize it and then hit me . . . that's awesome. That's unbelievable."

During the season, the Mets had already had bench-emptying brawls with the Dodgers, the Pirates, and, just one week before the Reds game, the Braves. Then there was the Cooter's mess. Rare in the history of the league was a team so enthusiastic in its pugilism, but even by Mets standards, the brawl in Cincinnati was a headline-grabber. It began with Davis and Knight, and might have stopped there—umpire Eric Gregg grabbed Davis from behind, keeping him from swinging back at Knight. But Eddie Milner, the Reds' batter when Davis stole third, hustled up the third base line as pitcher Jesse Orosco strode toward the pair, and that turned a two-man fracas into a full-on bench-clearer. A horde of Mets clashed with an equal contingent of Reds, the groups converging out near shortstop like sides in a rugby scrum.

Davis, later being held back by bullpen coach Bruce Kimm, was still on the fringe of the bunch, seeking out Knight, and would for days talk about how much he regretted not getting a chance to slug Knight in retaliation. Mets utility man Kevin Mitchell hurled himself into the mix, began punching a Red, then was taken down and set upon by three other Reds, including John Denny, who happened to be a karate expert. It was not until home plate umpire Gerry Davis stepped in and boomed, "The next guy who throws a punch gets suspended," that détente was achieved. With the Mets prepping for the playoffs and the Reds fighting for the NL West, Gerry Davis's warning was enough to simmer tensions quickly. No one wanted to be suspended. Already, the Mets had lost Darryl Strawberry to an ejection from the game for arguing balls and strikes. Now, Knight was tossed, as was Mitchell. Davey Johnson had no options remaining among position players, and stuck Orosco in right field, with Roger McDowell on to pitch. Johnson shuffled Orosco and McDowell between the outfield and mound, and pulled Carter from his catcher's spot to third base. It was a shoestring operation, defensively, until finally, the Mets came up with a three-run homer from Howard Johnson in the 14th to win the game.

When the Mets completed the sweep of the Reds the following day, they could gain some comfort from knowing that, though they were leaving yet another town heaped with disdain from rival players and local fans, they were pretty good at backing up whatever trash-talk they laid out. "People say we're one of the cockiest teams," Howard Johnson said. "They talk about how arrogant we are and they want to get the chance to retaliate. We enjoy fighting and if that's what it takes, we'll fight. We won't be pushed around." Of course, part of the fans' disdain for the Mets all across the country was cultural. They were from New York. "Everybody," Mets manager Davey Johnson said, "hates teams from New York."

There was one player who was notable for his absence from this fourth Mets brawl: veteran slugger George Foster, the highest paid player in the league. Foster had hit just .182 in his previous 21 games, and would appear just once in the Cincinnati series, as a pinch-hitter in the 14-inning game.

21

FRANK SINATRA WAS COLD, AND angry. He just wanted to get back to Pier 12. Things at the July 3 celebration on the waterfront of Governors Island had not gone smoothly, despite the best view of Liberty Island anywhere in New York City. This was to be the most dazzling part of what was being called Liberty Weekend in New York, the A-list VIP party: the president and first lady were the stars, and mingling in the crowd were Gregory Hines, Johnny Cash, Steven Spielberg, Mikhail Baryshnikov, Robert DeNiro, Shirley MacLaine, Dr. Ruth Westheimer, Neil Diamond, and a slew of others. It had been one hundred years since the citizens of France gave the Americans the Statue of Liberty, so it made sense French president Francois Mitterand was there, with his wife, Daniele, though neither was very comfortable—Mitterand did not get along well with President Reagan, and his wife was a pro-Communist who was not exactly taken by the crass display of American capitalism. Of course, Mayor Ed Koch was there. Liz Taylor was on hand, in a similar mood as Sinatra, her neck wrapped in a supportive collar because she had been injured shortly before while filming a movie. It had been unexpectedly frigid for July. The wind was persistent and earlier rains had left a tented area unwalkable. That area happened to be where the food buffet was housed. But then, the buffet was cold, too, mostly unappetizing, and rare roast beef was being served by caterers who somehow forgot to bring knives for the guests. Sod had been laid out in other areas, generously called a "lawn," but it kept sinking into the ground below. As one partygoer noted, "Anybody with heels on is in trouble." The wind was so brisk the Red Cross handed out silver foil blankets (Lee Iacocca was tucked under one, with his daughter, Lia), but only two hundred were available for a crowd of twenty-five hundred, which left the normally dignified upper crusters to tear the red cushions off the bleachers and erect makeshift fortresses to protect them from the gusts.

This was the viewing party, at a cost of $5,000 per ticket, for the relighting of the Statue of Liberty, which had spent the past four years undergoing a refurbishing program in time for its centennial celebration. President Reagan was charged with officially unveiling the new-look statue, and was presented with a large red game-show-style button to initiate the show. (One malfunction, a White House aide joked, and there goes Star Wars.) Sinatra had taken a turn on stage at the soggy gala, doing a rousing version of "The House I Live In," but he wanted to bolt the island as quickly as possible once the statue ceremony was over. Problem was, so did just about everyone else on hand. With boats crowding the waters and winds kicking up whitecaps on the short stretch of bay between Governors Island and the Red Hook section of Brooklyn, what had been a five-minute ferry ride out to the party from the pier hours earlier was now a forty-minute trek back. And so Sinatra stood with the crowd, impatiently signing autographs, waiting and waiting for the boat to get them back from their expensive night of miserable revelry.

Two days earlier, Jimmy Breslin had trucked out to the housing project at Red Hook, about a half-mile from Pier 12. There, he found Pedro Marrero, a former Marine from Puerto Rico who was lamenting the situations of the locals. They should have had the best real estate in the city for Liberty Weekend ceremonies. Instead, the streets all over Red Hook were festooned with No Parking signs, and, under orders from the Secret Service, police were stationed on the corners to prevent pedestrians from passing. Inside the housing complex, signs warned residents that anyone who went on the roof during the lighting of the Statue of Liberty or the fireworks that followed would be thrown out of the project. What should have been one of the few perks of life at the Red Hook project—the harbor view—was taken away. "For a celebration of liberty," Marrero told Breslin, "we don't have the liberty to celebrate." All around Red Hook, there were dormant piers, empty parking lots, and abandoned warehouses. Those had been bought up for big money by corporations for expensive parties, none as expensive as the president's big night on Governor's Island. In the project, Breslin went to different apartments trying to find places where the Statue could be viewed. He found only a couple, and they required almost impossible contortions of back and neck to get even a glimpse. "The sleek will enjoy the Liberty Weekend," Breslin wrote, "in as much comfort as can be given them—which, as those running the weekend insist, is quite proper, for the idea of Liberty Weekend is to cater first to people who can pay $5,000 a seat and show that as true Americans, they have finally learned to love themselves first. And the belief is, the more they do this, the more they spend on themselves, and the more properly they manage the task of acquiring money, the better it is for the entire society because that means that all of society has a segment of it that is rich, and of course the rich are good for us all."

On the Fourth of July, with New York's harbor at the ready for Operation Sail—the procession of Tall Ships from all over the world sent to pay respect to the newly redone Statue—the place to be was the *Highlander*, the 151-foot yacht recently bought and redone by publisher and entrepreneur Malcolm Forbes. If, indeed, you got an invitation, you were greeted, again, by the skulking face of Daniele Mitterand, who seemed out of place. Being French, she was enthusiastically taken to the wine cellar by Forbes. When Forbes said, "Look at all these lovely Bordeaux," Madame Mitterand frowned and said, "I'm from Burgundy," and of course, she left the boat soon after. Most others were happier. Brooke Astor mingled with Shelley Winters, white-collar gossip among what was called "the cigar crowd" (Rupert Murdoch, Don Hewitt, David Rockefeller, and the like) was passed about, and former secretary of state Henry Kissinger lingered (because who wouldn't want to see Kissinger on a boat on a July afternoon?). President Reagan and Nancy had asked about joining the Forbes party, but the Secret Service would not allow it—instead, their son, Ron, was on deck as a correspondent for *Good Morning, America*. Climbing onto the gangplank of the massive boat, guests were greeted by a pair of kilt-wearing bagpipers Forbes had flown in from Scotland. There was lobster, smoked salmon, and caviar (thirty pounds, which made the on-board chef wonder if there would be enough) at breakfast, and lunch would see filet mignon and chicken salad. Desserts were served in brass Thai goblets that gave off plumes of smoke from dry ice tucked inside. All over the harbor area, as many as forty thousand boats were crammed, but they parted for the *Highlander*. From one British boat, a banner was hung: OK U.S. IS FORGIVEN. COME HOME COLONIALS. TEA AND CRUMPETS AWAIT. At one point, as the *Highlander* was moored off Governors Island, it was approached by another vessel, a small police boat. From a bullhorn on the boat, a noise rose like a screeching harpy: "Malcolm! Malcolm! Hi!" It was New York's mayor, Ed Koch, and it was quite a coincidence—Koch's latest book, *Politics*, was included in the Capitalist Toolbox gift bags Forbes was giving out to guests. Forbes shouted back to Koch that he was putting on a very nice party in the city. Koch replied, "I think we'll do it every year."

The refurbishing of the Statue of Liberty was not Koch's project (Iacocca had headed up the refurbishment drive, though he had been fired near the end of the project), but the city had been assigned the task of arranging the festivities of the weekend, dealing with the onslaught of tourists, keeping the trains running and closing down traffic lanes for most of Lower Manhattan. It was a massive financial layout, with one cost estimate at $13 million to the city not counting all the overtime pay. Over the previous six months, Koch leaned on Liberty Weekend preparations like a crutch, churning out press releases with the grim hope that attention to the Statue of Liberty centennial would be a distraction away from the misery that municipal government had been since the New Year. There were obvious drags on the weekend, starting with the unseasonably chilly weather. But the weekend did bring into sharp relief the problem of class in New York City—while the *Highlander* was tooling around the harbor, an encampment of the homeless was set up in Battery Park, and they protested throughout the weekend. When folk singer John Denver, who was aboard Bill Fugazy's yacht, the *Princess*, with Lee Iacocca and Bob Hope, was asked if any groups were underrepresented over the weekend, he said: "The poor, the homeless, the American Indian." Still, Liberty Weekend was Koch's big chance to push aside Donald Manes and Stanley Friedman and Geoffrey Lindenauer, and he had been eager for it. He would not let it be spoiled. In May, Koch had told reporters, "When the best city in the world throws the best party in the world, the entire world is invited." He then added a bit of gallows humor: "They're stuck with us."

22

RON DARLING ACHIEVED A RARE double as the Mets pulled themselves out of their July doldrums and headed into baseball's final stretch: He opened the month of August on the cover of *GQ*, well coiffed in a tan-and-navy houndstooth suit and, weeks later, in full uniform at the peak of his pitching motion on the cover of *Sports Illustrated*. The *GQ* cover had been of greater concern within the Mets organization, however, because it had come with an in-depth interview in which Darling was less than complimentary about his manager. "Davey Johnson hasn't spoken to me three times all season," Darling said. "He doesn't believe in communication with his players. Some players, maybe—Ray Knight, Keith Hernandez—but not pitchers. Pitchers are not players, you understand, and Davey Johnson was a player." Johnson had been a star second baseman, spending his first eight seasons with the powerhouse Orioles of the late '60s and early '70s. He dealt plenty with pitchers in those days, playing behind a staff built around Jim Palmer, Mike Cuellar, and Dave McNally, three of the best of their era. But Darling was right to say that Johnson was not much of a talker. His managing style was to leave his players alone off the field, and herd them in the right direction when they needed it. He was not one to want to know what was going on with a player's wife or to play the father-figure role. That year, Johnson had coauthored a book about the 1985 season, *Bats*, and he had gotten some good-natured ribbing from sportswriters because in the book, he did not seem to know much about his own players. Johnson had called lefty Lenny Dykstra a switch hitter in the book, and referred to a Mets pitching prospect he had been watching only as

"Mars," which, most assumed, was a drawled version of Randy Myers. "I don't know *what's* in my book," Johnson laughed. But Darling probably had Johnson wrong when he told *GQ*, "I've heard that Davey was intellectually threatened by me. Why should he be? I'm not a clubhouse lawyer. I'm not going to start a coup to overtake his position." Johnson was no dumb jock—he had a degree in mathematics and was a very early devotee to the careful study of pitching patterns and sabermetrics, the advanced statistics that pushed aside many commonly held tenets in baseball in favor of more science-based conclusions.

Darling did intellectually intimidate many of his cohorts. He had gone to Yale, and Ivy Leaguers in the ranks of pro baseball were rare. Of Hawaiian descent, he was good-looking and married to a model, Toni O'Reilly, the kind of dream couple that drew coverage in *People* magazine and *USA Today*. Darling was dubbed "Mr. P" by catcher Gary Carter, with the P standing for "Perfect," a nickname Darling didn't much like (especially coming from Carter, who was nicknamed "Camera" for his eagerness to find a camera and microphone and absorb media attention). After two solid years with the Mets in 1984 and 1985, when he went a combined 28–15, but threw 218 walks in 69 games, Darling had shone in 1986, finally breaking out of the shadow of that other Mets pitcher who had come up in 1984, Dwight Gooden. While there was some mystery around why Gooden was not dominating in 1986 the way he had done before, Darling had developed enough trust in his command to throw more strikes and cut down on free passes. He closed July with his best effort of the year, a complete-game shutout with just six hits, no walks, and eight strikeouts for a win over the Cubs that put his record at 11–3. But Darling claimed to have much the same issue at the big-league level as Gooden—both were shy at their core, and not quite comfortable in their surroundings. Gooden had trouble shaking his inner-city Tampa upbringing, and Darling could not escape the Yale label. "I get sick of myself," Darling said, "even though I know I'm not the person I'm portrayed as. People think I'm a curio because I have what is perceived as an interesting résumé: Yale, English/Chinese/Hawaiian background, supposed Renaissance man, lives in Manhattan, married to a model, makes a million dollars. . . . If I win 20 [games], maybe I'll lose the Yalie tag and just be a pitcher."

Fortunately for Darling, Johnson was thick-skinned enough to let the *GQ* criticism pass. Darling would quickly claim his words had been taken out of context, though it is hard to see how else "Davey is intellectually threatened by me" could be taken, no matter the context. Johnson had his team comfortably in first place, and was banking on his stellar pitching staff to pull through the remainder of the stretch run and into the postseason. There would be no need to create an issue around Darling's interview. All year, the Mets' offense had been inconsistent and in 21 games from July 12 through August 5, the team batted only .247. But the rotation of Gooden, Darling, Fernandez, and Ojeda had been outstanding, and Johnson was not about to mess with that dynamic. Besides, Darling was not entirely wrong. Johnson (mostly joking) did have a thing against pitchers. "When I was playing in Baltimore," Johnson said, "I would say to McNally and Palmer, 'How come I can lose or win a game for you, but you can't do a thing for me?' That went over like a lead balloon. But think about it. The game is perceived—and rightly so—to have pitching as its most important ingredient. But pitchers don't play every day. I always figure that a pitcher has to be four times better than I am to be paid the same because I'm playing four times more often. Palmer and McNally did not agree."

. . . . .

For George Foster, his new reality had been settling in since the Mets' last brawl, the bench-clearer in Cincinnati. While his teammates had been backing up Knight on the Riverfront Stadium turf, Foster—thirty-seven years old, and having spent 11 seasons with the Reds—remained in the confines of the dugout, which had not gone unnoticed by his teammates. The previous week, when the team moved to sign ex-Mets outfielder Lee Mazzilli, released by the Pirates, Foster could see what was coming. He was being replaced. His pride was stung. He had been the National League MVP with Cincinnati in 1977, when he led the league with 52 home runs, tied, at the time, for the eleventh-most in big-league history. When he had gone to the Mets in 1982, as the highest paid player in the league, he had hoped to finish out his career strong and make a run at 500 total homers. He had only made it to 347. Asked about the Mazzilli move by a reporter, Foster dropped a bombshell he would soon regret. "I'm not saying it's a racial thing," Foster said. "But that seems to be the case in sports these days. When a ball club can, they replace a George Foster or a Mookie Wilson with a more popular white player. I think the Mets would rather promote a Gary Carter or a Keith Hernandez to the fans so parents who want to can point to them as role models for their children, rather than a Darryl Strawberry or a Dwight Gooden or a George Foster. The kids don't see color." Even after four and a half seasons with the Mets, Foster probably did not know he was picking at an old scab for the franchise, which had been accused of favoring white players for decades, and still bore the weight of having chosen catcher Steve Chilcott with the first pick ahead of Reggie Jackson in the 1966 draft (Chilcott was white; the Mets allegedly did not approve of the fact that Jackson, while at Arizona State, had dated women outside his race). Twenty years on, with Gooden and Strawberry key figures in the franchise's present and future, the Mets did not need racial resentments stirred up all over again.

After his statement hit the press, Foster explained to Johnson and Frank Cashen that he had not meant to say the Mets were making racist decisions, or that they were deciding who played based on skin color. Foster met with his teammates and said his quotes were (naturally) taken out of context. The thrust of what he was saying, Foster would later explain, was that center fielder Mookie Wilson had been injured in training camp, but was never given a chance to regain his job from Lenny Dykstra. (Wilson is black, Dykstra white.) It didn't much matter. Foster had lost the respect of several teammates during the Reds fight, and had not had much camaraderie with them before that. His performance at the plate—he was hitting .227—made it difficult to warrant keeping him on the roster. Not only was he losing his at-bats to Mazzilli, he would lose his roster spot, too. While on the road in Chicago, the Mets released him. Knight, who had played with Foster in Cincinnati, tried to put the move in perspective. "He was very hurt," Knight said. "I've known him for a long time, and I believe him when he says it came out the wrong way. I never knew him to say or do anything that had any racial connotation. In Cincinnati, he felt Johnny Bench and Pete Rose and other guys were getting all the publicity. He had all those big years in Cincinnati, then came here, and they expected big things. He'd hit two home runs in a game, and nobody would say, 'Great going, George.' They just expected it of him. That, and the big contract. I know George wasn't the most popular person here. He was a loner, an introvert. But he is a warm, good human being. I hate to see what happened to him under these circumstances. I can't believe he'd say anything bad. In the dugout yesterday, George looked out to the field and said, 'Mitchell's color is the same as mine.'"

23

ROY COHN WAS NOT AROUND, but that did not mean Donald Trump did not know what to do. When the six jurors shuffled back into the courtroom of Judge Peter Leisure after forty-two days of testimony and deliberation, they had sent a shock through sports by announcing they had found the NFL guilty of running a monopoly in pro football, and the jury found it had injured the USFL in doing so. That pronouncement was a blow to the venerable old league and Pete Rozelle, who slipped out of the courtroom and into a limo thinking his league had been defeated. He had no interest in watching USFL executives celebrate on the courthouse stairs. But then a second report came in: The jury had awarded the USFL damages of just $1. Rozelle perked up and yelled to the driver, "Turn this goddamned limo around and let's go to the courthouse!" Trump had been standing in the back, arms folded. He had been glad-handing media members throughout the trial, but when the damages were announced, he bolted. He would issue a statement, using the well-worn Cohn techniques: claim victory, even in defeat; take no personal blame; promise more legal action. "We won a great moral victory," Trump's statement read. "But now with the confusion and what seems to be a hung jury, we expect to win a total victory."

Trump was right in one respect: There was confusion. But a confused jury is not a hung jury. One juror claimed that the panel did not fully understand their instructions—her expectation, she said, was that Judge Leisure could raise the $1 at his own discretion. Other jurors contradicted her view, expressing an understanding that though the NFL had established a monopoly, the USFL had been responsible for its own demise through poor business practices. "We awarded the $1 as a token amount," the juror explained. Another juror labeled it "a sort of rap on the knuckles of the NFL." So the USFL, after having lost in the neighborhood of $200 million, was later given a check for $3.76 (treble damages, including interest) from the NFL. While Trump declared victory, Memphis Showboats vice president Rudi Schiffer was more realistic. "We're dead," he said. "How else can you interpret it?" The USFL had begun just four years earlier, with the modest goal of building up popularity for a spring football league. But once Trump got involved, he manipulated the new league into fulfilling his own end—a domed stadium in Queens with an NFL team, owned by Trump, to occupy it. Most of the other owners took serious financial lumps, while Trump escaped with just a small fraction of his personal wealth lost and a well of attention and publicity for his properties that was impossible to price. In the end, he had used the USFL for his own ends and his inability to tell the truth hurt the league's longshot lawsuit when he testified.

As former New Jersey Generals broadcaster Charley Steiner, comparing Trump to notorious loud-mouthed boxing promoter Don King, said: "There isn't a goddamn difference between Don King and Don Trump. One guy's hair goes north and south, the other's goes east and west."

PART IV

Battle

24

In his eleven years with the Giants, Harry Carson had managed eight career interceptions. His last one had come in Week 11 of the 1984 season, but with the Giants facing the Jets in a late August preseason exhibition game in the Meadowlands—with seventy-four thousand fans on hand for the intra-stadium rivals—Carson had a bit more pep in his gait. In the third quarter, Jets backup Pat Ryan was in for starter Ken O'Brien and Carson managed two interceptions within minutes, as the Giants took a 20–16 win in the seventeenth preseason meeting of the teams. The Giants were just two weeks away from the beginning of the season, and Carson was feeling rejuvenated. He would turn thirty-three in November, making him the second-oldest of the Giants, and its most steadying influence. "Harry Carson is like the Rock of Gibraltar," Giants safety Kenny Hill said. "He's about as old as the Rock of Gibraltar, too." Carson had seen plenty of struggles in his time with the Giants, but 1986 was set up to be different. With just weeks to go before the opening of the season, Carson was prepared to help his team build off the playoff loss to the Bears the previous January. He had spent the summer putting in extra work around his house in New Jersey and back at his family home in South Carolina. "I was as ready for that season as any of the seasons I had," Carson said. "When we got to camp, no one really said anything, but you could tell, we all had put in a little more work and come in a little more focused."

Because of his lengthy tenure with the Giants, Carson had cultivated a different kind of relationship with head coach Bill Parcells, who had been his defensive coordinator since 1981, before Parcells was named head coach in 1983. Carson had always appreciated the trust that Parcells—and Giants linebackers coach Marty Schottenheimer before him—had put in him. Carson had been the starter at middle linebacker, making the transition from defensive line, since his rookie year, and soon after that had been entrusted with play-calling duties. "I was a black guy playing that position, and that was rare," Carson said. "At that time, that position was still reserved primarily for white guys, because it was a thinking man's position. I was able to, with the help of Marty Schottenheimer, to play that position. But most of the linebackers of that era were white." Carson always felt he could approach Parcells, and he did so more than any other player on the team. In the depths of an especially grueling training camp, Carson went to Parcells after one session and made a request. Players had been working hard, so he wanted permission to do something special—bring in a couple of kegs of beer and some female "entertainment," to allow the guys to blow off some steam. Carson was not a drinker, nor was he a strip-club guy (he preferred a booth and a $7 steak at Beefsteak Charlie's), but he had seen ads for dancers in the back of *New York* magazine and figured the whole thing would not be hard to arrange. When Parcells processed what Carson was asking for, he shot his linebacker a stunned glare: "You want to do *what?*" Finally, Parcells heaved a sigh and told Carson, "If there is any damage, Harry, I am holding you responsible." The evening, it turned out, went off without a hitch. "The guys even cleaned up after themselves," Carson said.

Entering the 1986 season, though, Carson knew he could be on the brink of something special. His age dictated he would have to start thinking about retirement, but he had also been thinking, throughout the offseason, about life. He had been rattled in 1983 by the death of former teammate and running back Doug Kotar at age thirty-two— Carson had visited Kotar regularly when he was hospitalized in Newark fighting a brain tumor, and even after Kotar was moved to western

Pennsylvania, where he lived, Carson continued to fly there to see him. Carson, who was a pallbearer at Kotar's funeral, never really forgave those teammates who had not supported Kotar when he was sick. Later, Carson observed that what he learned from being at Kotar's side at the end of his life was, "If I had a zipper in my head and needed the support of my teammates or friends, a few true friends would rise to the occasion while others probably wouldn't give a fuck." Another ex-team-mate, John Tuggle, was also battling cancer, and would pass away just a week after the Jets-Giants exhibition. Carson had witnessed the effects of Lawrence Taylor's struggles with cocaine the previous year, and was struck when Maryland basketball star Len Bias (just drafted by the Celtics) and Browns safety Don Rogers (a first-round pick in 1984) both suffered cocaine-related deaths that summer. What struck Carson was that they were so *young*. "You find out you're human," Carson said. "You may think you're tough on the field, but your life is fragile. So you take advantage of every opportunity to get something done."

If Carson had come to camp with extra motivation, it was not all derived from meaning-of-life epiphanies. Some of it came from what the Giants had done in the draft the previous spring, loading up on defensive players, even in the middle where the team was strongest. He and his veteran defensive teammates had the same reaction two years earlier, when the Giants used the third pick in the draft to take a line-backer, Carl Banks. Now he was looking at the incoming rookies, five defensive players in the first two rounds. The one who concerned Carson most, though, was the one he knew was coming after his position, the one already dubbed his heir apparent: a second-rounder from Ohio State named Pepper Johnson. "I kept my eye on Pepper that entire training camp, that was for sure," Carson said.

· · · · ·

For the Giants, the 1986 season started with an appropriate test in front of a national audience on Monday Night Football. If the team was a true contender, it would have to first surpass the team that won the NFC East the previous season, the Cowboys, in Dallas. It would be a challenge. New York was just 3–13 in its last sixteen visits to Dallas, and had suffered an especially distressing defeat the previous December with a chance to seize control of the division, by a 28–21 score. There were mistakes galore in that one, including an interception returned for a touchdown by the Cowboys, a dropped would-be score by normally sure-handed receiver Phil McConkey on a deep pass from Phil Simms, and a bad snap on a Giants punt from the end zone that yielded a Cowboys touchdown in a loss that secured New York's reputation, spelled out in a *Post* headline: WHY CAN'T GIANTS WIN THE BIG ONE? That mental hurdle lingered in the background, while on the field, the Giants were carrying more tangible baggage. Running back Joe Morris, coming off the best rushing season in franchise history, had held out all of training camp for a new contract, and the running game was lacking without him. Linebacker Lawrence Taylor remained a wildcard, too, after his stint in rehab. Whether he could return to the production he had put up before his drug-addled 1985 would go a long way toward determining what kind of 1986 the team would have. The Cowboys were aging, but they would be getting an injection of excitement in the backfield—they had signed running back Herschel Walker out of the ashes of the USFL. "One game does not a season make," columnist Jerry Izenberg wrote in the *Post*, "but given the right circumstances this match could sure as hell break one for somebody."

It had the makings of a break for the Giants. They had gone into the day unsure whether Morris would play. He had accompanied the team to Texas, but he skipped the walkthrough on Sunday and while the rest of his teammates were going through their morning meeting on game day, Morris was holed up in his hotel room, awaiting word from his agent, Tom Toner, on whether there would be a new deal. Morris eagerly answered the phone in his room that morning during the team meeting when *Post* reporter Hank Gola called. Disappointed it was not news of an agreement, all he could say was, "I am at the meeting. My own meeting." Morris made the trek to Cowboy Stadium at 4:00 p.m., even without a contract. It was not until 6:15, two-plus hours before the game, that Morris finally got word from Toner: The Giants had awarded him a four-year, $2.2 million deal with incentives. He could sign it, and play, to the relief of his teammates and coaches. But the distraction of Morris's dramatic return hampered the Giants. "This is football season, not contract time," Carson said. Dallas took a 14–0 lead to start the game, but the Giants rallied to tie on a pair of Phil Simms touchdown passes. The Giants took their first lead in the third quarter, on a touchdown run by Morris (who was solid with 87 yards rushing), but the Cowboys came back with a touchdown early in the fourth quarter. It was Simms—who threw for 300 yards, just the eighth time he had hit that milestone in the last five seasons—who brought the Giants back again with a 44-yard touchdown pass to Bobby John-son with just over five minutes left to play, and New York now ahead, 28–24. But for all the fretting about the impact of Morris's holdout, it was the Giants defense that let the team down, allowing Dallas a 72-yard drive that began with just over two minutes to play and fin-ished with the game-winning touchdown a mere 54 seconds later, on a 10-yard trap play to Walker on a third down from a shotgun formation. The play had the Giants, expecting a pass as time wound down, com-pletely fooled. They lost, 31–28, allowing four offensive touchdowns, which had happened only twice the previous season.

The cleanup from the Cowboys loss was messy, and if the Giants defense had been exposed by Walker (64 yards on 10 carries, plus 32 yards as a receiver) on the ground, they had little time to wallow in it. They were preparing for an onslaught from the air the following Sun-day, facing the Chargers, who had just shredded the Dolphins for 500 total yards of offense and 50 points in their opener behind quarterback Dan Fouts and the intimidating vertical offense of coach Don Coryell. The Chargers' performance against the Dolphins in Week 1 had been so impressive that coach Bill Parcells had showed his lackluster defense San Diego's Week 1 tape repeatedly. On the night of the game, when the Giants were checked into the Woodcliff Lake Hilton, where they stayed as a team before home games, Parcells was showing it again—what *Times* columnist Dave Anderson called "a horror movie." Parcells spoke throughout the film, but by the time he got to the opening series of the second half, nose tackle Jim Burt had enough. "I can't watch this track meet anymore, Bill," he said. "It makes me sick to my stomach." Parcells turned off the projector. He had gotten his defense, which had not taken the Cowboys seriously enough, in the right frame of mind.

After the Week 1 loss, Harry Carson had spoken up in a different way, hoping to rally not just the defense, but the team as a whole. The Morris contract situation had been a problem for the team, but Carson also felt his teammates were taking too much for granted—they had played a tough game against the Super Bowl champion Bears the previous January, they were widely picked to challenge Chicago again this year, and even to go to the Super Bowl. They had steamrolled through training camp like a team with a laser focus. "Guys checked their egos at the door," Carson said. But they had played the first week like their ticket to the postseason was already punched. Days after the loss to Dallas, Carson got a letter from a man in Rahway, New Jersey, and was taken aback by its contents. The Giants, the letter said, would never win because there were too many "niggers" on the team, and the white players were not much better. "He called them 'fuck-offs,'" Carson said. "He wasn't sparing anyone." Normally, Carson would have thrown a letter like that away, he said, but the team needed to refocus. "I wanted to share it with them because I wanted them to know how some people felt about them," Carson said. "Because it was a racist letter, but they were attacking the team, period. I felt like it should be something shared with the team to let them know how certain fans or people felt about them. I don't know how much it galvanized us as a group, how much it pulled us together. But it reminded us, we did not see black or white, we just were Giants, we were red, white and blue, you know? Deep down inside, there are differences, but those guys were my brothers, and whatever affects me, affects them, and whatever affects them, affects me."

On the Thursday night before Week 2, *Sports Illustrated* was holding a party in Manhattan for its advertisers, and invited Carson to attend, offering door-to-door car service and a $500 check for his time, which would only amount to a few hours—he was promised to be returned home by 10:00 p.m. Carson turned them down though, instead spending that night watching more of those Fouts horror movies. On Sunday, refocused, ticked off about the Week 1 loss and duly educated on the threats posed by Fouts and the Chargers, the Giants dominated defensively. Fouts completed just 19 of his 43 passes, and had five passes intercepted (most in his career) and his worst quarterback rating as a starter in twelve years. The Chargers managed just 262 yards of offense, and the Giants held the ball for 39:44, nearly twice as long as San Diego. The offense was plodding and methodical, but with the defense operating at such a high level, the Giants were in control of the 20–7 win from the beginning. "Fifty points," Carson said back in the locker room. "I have never been so glad to get off the field with a win and I have never had as much to think about going in. You know what it's like to sit in those meetings and watch that guy ring up 50 points? That adds up to a lot of sleepless nights."

The Giants were back to 1–1, and could rest easy. They looked like the team they were supposed to be coming into the 1986 season.

25

When it comes to the Mafia, G. Robert Blakey takes the long view. As a kid growing up in North Carolina, he had very little exposure to different ethnic groups, and it was not until he went on to college at Notre Dame in the 1950s that he was asked (by his future wife) about his ethnic origins. "She asked me what I was and I paused and said, 'American,' because I did not know any better," Blakey said. "She thought I was being flip. Where I came from you were either black or white and everyone was some version of Protestant. Ethnic groups clustering together, that was not something I understood. I started reading about this stuff about the Mafia, burning things into their hands and their different codes and traditions and *omerta*, and I did not know if I should believe it. It was so foreign to my experience." But Blakey did develop a fascination with the Mafia and, after college, in 1960, landed a job with the Department of Justice as a special attorney in the Organized Crime and

Racketeering Section. He remembers having lunch one afternoon with Henry Petersen, who was then the chief of the section. Blakey asked Petersen directly: "Henry, do you think there is a Mafia?" Petersen shook his head. "No," he said. "There are just loose associations within cities, and a lot of it is familial, based on marriages and relations. But there is no Mafia." It was the general belief of the group dedicated by the Justice Department to battle organized crime, then, that the idea of a Mafia was a myth. It was a widely held belief, and a tribute to the ability of Mafia members to honor the principle of *omerta*, or silence. "Of course," Blakey said, "that was wrong."

As Blakey sees it, the Mafia got a little too full of its own behind-the-scenes power and committed an overreach it would pay for. It took more than two decades, but Blakey believed the Mafia was involved in the murder of President John F. Kennedy in 1963, and that led, eventually, to its demise. Blakey was chief counsel on the House Select Committee on Assassinations in 1977, which looked into the Kennedy killing, and concluded from his time in that role that the Mafia was at least in part involved. "And they got away with it," Blakey said. "That was what I thought years ago. But I've come to the conclusion on reflection in my old age that they didn't get away with it." How? Before Kennedy was killed, his brother, attorney general Robert Kennedy, had been pushing toward fighting organized crime, a mostly uphill battle. After Kennedy was killed, Robert Kennedy resigned (he did not get along with new president Lyndon B. Johnson) and went to the Senate. When he left, many of those who had been working on his task force on the Mob left, too, and they spread out into different parts of the government. (Blakey went to Notre Dame as a professor, and taught an organized crime class his students lovingly called "Gangbusters 101.") In doing so, they influenced the thought process of decision-makers in all branches of government. When Johnson, afraid of appearing soft as crime rates rose during the '60s, put together a commission to battle crime, he was persuaded to include organized crime in that battle. That was when Blakey returned to the government, as the chief counsel to the Senate Subcommittee on Criminal Laws and Procedures, his years of teaching having given him some bold new ideas on how to approach the Mafia.

"What I saw was that organized crime was like a merry-go-round at an amusement park," he said. "It was spinning. It was always spinning. There would be a crime and someone would get brought in, they'd go to jail. Maybe you'd send a bunch of mob guys to jail in a year. So they got off the ride. But you know what? The merry-go-round is still spinning, you haven't done anything to stop it. We were arresting and prosecuting the guys who were carrying out crimes, but not the whole criminal organization. There was no tool for that. First, you could not get evidence that showed that there was an organization. Then, you did not have a statute that covered the entire organization."

Two concepts arose from this realization. To gather information on the operation of an organized crime unit, electronic surveillance and bugging were required. Part of the Mafia code of *omerta* dictated anyone who went in front of a judge or jury must never even acknowledge that the Mafia exists, let alone point a finger at the higher-ups who ordered the crimes that were being prosecuted. It was nearly impossible for law enforcement to get low-level criminals to flip on their superiors. The only way to crack that silence was to break into the places where the Mafia kingpins did business and place listening devices. Blakey pushed for a wiretapping procedure to be part of the new crime legislation, called Title III. This was highly controversial, but conservative Democratic Senator John McClellan, chairman of the committee, was skilled at navigating bills to passage. No one in Congress wanted to be seen approving the government's right to listen in on conversations of private citizens, but McClellan managed to guide the bill through the Senate, and it was attached to a crime bill in the House in the spring of 1968. It might have died there, except that tragedy struck the country with the assassination of Martin Luther King Jr. His murder unleashed riots in Washington, DC, and around the country. As distasteful as Title III surveillance might have been to House members, the riots changed the politics. Now, members of Congress did not want to vote down an anti-crime bill as DC was burning in the backdrop.

The second concept Blakey brought back to Washington was the Racketeering Influence and Corrupt Organizations statute, known as RICO. The goal of RICO was to go after the entire merry-go-round, as a complete enterprise. It gave the government the authority to prosecute those enterprises as whole units if it can be shown that they engage in a pattern of criminality—that is, they have committed two or more crimes within a ten-year period from a list of thirty-five offenses, including Mafia staples like gambling, racketeering, money laundering, theft, and murder, as well as slavery, counterfeiting, embezzlement, bribery, and arson. Penalties would be severe, beginning at twenty years in prison, with hefty fines often attached, too. "Going for the money was important, too," Blakey said. "These are organizations that are founded on greed. There is talk about honor and family, but the Mafia is about greed." Show that an organization (a Mafia family, for example) has run a gambling ring, authorized a murder, and conspired to commit theft within a ten-year period, and a RICO charge can be brought against everyone who can be proven to be a relevant part of the organization, in particular those who were running the organization at the top, each offense earning a twenty-year term. McClellan was able to make enough deals to get RICO passed in 1970. With Title III on the books, law enforcement had the ability to secretly collect evidence to prove an enterprise, thanks to the wiretapping statute, and to prosecute the heads of the enterprises for all crimes committed under RICO.

For Blakey, 1970 was a triumph. At least, until 1971 passed and no RICO cases were brought. Same with 1972, and every year of the '70s. To his frustration, Blakey found that no prosecutor in the nation was willing to put the law to the test. Blakey left government to return to teaching in 1973. "Prosecutors are the worst," Blakey said, "because they do not want to try anything that has not been done before. No one wants to go first. So no one went first." But that began to change in the late 1970s and early '80s, when Blakey was teaching at Cornell and had decided his mission had to be to proselytize for RICO. It was not easy. Such was the resistance to the idea that, when Blakey met with US Attorney Whitney North Seymour in Manhattan to make a presentation on the use of RICO, he did not even finish before Seymour told him, "You don't know what you're talking about." Blakey was stunned. "He threw me out," he said. "Literally." Eventually, Blakey had a breakthrough with the FBI in New York, led by Neil Welch (who was named to take over the office in 1978). Welch began to see RICO and the wiretapping law for what they were meant to be, powerful tools against organized crime. That was when things began to change on the investigative front, when agents began hitting the heads of the five families in New York with bugs and surveillance.

Shortly after the FBI bugs were in place, Rudy Giuliani took over as the US Attorney for the Southern District, got a sense of what law enforcement had gathered from the bugs, and became an enthusiastic convert to the movement toward RICO cases, especially the concept of trying multiple families together. "You have to give Giuliani credit," Blakey said, "because all these prosecutors were too afraid to bring a RICO case. He wanted to try it." Of course, Giuliani tended to heap more credit on himself than he deserved, and had little trouble angling his way into cases being made in other districts to benefit his own reputation. "He was totally consumed with his own ambition," said Ed McDonald, who was in the Eastern District at the time, "and didn't have any real commitment to the criminal justice system. He was trying to advance his own agenda and shoot his mouth off to sound like a tough guy. Prosecutors can always act like tough guys, but you have to be fair guys. Rudy didn't care about fairness. All he cared about was getting his name into the papers as many times a day as possible." Giuliani later said the idea for applying RICO to Mafia cases came to him when he was reading the 1983 book by former Bonanno family boss Joe Bonanno, *Man of Honor.* In his book, Bonanno included a long and detailed explanation of the ruling Mafia body known as the Commission, dating back to its founding in 1931, as a sort of board of governors for New York's major crime families, necessitated by the realities of new-world life. Such a ruling body, Bonanno wrote, "was not an integral part of my Tradition. No such agency existed in Sicily. The Commission was an American adaptation." In his own book, *Leadership,* and in a slew of interviews over the years, Giuliani said he had an epiphany when he read what Bonanno wrote. "I dreamed up the tactic of using the Federal Racketeer Influenced and Corrupt Organizations Act to prosecute the Mafia leadership for itself being a 'corrupt enterprise'.... I realized that Bonanno's description of how the families were organized provided a roadmap of precisely what the RICO statute was designed to combat. As soon as I became the U.S. Attorney I was able to hoist Bonanno by his literary petard."

Blakey scoffed at Giuliani's recollection. True, Bonanno's book provided a detailed history of the Commission, and from that, Giuliani may have gotten an outline of how to try all family heads in one case. But there were already many arms of New York law enforcement entangled in Mafia RICO cases when he arrived at SDNY. "If he wants to believe that, if that is how it went in his head, then that's fine," Blakey said. "But if that's the case, can you explain what the hell was I doing out there for 10 years, going around with no one listening, trying to get people to see RICO this way and use it against the Mafia? What was the FBI doing for years before that getting all the wiretaps and building up those cases?"

But no matter. Blakey had a New York prosecutor ready to use his statute to hit the mob where it had not been previously hit: at the top. Giuliani would bring the Commission case, prepared to prosecute four of the five family heads at the same time. This is where Blakey's long view comes into focus. RICO, born out of the Mafia's suspected involvement in the John F. Kennedy assassination and brought to the federal statutes after disciples of ex-Attorney General Robert Kennedy spread throughout the government, would be the country's greatest tool in bringing down the Mafia, twenty-three years later.

· · · · ·

On July 12, 1979, Bonanno crime boss Carmine Galante was having lunch at a long table in the courtyard of a small storefront restaurant on Knickerbocker Avenue in Brooklyn, Joe and Mary's, picking at his meal with a glass of Chianti, dressed in a white button-down shirt with his sleeves rolled up. As usual, he clenched a cigar between his teeth as he sat with two bodyguards, Cesare Bonaventre and Baldo Amato, transplants he had brought over from Sicily. Customers were dining inside, but no one else was in the courtyard with the men, the other tables stacked in a corner to ensure Galante's privacy. Galante himself was not Sicilian, but his father had been a fisherman there, and as he rose in prominence in the criminal underworld, he was increasingly surrounded by Sicilian soldiers, known as "zips" because they spoke Sicilian so rapidly. This had been a tradition passed on from the previous Bonanno boss, Joseph Bonanno, to his underboss Galante. But for Galante, it had little to do with nostalgia and connection to his roots. No, Galante liked the Sicilians because he believed the American Mafia had gotten too soft, too engrained in workaday businesses, too beholden to its decision-making Commission, now nearly fifty years old and out of touch with the opportunities presented by modern crime. Zips were cold-blooded, and had the added benefit of having no criminal records in the United States. Galante, only five years removed from a twelve-year prison sentence on a trafficking charge, had little use for the careful temerity that guided most of his fellow mobsters. Tough, fearless, and brutal, Galante had a brick wall of a face and a hair-trigger temper that inspired both fear and disdain among his peers. He was in good condition compared to many of his jiggly fellow bosses, known to jog the East River or play handball at the YMCA. His toughness set him apart. A police lieutenant described Galante in 1977: "Not since the days of Vito Genovese has there been a more ruthless and feared individual. The rest of them are copper; he is pure steel."

While Galante had been in prison, Carlo Gambino of the Gambino family—the most powerful of the bosses—had pushed the Mafia away from the heroin trade, fearing the attention it drew from federal investigators. But Gambino died in 1976, and in his absence, Galante sought to restore drug trafficking, which had been his specialty since the 1950s, as the Bonanno family's cash cow. So did the Sicilians, who had easy access to opium from poppies grown in Turkey, which could be processed into heroin without molestation in the rugged hills of their home island, and moved on to New York through the Bonannos' already established links with the Old World. Just years earlier, the main source of heroin into the United States had been the French Connection, which routed from Turkey through the French port of Marseilles and into the United States from Canada. But arrests and murders had dried up the French Connection in the early '70s, and the more direct route from Sicily had fewer impediments and greater profits. For Galante, the heroin business was booming and his aspirations were growing. With Gambino gone, he saw the opportunity to seize more control over the entire Mafia and return the Bonannos, who had been in disarray since the forced retirement of Joe Bonanno in 1964, to the top of the hierarchy of families. But Galante's grab for control would prove to be his undoing. The heads of the other families had grown wary of his increasing power, still fearful of his willingness to dive headlong into the perilous heroin business and, with Rusty Rastelli (then in prison) also having a claim to the title of Bonanno boss, Galante's legitimacy as the family head was questionable.

As Galante ate at Joe and Mary's, with his bodyguards, Giuseppe Turano (Galante's cousin and the "Joe" in Joe and Mary's), and a family friend, Leonard Coppola, a Mercury Montego pulled up on Knickerbocker Avenue, and three men wearing ski masks leapt out. They stormed through the restaurant into the courtyard and began to open fire on Galante. To his certain shock, Bonaventre and Amato, his loyal zips, unholstered their guns and fired on Galante, too. Turano and Coppola were killed. The masked men and the bodyguards all quickly moved out of the restaurant and into the Mercury, speeding off. Galante, it turned out, had not only angered his fellow bosses with his play for control of the heroin trade. He had angered the Sicilians, who wanted a more generous cut of the profits, and they made him pay.

For Giuliani and his top assistant, Michael Chertoff, who had been chosen to be second seat in the Commission trial, the Galante murder was critical to building the case against the city's Mafia bosses. To prove a RICO case, they needed to establish both that the Commission represented an enterprise, and that it had committed predicate offenses. The murder of Galante would be the peak of offenses, if it could be pinned on the Commission. Over the years, it had been nearly impossible to trace murders carried out by La Cosa Nostra back to bosses, though. There was a chance to make that case with the Galante murder, based on Galante's status as a boss—informant information held that only the Commission could sanction the killing of a boss, and therefore, the Galante murder had to come on orders from the Commission. "It was the hardest part of the case," Chertoff said, "because you didn't have tapes. You were doing it on circumstantial evidence." They did have three prongs to make the Galante case, which would have been a tough one to win if it had been brought on its own, without the context of a RICO trial:

- A videotape of Bonanno capo Bruno Indelicato shortly after the Galante killing, taken by law enforcement surveillance of Gambino headquarters at the Ravenite Social club. "You had some Bonanno guys," Chertoff said, "including Bruno Indelicato, meeting with Neil Dellacroce, who was the underboss of the Gambino family, and they were there shaking hands and patting each other on the backs, and it looked like congratulating them—probably on the hit."
- Mafia Commission politics. The officer who had posed as a Bonanno gangster named Donny Brasco—Joe Pistone was his real name—had reported that the Galante murder had to have been a Commission order, and that the Indelicato family got a promotion thereafter, the easy inference being that they were taking a reward for Galante's death. "We had Joe Pistone, who had been undercover," Chertoff said, "with information that he had gotten that the Bonanno family had been involved with the murder of Galante, it was a sanctioned hit, the Commission ordered it. . . . One thing this meant was that the Indelicatos rose up in the Bonanno family because Galante was now out of the way."
- A palm print matching Indelicato from the Mercury that had been involved in the killing. This was the only hard evidence linking Indelicato to the Galante murder, and the case probably

would not have been made without it. "We exhumed the old file from the original police file on the Galante murder," Chertoff said. "The New York City police department worked on this with us, as well as the FBI. What we learned from looking at the file was there was a woman in the apartment across the street, and what happened was the car drove up, three men got out, one remained in the car, they went in the back, they killed Galante, came out and sped off. The woman got the license plate number and gave it to police, and within a matter of hours, the police went and found the car abandoned somewhere.

"There was a set of prints from the back door, and they tried to match against a bunch of people without any luck, then they tried to match it against Bruno Indelicato because there was informant information that he was involved in the murder. He was a killer. They couldn't match it. We were looking at this stuff in the office, it was pretty straightforward information that he was the shooter. So I said, 'When you guys took his prints to match, did you just take tips or did you take major case prints?' Which were palms. And it turned out that they had just taken tips. I said, 'Well, when you open a door, you don't use your tips, you use the palm of your hand, so let's get him back and take major-case prints.' So we did, and, bingo. They matched. We had [Indelicato] in the back of the car."

The murder of Galante was tough for prosectuors to prove. But behind it was the same driving force as the rest of the Mob's operations. The day after the murder in 1979, above a photo of Galante's bullet-ridden face and blood-soaked shirt, the *New York Post* announced the motive behind the hit in bold type that blared across the page: GREED!

26

IN 1961, WHEN THE METS were building their original expansion franchise, columnist Dick Young had a conversation with new team owner Joan Payson. "Expect nothing," he told her. The cast of players the Mets had assembled was wretched, castoffs from bad franchises or name players well past their primes. Payson wondered if, just maybe, the Mets had enough to beat out low-level teams like the Cubs or Phillies. Young told her, no. Payson asked if the team might beat out the other expansion bunch, Houston. "No," Young said, "I told you to expect nothing." And Young was right. That team was one of the worst in the history of baseball, and by Young's estimation, it was exactly what New York needed. Too many fans had grown weary of the dominance and corporate-style approach of the Yankees, a team that was seen as mostly soulless. The 1962 Mets, in their ineptitude, inspired a legion of supporters eager to root on the underdogs, with their many warts and foibles. It was almost as though the worse those Mets played, the more enthusiastic the support. For Young, much had changed in the intervening twenty-five years. He was still putting out columns (for the *New York Post* after leaving the *Daily News* in 1982), but now, the Mets had developed into a juggernaut, and cruised into late August with a string of eleven wins in twelve games that left them 20 games and miles ahead of the second-place Phillies. Even with all that had gone right, the Shea Stadium crowds still had complaints, and with Foster gone, one player more than any other bore the brunt of those complaints: All-Star outfielder Darryl Strawberry.

In a stretch of 38 games from July 13 through the end of August, Strawberry hit just .188 and struck out 47 times. He had knocked six home runs and drove in 27 runs, but for fans, Strawberry failed too often in clutch situations, could not hit left-handed pitching (just .209 on the season), and his generally easygoing manner left the impression he was not hustling. Strawberry struggled, particularly, at home, where he hit .227 with a .445 slugging percentage—on the road, that was .284 with a .557 slugging percentage. At one point, Strawberry fell into an

0-for-47 slump at Shea Stadium, and fans in one section stood and taunted him with chants of "*O! For! 47!*" So he was booed, with vigor. Johnson could understand that. Strawberry in 1986 was a considerable challenge for the manager. As he had done with Dwight Gooden in 1984, Johnson had pushed for Strawberry to come up with the team in 1983, even though he was just twenty-one years old and had only two full pro seasons since coming out of high school as the number one overall pick in 1980. Like Gooden, Strawberry had arrived with emotional baggage that was proving difficult to carry in New York. He had an abusive, alcoholic father and a rough upbringing in South Central Los Angeles, and a hard time finding role models as a big-league player. Strawberry was, like his teammates, a drinker, and had begun to dabble with cocaine early in his career. But he was the most naturally gifted of the Mets' position players, and Johnson did not want to see that go to waste. "He was like my son, because I was always scolding him all the time," Johnson later said. "Because he was a tremendous talent, the best talent I'd ever seen in my life."

Young had used his perch as a press box leader in the '60s to protect the Mets from too much criticism, but now, he supported the bitterness directed at Strawberry. "Players, many of them, take the booing hard, much too hard," Young wrote. "I'm not suggesting that Darryl Strawberry should jump up and down with glee when the boo-birds start pecking at him. Hell, nobody is that masochistic. But he could take it a lot better than he does." The booing became an issue for Strawberry on the final weekend of August. In a 6–3 win over the Dodgers, Strawberry had suffered through an awful afternoon. He struck out in the third with a runner on first to halt a two-run Mets rally, then ended another rally in the fourth when he flied out with two outs and the bases loaded. He struck out in the sixth—the booing got heavy then— and really drew the wrath of the crowd in the eighth inning, when he allowed a hard grounder to right field by Bill Madlock to slip past him for an error that set up a Dodgers run. The next day did not go much better, as Strawberry went 0-for-4 with a strikeout, two popouts, and a groundout. That left him 0-for-11 in the Dodgers series. After the game, Strawberry's frustration with the fans boiled over. He pointed out that he was in a pretty troubling spiral, where if he stayed silent, his anger would fester, but if he complained about the fans, he would be labeled as a whiner and would only invite more intense fan disdain. Still, he told reporters, "Maybe it's time to be somewhere else, if I'm not wanted. You realize this is a business, but there are a lot of places where you could be happy. I'm the only one on this ball club? That's a bunch of bull."

. . . . .

The Mets picked a terrible time for a four-game losing streak. On September 10, New York won its 93rd game, dropping their magic number to two for winning the National League East and securing a spot in the playoffs for just the third time in franchise history. With three games slated to be on the road against the second-place Phillies, it seemed safe enough to ship along eight cases of dry champagne ("Nothing too expensive," the team's PR man assured) on the team's charter buses to the visiting clubhouse in Philadelphia. But in the first game, Gooden gave up five runs in five innings and was tagged with the loss. The bubbly sat on ice throughout the game, but was just bobbing in pools of water by the time the 6–3 loss was final. In the second game of the series, it was reliever Roger McDowell who was the culprit, giving up four runs in two innings of a 6–5 loss. The champagne corks seethed, but remained wired shut. Sid Fernandez gave up four runs in four innings the following day, and Phillies pitcher Kevin Gross threw a shutout, forcing the Mets' equipment staff to pile the champagne in with the team's gear and take it on to their next stop, St. Louis. By now questions began bubbling up. There was still no danger that the Mets would lose 23 straight games to blow the NL East lead. But had they been playing above their heads all this time? Did this team have enough ability to win tough games in the clutch to be a real threat in the playoffs? The Mets opened their series against the Cardinals still in a funk, shut out over 13 innings of a 1–0 loss. That made 23 straight scoreless innings, a stretch that would run to 25 innings, the longest streak of

Davey Johnson's career as manager in New York. "You play 140 games as hard as we did," Johnson said, "you might be a little nervous."

The Mets salvaged a win against the Cardinals, 4–2, behind a good outing from Rick Aguilera in the last of their five-game road trip. They would bring the champagne back to Shea Stadium, at least having guaranteed a tie in the NL East ahead of a September 17 visit from Chicago, who came in as one of the worst road teams in the league, at 25–48. The Cubs served their purpose, putting up little resistance as heralded prospect Dave Magadan made his debut as a starter, going 3-for-4 with two RBIs and earning a curtain call, while Gooden struck out eight (and walked five) for a complete-game, 4–2 win. Gooden had to calm himself in the ninth inning with deep breaths as the crowd surged, telling himself, "'Just relax.' That's how excited I was." On the television broadcast of the game, play-by-play man Steve Zabriskie addressed the concerns the Mets had expressed, before the game, about getting off the field should they win. "They've got a lot of ushers and security people out," he said, "but they are obviously greatly outnumbered." As the game wrapped up, with forty-four thousand fans chanting, "We're Number 1!" a banner from the upper deck unfurled: FINALLY. Yes, finally, after a week of anticipating, and finally after thirteen years without a spot in the playoffs, the Mets were back. Gooden was met at the mound first by Kevin Mitchell and first baseman Keith Hernandez, and soon by the rest of his infield, their hands raised as they jumped and embraced. But within moments, the players were mobbed by a stream of hundreds of fans—as many as six thousand according to Frank Cashen—who barreled past the two hundred or so security people and over the dugouts to the field even before the final out was made. Gooden got lost in the mass of humanity. "I was scared," he said. "For five minutes, I felt people pounding on me, and I couldn't get up. After a while someone let me get up. I don't know who it was, but I headed right for the clubhouse."

The Mets clubhouse had been sealed with plastic sheets and transformed into a deluge of Korbel and Great Western. Before the crowd of reporters entered, Magadan was pulled into a television interview with Tim McCarver, and as McCarver was in mid-question, Darryl Strawberry approached from behind and climbed onto a lift behind Magadan, soaking him with champagne. After Gooden recalled his escape from the field, he told reporters, "It's a great, great thrill," and it was Strawberry again approaching from behind and pouring champagne over Gooden's head, saying, "I know it is, buddy." McCarver struggled to keep his composure through the sting of cheap wine in his eyes, but was able to pull Strawberry aside and asked him about his recent struggles in September. "I felt I did struggle a little bit," Strawberry said. "I just have to keep confidence in myself and keep believing that I can contribute to the ballclub." Strawberry told McCarver that winning the pennant was the biggest thrill of his life and added, "You deserve some champagne," giving McCarver yet another dousing.

Making a surprise dugout showing was Mayor Ed Koch, who admitted his ignorance when it came to baseball but, like Mayor John Lindsay before him with the Amazin' Mets World Series winners in 1969 (who helped sweep him back into office in a tough reelection fight), was hoping that the reflected glow of a playoff baseball team would blind some of the citizenry to the struggle of his third term. Never much of an athlete, Koch said he was the kind of kid "you would choose last" when fielding a team for a pickup game. "When reporters ask me about baseball," Koch said, "I think to myself, 'You dog you,' except I use a different word than dog." But Koch had been learning, he promised. "I will eat hot dogs, which I love," he said, "and I will cheer." Asked if he knew when to cheer, Koch said, "When the other people cheer." When Ralph Kiner, interviewing Koch, brought up how Lindsay had latched onto that team, Koch said, "That is true, but I'm not running this year. I'm here because I love the team." Koch then added a prediction: "We're going to have a ticker-tape parade here when they win the World Series." Shortly thereafter, of course, Dick Young reported, there was "Darryl Strawberry pouring champagne over Mayor Koch's bald pate. Only in my America."

Outside the clubhouse, the scene got ugly. The Mets fans who stormed the field tore up the playing turf, pulling up whole sections of sod in both the infield and outfield. After most of the fans had faded out of the park after midnight, groundskeeper Pete Flynn was left to inspect the damage with his crew. "It looks like bombs were dropped on it," he said. Flynn and his men worked until 3:00 a.m., and were back at work at 7:00 a.m. the following day, trying to patch the damage well enough for a game that afternoon and enough to carry the Mets through the final two-plus weeks of the season. Cashen could not quite wrap his head around the impulse that led fans to rip up their team's own home stadium. "This only happens in New York," he said. "It is some kind of mob psychology. I can't understand it. You'd have to speak to a psychiatrist." But he did worry that the field, no matter how well patched it was by Flynn, would be subject to quirky bounces, even in the postseason. "It is a shame that after such a wonderful season, we have to play in the playoffs on a field in this condition," Cashen said. "There will be soft spots. There will be uneven patches. There will be bumps. The Houston club will complain, and they have a right to complain." And if the Mets got to the World Series, their opponent there might have something to complain about, too.

. . . . .

When Astros starter Mike Scott, on the advice of then-manager Bob Lillis, went to visit recently retired pitching coach Roger Craig after the 1984 season to learn a new pitch that would change the trajectory of his career, Craig gave him a warning. "Roger Craig told me," he said, "that guys would say I was doctoring the ball."

They did. Most notably, Cubs first baseman Leon Durham was said to have found a small strip of sandpaper near the mound once during a Scott start. The reasons for suspicion around Scott were obvious. For the first six years of his career, Scott had been an unremarkable pitcher, a hard thrower with a good build (6-foot-2, 210 pounds) but lacking a go-to pitch that could keep hitters off-balance and extricate him from tight situations. He was with the Mets for his first four years in the big leagues, and went to the Astros in a trade in 1983. Before meeting with Craig, Scott was 29-44 in his career, with a 4.45 ERA. "I was just a guy who kind of hung on," Scott said, "sometimes as the 10th guy on a 10-man staff. The way I was pitching, I never knew from one game to the next whether I'd be looking for a new line of work." But after he spent the 1984 offseason learning the pitch that was making Craig a minor celebrity—the split-finger fastball—Scott returned to Houston a different pitcher. He went 18–8 in 1985, with an ERA of 3.29 and 137 strikeouts. In 1986, though, he had truly ascended. He was just 6–5 in June as the Astros struggled to find an offensive rhythm, but his ERA was 2.51, among the best in the league. Heading into his September 25 start against the Giants (now managed coincidentally by Roger Craig), the Astros had improved and Scott had won twelve of his last seventeen starts as Houston's offense came together. He took the mound at the Astrodome, seeking to clinch the NL West and a championship series matchup with the Mets.

Scott threw the best game of his career, a 13-strikeout no-hitter for his 18th win. Craig, his split-finger guru who had been around pro baseball for 35 years, was in awe. "He threw the split-finger harder than I've ever seen," Craig said. "I've seen a lot of no-hitters, but I've never seen one under these circumstances. That might be one of the most dominating no-hitters I've ever seen, especially in the situation where they were trying to win the pennant. . . . I sensed it early. He was ahead of the hitters and pitching with no fear. He showed me some balls. That's what you call supreme confidence in himself, what he did today." Down the stretch for the Astros, Scott was as confident as he had ever been. He finished the year on a 5–1 string in his final seven starts, striking out 71 batters in 54 innings and allowing opponents to bat just .155. He would be leading the Astros—expected to be a bottom-dweller in the NL in 1986—to the postseason.

"Somebody pinch me," infielder Billy Doran said.

"Me too," manager Hal Lanier said, before reconsidering. "No, somebody slap me. I still can't believe this."

27

TOM PUCCIO FIRST MET RUDY Giuliani in the early 1970s, when they were young attorneys in New York federal prosecutors' offices, Puccio working in the Eastern District and Giuliani in the Southern. Traditionally, the two offices were at loggerheads, the SDNY (Manhattan) treating itself as the gold standard of federal offices and the Eastern District (Brooklyn, primarily) seeing itself as the bunch that did the yeoman's share of prosecutorial work in the city while the SDNY preened for attention. But Puccio and Giuliani, teamed to work with an informant who was exposing police corruption, established a quick kinship. Both were of the same generation, hailing from middle-class Italian backgrounds, and had become friends. Their personalities meshed. Giuliani became known for his sizable ego, and Puccio had an ego of his own to match. "He was the world's most unforgettable character," said Ed McDonald, who had been Puccio's deputy in the Brooklyn Strike Force. "He was a brilliant guy, great investigator, totally Machiavellian, four steps ahead of anyone he ever dealt with. Incredibly smart. And he was a great trial lawyer. He was a difficult guy because he was arrogant and opinionated, and a lot of people were put off by him because he didn't suffer fools gladly." Nor did Giuliani.

Puccio went on to gain national acclaim for his work spearheading the Abscam case that netted a slew of federal and local officials accepting bribes, and turned into a celebrity when he successfully defended Danish socialite Claus von Bulow from charges that he had killed his wife. Giuliani had made his name in 1974, when he so thoroughly picked apart Rep. Bertram Podell in cross-examination on a bribery charge that Podell broke down and confessed on the stand. He had gone on to be the number three man in the Justice Department under Ronald Reagan, but was able to persuade his federal bosses to give him the job heading up SDNY in 1983, a step Giuliani saw as important to kick off a political career. In the meantime, Giuliani and Puccio each had tried to boost the other's careers. When Giuliani was attempting to get a federal judgeship in 1976, Puccio made phone calls on his behalf. When Puccio sought an appointment as the US attorney in Washington, DC, Giuliani attempted to pull strings for him. When Giuliani was still in Washington at the DOJ, he had quashed an indictment against then-congressman from Brooklyn Chuck Schumer after a series of *Village Voice* articles exposed Schumer for breaking the law by using state employees as campaign workers. After returning to New York, Giuliani found that *Voice* writers Jack Newfield and Wayne Barrett were holding a grudge against him over the Schumer case, until Puccio took the three out to an Italian meal where they ironed out their differences. They were not buddies, but Giuliani held Puccio in high enough regard that he invited him to his 1985 wedding.

Now, though, as early fall sunk in over the Northeast, the two were adversaries. Months earlier, when he had to choose which would be the first case he would personally litigate in his three years running the Southern District, Giuliani had surprised many by turning his focus to Stanley Friedman's Parking Violations Bureau case and leaving the lead prosecutor's role in the Mafia Commission case to a relative newcomer, Michael Chertoff. Giuliani had made going after the Mob a central theme of his tenure, but his calculation was that municipal graft cases were more complex, and if his office lost the case against Friedman, prosecuting further corruption cases might not be possible. The Commission case was to be groundbreaking, but there would always be Mafia cases to be tried. There was more at stake in the Parking Violations Bureau trial, and its importance grew when Friedman hired Puccio to defend him in March. Giuliani had faith in his prosecutorial team, but Puccio was too intimidating an adversary to leave to his young employees. In previewing the start of the PVB trial in late September, the *New York Times* focused on the lawyer-to-lawyer matchup, dubbing it, "a battle of the Titans, a heavyweight championship fight, a fall classic." (Not that Giuliani relished the chance to go up against Puccio. He had filed an earlier motion trying to get Puccio removed from Friedman's defense, on the grounds that he had previously represented another figure in the case, which was denied. He had also had a witness who was meeting with Puccio attempt to entrap him into making the witness a bribe offer while his office was bugged. Giuliani disclosed the bug in a pretrial conference, angering Puccio.)

The Titans would not battle in New York City, though. Earlier in the year, Puccio and Friedman had done polling, and determined there was little chance Friedman could get a fair trial in New York, with news of corruption in the city flooding the airwaves and front pages for months. Even if Friedman were tried on the evidence's merits, the thinking went, a New York jury would be too willing to look at him as the face of all city corruption and would be inclined to find him guilty. In June, Puccio had pushed for a change of venue on those grounds, and Giuliani had not resisted—in fact, Giuliani had even suggested it before Puccio brought his motion. From Giuliani's point of view, trying the case in the city would be more difficult, because the jury would be more inured to municipal corruption. In the past year, Giuliani had already seen plenty of low-level corruption charges yield either not guilty verdicts, or result in sentences so light as to barely qualify as punishment. Besides, Giuliani was well aware of Friedman's connections. He had been a law partner of Roy Cohn, who had among his clients one of the defendants in the Commission trial, Genovese boss Fat Tony Salerno. If the trial went badly for Friedman, Giuliani had reason to worry that Friedman or an associate could get to a juror with either threats or bribes and bring on a mistrial. If Puccio and Friedman wanted to move, that was fine with Giuliani. One of his assistants on the case, David Zornow, remembered, "Rudy knew that juries outside New York were more pro-government. His instinct was: 'Fine, let's do it. It will be a pox on these New York guys.'"

Judge Whitman Knapp (himself a Titan, having overseen the Knapp Commission hearings on New York police corruption in the early '70s) agreed, reluctantly, to have the trial moved, first to Hartford and then to New Haven because of scheduling conflicts. And so the future of Stanley Friedman, ultimate New York political deal-maker, and likely the future of Rudy Giuliani, aspiring New York politician, was all to be sorted out in a trial conducted among the leafy collegiate groves of New Haven. There was still overwhelming interest in the case back in the city, mostly because of the gruesome details of Donald Manes's suicide. That meant city desks at the four major New York papers sent up their own teams of reporters, and the local television stations did the same. To justify the expenses, every day the papers bulged with coverage of the New Haven trial. That added to the battle-of-the-Titans air around the Puccio-Giuliani duel. In late September, the two sides took up their headquarters, the defendants at the small Colony Hotel just across the New Haven Green from the courthouse, the prosecutors and their witnesses at the Park Plaza, and prepared for the fight.

.....

Donald Manes was the ghost that haunted the federal courthouse in New Haven. Dead for seven months as the trial opened, the case would give him one last return to prominence, and for both the prosecution and defense, Manes would be manipulated in ways that would benefit their arguments, but provide some final sullying insults for Manes's memory and legacy. For Giuliani, Manes was the tyrant who extorted friends and neighbors, and teamed with Friedman to exploit feeble-minded PVB employee and lead prosecution witness Geoffrey Lindenauer. For Puccio, he was the real target of the prosecution's case, the guilty man who should be on trial. It was only because of Manes's suicide, as the defense portrayed it, that Giuliani scrambled to find a target, and came up with Friedman out of a necessity to hold someone, *anyone*, responsible for city graft. But in the tug-of-war over Manes's role in the case, shocking details about Manes's private life came forth. Manes had a range of swindles running in the city government—not just parking tickets, but shady deals involving city towing contracts and a Queens cable television contract, among other kickback scams. He had professed to Lindenauer that he "might face bankruptcy" because of how thinly stretched his income was, with hefty mortgages on two homes and kids in college. His sins went beyond pilfering money from taxpayers, too. He had been living a double life for years, countering his well-crafted image as an affable family man with the reality that he was a drug user and a serial adulterer. Manes's suicide appeared to be a direct result of being implicated in Giuliani's PVB investigation after Lindenauer agreed to be a prosecution witness, but as more dirt on his life was exposed, a different possibility arose, too: Manes was afraid that his embarrassing secrets would be revealed as part of a pressure campaign against him, that he saw death as his only way to protect his wife, Marlene, and children from the humiliation.

Manes, who had been eyeing the mayor's seat or perhaps a spot in the US Senate only weeks before his first suicide try, had virtually no check on his power in Queens, and he took advantage. His career would be devastated if his deviances were exposed, particularly his appetite for sex—as writers Barrett and Newfield put it, Manes's "addiction to sex was well known." FBI tapes showed that the original source of the entire PVB mess, contractor and prosecution witness Bernie Sandow, had tried to get Manes involved in a session of multi-partner sex as a Caligula-style means of firming up a government agreement, what he called, "a chance to fuck together and seal up the whole situation." Manes had a kindred spirit and pliable cohort in Lindenauer. When Manes hired Lindenauer to join city government, he did not find him at an accounting firm or a law office. He found him at the Institute for Emotional Education, a snake-oil psychotherapy community Lindenauer had established in 1967, with about thirty-five staff members and 125 clients. Some patients, in an effort to get them to experience "healthy love," were encouraged to have sex with each other, and with their doctors, as part of their treatment. It was Marlene Manes who first visited the clinic, in 1974, and struck up a friendship with Lindenauer that grew to include her husband. Though Lindenauer would deny he ever treated Marlene Manes, she and Donald did secretly invest $25,000 in the clinic. But it was Manes who had pulled Lindenauer out of the psychotherapy world and into the sprawling city bureaucracy in 1978, first in the Addiction Services Agency, then, by calling in a favor from Friedman, into the PVB. And it was Manes who first got Lindenauer to act as his bag man for PVB bribery, beginning with a $500 payout from former city transportation commissioner Michael Lazar.

(Above) Investigators lean over the body of murdered Bonanno boss Carmine Galante in the courtyard of Joe & Mary's Restaurant in Brooklyn in 1979.

(Left) Anthony "Fat Tony" Salerno, figurehead boss of the Genovese family, leaves the courthouse after his arraignment as part of the Commission case in February 1985.

(Below) The body of Gambino boss Paul Castellano is wheeled on a stretcher outside of Sparks Steak House on 46th Street in Manhattan in December 1985.

In a crass political stunt, US Attorney Rudy Giuliani (center) and New York Sen. Al D'Amato (right) went "undercover" in a Harlem neighborhood in July 1986 to demonstrate how easily crack cocaine could be bought in New York. Also pictured, at left, is US Parole Commission Chairman Benjamin Baer.

Fresh off his win in the Parking Violations Bureau case at the end of 1986, Rudy Giuliani stands in front of thirty-three-year-old Michael Chertoff, who led the Southern District's case against the Mafia Commission at the same time, resulting in convictions across the board. Assisting Chertoff were John Savarese (left) and Gil Childers (right).

Ed Koch publicly kissing former Miss America Bess Myerson during his 1977 campaign for mayor. Koch's flirtation with Myerson was a ploy to combat rumors that he was gay, and the lie of their relationship lingered over Koch when Myerson faced legal and personal strife in Koch's third term.

Mayor Ed Koch (left) stands with Donald Manes in January 1980 at the opening of the Jimmy Carter reelection campaign headquarters in New York City. Manes was a key Carter ally, but Koch repeatedly undermined his bid to remain in office.

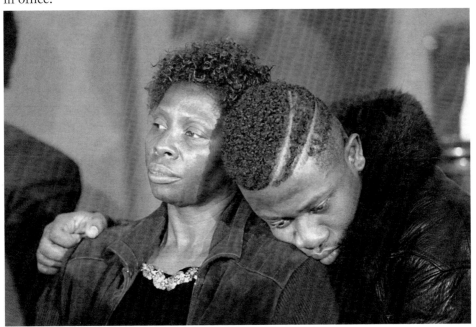

Anthony Griffith, the younger brother of Michael Griffith, rests his head on the shoulder of his mother, Jean, at a Brooklyn church on New Year's Eve 1986. Michael Griffith was slain by white teenagers in Howard Beach, an incident that touched off months of racial strife in the city.

Donald Trump's lawyer and political fixer, Roy Cohn (left), pictured in 1971 with law partner Tom Bolan.

Donald Trump, owner of the New Jersey Generals, speaks to reporters during the USFL's antitrust lawsuit against the NFL in 1986. Trump had forced the league into the legal confrontation, which the USFL technically won, but was awarded just $1 in damages, bringing about the end of the USFL.

In order to sway public opinion in his favor, Donald Trump (left, with shovel) agreed to rebuild the woebegone Wollman Rink in Central Park in the spring of 1986. Here, with Parks Commissioner Henry Stern, Trump celebrates the pouring of the cement at the rink, one of many photo-ops he called for the revamping of the rink.

Mets pitcher Dwight Gooden gets a hug in the Shea Stadium locker room after beating the Cubs to clinch the team's 1986 National League East championship. Below, Mets fans tear up the turf at the stadium to celebrate, leaving the field in disrepair.

Third baseman Ray Knight, the Series MVP, hits a tiebreaking seventh-inning home run in Game Seven of the 1986 World Series, giving the Mets a lead they would not relinquish for a stunning comeback series win over the Red Sox at Shea Stadium

Catcher Gary Carter leaps into the arms of pitcher Jesse Orosco after the final out of the World Series is recorded in Game Seven at Shea Stadium. But the celebration would be difficult for pitcher Dwight Gooden, who missed the team's ticker-tape parade while using drugs, and was involved in a brawl with police back near his home in Tampa in December.

Jets owner Leon Hess, right, walks with NFL Commissioner Pete Rozelle in the summer of 1986. Earlier that year, Hess had been presented with plans for a new football stadium in Queens, to be built by Donald Trump, but Hess torpedoed the idea when he found that Trump wanted local fans to finance the dome through seat leases.

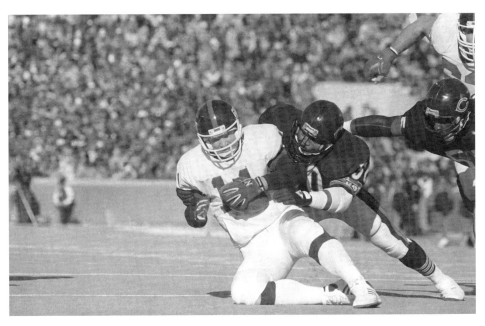

Giants quarterback Phil Simms is sacked by Bears linebacker Mike Singletary in an NFC divisional playoff game in Chicago in January 1986. Little went right for New York, which lost, 21–0, but the game served as motivation for the team's run to Super Bowl XXI the following season.

Linebackers Lawrence Taylor (left) and Harry Carson (right) open fan mail in the Giants' locker room ahead of the Super Bowl in January 1987. Carson and Taylor had a sometimes contentious relationship, but Carson was ultimately a mentor to Taylor.

Giants coach Bill Parcells, nearly fired three years before, is carried off the field at the Rose Bowl in Pasadena, California, in January 1987 after his team defeated the AFC champion Broncos, 39–20, for the Giants' first Super Bowl title.

Lindenauer would be the star witness for Giuliani, and Giuliani had braced Lindenauer to be pressed hard on his own sordid past and the deeds he had carried out with Manes. The goal for Giuliani was to lash Manes's misdeeds to Friedman and make the jury see the pair as crooked pols working in tandem, manipulating underlings like Lindenauer. Puccio's goal was to pin Manes to Lindenauer, and allege that Friedman was the victim of an overzealous prosecution that had lost its target to suicide, made a plea deal it could not undo with the real criminal, Lindenauer, and picked Friedman to fill Manes's void. Back in January, Ed Koch had declared Manes a crook, before he had had the benefit of a trial. This was as close to a trial as Manes, posthumously named as an unindicted co-conspirator in the case, would get.

· · · · ·

The differences between Giuliani and Puccio were on display right from the opening statements. Giuliani had brought to his job a moral absolutism rooted in his Catholic sensibilities—he had originally intended to be a Catholic priest, and did not give up that ambition until his sophomore year in college, when he decided that celibacy was not for him. But his holy intentions still guided his various white knight campaigns in the city. There were no squishy parts to the law, as Giuliani saw it, there was only the hard divide between right and wrong. He had been willing to sing his own praises on those grounds, of course, using his perch to sell himself as a future political candidate to anyone who would listen. "I don't think he ever missed an opportunity to speak anywhere," one former prosecutor said of Giuliani. "He'd go up to Albany to speak to five Boy Scouts." Even as their career paths had diverged since they had worked together, fifteen years earlier, that was clear to Puccio. "We were probably equally ambitious, though I never shared Rudy's obsession with politics," Puccio later wrote. "We both had strong egos and a love of courtroom litigation. Only one of us, however, regarded his career as one long moral crusade." Puccio had a sharper mind and was much better suited for the courtroom than

Giuliani, quicker on his feet and with a better sense of how to work a jury. He could be relentless on witnesses, picking out key phrases to repeat for the jury until they stuck. One observer wrote of Puccio's style, "His credo is: Hit 'em quick, hit 'em hard, hit 'em often, leave 'em bleeding."

This was what had attracted a packed courthouse to a college city seventy miles north of New York (Puccio would later refer to New Haven as "The Land of Steady Habits"), where the New York press was angling and elbowing for scoops and analysis while puzzled locals looked on. Giuliani's opening statement was detailed and methodical. He had a difficult challenge, focusing on Friedman while also looping in the four other defendants in the trial, each with different connections to the rigged Citisource contract or bribes at the PVB. He had to be methodical in explaining the case to twelve Hartford-area jurors (they had been bused in to New Haven) who had no background in the operation of New York government. Giuliani's presentation began by outlining the misdeeds of the co-defendants, building toward the climax: Friedman's entry, as a "bribe broker" into the trough of public corruption the PVB had become under Manes's orders. Working from a pair of large loose-leaf binders, Giuliani calmly presented his case over seventy-five minutes, telling the jury that the bureau had been turned into an "enterprise for illegal plunder." He acknowledged Lindenauer was no model witness, but made the plea to the jury that "This case will not turn on one or two witnesses. The key to this case is viewing the whole picture." Writing in the *New York Post*, columnist Ray Kerrison said, "By the time he had finished, I could taste the greed in my own mouth."

Where Giuliani had been mechanical, standing at a courtroom podium with his coat buttoned, Puccio dazzled in his opening, striding around the available space. Lindenauer's lack of credibility was his target, and he hammered it. He gave the jury a version of "good old Geoffrey Lindenauer" as a sort of maniacal savant of manipulation, coaxing patients to have sex with him at his bogus psychological clinic before moving to his spot within the Parking Violations Bureau, where he could feast on public money. It was Lindenauer, Puccio claimed, who had pointed to Friedman and manipulated Giuliani to save his own skin, "to fill the empty chair filled by Donald Manes." Lindenauer, Puccio insisted, was a pathological liar. "He lied to his friends, he lied to his family, he had lied to his colleagues. He had lied to his patients." Puccio went so far as to blame Lindenauer for Manes's suicide, as though he had coerced him into taking his own life like a Svengali in a city bureaucrat's cheap suit. Three times Puccio made the point: "Lindenauer knew Manes well. He knew that Manes, if put to pressure, would commit suicide. . . . He manipulated Donald Manes into committing suicide." As a capper, Puccio tried to infect everything that Giuliani told the jury with the lack of credibility of Lindenauer—again, making the subtle claim that Lindenauer had even manipulated the US attorney. He pointed, dramatically, at Giuliani, and said, "His mouth moved and words came out, but those were not his words. They were the words of Geoffrey Lindenauer." One Yale student who witnessed the two star lawyers work said, while Giuliani was good, Puccio was, "Wow . . . wow."

28

ONE REASON PROSECUTORS, FOR YEARS, avoided bringing wider cases against the structure of the Mafia was the sticky proposition of proving that there was a Mafia at all. As recently as 1983, in a case against Chicago's Mafia, the defense insisted that La Cosa Nostra (as the Mafia was frequently called) was a figment of the imagination of Hollywood and the media. Crimes happened. Cars were stolen, trucks were hijacked, victims were murdered, money was laundered, loans were sharked, labor was racketeered. But showing there was a wider organization to it all, showing links from this murder to that construction racket was difficult, and opened some easy channels of defense for the accused. Witnesses rarely flipped against Mafia members, and those who did were usually ex-mobsters themselves with long arrest records, generous plea bargain deals, and questionable credibility. But in examining the evidence that Rudy Giuliani's office had gathered and was prepared to deploy in the Commission case, lawyers for the eight defendants had concluded things were different this time. The prosecution would, of course, call witnesses. But that testimony would not carry nearly as much weight as the most powerful witnesses the prosecution had on its side: The words of the accused mobsters themselves, collected on tapes over the course of three years through the aggressive use of Title III wiretapping by state and federal agents. Witnesses can be impugned. Tapes can't.

Occupied in New Haven for the Friedman trial, Giuliani had turned the Commission case over to Michael Chertoff, a thirty-two-year-old assistant attorney just eight years out of Harvard Law. Despite his age, Chertoff had a serious and thoughtful mien that gave him gravity when he spoke, his nose punctuated by a tufty mustache and his hairline receded like a half-moon. At Harvard, he had been a brilliant student and skilled debater, and so impressed classmate Scott Turow that he would later base a law student character on Chertoff in his novel, *One-L*. "Chertoff was not reluctant to debate with anybody," Turow said. "He was self-confident, assertive, but never obnoxious." Chertoff had come to the Southern District with impeccable credentials, having clerked with Supreme Court justice William Brennan and appeals court justice Murray Gurfein. It was Gurfein who had sparked his interest in joining a US attorney's office, and he applied to the Southern District of New York in 1983, after Giuliani had gotten the job but before he had officially taken over. Chertoff had an offer from the Southern District of Florida in Miami, but preferred the prestige of the SDNY. He called Giuliani to report the Florida offer, and Giuliani quickly made him an offer. Chertoff was off to New York and now, three years later, he would be trying perhaps the most important case in Mafia history. "I had probably by that point maybe tried seven or eight cases," Chertoff said, "and it was like, 'Whoa, OK.' But it was the spirit of the office. They threw you into the deep end and you were expected to work really hard swimming."

For defense lawyers, with so many hours of tapes, a change of tactics was required. The tapes left no doubt about the existence of the Mafia, organized in New York into five families and guided by a ruling group, the Commission. There would be three Commission members among the eight defendants (a fourth, of course, was the recently murdered Paul Castellano, and because the strife-ridden Bonanno family had been temporarily removed from the Commission, there was no fifth family head). The tapes also left no doubt about crimes that were committed, especially in the manipulation of the concrete industry. Rather than lodging the standard denial, the defense determined it would simply acknowledge there is a Mafia, and move on to the next logical question: So what? The existence of a Mafia, as proven by the tapes, did not make any member of that group guilty of crimes. From that logic, the defense would show the Commission itself was little more than a group of elderly men, having coffee, working out business conflicts and the admitting of new members from time to time, as though they were bridge partners or a bocce club. Still, it was a difficult proposal for the bosses on trial to accept. One reason they had risen to their positions of power had been their adherence to Mafia rules, and one of the most sacred was the principle of *omerta*—silence. It was Tony "Ducks" Corallo, after all, who had pleaded the Fifth Amendment 120 times back when he was an aspiring capo testifying before Congress in 1957, and who, when asked by reporters whether he had a comment about the Commission trial as he exited the courthouse one day, responded, "Yeah. Go fuck yourself." That silence had helped preserve the organization for more than five decades. Now it would be broken, in federal court of all places. "I didn't know they were going to do that," Chertoff said, "but it didn't surprise me because they are on the tape talking about it so much, what are you going to say? So I guess they made a strategic decision, which makes sense, not to fight with what's on the tape but to simply say, there is no proof of these crimes. For most of them, there was just no defense because they were on tape so much."

Another tactic would be to defang the prosecution's charges on manipulation of the construction industry, the elaborate scheme known as the Concrete Club. By controlling the labor unions and delivery of concrete through one of seven chosen suppliers, the Mob first set the price for concrete in the city, then skimmed 2 percent of payments for concrete off the top of any construction project that topped $2 million. By some estimates, the labor and logistical issues that had their roots in the Concrete Club raised the price of building in the city by about 20 percent, costs that were eventually passed down to citizens. They paid the cost of real estate and watched their taxes filtered via abatements to developers greasing the palms of the labor rackets. (Mayor Koch had, back in January, attempted to fight this process by setting up a subsidized concrete supplier that would halt Mafia extortion by keeping prices closer to the national average—Koch joked, "I'm not afraid of concrete shoes.") This was the kind of arrangement, straddling the line between illegality and legitimate business, that thrived under Paul Castellano. With New York in a building boom in the early '80s, there had been plenty of projects to line the pockets of the family heads. But the tapes were unequivocal about the existence of the Concrete Club, and for the defense lawyers, that would require another unorthodox step. As they were doing with the Mafia, they would have to acknowledge its existence, but lay blame for it on corrupt contractors who were fiddling with building bids for their own ends, not on the Commission members.

For the Galante murder, the defense could use a more traditional argument, attacking the reliability of prosecution evidence against Bruno Indelicato, only linked to the scene through a handprint, and calling into question its connection to the Commission. With the defense plan laid out, Samuel Dawson, the lead defense attorney, stunned the courtroom in his opening statement by telling the jury, "This case is not about whether there is a Mafia. Assume it. Accept it. There is—right here in New York City." But Dawson moved quickly past that assertion, asking the jury, "Can you accept that just because a person is a member of the Mafia that doesn't mean he committed the crimes charged in this case?" Dawson disputed the notion that the Commission was a purveyor of violence or a tool of extortion. Its very purpose, he said, was, "to avoid—*avoid*—conflict." Dawson treated the Concrete Club charges as though they hardly had anything to do with the case at hand. "The government has this case upside-down," Dawson said. "This is really not extortion. It's a bid-rigging case."

In his opening statement, Chertoff stepped to the defendant's table, standing just feet away from some of the world's most powerful organized crime figures, men who had been responsible for dozens of murders in their careers. He looked at each one, introduced him to the jury, and ticked off the charges the government was making against him. He approached Fat Tony Salerno, seated alone. Salerno sneered back at Chertoff. "Ladies and gentlemen," Chertoff said, "this is Anthony Salerno, who is the boss of the Genovese family, and his nickname is Fat Tony." Salerno had undergone recent eye surgery, and his left eye was still red, the socket around it still had swelling. But it made Salerno look vulnerable and human. By approaching and standing alongside these godfathers, Chertoff was not just imbuing his opening with courtroom drama. He was stripping the bosses of their mystery, wiping away the gauzy romance of benevolent and fair Mafia dons, and showing the eight defendants were not guided by honor or love of family, but by money. "What you will see is these men," he said, "these crime leaders, fighting with each other, backstabbing each other, each one trying to get a larger share of the illegal proceeds. You are going to learn that this Commission is dominated by a single principle—greed. They want more money, and they will do what they have to do to get it."

29

WHEN THE ASTRODOME OPENED IN 1965, it was conceived as a glass bubble, one that could accommodate the beloved green grass and sunshine of the summer game, except without the two aggravations that infested baseball in Houston: the unrelenting moist heat creeping off the Gulf Coast, and the flocks of mosquitoes that were the scourge of

East Texas's low-lying bayous. In a clear glass dome, mosquitoes could be mostly shut out and the air could be cooled, while sun would keep the field as lush as any well-kept subdivision lawn. In reality, though, that sun was blinding through the glass of the Dome, impossible for catching fly balls (fielders had taken to wearing batting helmets during outfield practice) and withering to the yellowed grass below. An adjustment had to be made. The panes of the Dome were painted to reduce brightness, which also required a change in the playing surface. Without sun, grass was out, and the hard, synthetic green of Astroturf was in. Gone, along with the sun and grass, was any claim the building could make to baseball in the classic sense. Baseball in the reconfigured Astrodome—likened to a carpeted pup tent—would have as much in common with baseball in an open-air park as a submarine ride had with a trip on a daysailer. Astros coach Gene Tenace tried to explain the difficulty: "It's not easy to see in here. It takes time for your eyes to adjust. Did you ever read a newspaper in the sunlight and then step immediately indoors? You can't see. It's something like that." The Mets, once they wrapped up their 108–54 season, tied for seventh-best in baseball history, would begin their playoff quest here, thanks to a scheduling mishap. It was, according to National League rules of alternating home field edge, the East's turn to begin at home, but because the Astros were not expected to be a playoff team, no one had objected when the Astrodome's other tenant, the NFL's Oilers, scheduled a home game for October 12, which was slated for Game Four of the National League Championship Series. The league did not bother to negotiate a change with the NFL, which (as the USFL could attest) dominated the broadcasting world, and simply gave home field to the Astros over the Mets' objections, closing the matter.

More than home field, though, what really worried the Mets was Mike Scott, who had capped an impressive season by storming through the final two months of the year with his split-finger fastball, the most unhittable pitch from any pitcher in the league. The Mets had Dwight Gooden, and were encouraged by the way he had ended the season after a rocky start to the year off the field and a mediocre showing in June and July on it. Since August 1, Gooden had gone 7–2, with 93 strikeouts, a 2.66 ERA, and an opponent's batting average of .209. The Mets also had a sense of outrage on their side, a staple of the club. If there was a way to drum up us-vs.-them drama for this team, they would find it. On the day before the series started, the *Houston Post* published a survey of twenty-six players, coaches, and managers from around the National League, and found that twenty-three were picking the Astros. That probably should not have been a surprise. The Mets had bench-clearers with four of the NL's teams and had ticked off most of the rest. "The contempt other teams have for the Mets is unbelievable," Ray Knight said, peeved. "Just unbelievable."

Heading into the series opener, the Mets had proven that Roger Craig was correct when he told Scott that he would be accused of cheating. Scott figured he could use that to his advantage. Before the first pitch of the series was thrown, no subject was run through the media wringer as much as whether the key to Scott's success had been his use of sandpaper to scuff his split-finger before he threw it. "I know he doctors it," said Keith Hernandez. "I've seen the scratches on the baseball. He throws it off a fastball and makes the ball run." Doug Harvey, who would be the umpire in Game One, suggested that managers had taken to complaining about Scott as a way "to get to Scott's mind." But from the beginning of the series opener, all the chatter about scuffing had little effect on Scott, yet became a near-obsession of the Mets. Lenny Dykstra began the game with an attempted bunt that went for an out to first base, and Wally Backman reached on a throwing error by shortstop Craig Reynolds. But Scott mowed down Hernandez, who had balls-and-strikes complaints for Harvey through the entire game, on three pitches. Gary Carter was next and was so incredulous at the way Scott's second pitch dove that he asked Harvey to check the ball for scuffing. Harvey looked at the ball and found nothing amiss. Scott struck him out on the next pitch. So it went. Scott then breezed through the next seven hitters without allowing a baserunner. Gooden was in good form, too, yielding just one run on seven hits (a home run by Glenn Davis in the second) in seven innings and twice pitching out of bases-loaded jams.

But Scott was untouchable. Only three times in the game did the Mets get a runner past first base, including in the ninth inning when Darryl Strawberry knocked a one-out single and stole second. Mookie Wilson hit a sharp grounder to the right-side hole, but Davis dove and smothered the ball before it could get out of the infield. A throw from the knees to Scott covering first base barely got Wilson and moved Strawberry to third base. But Scott got Ray Knight to chase an outside split-finger for the final out, and the Astros had a 1–0 win. Scott struck out 14, allowed only five hits, and had demoralized Mets hitters physically and mentally. "That's the best movement I've seen on any ball from any pitcher this year," Carter said after striking out three times in four at-bats. "He had said before, if the hitters believe he is scuffing up the ball, it was an advantage to him."

....

Scott, even when he was not doing the pitching, loomed over the series. For Game Two, the Astros were throwing thirty-nine-year-old former Met Nolan Ryan, who had gone 12–8 with a 3.34 ERA that season (he missed time because of an elbow injury) and 194 strikeouts in 178 innings. In the game's early stages, it looked as though the funk into which Scott had sent the Mets might carry over, because Ryan set down ten straight Mets—five on strikeouts, including the now-befuddled Carter—to start the game. But Carter followed a pair of singles by Hernandez and Wally Backman by swatting an outside fastball to the wall in right-center field, bringing home Backman for the Mets' first series run. Strawberry followed with a sacrifice fly and the Mets were staked to a 2–0 lead. Lenny Dykstra was the catalyst in the fifth inning. He had rocketed one of Ryan's pitches toward the upper deck, but foul, on the first pitch of his at-bat, which Ryan did not much appreciate. He zipped his next pitch, a fastball, up and inside, causing Dykstra to tumble to the turf, giving Ryan a long stare as he got up. Dykstra followed with a hard single to the opposite field, winning his battle with Ryan and sparking the Mets. With Bob Ojeda crafty in working himself out of trouble in the first seven innings, when he allowed only one run despite giving up 10 hits, the Mets cruised, 5–1, and returned to Shea with a 1–1 tie. After two games, with the way the Mets had hit Ryan, the strength of Scott and the comparative weakness of the rest of the Astros pitching rotation, the series would turn on one question: Could Houston get a win in a game in which Scott was not pitching? That also left manager Hal Lanier to decide whether to go with Scott on short rest for Game Four, which would allow him a third start in a potential Game Seven. Lanier was coy on the subject, pointing out that Scott had not pitched on three days' rest all season, and that he had thrown 125 pitches in Game One. "At this stage of the season, the more days you can give a pitcher like that, the better," Lanier said. "We'll just have to wait and see what shape we're in."

The opportunity was there for Houston to get things in fine shape, indeed, in Game Three, despite the return to New York. The Astros jumped on Ron Darling for four runs in the first two innings and took that 4–0 lead into the sixth. But a big error by Reynolds at short after back-to-back singles from Kevin Mitchell and Hernandez gave the Mets their first run, and brought up Darryl Strawberry. Junkballing Astros starter Bob Knepper left his first pitch over the plate for Strawberry, who knocked it for a game-tying home run. Houston put up a run in the seventh, but in the bottom of the ninth, Wally Backman reached on a controversial bunt single—the Astros felt Backman had wandered out of the baseline to avoid a tag, but umpire Dutch Rennert ruled Backman safe. That brought up the 5-foot-10, 160-pound Dykstra, with nine career home runs to his credit. He would be the hero for the Mets, flipping an easy swing into Astros closer Dave Smith's low fastball and pulling it over the right-field fence. "The last time I hit a home run in the bottom of the ninth to win a game," Dykstra joked, "I was playing my Strat-O-Matic baseball game, rolling dice against my brother Kevin." The Astros were not much in a jocular state, having blown a chance to seize the series lead. General manager Dick Wagner complained about the Backman call, complained about some of the balls and strikes called by home plate umpire Frank Pulli, complained about the Mets playing music in the stadium while batters were in the box, and even complained about the bus that carried the Astros family members. "The bus that the wives traveled on to the stadium was not allowed in the area where the players' bus goes," he said, which forced them to walk a few hundred feet among Mets fans. According to the *Houston Chronicle*, "Wagner felt they were put in danger." Considering the call that Smith had received at the team hotel when the Astros first arrived in New York—"Some guy called," he said, "and said he was going to blow my head off with a machine gun"—Wagner might not have been completely wrong.

Short rest and all, Lanier was down, 2–1, in the series and now knew he had to pitch Scott in Game Four, which went exactly as the Mets had feared it would. Scott was dominant from the beginning, getting fourteen outs against the first fifteen batters he faced (only his own error in the fourth kept him from perfection) before he allowed a hit. Again, the Mets rarely even threatened, putting three runners past first base, and getting just one home, on a sacrifice fly by pinch-hitter Danny Heep (the player for whom Scott had been traded from the Mets to the Astros three years earlier). Mets starter Sid Fernandez was solid, allowing three runs in six innings, but Scott could not be matched. He did not rack up the strikeout numbers he had in Game 1 (he had five), but his split-finger's nasty downward break forced the Mets into 13 ground-ball outs. Houston won, 3–1, as Scott allowed only three hits in another complete game.

The Mets did not spend as much time complaining to umpire Dutch Rennert about scuffed balls during the game as they had to Doug Harvey in Game One, but instead, collected as many fouled-off balls as they could, with a plan to appeal to National League president Chub Feeney, allowing him to view the scuff marks himself. The matter took on greater consequence the following day when Game Five at Shea was postponed because of rain. That left Scott and scuffing as the only real topic for the gathered media to discuss. In the locker room, Backman and other Mets passed around banged-up baseballs to reporters, pointing out that grass does not scratch balls. There was the spectacle of Harvey, the umpire, holding a press conference to reassure reporters that Scott was not scuffing, that he had worked six games behind the plate with Scott and had checked around seventy of his balls without a mark. Harvey had a good track record on scuffing pitchers, too. In 1978, he had ejected scuffball master Don Sutton from a game in St. Louis, which led to Sutton threatening a lawsuit against Harvey. "Other than the spitter, it's the most explosive pitch I've ever seen," Harvey said of Scott's split-finger. "But it is clean." The managers' press conferences got a bit daft. Davey Johnson opened a drawer in his office desk and revealed the defaced balls. "Scuffed in the same spot," he said. He was asked whether the Mets had, possibly, doctored those balls themselves in an elaborate frame-up of Scott. "I'd take a lie detector test," Johnson said. When Lanier was told about that, he said, "Am I supposed to take one or what? Or should Scott take one?" Finally, Lanier offered the Mets some advice. "If they're such big fans of Mike Scott they have to save his used baseballs," he said with a laugh, "they ought to bring them over here so he can autograph them."

There was still a Game Five to be played, and an Astros win there would secure, at least, a Game Seven start for Scott. Dwight Gooden and Nolan Ryan, going head-to-head, were sterling. Gooden held Houston scoreless through four innings, though the Astros suffered another poor call, this time in the second inning, when Craig Reynolds was called out on a double play turn by umpire Fred Brocklander. It appeared that Reynolds beat the throw, which would have allowed Kevin Bass to score from third base, but before the call was made, first baseman Hernandez shouted "Out!" as a subliminal nudge to Brocklander's call. Hernandez would later admit that Reynolds probably was safe. But Gooden took advantage of his good luck from there. Ryan topped him by throwing four perfect innings to open, the Mets finally breaking through for the tie in the bottom of the fifth on a line-drive home run by Strawberry. The 1–1 tie held into the 12th inning, with Astros pitcher Charlie Kerfeld on in relief of Ryan, who went nine innings. Gary Carter, who felt he had been shown up by Kerfeld earlier in the series, came to the plate in search of redemption—the Mets had a runner in scoring position with one out, and Carter was determined to crack out of the 1-for-21 slump he had been in during the NLCS. Carter ripped a single up the middle, driving in the game-winning run.

Carter had been in the league for 12 seasons by that point. He had been part of history, the longest NLCS game in history. He was savoring it. "It's at the top," Carter said. "The top of all the games I've ever played in." It was a thriller, and put the Mets one win away from the World Series. But there was not much time to digest it. After the game, both teams had to hustle onto flights and get to Houston. Game Six, to be played under the shadow of a potential seventh game with Mike Scott on the mound, was coming to the Astrodome.

30

THE REAL GEOFFREY LINDENAUER DID not match up with the picture Stanley Friedman's defense lawyer Tom Puccio painted in his opening statement. Lindenauer was a central figure in the city's municipal scandal, yet he had never been interviewed or had his voice heard by New Yorkers. In the courtroom, he hardly looked like a master manipulator who had somehow puppeteered the decision of US attorney Rudy Giuliani to go after Friedman, manipulated Donald Manes into committing suicide, and orchestrated a fraudulent $22.7 million city contract for handheld computers that had not yet been created. Lindenauer was heavy, over 250 pounds, and spoke in a meek, soft voice that, according to *Post* columnist Beth Fallon, had the jury "in a trance." Fallon wrote, "His entire adult history is one of greed and bribes and fakery, yet the voice makes it all sound ordinary, even reasonable."

Lindenauer was the second witness to take the stand, after Queens PVB bribe-giver Michael Dowd, and to open, he recalled his early interactions with Manes, including the $25,000 investment Manes made in Lindenauer's quackish psychiatric clinic. When the clinic closed in 1974, Manes wanted Lindenauer to repay him, and even talked Lindenauer into hocking a $2,500 ring he had given his wife. To help pay him back, Manes petitioned Friedman (then Abe Beame's deputy mayor) to help Lindenauer get a job with the city. Lindenauer wound up in the Parking Violations Bureau, and once there, Manes, whom Lindenauer referred to as his "best friend," approached him about becoming a bag man for bribes from contractors. Lindenauer testified about the first bribe he received for Manes, given by co-defendant Michael Lazar, for $500, while Lazar was dressed in a bathrobe. Lindenauer gave Manes $250, operating under the impression they were splitting the loot. But an annoyed Manes asked where the rest of the money was. "He yelled at me, 'You're repaying the debt!'" Lindenauer said. In his second day on the stand, questioned by David Zornow of Giuliani's team, Lindenauer gave a gripping account of how he pondered suicide once federal investigators began closing in on the PVB scheme. It was Manes who suggested Lindenauer commit suicide, recalling how mutual Queens friend Shelly Chevlowe would have reacted if he had been in Lindenauer's situation—Manes held his thumb and index finger into the shape of a gun, and put it to his head.

The direct examination had gone well for Lindenauer. Zornow had addressed the sexual misconduct at his clinic head-on, hoping to take some of the sting out of the defense's expected attacks. Lindenauer's voice had remained steady, he had gotten emotional at only appropriate points, and he had had only minor slip-ups. He was a sympathetic character, far more a victim of Manes's bullying than a mastermind. But then it was Puccio's turn on cross-examination, and his rapid-fire peppering threw off Lindenauer from the outset. "Is it a true statement that you have engaged in lying, deceit, and manipulation?" Puccio asked. When Lindenauer answered that he had, Puccio fired right back, "On many, many occasions?" Lindenauer responded, "Yes, I did."

Puccio: Did you lie to people?

Lindenauer: I have lied to people.

Puccio: Have you defrauded people?

Lindenauer: I did.

Puccio: Have you manipulated people?

Lindenauer: I have not told people the truth.

Puccio: What do you understand manipulation to mean, Mr. Lindenauer?

Lindenauer: That's a difficult—I don't know.

Puccio: You don't know what manipulation means, is that your testimony?

With just a handful of questions, Puccio smashed the serene confidence Lindenauer had gained in his two days of testimony given to prosecutors. He tried to push Lindenauer on the gritty details of his clinic, and how he came to have sex with patients. Judge Knapp stopped him. "The details would be very engrossing," Knapp said, "but not very enlightening." Still, the questions had Lindenauer off-balance. There was also discussion of whether Lindenauer had suffered a nervous breakdown in 1983, which Lindenauer denied. From September of that year until April 1984, he had rarely shown up for work at the PVB and was at the Pawling Health Manor in Upstate New York. Embarrassed, Lindenauer admitted he had gone there to lose weight, because he needed a hernia surgery but was too obese to have it done safely. Lindenauer's discomfort over his weight was apparent. Puccio poked at the nature of his bribe meetings, which almost always happened over a meal. "Did you ever pay for a meal in your life?" Puccio asked. Angry, Lindenauer responded, "Many meals."

Lindenauer was also having trouble keeping dates straight, and Puccio called him on it. Lindenauer replied with "I don't recall" so many times that one of the other defendants' lawyers asked if he was having a problem with his memory. Lindenauer said, "I don't recall any problems with my memory," to the laughter of the gallery. Puccio hit Lindenauer on his willingness, after calling Manes his best friend, to turn on him and accept a deal from Giuliani. Lindenauer cracked. "I am very ashamed of what I have done," he said.

Giuliani and Zornow had coached Lindenauer carefully through his direct examination. Puccio wiped all that away in his cross-examination, and if Lindenauer had been let out of the witness box at that point, Giuliani's case would have been nearly dead. The problem for Puccio, though, was that there were four other co-defendants, each with his own lawyer. There had been no prior agreements about how to piece together the defense so it could be most effective for everyone. Each of the defendants' lawyers wanted his own shot at cross-examining Lindenauer, and he remained on the stand into the following week. The other questioners were not as skilled and sharp as Puccio, and Lindenauer grew more capable of withstanding attacks. By the second week of October, after Lindenauer spent an entire week on the stand, the prosecution's star witness rehabilitated himself. "He was batted around so much," Puccio observed, "that even I began to feel a little sorry for him at the end."

·····

Back at City Hall, Mayor Ed Koch followed the press reports of the trial in New Haven with bemused distance. He had called the trial "fascinating" and told reporters it would make "a good movie," but he did not weigh in on the details, except to point out what he had been saying all along: that the scope of the graft in the PVB was limited to a few bad apples. "There are only two people on trial out of the whole agency," Koch said, while conceding that the two involved in the trial were the most powerful PVB employees, the bureau's head, Lester Shafran, and Lindenauer, his number two man. Lindenauer rubbed a sore spot for Koch when he testified that Donald Manes, Koch's ally and the man Koch himself had said would be the best bet to succeed him as mayor, had told him he was hopeful of becoming mayor in 1989, and, then, Lindenauer said, "he would really show me how to make money." Koch got a boost during the trial on October 9, when a recorded tape of a conversation among Lindenauer and two of the instigators of the scandal, Bernie Sandow and Michael Burnett, was played in the courtroom—the tape from November 1985 that had started the PVB scandal in the first place. Burnett wondered whether they could persuade Koch to make Lindenauer PVB director after Shafran left as planned.

"You can't with Koch," Lindenauer said. "Absolutely, Koch, as good a mayor as he is, he's a [expletive]. There's no such thing as loyalty or friends."

But the revelations at the PVB trial had cast a chill over city government that Koch could not shake. Lindenauer had turned on Manes, Shafran, and now Friedman, and as other scandals around the government rose up and either fizzled out or gained traction, trust in one's fellow municipal bureaucrat was hard to find. "There was a little bit of McCarthyism attached to it," *Post* political writer George Arzt said, "in that everyone was seeing ghosts everywhere. Everyone was seeing what this guy might have done, this guy did this—there were ancillary investigations going on all over the place, not connected to PVB, but everything was being investigated. It was a paranoid time for city government, very demoralizing. People in government didn't know where to turn because suddenly everyone was being investigated. You didn't know who was wearing a wire and who wasn't wearing a wire."

The administration was paralyzed. The *New York Times* printed a list of serious issues the Koch administration was trying to handle, including the AIDS crisis, record-high homelessness, drug arrests leading to overcrowded jails, and an overtaxed mass transit system that left Midtown so crowded that some suggested entry fees for cars. Nothing, though, was happening. Koch nemesis Jay Goldin said, "The corruption phenomenon is consuming the administration's time, energy, and focus needed to deal with so many problems." Just as bad was the general weariness the scandals left among the public. There had been some hope that there would be collective outrage over the abuses, and that outrage could be a catalyst for real change. But that wasn't the case. Members of the Commission on Integrity in Government, set up jointly by the city and state to come up with safeguards against further major graft, were disappointed to find that while voters followed stories of politicians and corruption, they were mostly exhausted by it and not angry enough to throw the bums out. Felix Rohatyn, the investment banker who helped lead New York from the brink of bankruptcy in the '70s, agreed to join the group because he thought it would have a mandate from the public to make changes. "I was wrong," he said. "The stench that has come up is absolutely overwhelming, but people seem to be used to it."

．．．．．

After opening with titillating testimony from Lindenauer, both on direct and in cross-examination, the Friedman trial slowed considerably over the following weeks. Giuliani's methodical strategy revealed itself. He had put Lindenauer on the stand early, established the charges he would make against Friedman, allowed the defense to take their potshots at him, then steadily rebuilt Lindenauer's credibility with a series of witnesses who could back up what he had said. Those witnesses had believability issues, too, having all been involved in PVB bribery on some level and all given a deal for reduced sentencing by Giuliani. The defense could pick at the series of witnesses for that. But what Giuliani's witnesses lacked in moral fiber, they made up in volume. Giuliani had a parade of witnesses, all supporting different parts of Lindenauer's original account. Late in October, Giuliani had persuaded one more witness, former Datacom head Joe Delario, to testify in New Haven. Delario lacked the unseemly characteristics of the rest of the prosecution's witnesses, and for him, Giuliani had promised full immunity after originally threatening an indictment. Delario testified that, just about a year before, Friedman had demanded a bribe of $35,000 in "good-faith money" to be paid to Donald Manes and Lindenauer. Puccio began to worry. Giuliani had said in his opening statement that the key for the trial was a focus on the entire picture of the prosecution, not on the personal foibles of any one witness. If that line had stuck with the jurors, Friedman was in trouble. Even before the trial, Puccio had suspected that Friedman would have to testify, because there was no way to make a defense case without him, but the testimony of Delario sealed that decision.

Nearly two months into his own trial, Friedman took the stand in New Haven. Puccio had done his best to tinker with Friedman's image. Friedman had shaved off his familiar goatee to soften his look in May, and during the trial, Puccio tried several tactics to wring the aura of fast-talking big-city politician out of Friedman. He left his high-end cigars back in his hotel room, and toned down the level of designer in his designer suits. Each morning, heading to the courtroom, Friedman, Puccio, and Friedman's wife, Jackie, strolled across the New Haven Green, hoping to firm up his image in the eyes of news viewers back in New York—by the time the trio got halfway across the green, inevitably, they would be picked up by a pack of reporters—and in the eyes of any passing jurors. Puccio did his best, when questioning Friedman, to set him up not as a palm-greaser and bribe-taker, but as a standard-issue politician who swapped favors with other politicians and businessmen as part of the normal workings of government. "You don't really say, 'I want you to help,' if you're dealing with people you're friendly with in government or anywhere else," Friedman said. "You don't have to say any more for a friend to help a friend."

Throughout the trial, both Puccio and Giuliani had their frustrations with the flightiness of seventy-seven-year-old Judge Knapp. His handling of motions was inconsistent and, too often, he got too involved with direct communications with witnesses. "Giuliani and I used to look at each other and roll our eyes," Puccio remembered. "We knew Knapp was like a pendulum swinging back and forth every day. One day Giuliani would get hit, the next day it would be me. There was no rhyme or reason to Knapp's behavior." But Friedman did get worse treatment. After Puccio was done with his direct examination, Giuliani was prepared for cross, and the two lawyers were meeting in Knapp's chambers to discuss the parameters of topics Giuliani could cover—Puccio wanted him to stick to matters that involved the companies connected to the PVB scandal, while Giuliani wanted room to explore other aspects of Friedman's life. Knapp found Giuliani's request to be silly, saying, "I wouldn't do all this bullshit," but allowing that Giuliani should be able to ask the questions anyway. Puccio told him that some questions could be prejudicial. Knapp responded with an editorial on Friedman's testimony and Giuliani's strategy: "With the highly improbable story that your client told, I think that should be what we're talking about, not this bullshit." When the pool reporter who had been in the chamber emerged and relayed Knapp's sentiment, a firestorm in the courtroom ensued. Knapp asked the reporter, and the press corps as a whole, more than once not to publish what he had said. Speculation was rampant that Knapp's conduct would be grounds for a mistrial. Friedman, though angry, quickly quashed that notion. Considering the possibility of another two-month trial in New Haven, he said, "It would be cruel and unusual punishment to go through this again."

Friedman held his own, mostly, against Giuliani's cross-examination. As he had been throughout the trial, Giuliani was meticulous and detail-oriented, asking Friedman about specific dates and instances in which he had wielded his influence, from the mundane to the spectacular—his lobbying connections in the scandal-ridden taxi commission, for example, or the strings he had pulled to get a tax abatement for Donald Trump. The approach was tedious. When Giuliani began a question with, "Is it not true, Mr. Friedman, that on April 11, 1982 . . ." a courtroom spectator whispered, ". . . you left the shower curtain outside the tub." But Giuliani lodged some direct blows on Friedman, including getting him to testify that his income the previous year had been $914,000. He had a breakthrough against Friedman, too, when he asked about a $10,000 fee Friedman got for a lobbying job that only required him to get on the phone. Giuliani, feigning amazement, asked Friedman if he had really gotten all that money for making only two phone calls. "It was just one phone call," Friedman said, correcting Giuliani and wiping away the months of hard work Puccio put in to make Friedman come off less like a greasy city politician. Puccio called it a "hideous moment—the kind of exchange that causes defense attorneys to wake up in the middle of the night, sweating." Two days later, the defense rested.

31

New York was not Bob Knepper's kind of place, and he was as happy as any of the Astros to get back to the comforts of Houston for Game

Six. When he had come up with the Giants in the late 1970s, Knepper was on track for a stellar career, and went 17–11 in his second full season, with a 2.63 ERA. Teammate John Montefusco was ebullient in his praise: "Knepper might be another Sandy Koufax. He's got everything. The guys don't even want to face him in batting practice. A cinch 25-game winner someday." But inconsistency and struggles with his delivery overshadowed Knepper's early success, and he went just 9–12 in 1979. He had become a born-again Christian, uncomfortable in the Sodom and Gomorrah wasteland of the Bay Area, and the zeal with which he pursued his religion—as well as that of other members of the Giants' so-called "God Squad"—was part of a rift that developed in the San Francisco clubhouse. So devout was Knepper that he had even refused to throw at batters, part of the rough-and-tumble must-dos for pitchers in the game. As his performance suffered in what should have been the prime years of his career, teammates groused over his lack of emotion, his willingness to accept poor performances as, simply, "God's will." His religious sensibilities were soothed when he was sent to Houston in 1981, and from there Knepper was, well, resurrected. He was an All-Star in the strike-shortened 1981 season, won 15 games each in 1984 and 1985, and was a 17-game winner in 1986. He was no Koufax, but he had become a solid starter. Now, in Game Six, he was the one remaining prayer between the Astros and a Game Seven with a rested Mike Scott, who had allowed just eight hits and one run in 18 innings in the series. Knepper had left the team before Game Five to get back to Texas early and get some rest. Talking to reporters, Knepper feigned calm about the biggest start of his career. "I'm looking forward to it," Knepper said, "but I'm going to try to treat it like any other game."

Mets starter Bob Ojeda was approaching Game Six with some dread, however. He had thrown a complete game in Game Two, but since then, his left elbow had been throbbing. Cold compresses and rest had not helped it. There was no way he would miss his start, but it would be impossible to pitch with the pain. Ojeda needed something stronger than ice. He needed cortisone. Only the Mets team doctor could administer a cortisone shot, though, and he was in Washington, DC, for a conference. So Ojeda got on a plane, packing a syringe loaded with cortisone. The doctor gave him the shot at his hotel, and Ojeda flew back to New York in time to make the team flight to Houston. When he was warming up in the bullpen, though, Ojeda would later write, "It felt like I had two sandbags stuffed in my elbow. I was in trouble, I remember thinking, but I figured I had to try." Things looked bad at the outset. After a 1-2-3 inning from Knepper, the Astros started with a single by Bill Doran under the glove of shortstop Rafael Santana, and an out on an outstanding play at first by Keith Hernandez. But that was followed by an RBI double from Phil Garner. Two more singles and a walk, and the Astros jumped to a 3–0 lead with just one out and runners on first and third. Manager Hal Lanier, conscious of how critical each run had been in the series to this point, made what would be a disastrous decision: He had Alan Ashby attempt a suicide squeeze. Ashby squared expecting to see an off-speed pitch from Ojeda—Ashby would later say Ojeda had not thrown him a fastball at all in the first game. But Ojeda did throw a fastball, and a perplexed Ashby failed to get the bunt down. The Mets caught Kevin Bass charging toward home. Ashby lined out to shortstop for the third out, and Ojeda escaped.

For Game Six, Knepper had vowed to be the kind of guy his teammates back in San Francisco wanted. He would show emotion. He fist-punched the air when he ended the Mets' first inning. He stood at the mound and shouted, both fists clenched, when he struck out Kevin Mitchell to close the third. In the fourth, when Knepper missed on a 1-2 pitch to Strawberry with a curveball that was called outside, he squatted to the mound in anger, then pounded his glove when he struck out Strawberry looking for the third out. "You *never* see Bob Knepper doing this," Tim McCarver said of Knepper's "animated reactions" on the ABC broadcast. But never had Knepper been so locked in. Ojeda's elbow numbed after his rough first inning, and he allowed just two baserunners until he was relieved by Rick Aguilera in the seventh, but this game was Knepper's. He gave up a single and a walk in the third inning, and was perfect in every other inning, going into the ninth with a string of 16 straight batters retired and a 3–0 lead. "Scotty tomorrow! Scotty tomorrow!" became the theme in the Astros dugout. But on a 1-2 count to leadoff man Lenny Dykstra in the ninth, Knepper looped a curveball to the outside part of the plate and the perils of playing the field in the Astrodome came to the fore. Somehow, Dykstra reached out and caught the ball on the meat of his bat, lifting it to right-center. Center fielder Billy Hatcher took a bad angle, and the ball carried, over his head, to the wall. Dykstra motored to third base with a triple. Knepper had Mookie Wilson down in the count, 0-2, but Wilson hit a single out of the reach of Bill Doran at second base, scoring Dykstra. Hernandez followed with a double on a fastball over the middle, and with one out, Scotty tomorrow was in jeopardy, the score 3–2. Lanier called on Dave Smith, and Knepper got a standing ovation as he walked off, waving his hat. It was the last emotion Knepper would show, as he leaned, expressionless, against the dugout railing.

Smith should have been a plus for the Astros in the series. He was as good as any reliever in baseball to end the year, collecting a 2–1 record and 16 saves in his last 22 appearances, striking out 19 in 21 innings, with a 1.69 ERA. But he had blown Game Three to the Mets with Dykstra's game-winner, and was not focused to start his effort to rescue the game for Knepper in Game Six. He got two strikes on Gary Carter, the first batter he faced, but when Fred Brocklander called a ball on a pitch Smith had been sure was a strike, Smith lost his cool. He yelled at Brocklander. He walked Carter. He walked Darryl Strawberry, the next batter, loading the bases for Ray Knight with one out. When a 1-2 pitch that looked to be off the outside corner was called a ball, catcher Ashby groaned, hoping Brocklander would hear him. Instead, Knight took offense, turned and told Ashby to stop umpiring, as tensions were boiling at the plate. Lanier went to the mound. Shortstop Dickie Thon, Knight's old teammate in Houston, began walking toward the plate, shouting at Knight. "Ray said something to Ashby," Thon said. "I know Ray's very competitive. I just overreacted a little bit. He overreacted, too." Lanier pushed Thon back to his position, and when Brocklander came out to settle the situation, Lanier laid into him. Knight settled the matter by pounding a fly ball to right-center for a sacrifice fly that scored the tying run. Smith managed the final out, sending the game to extra innings, but he was seething. "It's hard to pitch to a guy," Smith said, "who has a floating strike zone."

. . . .

Game Six rolled past the four-hour mark. Sinkerballer Roger McDowell had kept the Astros off the board for four innings, only the second time in 1986 he had been on the mound that long. Larry Andersen had done the same for the Astros for three innings in relief of Smith. Thirty-seven-year-old Aurelio Lopez, signed in June, came on in the 14th inning, and immediately appeared out of his depth. He let up a single, a walk, and another single, to Wally Backman, driving in the run that would give the Mets a 4–3 lead. But Lopez settled in, getting a pop fly and a strikeout to avoid further damage. In the bottom of the 14th, the Mets called on Jesse Orosco, a two-time All-Star reliever with the killer lefty slider, who had lost his role as the sole closer to McDowell. Orosco had been nearly perfect in the series, allowing just one hit and a walk in three appearances. But with a chance to end the game in the bottom of the inning, light-hitting Billy Hatcher rocketed a 3-2 pitch to left field for a majestic home run. "It looked," Darling said, "like the final home run in *The Natural*."

By the 16th inning, exhaustion was taking hold. The rosters were expended. There had been nine pinch-hitters, and eight pitchers used, the guts of Ojeda and emotion of Knepper long forgotten. It was, again, former Astro Ray Knight at the plate in the 16th inning, and Lopez, who was gassed, on the mound. The guy the Mets could not give away in the offseason was now coming to the plate with Darryl Strawberry, having led off with a double, on second base, facing a guy who was not in the big leagues to start the season. Knight chatted with manager Davey Johnson before going to the plate, asking whether Johnson wanted to move Strawberry over to third base with a bunt. "Hell no," Johnson said. "Drive the ball to right field and get him home." Knight responded, "I can do that." Knight hit a line drive single fielded by Kevin Bass in right, and Strawberry came around to score easily when Bass's throw went up the third base line. That was it for Lopez. The Astros went to little-used lefty Jeff Calhoun, who could not locate his pitches. He threw two wild pitches (one scoring Knight) and a walk, gave up a sacrifice bunt to Orosco, a run-scoring hit to Dykstra to make it 7–4, and was fortunate to get a double play grounder from Mookie Wilson.

Orosco, too, was exhausted in the 16th, but needed three outs to get the Mets out of the vise grip of Mike Scott's split middle and index fingers and into the World Series. They did not come easy. He struck out Craig Reynolds in a dead-silent Astrodome, most of the fans having given up and filed out, to start the inning. He yielded a walk to forty-one-year-old Davey Lopes, pinch-hitting for Calhoun. He threw a fastball to Bill Doran that Doran laced to left field, moving Lopes to second. Hatcher, already a hero once, came to the plate and again Orosco offered a fastball. Hatcher pounded it to center field, scoring Lopes. Orosco got Denny Walling to ground out, but then let up another hit, to Glenn Davis, a soft fly to center that Dykstra misjudged, with a late jump. Now it was 7–6, with Astros on first and second, and two out. Kevin Bass, a switch-hitter with good power from the right side, was at the plate, and Johnson declined to make a switch to righty Doug Sisk. He stuck with Orosco. Hernandez, knowing Bass was a good fastball pitcher, and tired of seeing the Astros swat around everything Orosco threw that was not a slider, told Gary Carter, "Kid, if you call another fastball, I'm going to come to home plate and we're going to have to fight." Carter responded, "We're not going to fight." And so it was all sliders. One in at Bass's ankles for a swing and miss. The next so far outside it nearly jumped past Carter. A third back at Bass's ankles for another swinging strike. A fourth in the dirt that Bass managed to hold off. A fifth that hung off the plate and dove late, but too late for Brocklander to give him the strike call, running the count to 3-2. And finally, a near-perfect slider that dropped just out of the strike zone and got Bass to chase, for the game-winner. Orosco leapt, his hands over his head, his glove flung toward the heavens, or, at least, toward the painted glass of the dome. The Mets would be going to the World Series. They would not face Mike Scott again in 1986.

Johnson, speaking perhaps for baseball fans across New York, described the physical trauma of witnessing a game like that. "I came out of this one with a headache," he said. "Normally, the stomach gives me a problem, but this time I developed a headache in the ninth inning. I took some aspirin. And I took some more in the 14th." But with the win and a chance at the championship secure, Johnson said, "I just got a pardon."

PART V

Reckoning

32

To HIS FACE, YOU COULD call Carmine Persico "Junior" or "Carmine," but the moniker you would probably want to avoid was the one most used behind his back: the Snake. It was fitting, though, because all through his rise from a truant kid in the Red Hook neighborhood to the top of the Colombo family, Persico had been known as especially violent, quick-tempered, and duplicitous. That reputation could be traced back to the summer of 1961, when Persico had arranged a meeting with friend and associate Larry Gallo at the Sahara Club in Brooklyn. Persico and Gallo were supposed to discuss strategy in their battle against Mob boss Joe Profaci, who had been skimming too much profit from the rackets Persico and Gallo had been running. Instead, Profaci got to Persico and offered him a bigger cut of profits if he would betray Gallo. That was all it took. When Gallo entered the club, Persico jumped toward him from behind and wrapped a rope around his neck. It was Gallo's good luck that a police sergeant happened to enter the club before the hit was complete, and Persico bolted, leaving Gallo wheezing on the floor and opening a long, bloody war between the Gallo and Profaci factions. Persico, the following year, was ambushed while in traffic heading downtown, taking three bullets, including one to his teeth. He survived, though, and even spat out the bullet that hit his mouth. His attempt at the Gallo murder fell short, but Persico's reputation was made. He was the Snake.

Persico had been brought in late to the roster of defendants at the Commission trial, and he proved to be a beneficial addition for lead prosecutor Michael Chertoff. In the weeks before the trial, Persico let Judge Richard Owen know that he planned to represent himself. The lawyers and other seven defendants tried to talk him out of it, but it was useless. Of the chiefs of the five Mafia families who were facing trial as part of the Commission case the following month, Persico was the most hard-headed, and agreed to a hearing before Owen to argue for his ability to defend himself. Persico's reasoning was simple: He had been through the legal system so many times over the years, going back to his involvement in a truck hijacking in 1959, that he had as much expertise as any lawyer he could hire. Perhaps of more importance was Persico's drained legal fund—Persico and the Colombo family had only recently been found guilty on racketeering charges for a trial that had taken eight months, and Persico's lawyer, Frank Lopez, said he had not been paid for at least a year. Another motivation: Persico was not on any of the recordings that the prosecution would be presenting, because he had been in jail when most of the recordings were made. He would do well to keep himself separate from the others in the minds of the jury. At the hearing, Owen, who was skeptical of the request, questioned Persico closely, warning him that by representing himself he was taking away, from all defendants in the case, any right to appeal on the grounds of incompetent counsel. But Persico stood by his intention. "I've had quite a bit of experience with the Federal Government," he said. "I intend to try this case the best way I know how." And, because the law said that anyone could represent themselves if they were of sound mind, Owen had no choice but to accept Persico's request. Persico was pleased. His co-defendants were not. He shrugged them off, however. "I had a good attorney," Persico said, "but I just felt he was getting tired after all these years."

None of the defendants in the case were testifying, and the only voice jurors would hear from their table would be that of Persico. He was dapper for his opening statement, dressed lawyerly in a black pin-striped suit and red tie, with gold-rimmed glasses. He was fifty-three, but the scant hair on his head and bulbous bags under his eyes made him look older, more worn. He had notes, and flipped awkwardly through them, his abrasive manner smoothed by his soft, even tone. "I guess you all know my name is Carmine Persico," he began, "and I'm not a lawyer, I'm a defendant." After a pause and a consultation with his papers, he said, "Bear with me, please, I'm a little nervous." Persico was charming the jury, and if there was some hope to be taken for defense lawyers from his self-representation gambit, it was that Persico would somehow put a sympathetic face on the accused mobsters. Persico said the prosecution would try to intimidate the jury by attaching the word *Mafia* to his name. Do not, he warned, "be blinded by labels."

Persico added that no matter how the government tried to smear the defendants, if there were an underdog in the case, it was not the government. "They are going to bring people that committed murder, committed extortion, bribery, every crime you could think of," he said. They would use testimony from "dope dealers who polluted the city with dope, drugs," and it would all be paid for "with your money, and my freedom." The defense, Persico reminded jurors, could not recruit witnesses. "I can't tell a witness that's in jail, 'Come and testify for me, I'll give you freedom,'" Perisco said. "They're powerful people. Not me." If Persico was trying to score points with the jury, he appeared to be doing so in the early going. Actors James Caan and Robert Duvall, of *The Godfather* fame, came to watch Persico (Caan had also shown up at Persico's previous trial), and *People* magazine ran a feature article on his stint as a barrister, with New York University law professor Harry Subin saying Persico was coming across as an underdog. "The law is so stylized," Subin said, "that he may be doing a very clever thing. The jury may just want to hear someone tell his story."

But Chertoff figured he just needed to bide his time. "The problem you have when you represent yourself is you have yourself as a lawyer," Chertoff said. Persico was a man with a quick temper, which could not be suppressed over an eight-week trial. After listening to the first witness in the case, former Colombo associate Joe Cantalupo, testify about a beating he had been given by Persico's brother, Allie Boy Persico, in a Brooklyn social club over an unpaid debt, Persico seemed insistent on justifying the violence his brother had used. "You was angry because you was beat up, and you was beat up because you didn't pay back the money," Persico said. The statement from Persico, according to James B. Jacobs (another NYU law professor), "may have backfired by revealing Persico's own involvement in loansharking." Persico continued with the second witness to take the stand, Fred DeChristopher, who was married to Persico's cousin and had provided him a hideout at his house for three months when Persico was on the run the previous year. DeChristopher was a lynchpin witness against Persico, because there was scant evidence tying him to the RICO crimes. He testified that Persico told him the Commission had authorized the hit on Carmine Galante, though Persico said he was personally opposed. Eventually, DeChristopher turned in Persico, collecting a $50,000 reward, and when Persico had a chance to cross-examine him, the testimony got testy. Persico told DeChristopher, an insurance broker for whom Persico claimed to have supplied clients, that he had been so broke, "You couldn't even buy socks."

"You'd like to see me down in the sewer," an angry DeChristopher responded. "Wouldn't you like to see me down in the sewer completely?"

Persico paused and said, "I don't think the judge would permit me to answer that question."

"I know what your answer would be," DeChristopher said. "This ain't a sit [sit-down], this a court!"

"Do you go on sits?"

"No," DeChristopher said, still angry. "You do."

If Persico had created a well of goodwill in his plainspoken opening statement, that goodwill was dried up by the third week of the trial. That was the difficulty about representing himself. "Inevitably, what that does is, the advantage for the defendant is he gets to 'testify' without a cross examination," Chertoff said. "The disadvantage is the jury gets to see you. From Persico's interaction with DeChristopher, it was clear they know each other, because the body language, the human nature. So he wound up making the case against himself. Occasionally, he would slip and say, 'You knew when I said that, that was not what I meant.' Which, in a sense, subconsciously validates the testimony."

. . . . .

Chertoff put forward a painstakingly detailed case against the Commission. But the goal was to tell a story, create a narrative, and sweep the jury along in it. He had to demonstrate that the Commission was a disciplined, organized governing body, like a board of directors of a major company, not a loose and powerless group of elderly Italian men who just liked to meet up every once in a while. The plan he and Giuliani put together used Joe Bonanno's book as a guide. (Giuliani had tried to force Bonanno to testify but he refused and was briefly jailed; instead, Chertoff played Bonanno's interview on *60 Minutes* for the jury.) Chertoff went through the history of the Mafia in the United States, from the early arrival of organized crime at the turn of the century, to the formation of the Commission in 1931 to the progression of bosses of the five families over time, showing how one succeeded the other and how, through that succession, the Commission remained intact. That was important—the more he could emphasize the "organized" aspect of organized crime, the more effective the RICO case would be. He called seventy-five-year-old former Cleveland underboss Angelo Lonardo, whose connections to the Mafia dating back to the 1930s allowed him to discuss the careers of Mob-boss legends like Albert Anastasia, Vito Genovese, and Joseph Colombo. He gave gripping testimony about the traditions of the Mafia, describing an induction ceremony at the Statler Hotel in which he was presented with a cloth and, when the cloth was removed, a gun and dagger sat underneath. "That is the way you live now," he recalled being told, "you live with the gun and the dagger, and you die with the gun and the dagger." He described the dominance of the Commission over all facets of the Mafia, how it made the rules, "What you can do, what you can't do," he said. To show that the Commission carried weight even in Cleveland,

Chertoff had Lonardo point out the boss he recognized, the one who oversaw his group. He pointed to Tony Salerno. "People used to refer to him as Fat Tony," Lonardo said, "but he's a little thinner."

But the star testimony came from the defendants themselves, on the hours of tapes that Chertoff played for the jury. The tapes confirmed the structure and organization of the Mafia, with the Commission at the top. In one, recorded at Fat Tony Salerno's Palma Boys Club in 1984, Salerno is heard explaining to a Genovese capo the Commission's stance on the dysfunction in the Bonanno family, which was still heavily involved in the drug trade and had not fully settled its leadership question in the wake of Carmine Galante's murder. Rusty Rastelli had approached the bosses of the other four families to firm up his status as the Bonanno head, but Salerno was not ready to grant him status. "I told the Commission," Salerno said, "'Hey, listen, this guy wants to be the boss. He can be the boss as far as I'm concerned,' I said, 'but he cannot be on the Commission.' One vote is enough to throw it out, 'cause the Commission thing, it's supposed to be a sacred thing." Further evidence of the Commission's supremacy came in tapes recorded just after Joe Bonanno's *60 Minutes* interview. In discussing Bonanno's appearance, Tony Ducks Corallo told Lucchese underboss Tom Mix Santoro, incredulously, "He was even saying there was a Commission, he admitted there was a Commission." Castellano was similarly concerned about Bonanno's TV spot, caught on tape saying "They're going to make us one tremendous conspiracy." There was also a discussion between Corallo and Sal Avellino in the Jaguar from 1983, concerning a *New York Times* article about the infiltration of the Mafia into legitimate business. The story pointed out that Corallo was the Lucchese family head, with Santoro running its business enterprises in the Bronx and Christy "Tick" Furnari in Brooklyn. Avellino ticked off the aboveboard businesses Corallo was said to run—waste disposal, the Garment Center, construction.

"Yeah, sure," Corallo said to Avellino. "Didn't you know that?"

"Course I know that. I know it because I'm with you, but not everybody else knows."

"Yeah, well, they ain't *supposed* to know," Corallo said, laughing—and confirming his status as the head of the family.

The tapes also provided vivid descriptions of the Mob's criminal nature. Corallo and Avellino discussed what ought to happen to members of any family who are caught dealing in narcotics. "Now I couldn't be any plainer that I was with some of these guys 'cause I don't want anybody fucking with junk, they gotta be killed," Corallo said. "That's all." There were extensive discussions about the operations of the Concrete Club, the very existence of which was a pillar of the RICO charges levied against the Commission. There was a tape of one contractor, Sal D'Ambrosi, pressing concrete union president (and Colombo soldier) Ralph Scopo on being allowed to do a $12 million job. D'Ambrosi was not one of the seven chosen contractors in the Concrete Club, and was not allowed to take on a job worth more than $2 million. Frustrated, he asked Scopo, "Who do I gotta see? Tell me who I gotta go see?" Scopo replied, "You gotta see every family. And they're gonna tell you no, so don't even bother." Paul Castellano's dominance of the construction field (he had made nearly $1.5 million in a four-year span off construction projects) was a frequent topic, often frustrating his fellow bosses. The bug in Castellano's home had him expressing some concerns to a labor union official over Century-Maxim concrete, which was, according to Castellano, "raiding everybody." When Castellano said "It's a pain in the ass, isn't it?" the union official agreed. "You would think they'd be big boys," he said. "Go according to some rules like, right?" One Gambino family soldier, Angelo Ruggiero, was caught talking about underboss (and Castellano enemy) Neil Dellacroce's frustration with the Commission's focus on construction. "He's disgusted with construction," Ruggiero said. "He said, 'They meet for construction.' He said, 'I can't believe it. That's all they talk about is money. Money, money, money.'"

There were lighter moments, also on tape, though not all made it to trial. Ed McDonald, the chief of the Organized Crime Strike Force in Brooklyn, remembered when the Castellano bug first went up, he was certain agents would be privy to a constant stream of hits being planned and unions manipulated. Instead, McDonald said, "Audibility was difficult, and it was hard to come up with what they were talking about. And a lot of times, they were just talking about nothing. I mean, they were talking about what's better, Beck's or Heineken? They were talking about what they had for dinner the night before. Eventually, there was a goldmine there about Castellano and his racketeering activity. But when you first started listening, there was a lot about his grandkids, too."

At one point, Corallo was visiting with Salerno at the Palma Boys Club, and the two septuagenarian bosses commiserated over the insolence of the young members they were trying to keep in line. "Listen, Tony," Salerno said, "if it wasn't for me, there wouldn't be no mob left. I made all the guys." Salerno told Corallo he'd suffered the indignity of one underling calling him "Fat Tony" to his face. "I know the way he talks," Corallo said. "Shoot him. Get rid of them. Shoot them. Kill them. But you can't go on—it's disgusting." There was some irony, too. One tape had Salerno ruminating on Corallo's misfortune, after the bug in his Jaguar had been discovered. An associate told him, "Jesus Christ, you know you gotta be careful where you talk any place, you gotta be careful." Salerno said Corallo could hardly be blamed, though, because everybody talks in their car, and noted, as the tapes were rolling, "I talk."

The Jaguar bug also caught Sal Avellino having a philosophical moment with his boss, pondering the usefulness of the lives they were leading. "We have to think about it," Avellino said. "That the life was good enough for you, if we really believe in it, why wouldn't we want our son? If I were a doctor, I would be saying to my son, since he's a little kid, you're going to be a doctor. Or if I was a lawyer, I would be looking for my son to be a lawyer. So they must feel that if this life is good enough for me, I still want it for my son also. Otherwise, we're really saying that this fucking life is no fucking good. It's for the birds."

33

IN MOST SEASONS, THE METS and Yankees would find a date in the spring when both teams were off and take part in a charitable game for the Mayor's Trophy. It was a fundraiser to support amateur baseball in New York, but the Yankees being the Yankees, the game had proven too difficult to schedule for the past three seasons. The Mets gave up. Instead, they joined with the Red Sox and, on an open date back in September, traveled to Boston to play an exhibition at Fenway Park. When the game was planned, there was no way of knowing that the Mets would be dominating the National League, or that they would survive a dramatic six-game series against the Astros, with the final two games running 28 innings total and four of the games decided by one run. Nor could it have been predicted that the Red Sox, for much of the 1986 season, would be the top team in the American League, with 95 wins, the third-most potent offense in the league, and a surprisingly effective corps of pitchers. That the two franchises would be in this position had been the longshot hope of Boston general manager Lou Gorman, who had joined the Red Sox in 1984 after working under Frank Cashen in New York for four years. Gorman, a New England native and fan of the Red Sox as a kid, would never have left the Mets, he said, except for the Red Sox job. Before he left, he had helped construct the core of the current Mets, advising on the drafting of young stars like Dwight Gooden and Darryl Strawberry, the trades that had brought in Ron Darling, Sid Fernandez, and Keith Hernandez—and, yes, the less-stellar George Foster deal, but also the acquisition of budding prospects Lenny Dykstra and Kevin Mitchell. Watching the players he had helped bring together flourish in 1986, he marveled at how far they had come from his first spring with the team, which had lost 99 games the previous year. "We were starting at the beginning," Gorman said. "I remember going to training camp and watching the team and saying, 'We've got a lot of work to do.' The team had been spending no money. There wasn't much talent."

There was an overflow of talent at Fenway on the day of the exhibition, though. Before the game, on the mound, Gooden and Red Sox ace Roger Clemens posed for a forced-smile photo surrounded by whirring cameras. The picture was a what-if for New York, because the Mets had drafted Clemens out of junior college in the twelfth round in 1981, but had not signed him. Joe Torre and Bob Gibson, then the Mets' manager and pitching coach, went to watch Clemens pitch a high school game after the draft, but came away unimpressed and the Mets' offer to the hulking righty was not enough to dissuade him from going on to the University of Texas. Clemens recalled that his father had died around the time of the draft, and his family was reliant on his Social Security benefits. Had Clemens signed with the Mets, the benefits would be gone. It was too risky. It was a good decision, in the end. Clemens starred for the Longhorns for two years, and was a first-rounder for Boston in 1983. As he stood next to Gooden being pho-tographed, Clemens was the anchor for the Red Sox staff, had already hit the 20-win mark, and had set a record by striking out 20 Seattle Mariners back in April. "I struck out 16 once," Gooden said, "and I thought that was a lot."

The game itself was meaningless, of course. Boston pitcher Joe Sambito teased some of his former Mets teammates when he pulled open his Red Sox jersey to reveal the T-shirt he was wearing under-neath: "Houston Police 4 – New York Mets 0." Mets pitcher Bob Ojeda, who had left the Red Sox the previous season, was hit in the face with a pie in a friendly-fire sneak attack by Red Sox pitchers Al Nipper and Bruce Hurst. It was a nice boost, particularly for a Red Sox team trying to put behind it some of the tribulations of recent weeks. Just before the All-Star Game, pitcher Dennis "Oil Can" Boyd had a public meltdown when AL manager Dick Howser had declined to pick him for the game, despite his 11–6 record and 3.71 ERA. He accused Howser and baseball of racism, walked out on the team, and was sus-pended by the Red Sox. During that time, Boyd had a run-in with police after being spotted in conversation with a known drug dealer, and though Boyd insisted he was roughed up by police and did not have drugs on him, charges of disorderly conduct were filed. It was only by luck that Boyd was drug-free at the moment, it turned out. He had become hooked on crack cocaine during spring training in Florida, and admitted later to smoking crack throughout the 1986 season, including one game in May that he pitched while on crack. Boyd was on suspension for twenty-one days. He eventually apologized and returned to the team, but was much different. Hurt by the stories he had seen in the papers about him during his absence, he no longer joked and rambled with a grateful media. He was not quite the same on the mound, either, and still maintained that the police had injured his arm during their scuffle. In his final 14 starts, he went 6–5 with a 4.20 ERA.

The Mets won, 7–3. But for Lou Gorman, seeing the two teams he had helped build on the field together, with both leading their respective leagues, was a bit overwhelming. He was asked, what might happen if, a month later, the scene were to be reprised, only with a World Series at stake? Gorman could only shake his head. The thought was too much.

. . . . .

After Game Six in Houston, the Mets were beset by a dangerous mix of exhaustion and elation. In the Astrodome locker room, the bottles of Great Western champagne flowed freely, Jesse Orosco chatted proudly with reporters (he had won a record three games in the series), a crew of Dwight Gooden, Ron Darling, Sid Fernandez, and Rick Aguilera staged a dance routine, and Kevin Mitchell, for reasons unclear, had been in the team whirlpool with his uniform on, then stalked the locker room wearing a Mr. T mask. General manager Frank Cashen, somehow unmoved by the emotion of a trip to the World Series, was being interviewed by ABC when relief pitcher Randy Niemann strode up and doused him with champagne. Cashen grumbled. "It's always those who do the least who celebrate the most," Cashen said of Niemann on TV, taking on what *Post* writer Phil Mushnick called "a national image as a party-pooper." (Cashen, in his autobiography, referred to celebratory champagne showers as an "idiotic tradition.")

But Cashen's crankiness was just beginning. When the Mets finally rounded themselves out of the visiting locker room and into the team plane, the excess did not stop. Prior to the start of the playoffs, Cashen had been formally approached by Knight and Darling with a request that wives, forbidden to travel with the team, be allowed to join the team on the trips to Houston—they would be a calming influence, the argument went. Cashen acceded, reluctantly. On the team plane, though, the wives were partaking in hard liquor every bit as much as their husbands, and were no calming influence. Thirty years later, the *New York Post*'s Mike Vaccaro described the four-hour flight as "equal parts airborne clubhouse and rock-and-roll tour bus, with a dash of Caligula thrown in." Dwight Gooden would later say, "The plane was like the afterparty." Seats on the plane were broken, pillows were tossed, the seat pockets were filled with vomit. At one point, the door of the lavatory accidentally flew open, and one player was seen bent over a mound of cocaine. "We all saw it," Gooden said, "and we decided, 'Nope, we didn't see anything.'" Rumor was that the player was Wally Backman, who was so upset about the persistence of that chatter that he went to Cashen and told him it was not true. "I never got away from the rumor altogether," Backman would later say, ruefully. The ordeal was topped by a legendary food fight—salad items flung, dinner rolls hurled by major-league pitchers, cake splattered in the aisles and on the walls. When the team arrived in New York early the next morning, greeted by hordes of fans, the players and wives left a disaster scene in their wake.

Cashen, again playing the part of stickler vice principal, was so angry over the condition of the plane and the $7,000 in charges the airline levied against the team for cleanup that, the next day, he presented Johnson with a bill and said he thought the players should pay. Johnson brought the bill to his team and showed it to them. "Well," said Johnson (in one of many iterations of the story), "do you know what I think? I think in the next four games you'll probably put enough money in these guys' pockets to cover this. So fuck this bullshit!" Johnson tore the bill up, sending the Mets properly riled into the World Series matchup against Boston, which had managed to survive its own seven-game thriller of a series against the Angels in the American League. For both teams, there would not be much time for recuperation. Each series had closed on October 15, and the opener of the World Series was slated for the eighteenth. For the Red Sox, though, the difference was that their drama had unfolded in Game Five, when they trailed the Series, 3–1, and were losing in the game, 5–2, in the ninth inning. But they rallied to win that game and blew out the Angels in Games Six and Seven, by a combined score of 18–5. The Red Sox had momentum, while the Mets showed up for the final title push bleary-eyed from their epic in Houston and recovering from the flight that followed.

It showed on the field. In the opener, Red Sox lefty Bruce Hurst was untouchable, allowing just four hits over eight innings, while former Mets reliever Calvin Schiraldi pitched the ninth, allowing just one walk. The Mets mounted only minor rallies, the one with the most potential coming in the sixth inning, when Hernandez walked and Carter followed with a single. Darryl Strawberry had a chance to give the Mets a lead, but struck out watching a floating Hurst curveball to a chorus of Shea Stadium boos. Knight followed with a hard grounder to third base that went for a double play to end the threat. In the top of the seventh, Mets pitcher Ron Darling allowed a walk to Red Sox slugger Jim Rice, who moved up to second base on a wild pitch. Catcher Rich Gedman came to the plate to face Darling in a matchup he had been looking forward to for a while. Gedman and Darling had gone to competing high schools in Massachusetts, Darling to St. John's Prep in Danvers and Gedman to St. Peter's-Marian in Worcester. Gedman recalled facing Darling once, as a senior during Darling's sophomore year. But second and third base were open, so Darling gave him an intentional walk. "I hope I get a chance to swing the bat," Gedman said. With Rice on second, Gedman did, and poked a ground ball to the right side that evoked the trashing of the Shea infield back when the Mets clinched the previous month. The ball did not take the hop that second baseman Tim Teufel was expecting, and slipped underneath his glove. That was all the scoring Boston would need in Game One, winning, 1–0. Boston's bats were much livelier in Game Two, as the heralded matchup between Gooden and Clemens fizzled. Gooden was knocked around for six runs in five innings, and Clemens was pulled in the fifth, two strikeout masters combining for just nine in the game. Three hits from Rice and home runs from Dwight Evans and Dave Henderson helped the Red Sox cruise, 9–3.

Four days removed from their historic win in Houston and three days after Johnson tore up Cashen's bill, the Mets were reeling. They had been the best offensive team in the National League in the regular season, but after their struggles at the plate against the Astros, the bats remained silent against Boston. They were just 12-for-62 in the first two games, a .194 batting average, and all 12 hits were singles. Tension was building. From the Red Sox, outfielder Evans was accusing Lenny Dykstra of using a corked bat, a possibility the Astros had raised in the previous series. From within the Mets, Strawberry's home-field jinx, which had hung over him throughout the 1986 season, seemed to be back. He went 0-for-6 in the first two games, and the anger of the Shea denizens returned. Darling was not happy with the timidity of the crowd at Shea, which he surmised had been overtaken by yuppies who could afford the more expensive playoff seats. "People were sitting on their hands, it's a joke," Darling said. "These aren't the regular-season fans; these are guys in $500 suits. . . . I don't want guys out there talking about how much money they've made. Give me the guy with the T-shirt, the sweatshirt and the bottle of blackberry brandy." Knight was benched for Howard Johnson in Game Two, Davey Johnson explaining that he would need to get Howard Johnson some at-bats so he could be ready to act as a designated hitter when the series shifted to Boston. Knight was not buying it. He said after the game he was "hurt and frustrated." Asked about it, Davey Johnson said, "He said he didn't like me much today. I told him, 'I wouldn't expect you to.' But we're hitting .180 and that's a cause of concern for me."

Columnist Jerry Izenberg offered a theory on the Mets' struggles: Even now, this team was still being befuddled by Mike Scott. "Can it be," Izenberg wrote, "that the mystical dust with which the Astros' Mike Scott sprinkled them in the playoffs has become a sort of between-the-foul-lines type of athlete's foot that simply keeps coming back every time you think it's gone away? Scott may be out of their lives but the disease lingered on in Games 1 and 2."

34

IN SEVEN SEASONS SPENT AS an NFL quarterback in New York, one thing Phil Simms had learned was how to win the approval and love of the locals. "The way to get cheered in New York," Simms said, "is to be a backup. They love backups."

The problem for Simms was that, since he had been drafted out of Morehead State in 1979—a pick made by then-coach Ray Perkins, who was booed for making it—he mostly had been a starter. He took over as a rookie when the team started 0–5, and led the Giants to six wins in his first eight games before closing out on a three-game losing streak. For a team that had been looking to Joe Pisarcik, Randy Dean, and Jerry Golsteyn to man the quarterback spot in the years before Simms was drafted, his arrival was met with both wide-eyed excitement and nail-biting trepidation. He was very good in his rookie year, but you could pardon Giants fans, whose teams had not been to the postseason since 1963, for remaining wary. Their team had more than its share of Pisarciks, but it had also been sold on would-be savior quarterbacks who somehow arrived in the Giants locker room and were wiped clean of their ability to win football games. Fran Tarkenton had arrived in New York from the Vikings in 1967 as a twenty-seven-year-old in the prime of his career, went to four straight Pro Bowls, had just one season in which the Giants finished better than .500, and never reached the postseason. He went back to Minnesota at age thirty-two, and brought the Vikings to the playoffs in five of his final seven seasons in the league. Craig Morton was similar. He had been 10–4 in his final year as a starter in Dallas, before he lost the Cowboys job to Roger Staubach. He was shipped to the Giants during the 1974 season. In two-plus years with the Giants, though, Morton appeared to be washed up, the team posting an 8–25 record in his starts. The Giants sent him to Denver in 1977, where Morton went 12–2 and led the Broncos to a Super Bowl appearance.

With that history, Giants fans were justified to be more cautious than optimistic about Simms, and were assured that they were right when the team went 3–10 with him as the starter in 1980 and they watched him go down with a separated shoulder at the end of the season. He missed the last half of 1981 when he reinjured the shoulder, and when the Giants finally returned to the postseason that winter, it was with Scott Brunner as quarterback. Simms became a distant memory during the strike-shortened 1982 season, when a knee injury put him out for the entire year. Perkins, who had a stake in Simms's success, having risked a first-round pick on him, left the Giants after that season to take over for Bear Bryant in Alabama, moving Bill Parcells to the head coaching job. Simms, with just 10 games played in the past two years, was benched behind Brunner in Parcells's first season as coach, prompting a trade demand from Simms that won him few friends in the locker room, in the media, or among Giants fans. Parcells was set to give Simms a chance to earn the job by Week 5 of the 1983 season, but Simms broke his thumb in a backup appearance in a loss to the Eagles, and again he was out for the year. "As soon as it happened, I said, 'Damn it, there goes another season,'" Simms said. "Everything I ever wanted was right there in that game and to see it go was unbelievable."

Five seasons into his career, then, opinions of Simms ranged from him being either too fragile to handle an NFL starting job or simply being another monumental bust of a Giants quarterback. Linebacker Harry Carson remembered that, even when few cared about the Giants, when the team was consistently in the wasteland of fifth place in the division, the crowds still loved to harass Simms. "When the rest of the league was laughing at us, they'd introduce Phil, and he'd be booed," Carson said. "By the time we took the field, the fans would be throwing eggs, golf balls, and oranges." Not that it got better, necessarily, once Simms was healthy and granted the job unfettered by Parcells. He topped the 4,000-yard mark in 1984 and earned a Pro Bowl spot in 1985, but the love of the loge-dwellers remained elusive. That, Simms had come to understand, was just part of playing the position in New York, where everyone from Y. A. Tittle to Joe Namath had been booed. "They can be very mean," Simms said. "I've been called lousy so-and-so. I've been called everything. I've heard it so many times here. What can I do? What do you want me to do? All fans are fickle. They're all coaches. I've sat in the stands at other pro games here. The Knicks, the Yankees—you heard the same thing."

It was no surprise in Week 4 of the Giants' season, despite a win in Los Angeles over the Raiders to move to 2–1, that the fickle fans of the Meadowlands were letting Simms hear their disapproval once again with the Saints in town. Two weeks earlier, in the Giants' first win of the season, over the Chargers, he had been sacked four times and took one especially tough hit that had Simms on the turf. Receiver Lionel Manuel helped Simms up and told him he needed to come out of the game. "Lionel, I would never come out of the game," Simms told him. "I would not give the fans the fucking thrill of me coming out of the game." Things were expected to be easier against New Orleans. New York was a 10-point favorite over the lowly Saints in the game, but the team continued to look disjointed on both sides of the ball. The Joe Morris contract holdout had set them off course in the opener, but Morris had broken his nose against the Raiders, then had a bad reaction to medication given to him by the Giants' medical staff and remained bedridden. On the Giants' second possession, already trailing by a touchdown, with fewer than seven minutes elapsed in the game, the Saints ran a stunt blitz with linebacker Rickey Jackson, who split linemen and had a clear shot at Simms. Pressured, Simms hurried his throw, and no receivers reacted to help him. The ball floated into the arms of defensive back Dave Waymer, and as Simms hollered at his offensive line for the missed blocks on Jackson, the boos wafted down from the stands. After another New Orleans touchdown, Simms had a 3rd and-8 from the 35 yard line with about a minute to go in the opening quarter, and this time there was no blitz. Simms had time to survey the whole field, and when he finally threw to Solomon Miller, it was a low throw behind his target. Another interception, and more boos.

The Giants fell behind, 17–0, before Simms and tight end Mark Bavaro—who suffered a broken jaw in the game but returned to keep playing—got going. The Giants rallied for a field goal and a touchdown pass to Bavaro in the first half, and held the Saints scoreless in the second half, winning 20–17. Bavaro finished with seven catches and 110 yards. Comically tight-lipped even when he had not just broken a bone in his face, Bavaro did not have much to add after the win over New Orleans.

"I got to go for an X-ray," he mumbled when asked how he felt.

"I got to go for an X-ray," he answered when asked how his tooth, which was also cracked, felt.

"I got to go for an X-ray," he said, too, when asked how the injury had happened in the first place.

Bavaro had his jaw wired shut, but still played against St. Louis in Week 5, another slog of a win, 13–6. Bavaro caught only two passes, but drew double-teams throughout the game. Simms could not get the ball to his receivers, though, and was a miserable 8-for-24 passing for 104 yards. Two bits of good news, though: The game was on the road, and the Giants were 4–1.

35

BACK IN 1981, AS TRUMP Tower was taking its place on New York City's skyline, Donald Trump met artist Andy Warhol at one of Roy Cohn's birthday parties. Two months later, Trump and Warhol met again, and this time, Trump was interested in commissioning Warhol to do a series of paintings of Trump Tower that would adorn the residential portion of the building. "It was so strange," Warhol wrote in his diary. "These people are so rich. They talked about buying a building yesterday for $500 million or something. They raved about Balducci's lunch, but they just picked at it. . . . And they didn't have drinks. They all just had Tabs. He's a butch guy. Nothing was settled, but I'm going to do some paintings anyway, and show them to them." Warhol wound up doing eight paintings of the Tower—he later wondered why he had done so many—and Trump and his wife, Ivana, went down to see them. Warhol was proud of the work, black-and-white with tones of silver added, and even sprinkled with diamond dust. But when Warhol showed Trump the finished product, Trump did not seem to get it. "It was a mistake to do so many, I think it confused them. Mr. Trump was very upset that it wasn't color-coordinated. They have Angelo Donghia doing the decorating so they're going to come down with swatches of material so I can do the paintings to match the pinks and oranges. I think Trump's sort of cheap, though, I get that feeling. And Marc Balet who set up the whole thing was sort of shocked." Trump never bought the paintings from Warhol, who was resentful. He saw Ivana Trump two years later at another Cohn birthday party, and considered "telling her off," but Ivana managed to wriggle away before he could. A year after that, Warhol's opinion of the Trumps was settled: "I just hate the Trumps because they never bought my Trump Tower portraits. And I also hate them because the cabs on the upper level of their ugly Hyatt Hotel just back up traffic so badly around Grand Central now and it takes me so long to get home."

Buoyed by his manipulation of the USFL, which now lay in tatters in his wake, Donald Trump's celebrity blossomed nationally in the early and mid-'80s. For those who had experienced Trump up close, though—workers, journalists, fellow titans of the financial world—this was somewhat of a mystery. Warhol was not the only one who had grown to understand that Trump should be trusted at one's own peril. *New York Post* columnist Susan Mulcahy related the story of a meeting she and a colleague had with Trump in 1984, which began first with flattery, him mentioning how much he enjoyed the *Post*. Then, an attempt at modesty: He said he did not think his presence in the press was all that important. In the next breath, he asked if they had seen a feature about himself in the *Washington Post* (a three-page spread in which he was called "a paragon of energetic brilliance and the catalyst who brought back city living"), and pulled out a couple of copies of the out-of-town paper he just happened to have handy. Mulcahy was less interested in the flattery and more interested in rumors that had been floating about Trump buying land to be developed into a major project on the Upper West Side, and asked him about it. Trump shrugged. There was not much happening with the property, he said, at least not yet. Mulcahy went back to the paper and wrote about another Trump angle from their conversation. The next morning, she was flipping through the papers and was stunned to see a headline in the *Times*: TRUMP SET TO BUY LINCOLN WEST SITE. Insulted and angry, Mulcahy spoke to Trump by phone, and Trump explained he could not have told her about the purchase of the site because he had had a deal with the *Times*. Mulcahy later explained that "I don't think he realized that denying a story in an interview with one newspaper on the very day you're giving the same story to another newspaper is—how shall I put this?—not done. Not if you want to remain on speaking terms with the newspaper you screwed out of the story. . . . Either he didn't get it, or he got it quite coherently—and he didn't really give a damn. Take your pick."

Minneapolis Star and Tribune reporter Bob Sansavere had a bizarre encounter with Trump in 1985, as he was writing about the performance of quarterback Doug Flutie, a high-profile signing of Trump's New Jersey Generals who had been underperforming, and called the organization for a quote on Flutie. He was transferred to what was identified as an executive vice president of the Trump Organization, John Barron. In discussing Flutie, Barron freely let fly with his frustration about Flutie. Later, this Barron called back Sansavere to temper his earlier statements, saying that Trump himself was not pleased with the public criticism Flutie had gotten. But Sansavere—who had begun his career in New Jersey and had been to a number of Trump press conferences for the Generals—pointed out to Barron that his voice sounded exactly like that of Trump. Barron's response, incredibly: "Well, we went to school together, so we have the same intonations." Sansavere furrowed his brow. He had gone to school with plenty of classmates who did not come out the other side with the same voice as his. "I don't think the intonation had anything to do with it," Sansavere said, laughing. Curious, Sansavere called the Trump Organization the next day, looking to speak again to Barron. He could not be located, he was told, but without prompting, Sansavere was assured by one secretary that Barron, "absolutely exists." Sansavere took that to mean that Barron did not exist, that he was simply Trump speaking under a false identity. Sansavere had fun with it, though. He sought a spelling for his name, but was given three versions—Baron, Barron, and Barronne—by three people. He asked how long Barron had been with the company, and was first told he had been around a long time. He asked someone else, and was told Barron had just been hired. "I had a pretty good idea what was going on," Sansavere said. "Trump didn't deride Flutie's contract, but John Barron sure did. John Barron was quite vocal in saying how Flutie was not living up to what the contract was paying him. But Trump did not say it."

Well-respected longtime NFL writer Paul Zimmerman had a run-in with John Barron, too, when he called "Trump's PR man," with a USFL question. "Mr. Trump wants to know the tenor of your questioning," Zimmerman was told. "Tell Mr. Trump it's not a tenor, it's more of a baritone," Zimmerman joked, waiting for the chuckle at the other end of the line. Long silence. "Mr. Trump says he can't do the interview at this time," the unamused "PR man" replied.

Shortly after the release of his book *The Art of the Deal* in 1987, which had Trump's name on the front, but had been written by Tony Schwartz, Trump was putting on a press event to generate interest in an upcoming fight at one of his Atlantic City casinos. A pair of *New York Times* sportswriters approached him to thank him for the lunch spread, and began chatting. Trump brought up the success of his book to them, and said, "I guess that makes me a great writer, doesn't it?" One of the writers, Dave Anderson, replied, "Well, no, it makes Tony Schwartz a great writer." Trump, still unsmiling, stomped off.

. . . . . .

In 1938, more than a year after the death of her brother—William, the successful owner of the W. J. Wollman brokerage house, first in Kansas City, then in New York—a $5 million trust was set up to be overseen by Kate Wollman, who was directed by her brother's will to use the funds for "public charitable, educational or scientific purposes." Eleven years later, Ms. Wollman determined that one of those purposes should be a skating rink in Central Park, presented in honor of her parents. She wrote a $600,000 check to the city to cover the building of an ice rink in the southeastern corner of the park, near the lagoon, with the city providing $150,000 to establish infrastructure. The rink, a review at the time said, "fits gracefully into the rugged, natural contours, and the low, one-story semi-circular building to the north of the ice is neatly and cleanly designed." In addition to providing bathrooms, the building also "houses the refrigeration machinery which will make the rink usable for ice-skaters from October to late spring." When it was opened, just before Christmas in 1950 after a year of construction, it was hailed by Mayor Vincent Impellitieri as a "praise-worthy example of practical, public-spirited philanthropy."

Now, thirty-six years later, Mayor Ed Koch had accepted an unorthodox plan to refurbish the inner workings of the Wollman Rink. The original project was slated for two years and $9 million, with the goal of replacing a traditional brining system with a more efficient Freon tubing system, one that had never been tried before and involved laying twenty-two miles of coiled-up, thin-walled steel tubing filled with Freon underneath a concrete slab. The rebuilding got absurdly out of control. It was begun in 1980, and by mid-1986, the repairs were four years overdue and more than $3 million over budget. Installation of the new system had failed at just about every turn. In 1981, severe rain hit the rink and flooded the site, leaving the pipes covered in silt, which required a long and expensive cleaning process. In 1982, despite the pipes having been exposed for a year, the cement for the concrete slab was poured over them, and midway through the job, the contractor realized he had underestimated how much cement he would need. He diluted the rest of the cement to stretch it, and the resulting slab was too brittle and eventually cracked. Efforts to pressurize the pipes failed. There were too many leaks. In 1985, a regular Parks Department contractor—Arc Plumbing, keeper of Shea Stadium's dodgy pipes and employer of ace salesman John Gotti—was called in to add a gas line that might save the project. Instead, the new line made existing leaks worse, and because they were Freon, the leaks were invisible and very difficult to locate. The city spent $200,000 to have the problems further studied, and the resulting report determined that there was no way to tell what exactly had gone wrong, but that all the work that had been put into the rink to that point was useless. It would have to be torn up and restarted. The rink had become a fable for the inefficiency of government, and while the scandals of New York City had made Koch look somewhere between very naïve and personally corrupt, the bungling of the Wollman Rink job hit at the strength of Koch's reputation, which was that he was a very capable manager.

That is where Donald Trump inserted himself. To be clear: Koch despised Trump. "Ed thought he was a blowhard," Koch's press secretary, George Arzt, said. "Ed did not suffer blowhards well." Koch and Trump had a built a strange relationship over the years, built on dislike but bonded by political expediency. Koch had been good for builders in the city, and builders provided the bulk of his campaign financing. In the 1985 mayoral campaign, before the real political season had even opened, Trump donated $25,000 to Koch's reelection fund. It was money well spent. During his eight years in office, Koch had created a pro-business environment in New York from which Trump was one of the great beneficiaries, and Trump was not so blind as to ignore that. They had fought over the Trump Tower tax abatement, but at the topping-off ceremony for the building, Koch was there to read the toast and take pictures with Trump. Their battles had mostly been out of the public eye, and they usually offered tepid compliments of each other when asked. But things had changed for Trump as 1986 wore on. The levers he had relied upon in the past to gain favor throughout the city were more and more unavailable—Roy Cohn was dead, Stanley Friedman's trial was not going well in New Haven, and Trump's ability to pile up publicity as a pro sports owner was ending. Trump was going to have to begin going it alone. He went on a charm offensive, an attempt to win favor among the public in New York City, and with Koch's scandal troubles slapping down his own approval ratings, the mayor would make for an easy target.

In a letter dated May 28, beginning with the greeting, "Dear Ed," Trump wrote to Koch offering to repair the Wollman Rink himself if the city would allow him to take over the restaurant connected to the rink. "For many years I have watched with amazement as New York City repeatedly failed on its promises to complete and open the Wollman Skating Rink," Trump wrote. "During this six-year period I have constructed major hotels, apartment buildings and, in 26 months, Trump Tower, a highly sophisticated and complex mixed-use building containing shopping, offices and apartments. Building the Wollman Skating Rink, which essentially involves the pouring of a concrete slab, should take no more than four months' time." Koch found Trump's letter to be self-aggrandizing and obnoxious. That was always Koch's view on Trump, whom he later pegged as "a supreme, egotistical lightweight." Koch released Trump's letter to the newspapers, along with his own "Dear Donald" letter, which was packed with sarcasm, but broadly accepted Trump's offer. Hitting at Trump's penchant for slapping his name on any project he could, Koch admonished, "Remember, the Bible says that those who give charity anonymously or, if not anonymously, then without requiring the use of their names, are twice blessed," and finished, "With bated breath, I await your response." But Koch miscalculated. Where he saw Trump's me-first character in the letter containing the Wollman offer, the public saw generosity in the face of government incompetence. On June 6, the two sides sealed the deal. The city agreed to a $3 million deal with Trump, who said he would have Wollman Rink up and functional again by that winter. If the cost came in below the $3 million, Trump said he would donate the excess to a charity for the homeless. If it was over that number, Trump said he would pay it himself. Koch had to gulp deeply and swallow his pride to make the arrangement.

Trump got to work quickly on the rink. He induced contractors who had done big jobs for him in the past—and hoped to do more—to take on the task at above-average speed and with below-market rates. He had set a deadline of six months, and knew that without the oversight and regulations normally required for a municipal job, he could easily beat it. He did, by more than two months, and as the rink came together, Trump took every possible opportunity to let the city know it. By July, the site was recalibrated and in August, new pipes were beginning to be laid. Trump held a press conference to announce the beginning of the laying of the pipes, and to outline the remaining construction plans. In September, the pipes were finished and Trump held a press conference. The next day, the new slab for the concrete was poured, and Trump turned it into a ceremonial pouring of concrete, with the media invited yet again. Parks Department commissioner Henry Stern was there and noted he was glad the ceremony had not been scheduled for the following day, when the department was dedicating Diana Ross Playground. "I don't think Central Park is big enough for Donald Trump and Diana Ross in one day," Stern said. Trump had a press conference in late October to announce the ice was ready, and had another press conference three days later with skating champs Dick Button and Aja Zanova-Steindler. He went on CBS's *Newsmakers* program on November 9 to announce that the rink would open November 13, and that there would be a gala Grand Opening on November 15. "We went to the first few press conferences," Stern said, "but we stopped after a while. Normally, contractors don't call press conferences to announce their progress. But this was his reward."

36

AHEAD OF GAME THREE OF the World Series back in Boston, Red Sox second baseman Marty Barrett was asked about his expectations of playing for the championship, and how those matched up with reality. He was taken aback by the question. He had watched the National League's championship series, how the Mets and Astros battled, and he had been in the trenches of the AL's championship series, a seven-game win over the Angels. But through two games in New York? "I always thought that it would be filled with pressure," Barrett said, "that everyone would be out there saying, 'Oh, no, I hope they don't hit the ball to me.' It hasn't been like that at all. I remember just watching the Houston-Mets series on television and my palms would be sweating. I thought that's the way it would be, playing the game. It hasn't been like that at all." The Red Sox were up 2–0 in the series, which they had begun as 12-to-5 underdogs, and had not trailed or been tied. The *Boston Globe* ran a column from legendary writer Leigh Montville under the headline THEY MADE IT LOOK EASY, as though the thing had been won already. Mets first baseman Keith Hernandez was asked about losing two at home, and replied that the Royals had lost their first two in Kansas City the previous year and still won the series. True, the gathered media types told Hernandez, but those Royals had been the first team in World Series history to come back and win the championship that way. Hernandez sneered, "I didn't say it would be easy."

At his press conference for Game Three, Red Sox starter Dennis "Oil Can" Boyd, who had undergone his very public battles with the team and media over the summer, charmed reporters. He weighed a little more than 150 pounds, but even with his slight frame, Boyd liked to wear his uniform pants low, dangling over his socks. "I mean, there's an old-time feeling that kind of possesses me and takes me back to the '30s and '40s," Boyd said. "I think of myself as Satchel [Paige] or one of the old-time players from the Negro Leagues with their baggy uniforms. I like the primitive culture of baseball." Boyd also said, when asked about the Mets, "I think I can master those guys," a dose of confidence reflective of all New England's feeling about the Red Sox. He had not mentioned that he was up much of the previous night, smoking crack, but it showed during the game. His confidence faded quickly on the third pitch Boyd threw, with Lenny Dykstra leading off. Dykstra faked a bunt on the second pitch, but then reached out and knocked a home run into Fenway's tight right field corner for a home run and a 1–0 lead. That was the first of four straight hits before Darryl Strawberry struck out swinging, which was followed by an out from Ray Knight and another hit by Danny Heep. By the time Boyd got off the mound, he was down, 4–0, with the Red Sox unable to start anything against Bob Ojeda. Boyd recovered to pitch into the seventh, but a two-run single from Gary Carter and an RBI double by Knight gave the Mets a breeze of a win, 7–1. And there was an added bright spot heading into the rest of the series: Strawberry, after starting

0-for-9 with five strikeouts, finally broke through with his first World Series hit, a single to center field to start the eighth inning. Working with Strawberry in the cage under Fenway before Game Three, hitting coach Bill Robinson had him focus on keeping his shoulder tucked early in his swing, then had sharp words for reporters, saying, "I think it's unfair that you people are looking for a scapegoat. . . . He does have mental lapses as most young kids do. But he's still a baby as far as hitting." Strawberry was still grown up in Game Four, when he hit a big double off of Fenway's Green Monster wall in left field in the fourth inning, and scored on a Ray Knight single that gave pitcher Ron Darling a 3–0 lead. Strawberry was 2-for-4 in the game, but it was Gary Carter who was the star, with two home runs and three RBIs. Carter, a dead-pull hitter, was thriving at Fenway, with six RBIs in two games. He lived up to his nickname—"Camera" for his media friendliness—in the postgame press conference, when he arrived in the Series' auxiliary interview room and was asked to make an opening statement. "How much time do I have?" Carter asked.

For Game Five, Mets manager Davey Johnson did not even consider a change away from his scheduled starter, Dwight Gooden, on three days' rest. He had Sid Fernandez, an All-Star who had gone 16–6 on the season, in the bullpen, having pitched just one-third of an inning in eleven days. But because Fernandez was a lefty who would invite Boston's right-handed sluggers to pummel the tight left-field wall, Johnson stuck with Gooden, who had been yanked after the fifth inning of Game Two after giving up six runs. Neither option was appealing, but Gooden having been the ace coming into the year, Johnson stayed with him. The Mets' manager would regret his choice. Gooden labored to get through the first inning, throwing 22 pitches and seemingly shy about unleashing his fastball. He gave up a walk (but the runner was picked off) and two hits, then hit designated hitter Don Baylor to load the bases. But he got a high fly ball to left field from Dwight Evans to end the inning without a run. He pitched on the edge of disaster from there, though, giving up just one run in the second after a one-out triple by Dave Henderson, escaping first-and-second with one out by allowing just one run in the third, and pitching out of a first-and-third jam in the fourth. He gave up a run on three hits to lead off the fifth, though, and Johnson had seen enough. He called for Fernandez, who got a strikeout, yielded a double, then recorded 10 straight outs to get the Mets into the eighth. He gave up a single and a double, but not a run, before Fernandez finished the Red Sox with a sterling line: four innings, three hits, no runs or walks, five strikeouts. Boston's Bruce Hurst battled through a complete game, giving up two runs for the 4–2 Game Five win. Strawberry, pummeled with chants of "DAR-ryl!" by the Fenway Park crowd throughout (he tipped his hat to them in the outfield) managed another hit in the series.

But the story after Game Five was Gooden. He had almost certainly pitched his final game of 1986, and the worry that he was not— and might never again be—the same pitcher he was in 1984 and 1985 was gaining some steam. He labeled his fastball, only recently in a category with Bob Gibson and Sandy Koufax, only "average" in Game Five. Baylor said he had had a look at Gooden's fastball and "thought of at least 10 pitchers in the American League who throw better." Mets beat writer Bob Klapisch postulated that Gooden had been undone by his dropping into a three-quarters delivery, and by adding too much weight over the course of the season—he was 215, up from the 180 he had been when he broke into the league two years earlier. Gooden conceded that his conditioning had been lacking. He would change that, he said, when he went back to Tampa in the offseason. "This winter," he said, "I've got to prepare for 1987."

Everyone else would be preparing for at least one more game, maybe two, both home games for the Mets. The Red Sox, playing for their first World Series win since 1918, would have two shots at finishing the job and would have Roger Clemens, arguably the best pitcher in baseball in 1986, on the mound. In the travel day between Games Five and Six, the *Post*'s Lyle Spencer wrote an appreciative column about thirty-six-year-old Red Sox first baseman Bill Buckner, who had been a Dodger in the early 1970s and had fought through a torn-up ankle with LA in 1975 to come back and play 11 productive seasons—including 1986, when he knocked in 102 runs. Spencer had been a beat reporter in LA during Buckner's Dodger days, and now, Buckner told him he was taking two anti-inflammatories a day to cope with the ankle pain, which had been exacerbated by an Achilles tendon injury. Buckner also had nine cortisone shots just to get through the 1986 season (three per year is the recommended limit), and laughed off the national attention he was getting for his special-fit high-top cleats and his ever-present limp. Spencer chalked it up to his humility, and if the Mets were going to win a World Series title, they would have to take it from an admirable player like Buckner. "Here is a man you can relate to, America, a real working-class hero," Spencer wrote. "Win or lose, hit or miss, he has moved us in a World Series that hasn't exactly been loaded with drama."

And with that, back they went to Shea, which was still not recovered completely from the September turf-tugging party that took place when the Mets clinched the East.

· · · · ·

Like Game Six in Houston, the initial stages of Game Six of the 1986 World Series were forgotten by the time the real drama unfolded. The Red Sox jumped on Mets starter Bob Ojeda quickly with a single by Wade Boggs, but there was an inkling that this would be no ordinary game when a begoggled man in a white jumpsuit came circling down from the night sky near the upper deck of the stadium with Buckner at the plate. A roar from the crowd arose as he approached, and on the television broadcast, a baffled Vin Scully noted, "Boy, this crowd came here to make some noise tonight." But the crowd was rooting on musician-actor-screenwriter Michael Sergio, who had leapt out of a 1964 Cessna 182 above Queens about five minutes earlier, pulled the cord on his parachute and floated downward as a spray-painted sheet reading "Go Mets!" flapped in the wind behind him. Sergio planned to land on home plate, but found that Gary Carter was not budging from his spot there, and landed between first base and the pitching mound. He was grinning, pumping his fists and chanting, "Go Mets!" He was corralled by police, led into the New York dugout, and high-fived by Ron

Darling—who partly inspired the stunt, when a group of skydivers that included Sergio saw Darling's comments about the poor crowd noise for the first two games at Shea. Sergio was then arrested. The Red Sox did rally to bring Boggs home on a double, setting up a daunting proposition for the Mets: No team in the series had come from behind to win a game, and the task got even more daunting when Clemens started by striking out six of the first 10 batters he faced and took a no-hitter into the fifth inning. But that was ended when a walk and a stolen base by Strawberry were followed by a single from Ray Knight, and a single from Mookie Wilson that was bobbled by Dwight Evans, the game's best right fielder, allowing Knight to advance to third. He then scored on a double play and tied the score, 2–2.

The Red Sox scored in the seventh, giving Clemens a 3–2 lead. He finished the seventh and, with 134 pitches on his right arm, was lifted from the game in the eighth inning when his spot in the batting order came around with one out and a runner on second—Red Sox manager John McNamara called on Mike Greenwell to pinch-hit against Roger McDowell, pulling back Clemens, who had his batting helmet on. This instant would be mangled by decades of memory-crunching in New England, with Clemens claiming he was pulled because of a blister that had popped in the fifth inning and McNamara sticking by the story he had given at his postgame press conference: "My pitcher told me he couldn't go any further." Either way, Boston needed reliever Calvin Schiraldi to get six outs to secure a Red Sox win and earn a World Series title. Lee Mazzilli, brought in to take George Foster's roster spot back in August, hit a single to right to start the eighth, and went to second on a Dykstra bunt that Schiraldi misplayed. Wally Backman moved Mazzilli to third with another bunt, and the Mets tied the game with a Carter sacrifice fly. The game remained 3–3 until the top of the 10th, when Rick Aguilera gave up a leadoff homer to Dave Henderson and the Red Sox tacked on an added run with a single by Marty Barrett. It was 5–3, Red Sox.

That's when more memories begin to collide. McNamara still recalls his reaction to what he remembers as Clemens asking out of the game: "You gotta be shitting me." Clemens recalls getting his bat and preparing to hit before being told McNamara was going with a pinch-hitter. Oil Can Boyd recalls standing next to McNamara hollering onto the field for much of the game's climax, because he knew that he would either be celebrating with a World Series championship or preparing to pitch Game Seven—and according to Boyd, Clemens never asked out of the game. Don Baylor would long wonder why, in the top of the eighth with the bases loaded and two out, McNamara did not call on him to pinch-hit for Buckner against lefty Jesse Orosco. Buckner and McNamara would deny it, but word in the Red Sox locker room had been that Buckner talked McNamara out of pinch-hitting for him. And there was Davey Johnson. He drew the ire of Strawberry when, in the ninth inning, he pulled a double-switch, moving Mazzilli to right field and inserting Aguilera, allowing Aguilera to pitch an extra inning by putting him in the number five spot but leaving Strawberry out of the game. That sent Strawberry into the locker room early, where he seethed and would remain seething no matter what the rest of the Mets did in the game. He would later tell reporters, "This is the one thing I'll never forget in my career. From now on, [Johnson] can keep his distance."

Schiraldi started the 10th with ease. He got Wally Backman to fly to left on an 0-2 count with a soft, defensive swing. Hernandez slashed a fly ball to the warning track in center field that sounded like danger off the bat, but landed harmlessly in the glove of Dave Henderson, whose smile still had not faded from his homer in the top of the inning—he was set to be the hero, as he had been for Boston in the ALCS with a dramatic Game Five homer.

That was when Frank Cashen, as Mets general manager, had the elevator from the press box held while he stood with team president Fred Wilpon. Cashen had gone from his booth just off press row to visit Mets owner Nelson Doubleday and suggest that they go briefly to the Red Sox locker room to congratulate Jean Yawkey, who had taken over as team owner after her husband Tom Yawkey passed away. Doubleday declined and said, "Frank, you handle it," instructing him to pass along his congratulations. In a nearby box, Bart Giamatti, the new president of the National League but an ardent lifelong Red Sox fan, was quietly hoping this would not be another in the long line of spectacular bungles by the team. Among the writers, the UPI's Fred McMane had already worked out his lead sentence: "Dave Henderson, playing the hero Boston has sought for 68 years, homered in the top of the 10th inning Saturday night, to give the Red Sox a 5–3 victory over the New York Mets. . . ."

The Shea Stadium scoreboard, for only a split second, read CON-GRATULATIONS RED SOX., before flicking off. Hernandez, somewhat dejected, went back into the clubhouse where Strawberry was, turned into Johnson's office, lit a cigarette, and opened a beer. Kevin Mitchell was in the locker room, too, taking off his uniform pants and working on his flight plans back home to California. But he was yanked away from his locker, with no time to put on his cup, when Gary Carter hit a single to left field, and the team needed a pinch-hitter.

Mitchell completed his scramble from the clubhouse, took a hand-ful of warm-up swings with his bat weighted, then took the plate against Schiraldi. He fouled a check swing off on the first pitch and punched a curveball left over the plate into center field to put runners on first and second. As rolls of toilet paper unfurled from the Shea Sta-dium upper deck, Ray Knight stood in, and fell behind, 0-2. The Red Sox were one strike away. "I was really numb," Knight said. "Like in a trance." Schiraldi put a fastball up on the inside part of the plate, but not far enough inside, and Knight did all he could with it—fist it with as much strength as he could muster, the hand strength Bill Robinson had worked with him to develop the previous spring. He hit an inside-out single to center. Carter scored. The score was 5–4. McNamara had seen enough. He would pull Schiraldi and bring in Bob Stanley. Even in his uniform, even in the depths of a World Series, Stanley resembled the anchor of a typical duckpin bowling league team. He had been an All-Star as a starter in 1979, converted to the bullpen, and was an All-Star again as a reliever in 1983. But by 1986, at thirty-one, he had faded into mop-up duty. When he joined McNamara at the press conference podium for Game Five back in Fenway, he was asked where he thought he ranked on the list of players invited to the media podium. "Probably 24th," Stanley had joked. "Everyone else was tired. I was well-rested."

In the visiting clubhouse, risers were erected while the lockers were plastered over in plastic and duct tape for the post-series celebration. A podium was set up for NBC's Bob Costas, who would interview Jean Yawkey and some of the Red Sox executives and players. Boyd, rumor would have it, had snuck back to have an early tilt of champagne (he would deny it, instead saying he was in the tunnel smoking a cigarette). The World Series trophy had been wheeled in, and commissioner Peter Ueberroth was on hand. Costas asked his producer what he should do if the Mets tied the game. "Get your ass out of there," he was told.

Mookie Wilson, who had been standing just off the plate as Carter scored, came up to face Stanley. Stanley got ahead of Wilson with a fouled-off sinker, then missed with two high, outside fastballs. Wilson fouled off two more inside sinkers, and another that flitted outside. On the seventh pitch of the at-bat, second baseman Marty Barrett snuck around to attempt a pickoff of Knight at second base, but Stanley missed the sign and never threw over—Knight appeared to be too far off second and would have been caught if Stanley had made the throw. Instead, he came inside with a sinker again, which Wilson had to leap to avoid. The ball rolled to the backstop, and Mitchell came home to tie the score without a throw from Rich Gedman.

Costas bolted from the locker room. Yawkey was ushered out of the room. The trophy, almost as quickly as it arrived in the Red Sox locker room, was wheeled back out.

Again, the toilet paper fell, and again, with the score 5–5, Wilson fouled off two more good offerings from Stanley. Wilson finally put a ball in play on the tenth pitch of the at-bat, a roller to Bill Buckner at first base. The ball hopped in front of the plate, took a big bounce— again, that Shea Stadium turf—and landed again just short of first base. The ball hopped awkwardly on its second bounce, as if loaded with topspin, and as Buckner adjusted behind first base, the ball slipped between his legs and into short right field. Knight, arms flailing as though he were in the midst of the butterfly stroke, scored from second base. Schiraldi, dazed, watched from the visiting bench. On the television broadcast, there were more than three minutes of silence from Scully and his cohorts, as they let shock and camerawork tell the story. This time the scoreboard got it right: WE WIN! Knight sprawled out, exhausted, on the home bench.

There would be a Game Seven. The Mets, again, got a pardon. But it was hard to care just then. "The only thing I want right now," Knight said, "is a soft pillow."

37

RUDY GIULIANI DID NOT MUCH like Stanley Friedman. His sense of public service and the moral rectitude it required was offended by Friedman, an operative who freely admitted that he traded in political and financial favors, and did not see anything wrong with it. During a recess near the trial's end, Friedman said to reporters, "This is the system. It may be deplorable, you may not like it—change the system." As a crusading prosecutor, Friedman's attitude made an easy target for Giuliani. While Giuliani had been mostly close-lipped during the trial when it came to the media, Friedman had been hammering his prosecutor in the newspapers, which ratcheted up the ill feeling. Friedman's line of attack was that Giuliani had singled him out only because he needed a target for a corruption case that would then vault him into the Senate or the mayor's chair. "If not for the political motivations of the United States Attorney, Mr. Giuliani," Friedman said, "and the fact that I was a ripe subject, being a political leader, this case never would have come to an indictment." As the Parking Violations Bureau trial wore on into the eight-week mark in New Haven, nerves grew more and more frayed. When one of Giuliani's assistants, William Schwartz, got up to speak while Judge Whitman Knapp was speaking, Knapp snapped at him to sit. "Mr. Schwartz," Knapp said, "you should take some Valium." But the personal tension between Friedman and Giuliani was densest, and boiled over into a profane shouting match. As one account of a sidebar conference with Knapp had it, "the argument ended with Mr. Giuliani and Mr. Friedman shouting vulgarities at each other outside the jury's hearing." Giuliani found Friedman to be a self-superior fraud. "Friedman took his beard off during the pretrial process—I can only guess—in order to make himself look less sinister," Giuliani later said. "What he could not do, however, is change his personality. And his personality was always very arrogant. Stanley Friedman was in politics for one primary reason, and that was to make money."

That would be the crux of Giuliani's closing argument against Friedman and his co-defendants. They had betrayed public trust to line their own pockets. Yes, the witnesses called by the prosecution in the case were not exemplary citizens, but their combined testimony painted a clear picture of a government department transformed into a well of cash for crooked politicians. Giuliani told the jury, in an impassioned and quivering voice, "These defendants were important participants in the total and absolute corruption of an agency of government. They did it for money. They did it for greed. They did it out of a perverted sense of what government is all about." The defense had not put up much of a case, and its entire strategy relied on picking apart the testimony of unreliable and guilt-ridden witnesses bought by the government with plea-bargained sentence reductions. Giuliani had introduced a wide array of witnesses, giving Puccio and the other defense lawyers grounds to create reasonable doubt. The lawyer for Michael Lazar told the jury, "Don't be misled by the number of witnesses the government calls. Each of the witnesses who testified against Michael Lazar, I submit, had a motive to lie. The same lie told by 100 liars is still a lie."

Puccio took the same tack, speaking to the jury for two-and-a-half hours. He focused on tearing down the testimony of Geoffrey Lindenauer, which would have been easier for him to do had he not been questioned for days by the defense's other lawyers. He heaped blame for the entire PVB enterprise on Donald Manes. He labeled Manes a liar, and pointed out the instances in which Manes had lied to Lindenauer, who admitted to lying himself—if Lindenauer was a liar and was getting his information from Manes, another liar, who knows what the truth could be? Puccio kept up his shaky Lindenauer-as-manipulator theme, too. "Why did Donald Manes feel he had to lie to Geoffrey Lindenauer? Because Donald Manes had created a monster—he created a person he could not control, who ultimately led to his demise." Puccio tackled one of his case's other weaknesses by conceding that Friedman was an influence peddler, but asserting that was no crime. Friedman was a respected politician, and those who spoke out against him did so because they were guilty and sought to avoid jail time. The choice was simple. "Stanley Friedman," Puccio said, "head-to-head, against the dregs of the earth."

But Puccio, and the defendants, knew their chances of acquittal were slim. In retrospect, Puccio wondered whether he had been over-confident coming off his defense of Claus von Bulow, believing he could successfully defend anyone. The wise advice for Friedman would have been to plead guilty in search of a light sentence, and offer some other political scalp for Giuliani to chase. It was unlikely that Friedman would have accepted that advice, considering his distorted sense of his own innocence. That certainty, combined with Puccio's hubris, had made the two, in Puccio's words, "an unhealthy marriage." They had talked themselves into believing they would win an unwinnable case. After three days of deliberation, the Connecticut jurors returned, and found Friedman and his three co-defendants guilty on all charges. On the stairs of the courthouse afterward, Giuliani addressed the media, saying, "This verdict is a very significant victory for the honest and decent citizens of New York City, who have had to labor under the yoke of people like Stanley Friedman for too darn long." Friedman, certain that Giuliani was using him to launch a political career, would say of Giuliani, after seeing him shaking hands in his coat and gloves, "This guy will never be a politician. You never shake hands with your gloves on."

....

Originally, Michael Chertoff was slated to be one of Giuliani's assistants on the Mafia Commission case, but as the scandal in the Parking Violations Bureau grew in 1986, his unit chief Barbara Jones told Chertoff he should be preparing for the Mob trial as though he were the lead attorney. Once it was clear that the PVB case would go to trial, Giuliani decided he would take the lead, and put Chertoff in charge of the Commission prosecution. "I am surmising he had ambitions to run, a lot of people were saying it," Chertoff said, "and he thought it was a more visible case, probably a shorter case." Giuliani had gone to the Southern District in 1983 with the idea that he would spend four years in the job, build up his name recognition and résumé, and run for office. Even by late 1986, having eschewed a gubernatorial candidacy against Mario Cuomo, Giuliani was considering whether that office should be US Senate, where Democratic incumbent Pat Moynihan was strong, or a run against Mayor Koch. Despite Moynihan's popularity (he would go on to win reelection against a weak candidate in 1988, getting two-thirds of the vote), Giuliani considered a run carefully, and Donald Trump offered, in late 1987, to put up a $2 million fund to help Giuliani win the seat. There were other offers, too, including a chance to head the Securities and Exchange Commission and a nomination, if he had wanted it, to take over the FBI. But Giuliani had his eye on Koch's spot all along, and the aggressiveness with which he prosecuted both Friedman and Mafia figures were indicative of his desire to win high-impact verdicts that would resonate with voters in the city.

Giuliani also cultivated his media ties in ways none of his predecessors had done, to guarantee positive press coverage. He often drew the scorn of rival prosecutors for what appeared to be a need to put his own accolades ahead of sound compromises that could be beneficial to all involved. Manhattan DA Robert Morgenthau had encountered numerous battles with Giuliani. In the Eastern District (primarily Brooklyn), Ed McDonald had the same problem. Teams of lawyers had been working for months, for example, on the wiretaps that were monitoring Mafia bosses before Giuliani's arrival. But when Giuliani came in, he muscled other prosecutors out to bolster the cases he wanted to make in the Southern District. Because Giuliani had been the number three man in Attorney General William French Smith's Justice Department before taking the SDNY job, he had the upper hand in any argument over jurisdiction, which would be settled by the AG's office in Washington, and he freely leaned on that advantage.

When he showed up in New York, Giuliani had not expected economic sector prosecutions to be much of a factor in making his political name, not while working in the Justice Department of Ronald Reagan, hero of early-'80s acquisitiveness. Busting the Mafia, reviving anti-corruption prosecutions, and pushing against the drug trade in the city—those were his ticket to electoral success in New York, he figured. But the excesses happening at the Stock Exchange, just about ten blocks from his office at St. Andrew's Plaza, were too blatant to ignore, especially with SEC lawyers also looking into financial crimes and potentially stealing Giuliani's thunder. Focused on the difficult prosecution of Friedman for most of 1986, Giuliani generally delegated authority to pursue market law-breakers to his assistants (he had no contact with Chertoff throughout the Commission case). There was no shortage of targets. The knack that an investor like Ivan Boesky had for picking companies that were ready for a takeover, putting big sums of money into their stocks in anticipation of a stock spike and a buyout, had drawn the suspicion that many of the top traders on Wall Street were getting illegal insider information. In May 1986, Giuliani's office made the first move in what would be a domino-line of activity. He had Dennis Levine of Drexel Burnham Lambert arrested on charges of insider trading, and moved quickly to find whether Levine would be willing to cut a deal.

Levine did, and to the surprise of prosecutors, it took only three weeks to finalize his agreement. What's more, he implicated the biggest target in American stock trading: Boesky himself. While the Friedman trial was getting underway, Giuliani's office approached Boesky and found that he, too, was willing to make a deal, and for three months, he wore a wire, capturing conversations with longtime friends and Wall Street cohorts. When word got out, in the early winter, that Boesky had flipped, a pall was cast over Wall Street. He had had a slew of connections, had bent and broken too many rules with too many accomplices over the years for any major player in the financial world not to be a bit scared. To Giuliani's continued surprise, news about Boesky set off a wave of violators who were willing to make deals and implicate other violators. One, Martin Siegel, set what one prosecutor called the "all-time record" for turning on his cohorts. "We subpoenaed Marty Siegel at the end of the day on a Friday," the prosecutor said, "and he arrived ready to cooperate Monday morning."

Giuliani received ample criticism for his handling of white-collar Wall Street criminals. The deal with Boesky had been for three years in prison and a fine of $100 million, half of which he was able to deduct from his taxes and the other half payable with stocks rather than cash. For that Giuliani was criticized for going too light, but the deal belonged in part to the SEC, and all sides knew that the prosecution of insider trading cases was difficult. In February 1987, Giuliani OK'd the arrest of three traders in public, without giving them the opportunity to turn themselves in, furthering the accusation that he was using high-profile arrests as a ploy to grandstand for press coverage. "This was a terrible perversion of justice," said the lawyer for one of the defendants. "Really shocking." (Giuliani did not order the arrests himself, however, and he pointed out that if the arrests were made for publicity, he would have alerted the media, which he did not do.) He did take Boesky's information and bring in the biggest broker of insider-trading secrets on Wall Street, Michael Milken. In all, there had been twelve insider trading cases prior to January 1984, and there were forty-seven in the four years that followed. Giuliani's heart might not have been in them the way it was for Mafia or public corruption trials, but his willingness to prosecute showed he took the insider trading problem seriously. These cases helped Giuliani's standing in the city only in the sense that New Yorkers were pleased to see the country's modern robber-barons brought to heel—even on light sentences—but they didn't burnish his local credentials as much as the prosecution of city corruption and organized crime.

In May 1987, Giuliani did an extended interview with *New York* magazine. The final question—or statement, really—was about how the rest of New York viewed his designs on his future. "You're often portrayed as unabashedly ambitious," he was told.

"That's very unfair," Giuliani said. "I see it as a criticism because I wouldn't step on anyone or do anything improper or unethical to further myself or my career. The things I've achieved, I've achieved on the merits of doing a good job. I've no family connections, no wealth. I didn't end up getting appointed for jobs because I knew the right people. I got appointed because I worked very hard. And if I never hold another public office in my life, I can look back on this public office and say, 'I did a really good job.'"

38

THE NOVEMBER 10, 1986, ISSUE of *Fortune* magazine featured what was, for a sober publication dedicated to the business world, an odd cover. It was a photo of Tony Salerno in a fedora, cigar clenched between his teeth, his eyes drooping and pointed away from the camera. The headline: THE 50 BIGGEST MAFIA BOSSES. Inside, two *Fortune* reporters ranked the bosses, nationally, according to their "Wealth, Power and Influence." Salerno, as the cover indicated, was number one, though there were some problems with that. To begin with, Salerno was only the frontman for the Genovese clan. He acted the part of the boss, and attended Commission meetings, but it was Chin Gigante who made the decisions for the Genovese family. Gigante was the most careful of Mafia dons, and was glad to have Salerno around to keep law enforcement away from him. (Salerno, poking fun at Gigante's insanity act, once sent out Christmas cards that featured himself in a robe with a baseball cap on and a cane in his hand.) Another problem was that Salerno was immersed in a trial that could force him to spend the remainder of his life in prison. It was a problem for most of the top mobsters *Fortune* named. Of the first eleven, seven, including Salerno, were on trial in the Commission case: Tony Ducks Corallo (3); Gerry Langella (5); Carmine Persico (6); Christy Furnari (7); Tom Mix Santoro (8); and Ralph Scopo (11). Bruno Indelicato, a defendant in the case for his involvement in the murder of Carmine Galante, was twenty-fourth. The New York papers focused on the fact that new Gambino head and media star John Gotti was just thirteenth. The headline in the *Post*: GOTTI'S NO BIG SHOTTI, SAYS MAG. "His superstar status is more image than substance," the *Fortune* article read. "He does not seem qualified to run the Gambino family's complex businesses, which range from meat and poultry sales to a garment industry trade association."

Not only were these heavy hitters on trial in federal court, but they could sense their impending doom. The evidence against them was overwhelming. Chertoff and his team had called more than forty witnesses and played more than one hundred tapes for the jury. The defendants seemed to wear down as the trial progressed, from defiant to bored to defeated. The team of defense lawyers called only one witness, the wife of Fred DeChristopher, and Chertoff easily negated her. When Persico questioned her, he was heavy-handed, repeatedly asking her whether her husband was deaf. She insisted that yes, he could barely hear anything, so there was little chance he could have heard much of what he had claimed Persico had said. When Chertoff got her on cross-examination, he said, "I am questioning her, and I said, 'Let me ask you, you said Fred's deaf? So he really could not hear any of this stuff?' So I said if you were like Fred and you were sitting there, and I am here talking to you right here, you are telling the jury, Fred could not have heard anything I said? She said, 'That's right.' Well, the jury had watched Fred testify for three days."

The prosecution case had gone for seven weeks, but the defense lasted just three days before final arguments began. All the defense could do was pick holes, where they could be found, in the testimony of prosecution witnesses and hope that some piece of the prosecution's case—the Carmine Galante murder, the categorizing of the Commission as the head of an enterprise, the nature of the Concrete Club—did not hold up with the jury. In the meantime, as the trial went on, the defendants got testy. Salerno had grown weary of the low-grade deli sandwiches that had been his only lunch fare for two months, and pleaded with Judge Richard Owen for a reprieve as court went on break one afternoon. "What about a hot lunch, judge?" Salerno said. "Can't we have a hot lunch?" Throughout the trial, the subtle rustle of paper wrappers could be heard coming from the defense table as Salerno opened another Mars bar or Baby Ruth. Once, as the defendants waited for the jury to be returned to the courtroom, Salerno pulled out an Almond Joy and began to eat. One of the prosecutors approached him with a granola bar and said, "They're much better for you, Mr. Salerno. Better than all that chocolate." To which Salerno, gauging the direction of the trial, said, "Who the fuck cares? I'm going to die in the fucking can, anyway."

Chertoff's challenge in his closing statement was to tame the mountain of evidence the prosecution had presented, and re-deliver it to the jury as a comprehensible story. In their closing remarks, a succession of eight defense lawyers (including Persico) had attempted to poke as many holes as they could in the argument that the crimes described were anything more than individual bad acts, not tied together by Mafia connections. Albert Gaudelli, attorney for Tony Corallo, said the prosecution had evoked images of the Mafia "to inflame and prejudice you," and added, "Membership is not a crime." Chertoff began there, in near agreement with Gaudelli, telling the jury, "Mr. Gaudelli said yesterday that the government threw in this Mafia stuff in order to prejudice you and inflame you and get you thinking about things you are not supposed to think about. Well, you know, the word 'prejudice' means prejudge, and when you came into this courtroom eight weeks ago, almost to the day, and I gave you my opening statement, I said to you to put out of your mind all of the baggage, all the media stuff, everything you think you know about the Mafia, because that doesn't belong here. . . . But you have listened to evidence for eight weeks, so it is not a question of prejudging anymore or preconceptions. It is a question of what you learned from the tapes, from the surveillances, from what these defendants said and did as you heard about it in this courtroom." The crimes the jury heard about, Chertoff said, were not isolated crimes, but were interdependent and carried out at the direction of the Commission of La Cosa Nostra. Where past Mafia bosses could avoid prosecution based on their lack of culpability for specific crimes, Chertoff was reasserting that the structure of the Mafia made it an enterprise, and the responsibility for crimes committed on behalf of that enterprise could be pinned on those at the top of the enterprise under the law. "You know," Chertoff said, "that the organization we are talking about here was not the Kiwanis, it wasn't the Elks Club, and that is important, too, because these men weren't just thrown together in this organization. . . . They took oaths to join this organization. They joined this organization which was disciplined, which had rules that were enforceable by punishment, including the punishment of death."

Flipping Gaudelli's words back on themselves, Chertoff said, "So it is not true to say that this case has nothing to do with the Mafia or the Mafia is irrelevant. The Mafia is very relevant in this case. The Mafia is relevant because it is the Mafia that makes possible this kind of concerted criminal activity. The Mafia is relevant because what racketeering is, the evil that racketeering laws are designed to prevent, is people banding together in an organized and disciplined fashion for one purpose: to commit crimes."

The twelve-member jury deliberated for five days, from 10:00 a.m. until after 5:00 p.m., each passing day weighing heavily on the defense (long deliberations generally favor prosecutors). Nearing the final day, Barbara Jones told Chertoff to prepare two statements, one for guilty and one for not guilty. "I said, 'I can't do that,'" Chertoff said. "I was not going to jinx myself. I was just going to wait and say something on the stairs when it was over." On the final day, the jurors asked to re-hear Chertoff's closing argument (a good sign, though they were not allowed to review it). When, finally, the jurors returned, just after noon, the defendants were stone-faced. Chertoff breathed a sigh of relief when the jury forewoman announced the verdict on the first count, a RICO enterprise, for all eight defendants: guilty. But there were 151 counts, and as Owen kept reading counts, the forewoman—tears welling in her eyes as she nervously sipped water—kept responding, guilty.

"It was a huge weight lifted off my shoulders," Chertoff said. "Here, Rudy had entrusted me with this huge case and I kind of felt like anything less than a perfect score and I would have to explain myself."

.....

In January 1987, the eight mobsters convicted in the Commission case were back in front of Judge Richard Owen for sentencing. He gave bosses Tony Salerno, Carmine Persico, and Tony Corallo one hundred years each. He gave Concrete Club bagman Ralph Scopo one hundred years, and Colombo underboss Gerry Langella one hundred years. Lucchese consigliere Christy "Tick" Furnari got one hundred years. Tom "Mix" Santoro could sense what was coming, and as Owen directed presentencing comments toward Santoro, he urged the judge to speed things along. Owen told him he was just doing his job. "And you're doing a good job," Santoro said with bitterness. Santoro got one hundred years. The leadership of the five families had been shredded, and there was no chance they would be able to continue to direct the activities of the Mafia from their cells, not with century-long sentences hanging over them. The only member of the convicted eight who did not get one hundred years was Bruno Indelicato, who had been one of five gunmen to carry out the assassination of Carmine Galante and two others in 1979. Indelicato got forty years. That a triple murderer got less prison time than the higher-ups sent a message about RICO to those who would take over for the likes of Salerno, Persico, and Corallo in the short term, and to any future Mob boss: You will be accountable for all crimes conducted by your underlings. The crux of a RICO case is to prove that there is an enterprise, and that enterprise is responsible for a pattern of crimes. The Commission case made it possible for the government to prosecute anyone on RICO grounds if it could be shown that the defendant was an active member of La Cosa Nostra (the enterprise) and that the defendant committed or authorized at least two crimes. Being at the top of the Mafia hierarchy was enough to prove that crimes had been authorized. The thrust of the convictions, and Owen's sentences (all of which held up on appeal in the Second

Circuit), was that simply being a Mob boss could line you up for a one-hundred-year sentence. Nationwide, prosecutors took notice, and city by city, the government pulled down the top tier of the Mafia. As Boston kingpin Gerry Angiulo said on an FBI surveillance bug, "It might be me, you, him, him, and him, too. Nobody knows. Under RICO, no matter who we are, if we're together, they'll get every fucking one of us."

Years later, Bob Blakey conducted a study on the effectiveness of RICO, and found that Mafia members identified in a 1969 Senate subcommittee hearing served, on average, forty-one months in prison. Members identified for another congressional committee in 1988, with RICO in play for about five years, served 101 months. Those who were brought up on RICO charges, about a third of all offenders, served 132 months, on average. For Blakey, it was a personal triumph, a validation of the law he had devised and fought so hard to persuade law enforcement and prosecutors to implement. "It changed everything, particularly in New York where the five families were located," Blakey said. "If you compare the jail time done by different levels of Mafia members, before and after RICO, you get an idea of what changed. Most Mafia bosses did only a few years here and there early in their careers, and it was the captains and soldiers who were sent off to jail the most. But with RICO, you see big sentences for the bosses. You're taking out a whole swath of their leadership all at once. That's what changed."

39

Before Game Six of the World Series at Shea Stadium, *New York Times* writer Ira Berkow approached Mets pitcher Ron Darling, who happened to live in his neighborhood, Murray Hill in Manhattan. "If there is a Game Seven, you will be pitching," Berkow said. "That's right," Darling responded. "How will you get to the park?" Berkow asked. "I'll be driving," Darling said. So Berkow asked if Darling would mind some company, and when Darling agreed, Berkow had himself a ride to Shea for Game Seven—in a 250SL Mercedes, driven by that game's starting pitcher. Of course, when Berkow was walking up to the parking garage where Darling kept his car, on 37th Street, he looked up to see a black-haired young man pulling away in a Mercedes. Panicked, he approached the parking attendant and asked if Ron Darling kept his car there. He was told yes, and Berkow helplessly said, "But Ron Darling just pulled out. . . ." Walking around the corner, though, he heard honking—there was Darling, waiting for Berkow on the street.

On the ride to Flushing, which lasted about a half-hour, Berkow began to poke Darling with questions. The clouds were thick and waterlogged, the somber weather only adding to the existential bent of the chat. Darling began talking about the pregame moment walking from the bullpen to the tunnel and onto the field. "In that walk," he told Berkow, "with the spikes echoing on the concrete, you feel very lonely. You wonder if it's going to be one of those days and you're not going to get anybody out." Berkow asked about the stress of the situation. Darling's family was in town, which added a layer of pressure to an already monumental point in his life. He was fatigued, too, because he had not gone to bed until 3:00 a.m. after the hurricane that Game Six had been. Berkow asked why he had not left Game Six early, as pitching coach Mel Stottlemyre had recommended he do, to get some rest. "If we lost, then I'd want to be with the guys," Darling said. He asked about the strain on his arm, pitching again on three days' rest for the second time and about the pressure of pitching a Game Seven, especially at age twenty-six. Darling shrugged off the short rest, and said his strategy was to "just tell your arm it's OK." He said nothing matched the nerves of his big-league debut in 1983, when he faced Philadelphia and retired Joe Morgan, Pete Rose, and Mike Schmidt, all perennial All-Stars, to lead off the game. Berkow asked about Darling's father, who was a machinist in Worcester, Massachusetts, when Darling was growing up, and the grind of the working life he had endured. "To feed a family of four kids, with modest means," Darling said, "that's pressure, too." By Darling's account, he did not know Berkow would be conducting a pregame interview as they drove—he liked to ride on days he was pitching in contemplative silence—but the questions, he later said, meant that,

"Right away I was out of my comfort zone." (When Berkow saw that, he wondered, "Did he really think I wasn't going to ask him any questions?") Darling was tired and irritable heading into Game Seven. But there was a blessing: The clouds had opened up and the rain was not stopping. The game would be postponed. Darling would still pitch, but he would have another day to get himself into his comfort zone before he did. Berkow wrote his column about Darling for the rain day, and found another way to the park for the rescheduled Game 7.

At the Grand Hyatt on 42nd Street, the Red Sox team hotel, news that the game had been delayed got Red Sox manager John McNamara thinking. Had the Red Sox not suffered their Clouseau-esque 10th inning in Game 6, starting pitcher Bruce Hurst would have been the series MVP. He had won both of his starts, allowing two runs in 17 innings with 14 strikeouts, keeping the Mets baffled by his array of breaking balls and control with his fastball. Scheduled starter Dennis "Oil Can" Boyd had struggled in his one World Series start, had not been great in his two starts against California in the American League playoffs, and had been on the downswing since his suspension from the team in July. McNamara determined he would make the switch to Hurst, but the problem remained: telling Boyd, who had gone AWOL when he was not named to the All-Star team. Boyd took the news badly. He stormed through the lobby of the hotel—friend and fellow pitcher Al Nipper tried to stop him—but Boyd skulked out into the New York night to, as could be done easily, find crack cocaine, crying as he walked. He was still crying the next day when he showed up for the game, uncharacteristically silent with reporters. He was comforted by the fact that McNamara told him he would be the first pitcher out of the bullpen. He did not know at the time, though, that pitching coach Bill Fischer had told McNamara that Boyd was drunk in the bullpen and could not pitch—and that Nipper had told him so. Boyd said he checked with Nipper on that, though. "I know that didn't happen," Boyd said later. "They're lying." Hurst and the Red Sox were entering Game Seven in a state of tumult, while Darling was still grappling with the pressure of the situation. Nine days earlier, the two pitchers had gone neck-and-neck in a 1–0 duel. But Game Seven was different.

Darling had a bad footing from the beginning, giving up four hard-hit balls—one for a hit, the others for outs—in the first, and heading into a second inning that got his mind working against him. Cleanup hitter Dwight Evans was at the plate and Darling got ahead of him, 1-2. Darling came back with a good sinker at the knees, and was certain he had struck out Evans. But umpire John Kibler thought it too low and called a ball. Darling remained stoic on the mound, but the call rattled him. Evans fouled off another pitch, took a bad pitch inside from Darling, and worked another good fastball into a foul. Darling came back with another fastball inside, but this time Evans did not miss it. He cracked it to left field, and Darling just dropped his head and kicked the ground. He did not turn to watch. He knew he had given up a home run. He gave up another to Rich Gedman in the next at-bat, one that landed briefly in the webbing of Darryl Strawberry's glove in right field but bounced out when Strawberry hit the wall. Darling gave up a walk and two more hits, but he escaped the second with some luck, as Mookie Wilson tracked down a hard-hit fly ball from Bill Buckner. The Mets trailed, though, 3–0, and watching Hurst throw at the outset of the game, there was some worry that those three runs might be all the Red Sox would need. Hurst allowed a single by Ray Knight in the second inning, but retired nine of the first ten Mets he faced. In the fourth inning, Boston put together another rally on Darling, who hit Dave Henderson with a pitch, got a fly ball out, and then had Henderson sacrificed over to second base on a bunt by Hurst.

Trailing, 3–0, with one out and a runner on second, Davey Johnson had seen enough. Sid Fernandez was warmed in the bullpen. Fernandez had been one of the great Frank Cashen/Lou Gorman moves of the Mets' rebuilding project, acquired in 1983 from the Dodgers for Carlos Diaz and Bob Bailor, each of whom had been sent away by the Dodgers by the time Fernandez came on to relieve Darling. He had accepted his move to the bullpen after a stellar season (16-6,

3.52 ERA) with grace, and had given Johnson four good innings of relief in Game Five, when Dwight Gooden had petered out—Keith Hernandez called Fernandez the "unsung hero" of the Mets' World Series. Fernandez walked Wade Boggs, but got the Mets out of the jam with a fly ball out. Hurst rolled through the next two innings with six straight outs (he had now set down fifteen of sixteen batters he faced), but Fernandez matched him, striking out four of the next six batters he faced to keep the Mets' deficit at 3–0. Even as they trailed, the Mets were confident. Hurst was on three days' rest and would wear down, the hope went, leaving the team to go against a Red Sox bullpen that had been scarred, perhaps permanently, by Game Six. Even Hurst knew it. "I wasn't conditioned to pitch on three days' rest," he would say later. "I haven't done it all season."

If McNamara's lack of faith in his relievers, no matter what he thought of Boyd's condition, needed confirmation, it came in the sixth inning. Hurst had not thrown many pitches (56) entering the inning, but his fatigue was obvious. Rafael Santana led off with a chopper up the middle for an out, but pinch-hitter Lee Mazzilli pulled a hit to left field, and Wilson followed with another hit, giving the Mets two baserunners for the first time in the game. McNamara stuck with Hurst, who walked Tim Teufel. Shea Stadium trembled with crowd noise as the Mets had the bases loaded with Keith Hernandez at the plate and Hurst exhausted. Hernandez clubbed a high fastball into left field for a two-run single. It was Hurst's turn to get lucky on the next play, though. Gary Carter hit a short, looping fly to right field that had Evans chasing hard. He dove, got his glove on the ball, and rolled over. The ball squirted out during the roll, but Evans's back blocked the play and the umpire could not make a call until he knew whether Evans made the play. Hernandez was stuck between bases, not knowing whether to move to second base or retreat to first. By the time the umpire signaled a hit, Evans was throwing to second base. A run scored, but Hernandez was tagged out, and shouted at umpire Dale Ford on his long walk back to the dugout. Only a diving catch by Jim Rice on a slicer to left by Darryl Strawberry ended the sixth. Still, the Mets had gotten to Hurst, tied the score, and eagerly awaited the appearance of the Red Sox bullpen crew.

After promising to use every facet of his pitching staff with the championship on the line in Game Seven, McNamara made a bizarre choice. In the bottom of the seventh, he went to the mentally shaken and physically spent Calvin Schiraldi. It was a shot at redemption, perhaps, but a tied World Series Game Seven is not an ideal spot in which to rebuild the confidence of a rookie reliever. Schiraldi reacted as one would expect. On a 2-1 count, he challenged Ray Knight with a fastball. "It wasn't where I wanted it," Schiraldi explained. Indeed, the pitch was waist high out over the plate, Knight's sweet spot. He laced it over the wall in left field to give the Mets the lead. After Lenny Dykstra reached on a single, the Red Sox put on a pitchout to try to catch Dykstra stealing. Instead, Schiraldi's pitch went four feet too wide for about as wild a pitch as possible, moving Dykstra to second. Rafael Santana knocked a single to score Dykstra, and after a sacrifice bunt, McNamara pulled the plug on his Schiraldi experiment. Joe Sambito entered the game, walked two batters (one intentional), and allowed a run on a sacrifice fly from Hernandez. McNamara even resorted to Bob Stanley for the final out of the seventh. The Mets led, 6–3, but with Roger McDowell giving up two runs in the top of the eighth to make it 6–5, they needed insurance.

That is when Strawberry stepped in, facing Al Nipper, who had started Game Four for Boston and had pitched well, allowing three runs in six innings of the Red Sox loss. It was obvious this was likely to be Strawberry's last at-bat of what had been a mostly miserable World Series—the strikeouts in the first three games, the taunting he had gotten in Boston, the double-switch benching that Davey Johnson gave him in Game Six, the complaints that followed despite the Mets' incredible win. When Nipper left a bad, 0-2 sinker over the plate for Strawberry, he turned on it with all his pent-up fury and drove it high into the night. In part to savor the moment, in part to show up Bostonians, in part to stick it to Johnson, Strawberry slowly strutted out of the batter's box, admiring as the ball kept carrying. It took Strawberry nearly forty-five seconds to trot his way 360 feet around the Shea Stadium infield, and when he got to the plate, he was greeted by Knight, who sensed the opportunity for a little healing. "Go in there," Knight told Strawberry, "and shake Davey's hand." Strawberry nodded twice to Knight and said, "OK." He was asked after the game if he had taken Knight's advice. "No," he said. (He was asked if he intended to. Same answer.) The Mets added another run on a single by relief pitcher Jesse Orosco, of all batters, one final insult for the Red Sox's woebegone bullpen, which had an ERA of 7.63 in the series, a good bit worse than the starters (3.61). Down, 8–5, the Red Sox put up no fight in the top of the ninth. A red smoke bomb whistled down from the stands, landing in left field, shrouding the field with a haze that gave the stadium the feel of Verdun circa 1916. Meekly, the Red Sox were retired: pop fly, groundball, strikeout, 14 pitches in all. As in Game Six in Houston, Orosco was again on the mound, again tossing his glove in the night air, and again being mobbed by teammates. This time, the NYPD brought out a brigade of cops on horses to keep fans from pouring onto the Shea turf while the players rejoiced.

The Mets were World Champions. Mayor Koch had already determined there would be a ticker-tape parade for the team. He did not know much about baseball, but the Mets had been a cocky and pugilistic bunch all season, one prone to adversity—though mostly of its own making. That rang familiar to Koch. Writing about the team, Koch said, "The Mets are the mirror of this city. In 1986, the sweet uses of adversity have produced a tough, vibrant, confident, resourceful team. . . . It's rare that a team so accurately reflects its city. It's true that many of the players are from other places, but so are many residents of our five boroughs. Being a New Yorker is not a matter of geography, it's a state of mind."

. . . . .

About fifteen miles across the Hudson River in New Jersey, Joe Jacoby was confused. The veteran Redskins offensive lineman was facing off against linebacker Lawrence Taylor, two of the top players at their positions. But Jacoby and some of his Redskins teammates had no idea that Game Seven of the World Series was being played over at Shea Stadium, and were befuddled by the cheers that went up over Giants Stadium, seemingly at random. The Redskins had started 5–0 before suffering a loss to the Cowboys, but entered the Meadowlands 6–1, a game ahead of the Giants. With Dallas already at 6–2, the teams were playing a nationally televised Monday night game for the lead in the NFC East. The Redskins were expecting an engaged, packed stadium. They were not expecting the portable televisions and radios that were keeping fans locked into Mets–Red Sox. "They're cheering now," Jacoby said, "and you're going, 'What's this about? There's no one on the field.' Or it would be in the middle of a play. A game, it has a certain rhythm and the crowd is part of that. So when the crowd starts going into a different direction, they're going wild and nuts, it is very weird. There were a lot of us who, you get so wrapped up in your season, you don't even realize there is a baseball game that night." It was when Knight homered for the go-ahead run in the seventh that the fans at Giants Stadium erupted while Redskins quarterback Jay Schroeder was calling a play. Jacoby, as anyone charged with blocking Taylor (who had three sacks in the game) would be, was jumpy. He moved quickly at the sound of the crowd for an offside penalty.

With the Mets having secured their World Series win by the fourth quarter, the fans could turn their attention to what was the team's most impressive performance of the season. The Giants had not yet put together a complete game against a good team on both sides of the ball, but that changed against Washington. The Giants built a 20–3 lead in the third quarter, focused heavily on putting the ball in Joe Morris's hands. That had been tough to do early in the year, when Morris was coming off his contract holdout and then suffered a bad reaction to medication after breaking his nose in Week 3. He had put up 116 rushing yards against Seattle before facing the Redskins, but torched Washington with 181 yards on the ground and five catches for 59 yards as a receiver. Simms was efficient, completing 20-for-30 passing for 219 yards, and was mistake-free for the night—the Giants had no turnovers, the Redskins had two. The Giants defense shut down the Washington running game (32 yards), forcing Schroeder to fling 40 passes. A big receiving night from Gary Clark (241 yards) helped the Redskins push their way back into the game, pulling even at 20–20 in the fourth quarter. But with four minutes to go, New York leaned on Morris, getting a 34-yard run to the Redskins' 22 to set up three more runs by Morris that were capped by a 13-yard sweep play for the go-ahead touchdown. The defense made it hold for a 27–20 win. "We could see the confusion in the minds of the Redskins," Harry Carson said. "They were wondering, what the heck are these people cheering for?"

The fans were celebrating the Mets' win. But the Giants were now 6–2 through eight weeks for the first time since 1963, which was also the last time they had finished first in their division. They were tied with Dallas and Washington, but had not been in such good position for a first-place finish in two decades.

PART VI

Crash

40

BILL PARCELLS HAD ONLY BARELY survived his first season as the coach of the Giants, in 1983, when New York went 3–12–1. By the middle of the 1986 season, though, he had achieved some job security and his comfort level allowed him to make a bigger personal imprint on his team. One of Parcells's strengths was his ability to read personalities, and he was especially good at understanding the media. Even in a saturated market like New York, Parcells had figured out how to best manipulate the coverage of his team. He had once considered a career as a writer, one he wisely decided to forgo in favor of football. But he had a feel for the business end that guided local reporters, and he approached his interactions with the media with a shrewdness that was belied by his sometimes blunt and dismissive demeanor. He understood that writers from some papers—the *Post* or the *Daily News*, for example—were under pressure to stir up controversies, and that outrageous stories on their back pages fueled sales. He would have to tread carefully with those questioners. He knew columnists from the *Times* or *Newsday* were more erudite, which would bring about a choice: give them the thoughtful, pithy quote they were looking for, or knock them down a peg with some sarcasm. He was once asked by a New York reporter about an injured player and said, "He's out." When the reporter asked if he meant out for the game, Parcells slumped his shoulders, cocked his head and said, "No, he's out of town. Of course he's out for the game!" Because he grew up in New Jersey and coached the Giants, he was asked at another time by an out-of-town reporter, what exactly was a "Jersey guy"? His answer: "A guy from New Jersey." When he had been questioned about his decision to focus on defense in the draft, rather than addressing glaring offensive holes (depth at wide receiver, for example), Parcells shrugged. Add defense, he quipped, "if you want to win. If you want entertainment, take your team to Broadway, like Bingo Long's All-Stars."

When Michael Katz of the *Daily News* asked him about the budding Giants tradition of players dousing him with Gatorade at the end of each victory, Parcells had a laugh. "Funny," he said, "the chairman of the board of Quaker Oats—they make Gatorade, don't they?—he sent me a gift certificate to replenish my wardrobe. I thought that was kind of cute." Katz asked the next logical question: How much? Parcells smiled. "More than $5, less than $5,000." That was typical of his banter. *Post* columnist Jerry Izenberg recalled that it was wise to arrive early for a Parcells press conference. "When it was just him in the press room, hanging out with reporters, he would sit and talk about any subject," Izenberg said. "Other sports, politics, he could talk about anything and you could have good conversation with him. He would even sit and pick games for us, he would pick three as long as we would not tell anyone. He had a good percentage, too. But once the television guys would get there and start setting up their cameras, he would put on his persona and be Bill Parcells. The reporters who were around him all the time knew that was more of an act. He would have disagreements and he might get mad at you. But he was always good with people he knew."

Parcells applied his people skills to his players, too, and no one needed it more than quarterback Phil Simms, even at the height of one of the best seasons in Giants history. Parcells would sometimes run a trick with Simms where, for the entire week, he would say hardly anything to his quarterback. Simms would start thinking: *What's wrong, am I doing a great job or am I horrible?* That got Simms more focused during practices and ready for games on the weekend. Heading into the tenth week of the 1986 season, the Giants were 7–2, tied with the Redskins on top of the NFC's East Division, though the Giants had the edge because they had beaten Washington at the end of October, on the night the Mets won the World Series. But Simms was struggling, and not in need of any of Parcells's mind tricks. In Week 7, a loss in Seattle, he had been sacked six times and threw four interceptions. In Week 9, a grinding 17–14 win over the Cowboys, Simms had felt the bottom dropped out. He threw 18 passes and completed only six of them, four going to his tight ends, Mark Bavaro and Zeke Mowatt. He finished with a 22.2 passer rating, the worst of his career. He was taking an average of more than three sacks per game, and had thrown as many interceptions (12) as touchdowns. His two best outside receivers, Lionel Manuel and Stacy Robinson, were injured, Manuel going down in Week 4 and Robinson in Week 6.

There had been talk about the Giants trading a high draft pick for disgruntled Rams receiver Henry Ellard, locked in a contract holdout, but instead, the team re-acquired Phil McConkey, who had been let go, to the dismay of Simms, on the last day of training camp and hooked on with the Packers. That gave Simms a sure-handed target, at least, but McConkey was not a speed receiver, not a player who could stretch the field. There was Bobby Johnson, who had caught 15 touchdowns in his first two seasons with the Giants, but who had fallen out of favor with Parcells. In the papers, Johnson's problem was described only as a trip to the Parcells doghouse (not uncommon), but Johnson would later explain to author Jerry Barca the real problem: He had gotten hooked on crack cocaine before the start of training camp, and used crack throughout the 1986 season. Even with his budding addiction, the injuries to Manuel (who returned for the playoffs) and Robinson (who came back in Week 11), Johnson was the best wide receiver Simms had for much of the year. The Giants had used two late-round picks on rookies Vince Warren and Solomon Miller, but both struggled to get open and dropped too many balls. Warren never caught a pass in his one season and Miller caught just 14 in his entire NFL career. Not that it mattered to Giants fans. They only saw the 6-for-18 from their favorite target for abuse, and let Simms hear it. Fans were chanting for backup Jeff Rutledge during the Cowboys win, never mind that Simms's receivers were McConkey, two rookies, and a crack addict. Writer Frank Litsky began a column after Week 9 with "What's wrong with Phil Simms, anyway?" Later in the column, Giants receivers coach Pat Hodgson answered the question for him: "Phil gets the brunt of it, and it's not all his fault. It's, 'Vince who?' and 'Solomon who?' But people know Phil Simms."

The following week, entering a game at Philadelphia, the focus on Simms was muted by rumors that Eagles coach Buddy Ryan had put out a bounty on Giants linebacker Lawrence Taylor. In the first meeting of the teams, Taylor had dominated in a 35–3 Giants win, racking up four sacks. The Eagles had tried to handle Taylor largely with rookie running back Keith Byars blocking him in that game, but the results were disastrous. At one point, weary Eagles quarterback Ron Jaworski peeled himself off the turf after a Taylor blow and, to lighten his own mood, asked Taylor, "So, how's your golf game, LT?" Manuel was asked after whether he was surprised by the Eagles' blocking strategy. "Was I surprised they tried to stop LT with just a running back, a rook against an All-Pro?" Manuel said with a grin. "Yeah, I told Lawrence he should buy Byars dinner." Early in their second meeting, it was clear Philadelphia was targeting Taylor. On a pitch to the running back, rookie guard Nick Haden stepped out toward Giants linebacker Harry Carson, but quickly circled back and, as Taylor was chasing down the play, walloped Taylor from the side. "I tell you," analyst John Madden said during the game's broadcast, "No. 56 is a marked man." On the next play, Taylor—irked by Haden's cheap shot—threw off a block from tackle Joe Conwell, cut inside past Haden, and sacked Jaworski. If there was a bounty, it could be said that the Eagles had better luck with Taylor than in the first meeting in the sense that he had three sacks instead of four. The defense pulled the Giants to a win again, 17–14, in what would be the final game in Philadelphia for Jaworski, who tore a tendon in his throwing hand.

For Simms, the problems persisted. He threw 18 passes for the second straight week (in the first four weeks of the season, he had averaged 38 passes per game) and completed only eight, four to Bavaro, three to his running backs, and only one to a wide receiver. Parcells had grown to appreciate the thick skin Simms developed over his years of coping with injuries and jeering fans. It was something Parcells had seen often. "Hell, they booed (Joe) Namath," Parcells said of New York fans. "They boo everyone, and when Phil's gone, they'll boo whoever the next guy is and say, 'Yeah, he ain't as good as Simms.' The thing about Phil is, he's so *tough*." But after the win over Philadelphia, Parcells determined his quarterback, toughness and all, had been beaten down by the ineptitude of his receivers and the blame he was absorbing for the passing game's failures. He was in need of a pick-me-up. "He could have been 13-for-18—they dropped five passes on him—but he got hammered in the papers, 'What happened?'" Parcells said about the Philadelphia game. "I called him in and said, 'Look, I think you're a great quarterback, and the way you got to be great was by being fearless out there, and resilient. Don't worry about the things you can't control, like drops. Be yourself.'"

His teammates, too, rallied around Simms. Said safety Kenny Hill, "He's been denigrated and castigated by the press because of what they perceive as his lackluster effort. He's been subjected to unfair abuse." Simms responded the following week, when the Giants traveled to Minnesota to play the Vikings, one of the league's best defensive teams. Robinson was back, and just in time—the game plan for the Giants called for them to attack Minnesota's zone coverage by throwing underneath the zone with short and midrange passes. To open the game, Simms shook off his struggles from Weeks 9 and 10. In the first half, he was 11-for-15 passing, for 173 yards, nearly matching his combined output from the previous two weeks. But the Giants sputtered when they got into scoring range, and had settled on three field goals. They led at halftime, 9–6. Minnesota would seize the lead to open the second half with a touchdown, but the second half would prove to be rough for Vikings defensive back Issiac Holt. He intercepted his second pass of the game, but was hit by Bobby Johnson and fumbled the ball back to the Giants in Vikings' territory. Four plays later, the Giants had another field goal, and the score was 13–12 heading into the fourth quarter. Just as they had done to Jaworski in Week 9, the Giants relentlessly chased down Vikings quarterback Tommy Kramer, and on the second play of the fourth quarter, Kramer was sent to the sidelines with an injured thumb on a hit from Taylor. Minnesota's backup, though, was Wade Wilson, a veteran who did not shrink in relief of Kramer. After the Giants took a 19–13 lead on a touchdown pass to Bobby Johnson, Wilson led the Vikings on an 80-yard drive, completing three passes for 68 yards, including a 33-yard touchdown with just under seven minutes to play.

The Giants were still trailing, 20–19, when McConkey took a punt to the New York 41 yard line with just over two minutes to play. Simms moved them into Minnesota territory with a pass to Johnson, but picked up only two yards in the next two plays. With 1:18 to go and the decibel level at the Metrodome making it nearly impossible to hear, Simms lined the team up for a 3rd-and-8 play. The Vikings blitzed. When Simms dropped back to pass, within two seconds, defensive ends Mark Mullaney and Doug Martin (George Martin's brother) had broken through the Giants' offensive line. Simms never had a chance. He slid to his right, where linebacker Chris Doleman was waiting. Three Vikings collapsed on Simms back at the Giants' 48 yard line. It was a loss of nine yards, setting up a 4th-and-17 situation with 1:12 showing on the clock. The Giants did not have many options. They knew the Vikings would drop back into coverage to make it tough for Simms to find a target. They pulled out a play that was, according to Simms, one of the first plays they had installed in training camp: Half Right W Motion 74 X In. As soon as Simms took the snap, there was confusion on the offensive line—with the Vikings playing six men back in pass protection, Simms would have at least expected some time to throw. But Mike Stensrud, all 6-foot-5 and 280 pounds of him, busted through Mark Bavaro's block attempt and Simms had to get rid of the ball quickly. On the right sideline, he saw Johnson running into the space between the two levels of the Vikings zone. Simms threw a floater, hoping to drop it over Holt. With the ball in the air, Holt tentatively reached up but pulled his hand back. Johnson had settled his two feet just inside the sideline. He made the catch. It was a first down, to the 30 yard line. "He just threw the ball perfect," Holt said. "We had an under and over-the-top coverage. There was a little hole in there." Johnson had found that hole and could not believe it stayed open as long as it did. "It seemed like the ball took an awful long time to get to me," he said. The Giants ran three plays down to the Minnesota 16 yard line. Kicker Raul Allegre made the field goal, his fifth of the game. The Giants had an improbable win, 22–20. Lineman Jim Burt, breaking protocol on the athletes' rule against looking too far ahead, said after the game, "It looks like a Giants-Mets year."

Simms was a quarterback reborn. In the six weeks before the Vikings game, he had completed 53 percent of his passes, with 924 yards, four touchdowns, and a passer rating of 61.8. In the final six weeks of the season, he completed 59 percent of his passes, threw for 1,438 yards and nine touchdowns, and had a rating of 84.8. After beating Minnesota, the Giants played three straight games against playoff teams Denver, San Francisco, and Washington, and won all three. They closed the year with blowouts of the cellar-bound Cardinals and Packers, winning by a combined 51 points, taking a nine-game winning streak into the postseason. Simms loosened up along the way. He was invited to be a guest VJ on MTV with some of his teammates in December, and Simms—who, early in his career, worried that going from Kentucky to the big city would make him "New York slick"—showed up wearing sunglasses and a headband, poking fun at Bears quarterback Jim McMahon. "I don't want to become any personality," Simms said. "It's just not in me. I think Joe Namath ruined it for all of us."

41

It was the offseason, so Dwight Gooden was back in Tampa, a week before his twenty-second birthday in early November. He was sitting with *Tampa Tribune* writer Tom McEwen, a local legend who had been following Gooden's career since he was in Little League and who helped popularize the nickname "Doc." Gooden had a comfort level with McEwen he didn't have with the media in New York, and after a few conversations with McEwen, his trust in the Mets press corps deteriorated further. McEwen told of how the papers in New York, throughout the 1986 season, had been calling the *Tribune* to ask "whether Dwight was into drugs," and quoted one informer saying Gooden was known among reporters as the "Rock Star," with "rock" being slang for cocaine. One New York paper sent a team of investigators to Tampa to unearth connections between Gooden and drugs. A Boston paper had called the *Trib*, too, to insist they had it on "good authority" that Gooden had checked into the Betty Ford Institute. When McEwen told Gooden, he looked puzzled. "What's the Betty Ford Institute?" he asked.

While McEwen moralized about the intrusive media from up north nosing around Gooden's private life in Tampa, Gooden sat for an interview with him and fed him lie after lie. He did confirm some news that had been circulating through the rumor mill—that he and Carlene Pearson, his high school sweetheart, were calling off their wedding, which had been planned for November 18. That news came after it was revealed that Gooden had fathered a child, born in April, from a dalliance the previous year with another high school friend. When the Knicks honored the Mets at a game on November 11 at Madison Square Garden, Gooden was among the six players who appeared, but would not talk to New York reporters. Instead, the Mets released a statement on his behalf that read, "I have an 8-month-old son and I'm proud of him. I'll support him. My wedding is postponed. Aside from that, it's a personal matter." Gooden got a standing ovation when he and Jesse Orosco went to center court for the ceremonial tipoff. But that was not the story Gooden was trying to tamp down by talking with the *Tribune*. He was using McEwen to address the drug rumors that had begun in the summer and were gaining in intensity, especially after the Mets wrapped up the World Series championship and Gooden failed to appear with his teammates at New York's ticker-tape parade the next day. In the post-championship euphoria, the Mets had trouble getting their stories on Gooden's parade absence straight. The *Times* related that, "Mets officials said [Gooden] had overslept." The *Post* reported that clubhouse attendant Charlie Samuels took a call from Gooden and relayed a message to Davey Johnson that Gooden was sick and could not come. Samuels wanted to know what he should tell Gooden. "I stopped being the manager last night," Johnson said. "Tell him anything you want." Mets PR man Jay Horwitz told beat reporter Bob Klapisch, "Dwight called me and said he wasn't feeling very well. We've had some kind of flu going around the team. Wally [Backman] had it over the weekend. I know Dwight wanted to go. Some people might make a big thing out of this, which is too bad."

Some did make a big thing of it, so Gooden addressed it with McEwen. After Game Seven, Gooden was supposed to be at the park sometime around 8:00 a.m. "I partied with beer and stayed up till 5 a.m.," he told McEwen. "I also got a bad stomach. I got up at about 9 or 9:30 and called Jay and told him how I felt. He said he'd handle it. I just wasn't up to it physically. I wasn't hiding because I hadn't won any games." In his autobiography, Gooden would reveal what a monumental lie that was. When he left the Mets clubhouse, he had planned to meet his fellow players at Finn McCool's, a bar in Port Washington that had become a regular hangout for the team. But he had pulled off the Long Island Expressway early, to visit the projects where his drug dealer lived. He had decided he needed cocaine. He bought some and stopped at the apartment of a friend who lived in the project to snort a bit before heading to the bar. But a couple of lines became a couple more. There was alcohol passed around, and more lines. Gooden lost track of time, and was stunned by each glimpse he got of the clock, warning him how fast the hours were moving. Finally, he saw the sky lighten outside, the sun beginning to break through, and pulled himself away to leave. By the time he made it back to his place, he had already gotten calls from Horwitz, from his mother, from Pearson. All were looking for him. But he was too wired, too paranoid to leave. As Gooden explained to ESPN in 2011: "Then the next thing you know the parade's on and I'm watching the parade on TV."

But Gooden continued to lie about the parade in his chat with McEwen. He boldly denied having an issue with alcohol at all. "Beer is what I drink and not much of that," he said. "Wine makes me sick." What about drugs? "No," Gooden said. "I never use them and I never will." And then Gooden took a gamble. The previous spring, when he was negotiating his contract for 1986, the Mets wanted an agreement from him that allowed for drug testing. Because baseball had no formal testing policy, Gooden was not obligated to go along, and he declined to have that provision added. The Mets had pushed him to accept it, having received word of his association with seedy characters in Tampa in the 1985 offseason from the commissioner's office. Now, though, he told McEwen, he welcomed it. "I told my agent, Jim Neader, I want a drug testing clause in my new contract," Gooden said. "It can be for a test every week, every two days, as often as they want and it can be forever." Gooden had not, of course, told any of this to his agent. He had not run it past the union. Still, to stave off speculation on the reality of his drug use, Gooden created a fantasy in which he had no drug problem, and somehow got himself to believe it. Gooden was now on record: He would not only accept, but would insist upon, drug testing in what would be a very generous contract coming in the following months.

The line written by Dick Young back in April was prescient: "Now that he is 21, a man, does he think he can get away with things?"

· · · · ·

For Gooden, the winter of 1985 and spring of 1986 sprouted enough minor controversies—the mysterious sprained ankle, the phantom car wreck to explain a missed spring game, the confrontation with a rental car attendant at LaGuardia—to harden him to the difficulty of life as a celebrity in New York. But his winter following the 1986 season was different. He was discovering the difficulty of being young, black, and successful anywhere in America, while also managing a substance abuse problem without help. When he arrived back in Tampa after the World Series, Gooden noticed he had company when he drove around the city. Usually there would be some bulky Ford following him for a few blocks, then maybe another. Mostly, it amounted to nothing, but Gooden knew they were unmarked police cars. Driving a $50,000 Mercedes 380SE, very often in some of Tampa's more downtrodden areas, made Gooden an easy target for a mostly white police department with a deep history of race-related incidents.

On December 13, Gooden's patience finally broke. He had been with his nephew, Gary Sheffield (then a minor leaguer in the Brewers' organization), and two friends at a Chili's for some beers and food, then planned to drive to visit a party an acquaintance was having. Gooden was making a left on Nebraska Avenue when he saw the lights of a police car that had been stopped at an intersection. Gooden thought the cops, Jeffrey Smith and Tim Cotter, were pulling over Sheffield, who was in a Corvette ahead of Gooden. Instead, the car dropped back and pulled over Gooden. Sheffield initially pulled over, but seeing Gooden at the side of the road, he pulled away, prompting Cotter to call for backup. Gooden could not calm himself as Smith asked for his license and registration. He wanted to know what he had done wrong that warranted the traffic stop—the police would later say he and Sheffield were "weaving," but Gooden said they had done no such thing. The officer told him to "Shut up," and threatened him with jail. Gooden insisted on asking what his violation had been. The more he asked, the angrier Smith got. Other officers had joined him, standing back and watching. Finally, he got Gooden out of the car and, again according to the police report, Gooden "started yelling, using profane language, accusing [Smith] of police harassment." Gooden saw the officer move for his handcuffs. Smith was going to arrest Gooden for asking why he had been pulled over. There was a back-and-forth, Gooden upset at the situation. Smith put his hand on Gooden's chest, and at that, Gooden reached for the officer's hand, according to the report, saying, "You don't fucking touch me." When nearby officers saw Gooden's move, they swarmed.

Gooden was beaten by nine officers. He was hit with a flashlight, nightsticks, fists, knees. He fought back, futilely. He would later describe the beating as "Fourth of July going off on my face." Sheffield and Gooden's other friends moved to defend him, but they, too, were arrested, and Sheffield was beaten. Gooden suffered an injury to his eye, bruised ribs, bruises and abrasions on his face and head (he would need twenty stitches), and, he said, had a tooth knocked out. According to the police file on Gooden, one of the officers involved in the drubbing of Gooden, James Thompson, egged on another officer who had Gooden's arm yanked behind his back. "Break his arm!" the officer shouted. Thompson defended that taunt by saying later, "Well, you know, just trying to make him stop is all I was trying to do. I didn't mean to snap his arm off." (Gooden pointed out, though, that it was at least his left arm, not his pitching arm.) Another officer shined a flashlight in Gooden's eyes and pretended to be a broadcaster conducting a mock interview. By Gooden's account, one of the cops pulled a gun on him and told him, "Say your prayers, motherfucker," but did not pull the trigger. One witness reported that Gooden kicked an officer in the groin and told him he was going to kill him. Another witness supposedly overheard one of the officers say, "Give a nigger a little money and he gets pig-headed." The police report indicated one of the officers put Gooden into a chokehold, and Gooden claimed that, to stop the beating, he pretended to pass out, which frightened the officers enough to get them to back away. When the ruckus finally was over, as Gooden recalled, he was driven to a parking lot, where two black officers were called in. They drove Gooden to the hospital, to make the matter look less racially motivated.

Even before Gooden's arrest, tension between the police and blacks in the city was so pitched, one black man told the *Tribune* he feared a "big explosion" was coming. In the month before the Gooden incident, there had been four people shot by Tampa police, and three were black. One, who was sixteen, was killed. Bob Gilder, president of the Tampa chapter of the NAACP, filed a request with the Justice Department to investigate the Gooden arrest. "I know one thing," Gilder said, "Tampa needs to get its head out of the sand. There is a race relations problem here. People sit around and say this is where the good life gets better every day or some other bullshit like that, but this reminds you that the problem is something we have to deal with." As the case drew more and more national attention, though, Gooden wanted to defuse it quickly. He was, after all, a naturally shy twenty-two-year-old who happened to be developing a cocaine habit. He wanted to have his record cleared (he had been charged with battery on a police officer, resisting arrest, and disorderly conduct, and eventually got only probation) and be done with the case, not play the part of a national symbol for racial injustice. The FBI sought to interview him about his allegations of civil rights violations, but Gooden turned them down. Eventually, his lawyer won two civil rights violations suits on his behalf, and Gooden gave the money to charity. Of all the officers involved in Gooden's beating, only one was reprimanded—lightly, with a "letter of counseling." That was the officer who had done the mock interview. The officers involved in trying to break Gooden's arm were not reprimanded because, according to Tampa's assistant police chief, the comments were made "in the heat of battle." When Gooden met with the media on December 19, six days after the incident, his eye was still bloodshot, but he would not discuss the specifics of the case. Instead, he said, he was focused on 1987. "It's still going to be in the back of people's minds," Gooden said, "but hopefully things will be better. It's tougher on my family than it is on myself. Hopefully, being back on the field, I'll be a little more relaxed."

With that in mind, in late January, Gooden invited Sheffield to take a trip to New York with him, to get away from tensions in Tampa and relax in the big city. When he landed at LaGuardia Airport, however, he was met by a half-dozen agents in dark suits, asking if he was Dwight Gooden. He had no idea what the trouble could have been, but given what had happened in Tampa, he feared the worst. He was informed that Carlene Pearson, who had run into the man giving Gooden a ride from the airport that night, had been waiting in the terminal to meet him, without having told him. In her purse was a loaded two-shot .38 Derringer, and she was arrested when she ran her bag through the scanner. Gooden's relaxing getaway back to New York began, then, with a trip to bail out his ex-fiancée. So far, 1987 was no improvement on 1986.

42

ON THE NIGHT OF DECEMBER 19, while much of the insulated Queens neighborhood of Howard Beach—mostly Italian, set off from the rest of the city by JFK Airport to the east, Jamaica Bay to the south, and Spring Creek Park along its western edge—went about its pre-holiday business, a 1976 Buick broke down on the side of Cross Bay Boulevard. In the car were four black men: twenty-three-year-old Michael Griffith, thirty-six-year-old Cedric Sandiford (the boyfriend of Griffith's mother), eighteen-year-old Timothy Grimes, and Griffith's cousin Curtis Sylvester, twenty. Sylvester remained with the car while the other three went back into Howard Beach to find help. An initial attempt to fill the radiator with water had not worked, so the men tried again. On their walk, they had encountered a carful of white teenagers, and the two groups exchanged insults before the teenagers drove off. The black men came to New Park, a rundown pizza place, ordered some slices, and sat down to eat. Spotting the three, a local resident called the police to report suspicious men in the area, and a car was dispatched, but officers quickly left when they were told the men were simply having something to eat and there was no problem.

It was 12:40 a.m. when they left the pizza parlor. Once outside, they were surprised to find some of the young men with whom they had had a run-in earlier, a group of about twelve teenagers, all white, all slightly drunk, some wielding baseball bats, others with tree limbs. Grimes had a knife and pulled it out, but one of the white youths knocked it to the ground. Grimes heard one of the teenagers shout "Get the nigger!" and turned to run. With that, the teenagers set upon the men. Sandiford was hit in the thigh, and he and Griffith managed to run, chased on foot by some of the mob of kids, and in cars by others. Sandiford, slowed by his heavy boots, was caught first, and the group continued the beating until Sandiford pretended to be unconscious. Griffith had been well ahead of Sandiford, but doubled back and tried to climb the fence separating the neighborhood from the Shore Parkway. The mob of teens pulled him off the fence and beat him until he managed to get through a hole in the fence. With the white youths swinging at him, Griffith ducked onto the parkway, attempting to reach the other side. From there, his movements are hazy, but his fate was certain. At 1:03, a caller dialed 911 and told the operator there was a body lying in the westbound lane of the parkway. It was Michael Griffith, struck dead after having been hit by a car.

New York was not well prepared to handle the death of Griffith. The class divisions that were exacerbated during the early 1980s by the federal government's economic policies cut along racial lines in the city. Whites were benefitting more from the booming economy, while the flip side of that boom—crack addiction, for one thing, and home-lessness for another—disproportionately affected black neighborhoods. For blacks in the city, Mayor Ed Koch lacked the credentials to lead when a racial crisis hit. For all his successes, Koch had failed to make meaningful connections with minority communities, and had been accused of playing to racial stereotypes to win votes in his three may-oral victories. He had started on a poor footing in his first term with the 1980 closing of Sydenham Hospital in Harlem. It was, for a mayor who had vowed to balance the city's budget coming out of the fiscal crisis of the '70s, an easy decision—Sydenham was old and decrepit, the small-est of the city's seventeen hospitals, mostly used only by drug addicts and alcoholics, rarely ran at capacity, and was costing the city about $9 million per year. But Koch failed to recognize the significance of the hospital to the surrounding community, especially for black doctors. In the '40s, Sydenham had been the first hospital to integrate, and even as it declined with the passage of decades, it remained important to black doctors who had trouble getting admitting privileges at the other hos-pitals in Manhattan. But Koch had won the mayoralty in 1977 with a promise to swing a heavy budgetary axe, and, worse, he was notoriously stubborn. As objections to the closing of Sydenham grew into orga-nized demonstrations, including the occupation of Sydenham offices,

Koch became more dead-set on closing it, if only to prove he would not be pushed around. In a later conversation with Harlem congressman Charlie Rangel, Koch acknowledged his error. "The perception of what was happening to my community," Rangel said, "was far more important than anything that could come up on the balance sheet." Koch agreed with Rangel. "I said subsequently, after I left office, it was a mistake," Koch said. "Not that it wasn't right on the merits, but that I didn't take into consideration what the hospital meant psychologically to the community."

Koch's standing in the black community never recovered from the Sydenham closing, and in the spirit of his stubbornness, he did not do much to win back that support. As crime became a bigger problem in New York in the mid-'80s, Koch pointed to black communities as the problem. Congressman Major Owens explained Koch may have not had a personal problem with race, but he did have a political problem. "Koch has no trouble interacting with black folks," Owens said. "I'm from the South. I've met racists. . . . Koch is not a racist. He has black friends. I am sure there is no problem with his emotional framework. He's an opportunist who will not hesitate to use racism to consolidate his political base and to deal with problems as they come up, scape-goating. He does not hesitate when the time is right to inflame situations, equating black crime with white racism—in essence, saying to the people of the city, 'The crime problem we are all concerned about is blacks against us.'" Throughout 1986, as the municipal scandals dominated Koch's administration, the city's largest black paper, the *Amsterdam News*, ran a front-page editorial under the headline KOCH MUST RESIGN, every week, sometimes with guest authors. His handling of the scandals in the Parking Violations Bureau and elsewhere were just one reason. His history of race-baiting was the other. Koch's police department had undergone serious racial convulsions: the killing of an elderly black woman, Eleanor Bumpurs, during an eviction; the beating death of subway graffiti artist Michael Stewart by six transit cops in 1983; and the torture of a black prisoner later shown to be innocent by five white officers using stun guns in the 106th precinct, not far from Howard Beach. The major crime stories of 1986, from the PVB to the busting of the Mafia Commission to Meade Esposito's bribes and Wall Street insider-trading schemes, had mostly involved well-heeled white criminals, and were all federal cases. But one black leader even held that against Koch. Blacks could not be accused of abusing their power, because Koch had given them none. "Hell, no, you're not going to see any black of consequence indicted in this corruption scandal," one prominent black politician told the *New Yorker*. "We never got invited to the table when the pie was being divided up. We didn't even know there was a pie. . . . Candidly, Koch didn't even give us an equal opportunity to steal."

The city was—and always is, really—on a razor's edge when it came to racial tension, and Koch was never going to be the right mouthpiece to cool the situation. When Griffith was killed, Koch, who had marched in support of the Voting Rights Act in Montgomery in 1965, overreached in his rhetoric, saying, "The survivors were chased like animals through the streets," and harkened back to the '60s by also saying the incident was "the sort of thing you would expect to happen in the Deep South." He labeled Griffith's death "a racial lynching," and "the most horrendous incident in modern times." Aides tried to reel in Koch on the topic. "We were all trying to temper Ed in his remarks and keep things under control," said George Arzt, by this time Koch's press secretary. Koch lacked credibility on the subject, and the story spun out of his control, so that every act of political conciliation was met with backlash ranging from suspicion to outrage. Koch met with a group of twenty-three black leaders days after the murder, and on January 1, he released, jointly with the group, a statement condemning pervasive racism. But that drew fire from more outspoken black leaders, including Rev. Al Sharpton, who charged that all the leaders in Koch's group were moderates and labeled the meeting a "coon show." Koch urged that the teenagers responsible for the beatings be brought to justice and offered a $10,000 reward. Three teenaged boys from John Adams High

School were arrested, and charged with second degree murder, but the case had to be assigned to a special prosecutor when Queens District Attorney John Santucci could not get witnesses to cooperate.

Despite his efforts, Koch was knocked down at every turn by Alton Maddox, the lawyer for Cedric Sandiford, who made some outrageous false claims (that the car that killed Michael Griffith had been one of the cars chasing him earlier; that the teenaged attackers were really in their twenties), and sought to capitalize on black outrage with the government by accusing Koch and police chief Benjamin Ward (who was black) of being part of a cover-up to protect the white assailants. They were not, but Maddox grabbed headlines and worsened mistrust with his rhetoric. "The Mayor, the Police Department, the Queens District Attorney's Office, the Police Commissioner and some of our Negro leadership have all formed a new lynch mob," Maddox said. "And they are hounding and chasing the messengers for speaking the truth. We have a lynch mob that is running loose in New York City."

Just after Christmas, Koch sought to ease tensions by having an open dialogue on race, with the idea of visiting two churches, one black and one white. It took some courage. Koch was accustomed to his problems with blacks, but after labeling the whites of Howard Beach racists, he now had a problem with whites. He went to Our Lady of Grace church in Howard Beach, a mostly white Catholic congregation, and was greeted with jeers and shouts so loud he could barely be heard—a rarity in Koch's legacy. "Go home!" he was told, and "Resign!" He maintained his plea for discussion. "There is a discourse that should be had more often," he said, "where one can talk about the anxieties and the fears and the frustrations. That's what I'd like to talk about and to have you, if you will, respond." But many in the angry crowd walked out, and Koch accomplished little. "You want another racial war?" one woman asked. "You want another '60s on your hands with that attitude? Leave it alone! Leave it alone!" He was better received at the Morning Star Baptist Missionary Church, but still was asked some pointed questions. One man asked Koch why it took a crisis to get him to take action on the topic of race, and Koch could only demur.

Another told him racism in New York "is worse now than 25 years ago." Koch replied, "I don't think that's true."

Koch was a month removed from the Stanley Friedman verdict, and had been hopeful that the new year, with New Yorkers buoyed by a world champion baseball team in Queens, would allow him to restart his third term after a lost 1986. But throughout the unfolding of the Parking Violations Bureau scandal, Koch could be feisty with the media, and vigorously defended his administration over his commissioners and their bad acts. There was no retort he could muster that would help his situation after the killing of Griffith, and as more racial attacks followed—blacks on whites and vice versa—Koch had no answers. Politically, the Howard Beach incident left Koch wounded even further with the black community, and his fumbling attempts to address, head-on, the racial fault lines in New York backfired, alienating the outer borough whites who had been overwhelmingly supportive of him.

"Racial politics is always fragile in New York City, and in the country, as we found out," Arzt said. "When something like this happens, everything sort of unravels. We were just trying to keep everything under control, meet with the right groups, talking to people. Meeting with ministers, meeting with African-American commissioners and officials in our administration. But it was a very tense time."

43

YEARS LATER, HAPPY IN RETIREMENT, Redskins left tackle Joe Jacoby was playing in a charity golf tournament in Williamsburg, Virginia, and was seated at the clubhouse bar with some of his former teammates. From the corner of his eye, he saw a familiar face enter: ex-Giants linebacker Lawrence Taylor, a Williamsburg native and a known hater of all things Redskins (as a kid, Taylor had been a Dallas fan growing up in Redskins country). Jacoby and Taylor entered the NFL together in 1981, Taylor as the number two overall pick and Jacoby as an undrafted free agent who quickly earned a starting job. They had both retired at the same time, too, in 1993. In the intervening years, they had gone nose-to-nose nineteen times in one of the best lineman vs. linebacker rivalries in NFL history. But throughout their careers, they had never spoken a word to each other. Jacoby, for all his grit and mettle, was known to have a quiet demeanor, and no matter how much trouble Taylor found off the field or havoc he caused on it, he was not much of a trash-talker in Jacoby's experience. At the bar, Taylor pulled up a chair next to Jacoby, who waited, silent, for the linebacker to have the first word. Finally, Taylor turned and said to him, "You're one tough son of a bitch." Jacoby nodded and said, "You're not too bad, either." To Jacoby's memory, those might be the only words the two have spoken to each other.

Twice during the 1986 season, the Giants had beaten the Redskins in rugged games they were able to control with their defense. Washington had never taken a lead in either game, and the wins marked the first time New York swept the matchup with the Redskins since 1977. The first one had been the jumpy game at the end of October, when the Mets were playing Game Seven of the World Series. The second had come in December, and of all the games Jacoby played that year—maybe of all the times he had played Taylor in his career—that one had been the toughest. What set Taylor apart, Jacoby found, was the way he sought out contact. Taylor was not just a great athlete and linebacker, he was a genuine connoisseur of football violence. Giants defensive coordinator Bill Belichick explained: "In defensive meetings, while we're studying film, all of a sudden Lawrence will say, 'Ah, Bill. Run that play back again,' And I'll realize he's looking at some guy—20 yards away from the ball—a wide receiver who was knocked off the screen by a defensive back. I've even seen him get his thrills watching one of our own guys get dusted." Jacoby, being a human being in possession of emotions like empathy and compassion, had not dealt with a player of Taylor's mindset. He mostly enjoyed it. But in that December game, he had been assigned to stop Taylor one-on-one, without much help. Over the years, he had figured out some weaknesses of Taylor, some ways to turn his athleticism against him. Jacoby had about as much speed as a 6-foot-7, 300-pounder could have, and when Taylor would try to blow by his outside hip, as he could do to most linemen, Jacoby was able to shuffle his feet to keep up with him. Jacoby also had vise-grip hands that, when they laid into Taylor's shoulder pads, allowed him to redirect Taylor away from the Redskins' play. But in the Redskins' loss in December, Jacoby had struggled. He got caught up in his footwork a few times, and dropped his head too often, a habit that leads to lineman mistakes. At some points, quarterback Jay Schroeder was at fault for scrambling into the area where Jacoby was at work, allowing Taylor to make a play. Taylor wound up with three sacks and pressured Schroeder into throwing six interceptions. Jacoby was asked if the game had been an embarrassment. "I don't know if I would call it embarrassment," Jacoby said. "Maybe just a bad day at the office."

Even with the struggles of Jacoby and the Redskins offense as a whole in that game, when it was over, Taylor had told Bill Parcells, "It's going to be us and the Redskins." The Giants had controlled both matchups with Washington, and had a much more difficult time beating the likes of Minnesota and New Orleans, but Taylor knew Washington was the best team they had played that season. When the playoffs got underway, the Giants made fast work of the 49ers, a game that may have been decided on San Francisco's opening possession, when normally Velcro-handed receiver Jerry Rice dropped a pass on a slant pattern that had him set up for a near-certain touchdown. The 49ers never recovered and lost, 49–3. Joe Montana and backup Jeff Kemp combined to go 15-for-37 on passes, and San Francisco's plan to run the ball away from Taylor did limit Taylor's tackles, but set up Carl Banks for a big day with five solo tackles and two assisted tackles, as the 49ers wound up with 29 rushing yards on 20 carries. There was, perhaps, some disappointment for the Giants when the Redskins went to Chicago and throttled the Bears, who were playing with Doug Flutie at quarterback in place of Jim McMahon. That ended the Giants' chance to avenge the embarrassing loss in Chicago the previous season, but it was not a surprise to see the Redskins earning a spot in the NFC Championship Game. "A lot of our players thought it would be them,"

Bill Parcells said. "I thought so, too. They don't die easy. . . . They're the best team we played all year."

Two weeks earlier, in the Redskins' wild-card playoff win over the Rams, Jacoby had broken two bones in his hand and had to wear a cast over his arm to keep playing. There was some pain, and Redskins trainers gave Jacoby a ball of foam to grip with his hand while blocking to dull the pain of contact. That ball, though, would keep him from getting the palms of his hands into Taylor the way he liked. Worse, the cast would get heavy as the game wore on, the soft inside material weighed down by sweat and the heavy outside frozen by brisk winter temperatures. Jacoby was not the only one with problems, though. Just as the Redskins' offense was focused on containing Taylor, for the Giants' offensive line—lovingly dubbed the Suburbanites by Parcells— Redskins defensive end Dexter Manley was central to the game plan. Manley had been second in the league in sacks (18.5), and, unlike Taylor (the league-leader with 20.5), might have ranked first in trash talk. But during the season, Redskins coach Joe Gibbs had publicly requested that Manley tighten his mouth and keep his focus on the field. Manley complied, but produced only one sack in the five games that followed and had been so effectively limited by lineman Brad Benson when the Redskins and Giants met in December that Benson was named NFC Offensive Player of the Week, a rare honor for a lineman. Still, even with his manners tamed by team-ordered mandate, Manley's taunts of the Giants from earlier in the season stuck with the team. In the conference room where the offensive line put together its weekly strategy, a sign hung on the door reading, "Dexter Manley: You wanted the Giants, you got us." When, in the days before the NFC Championship, Benson strode into the media interview room, fellow lineman Jim Burt took the intercom microphone and announced to gathered reporters: "The best against the best. Benson vs. Dexter. Whoever wins the battle decides the game." Burt was not entirely joking. With temperatures around freezing and winds of about 25 mph expected at the Meadowlands, the game was set up to be won or lost at the line of scrimmage.

It could be argued that the game was decided by the toss of the coin. The Giants won it, and Joe Gibbs would later say, "I think the coin toss was the biggest play for them." Parcells ceded the first possession to the Redskins and opted to take the wind at his team's back for the opening quarter. That would limit Jay Schroeder as a threat, at least when the wind was in his face. In the two losses, Schroeder had tallied 729 yards passing against the Giants, which accounted for one-fifth of the passing yards they had given up on the year. Going into the wind to start the game, Washington went three-and-out, but when punter Steve Cox lined up for his first kick, from his own 24 yard line, the wind pushed the ball to the outside of his foot, and shanked to the sideline at the Redskins' 47 yard line. That set up the Giants for a field goal, continuing their season-long streak of never trailing the Redskins in three meetings. Another fruitless Redskins possession led to another punt for Cox, who had averaged 43.6 yards during the season, fifth in the NFL. This one was not much better. Cox kicked from his own 11 yard line, and sent the ball wobbling for just 27 yards. The Giants put together a steady drive to cover the 38 yards, with Simms throwing an 11-yard touchdown to Lionel Manuel, establishing a 10–0 lead. As *Washington Post* columnist Tom Boswell wrote, "Can 10–0 feel like 100–0?"

The wind ensured the much-hyped battle along the lines was the game's critical factor. The Redskins altered their blocking scheme, and Jacoby was able to keep Taylor (who injured his thigh in the second half) in check and without a sack despite 50 pass attempts. Manley, too, despite his repeated verbal jabs at Benson, was quiet on the stat sheet. He did not have a sack. Phil Simms only threw 14 passes, and completed seven for a modest 90 yards. Schroeder completed only 20, for 195 yards. But the Giants won the field-position game, and suffocated the Redskins' running game, which had put up 134 yards on the Bears' brick-wall defense the week before, but managed just 40 against the Giants. Benson and the Suburbanites were able to grind out enough of an advantage to help Joe Morris to 87 yards rushing, the bulk of New York's 117 rushing yards on the day. It was an unsightly game, but the Giants controlled the line of scrimmage and won, 17–0. For the first time, the team would be going to the Super Bowl, doing it behind a defense that was getting better as it went along, developing a ruthless ability to identify the other team's strength—for the Redskins, it was running the ball—and shut it down. Long after the game, as the last stragglers in the locker room cleared out, Giants president George Young was asked if the win over Washington had reminded him of anything in particular. "Alexander the Great against Darius," Young said. "Alexander had 14,000 troops. They say Darius had an army of a million. Alexander sent his men to the center of the lines and told them, 'Look for the elephants.' He knew that where the elephants were, that's where Darius would be, too. Kill the emperor and it's an enormous psychological blow. His troops would panic."

That's what the Giants' defense had grown accustomed to doing: Finding its opponent's emperor. And killing him.

44

IT WAS SAID THAT WHEN Ed Koch was vying to be mayor in 1977 as a reformer running against entrenched party interests, the deals he made to gain the support of the three major party bosses—Donald Manes in Queens, Stanley Friedman in the Bronx, and Meade Esposito in Brooklyn—amounted to a Faustian bargain. Koch rankled at that characterization, insisting there was no quid pro quo involved, and he had given nothing away in gaining the support of the leaders. But the bargain Koch could not deny, the one for which he did sell a bit of his soul, was his public flirtation during the campaign with Bess Myerson, who had become a hero around the nation in 1945 when she won Miss America, the first Jewish woman to win the honor. She had entered politics in the late 1960s, joining the Lindsay administration in the Department of Consumer Affairs. Myerson had agreed, with convincing from campaign manager David Garth, to make some appearances with Koch in what was still a longshot bid for the mayoralty. But when

Koch began gaining ground on Mario Cuomo and others, Myerson was easily persuaded to make more appearances. She was not just a Koch supporter; she became Koch's cover story to thwart allegations he was gay. Garth had set up the pair, Koch had run with it, and Myerson indulged her renewed celebrity. When cameras were around, Koch could be seen holding Myerson's hand and cooing with her in public, inviting questions about their potential matrimony. At rallies, Koch would sometimes appear with Myerson and ask the crowd, "Wouldn't she make a great first lady of Gracie Mansion?" Koch was asked on television, just ahead of the 1977 vote, whether he might marry Myerson. "It's always a possibility," he said. The rumors of Koch's sexuality persisted, but Koch's play-acting courtship of Myerson was an effective response, and a major reason Koch beat Cuomo in November.

It was also a total fabrication, a political hoax. There would be no marriage, and the Koch-Myerson relationship mostly dissolved into a cordial friendship after the 1977 election, with Myerson hanging onto a job as the Cultural Affairs commissioner at City Hall. That made her a lingering vulnerability for Koch, the woman who knew the truth about Koch's private life and the public sham in which she had participated 10 years earlier. In January 1987, it was reported that when Myerson was brought before a Rudy Giuliani-led federal grand jury investigating sewer contractor Andy Capasso—with whom Myerson had been in a relationship since 1980, when Capasso was still married to his now ex-wife, Nancy—and the $53 million worth of city contracts his company received for a project in Brooklyn, she had taken the Fifth Amendment and refused to answer questions. This put Koch in a bind. The previous year, he had told reporters any commissioner in his government who pleaded the Fifth would be fired because Koch did not know if he could trust them. But Myerson had to be handled delicately, and there was some relief when she agreed to accept a three-month leave of absence while a special prosecutor, former judge Harold Tyler, investigated the matter. Capasso pleaded guilty to four charges of tax evasion, hoping Giuliani would be satisfied and stop his probes into other aspects of the case. Giuliani did not.

In April, Tyler delivered his report to Koch, who kept it private, issuing only a terse, 156-word statement acknowledging "improprieties" on Myerson's part. In June, though, the Tyler Report was leaked to the *Village Voice*, and its primary finding produced another round of woe for Koch. During the Capasso divorce proceedings, Myerson had befriended the judge, Hortense Gabel, who would be ruling on Capasso's alimony payments to his wife. Myerson brought the daughter of the judge, who had struggled with depression and had been unable to hold a job, into the Cultural Affairs department, gave her a job, and lavished her with praise and attention. Shortly thereafter, Gabel ruled in favor of Andy Capasso, cutting his payments to his wife from $1,500 per week to $500. Tyler found Myerson had used her office to "improperly influence" Gabel's decision.

Koch did not need more headaches. It probably should not have been a surprise to find Capasso in the throes of scandal—he was a close friend of Manes and had been a tennis partner of Friedman—but his connection with Myerson had the potential to deal the kind of personal blow to Koch he had been able to dodge with the other city scandals. Worse for Koch, the Myerson scandal had the full attention of Giuliani, still carrying the glow of his office's wins in Friedman's corruption case and in the Mafia Commission case. It had been an open secret that Giuliani had come to New York to kick off a political career, perhaps with a run for Cuomo's seat in Albany in 1990 or with a run for Senate against Patrick Moynihan in 1988. Both would be formidable opponents. Koch would not be so formidable, though, wounded as he was by scandal and facing a potential political death knell should details about his private life emerge. Giuliani had been careful, going back to his first entry in the city's municipal scandal through the guilty verdict against Friedman, not to point a finger at Koch for the corruption that had overcome parts of his government. That was just good sense. Giuliani had no evidence Koch knew anything about the payout schemes in the Parking Violations Bureau, so when he was asked, he routinely came to Koch's defense, and Koch would proudly repeat his findings. Still, as Geoge Arzt recalled, "I think Koch was wary of him. I think Koch suspected that he wanted to run for Mayor at some point." If Giuliani could get something truly damaging on Koch, something that might pave his way to the mayor's office, Giuliani would have to consider it. And Koch's personal life, especially if it could be shown that he was gay and had been lying about his sexuality for more than a decade as mayor, had the potential to do the most political damage.

Koch had a complex relationship with his sexual identity. As Andy Logan of the *New Yorker* once wrote about rumors of Koch's sex life, "There is no solid evidence of the Mayor's having had any passion in life other than politics." His experience in the 1977 election—the questions about his homosexuality, the "Vote for Cuomo, Not the Homo" posters—scarred him. He was almost universally consistent every time the topic of his sexuality came up. He was never outraged by the questions, but handled them in a style that was typical of him: plucky, blunt, and ribald, with a rhetorical flourish. In an interview done just before his death in 2013, Koch was asked about keeping his sexuality private, even after social mores had changed so much. Koch's position was that if he had answered the question, he would be making it acceptable for any reporter to ask any politician about his or her sex life. Koch did not identify himself as a gay man, did not want to be identified as the gay mayor, and did not believe sexuality should be a political litmus test. "I am not going to let it happen if I can prevent it," Koch said. "And so I have taken the position, in response to the basic question, it's none of your fucking business." Koch recalled appearing on CNN's *Reliable Sources* in 2000 with Howard Kurtz and Bernie Kalb, who pressed him on the issue of public figures keeping their sexuality masked. Koch turned the tables, asking Kurtz if he was married. When he said he was, Koch asked, "Well, when was the last time you performed oral sex on your wife?" When Kurtz recoiled in shock, Koch told him, "It's a terrible question, don't answer it." But his point was made. "There are things you don't have to answer," Koch said.

This was one thing he would not be answering, at least, unless Giuliani got his hands on enough solid information to go public. The more Giuliani looked into Myerson's history, the more pressure that could be brought to bear on her, the closer Koch would be to having his nightmare—a stream of questions about his sex life going back to his charade with Myerson—made a reality.

45

IF THE WORLD SERIES PARADE through Manhattan had been the harbinger of personal disaster for Mets star Dwight Gooden—whose woes began when he missed the festivities after spending the night on a cocaine bender in a Long Island housing project—then maybe Mayor Ed Koch was doing the Giants and drug-troubled players like Bobby Johnson and Lawrence Taylor a favor. Long before the Giants had beaten the Redskins and punched their ticket to the Super Bowl, Koch had said he would not put on a ticker-tape parade up Broadway if the Giants (or the Jets, for that matter) won a championship. He called the Giants, playing as they did in New Jersey, a "foreign team," and added, "I would probably go to a ticker tape parade in Moonachie. But if they want a ticker tape parade in New York City, they will have to play in New York City." Koch punctuated his disdain for the other side of the Hudson by pronouncing Moonachie as "mah-NOO-chee" rather than the correct "moo-NAH-kee." It was a silly controversy, especially as more serious problems like the racial attack at Howard Beach were dominating the mayor's priority list. But it was the kind of controversy the papers liked to debate. The Giants had New York in their name, and were listed in the Manhattan phone book. PR man Tom Powers harkened back to the team's days at Yankee Stadium in the Bronx. "It's the same franchise that has represented the area for its entire history," Powers said. "We are now six miles west of the Empire State Building, where we were previously six miles north." But the franchise mailing address was in East Rutherford, New Jersey, along with its headquarters and stadium. When the Giants played in the NFC Championship, signs read DROP DEAD ED! NEW JERSEY #1! and MAYOR KOCH: LOVE THY NEIGHBOR.

Lawrence Taylor, that astute political pundit, observed, "Mr. Koch, or whatever he calls himself, he's something else. He's a great bandwagon player. He'll probably change his mind if he finds out it means enough votes for him." Taylor was right. With the mayor being stung by the criticism, most notably from Donald Trump, that he was allowing major companies—he was fighting to keep NBC in the city—to escape Manhattan for the asphalt flats and cheap rents of New Jersey, he held to his stand on the Giants. The Times and CBS ran a poll of New Yorkers, and found support for a parade in the city had a narrow edge, 46 to 42 percent. American Express stepped in with a compromise, offering to pay $700,000 in cleanup and police overtime for a parade in New York. Koch agreed to that, and rolled back his earlier potshots on the Garden State. "The foreign state I love the best," he said, "is New Jersey, because I used to live there." But by then, the Giants had already been stung by Koch's preemptive parade denial. When the NFC championship was settled, the Giants put out a statement: "The only logical place for a Giants celebration is here at Giants Stadium in the New Jersey Sports Complex." The issue was settled. Koch was ambivalent. It was pointed out to him that he would be in Poland when the Giants played the Super Bowl. He responded that he would be among people who cared as much about the game as he did.

· · · · ·

Harry Carson has a favorite photo, taken at the 50 yard line of the Rose Bowl in Pasadena, at the captains' meeting and coin toss before Super Bowl XXI in January 1987. Moments earlier, he had been talking with coach Bill Parcells about what he wanted if they won the toss. Carson paused, waiting for some of the other captains to join him. Instead, Parcells said, "Go ahead!" So he went out to the middle of the field, alone, as the crew of Broncos captains approached. Alexander vs. Darius. In the photo, he is shaking hands with the quarterback of the AFC champion Broncos, John Elway. Looking on are four other Broncos: defensive back Louis Wright, linebacker Tom Jackson, receiver Steve

Watson, and kicker Rich Karlis. "I'm standing there for the coin toss with Jerry Markbreit, who was the official," Carson said, "and you had five Denver Bronco captains that I was going up against there. I run into Giants fans and they tell me, 'The coolest thing was when you went out for the coin toss by yourself.' I think people wonder, what was Bill Parcells thinking, what was he trying to achieve? I think he just liked that image, one Giant against all of those Broncos. It really is a great shot for me." It also brought Carson back to his first days with the Giants, when the franchise could do almost nothing right and he wanted nothing more than to be traded elsewhere, to be given a real chance to win. It brought back the pain of the loss to the Bears the previous January, when the Giants had flattened against a team they felt they could have at least challenged. Now, he was calling the coin toss in the Super Bowl. "I have had fans tell me," Carson said, "they knew we were going to win just seeing me alone out there."

The game against the Broncos would not be so easy. The Giants knew, because they had played Denver in December and had been chewed up by Elway, who threw for 336 yards and ran for another 51. The Broncos defense had been tough, sacking Phil Simms three times and limiting him to 148 yards passing. The offense could muster only four field goals from Raul Allegre, but the margin in the 19–16 win came thanks to a 78-yard interception return for a touchdown by George Martin. When the Super Bowl began, Elway took advantage of the Giants' defensive scheme, which called for its defensive backs to give plenty of cushion to Broncos receivers to take away deep balls. Elway made the Giants pay with short throws in front of the defense, and completed his first seven passes. Karlis started the scoring with a record-tying 48-yard field goal a little more than four minutes into the game, but Simms brought the Giants right back, completing passes of 17 yards to Lionel Manuel, an 18-yarder to Stacy Robinson, and another 17-yard pass to Mark Bavaro to set up a six-yard touchdown pass to Zeke Mowatt. Elway returned fire with a six-play, 59-yard drive that yielded Denver's first touchdown, with just over two minutes to go in the opening quarter.

During the week leading up to the Super Bowl, Broncos coach Dan Reeves had gotten so fed up with media questions about the impossibility of scoring on the Giants defense (which had allowed three points in its two postseason wins) that he finally answered, "We're gonna run all trick plays, because we can't score on 'em any other way." But through one quarter, the Broncos had put up 10 points and held a lead. Elway nearly built on that lead on the team's next possession. He hit Mark Jackson over the middle for a 54-yard completion and got the Broncos to the 1 yard line for a first-and-goal. The defense, dazed by the passing of Elway, snapped into focus with Denver on the verge of taking early control of the game. The Giants got some help from Reeves, whose play-calling broke the Broncos' momentum when he started the series by calling for an Elway rollout run that went for a one-yard loss, then called for running back Gerald Willhite up the middle, who was stopped for no gain. On third down, rather than going back to the passing game that had gotten the Broncos into position to score, Reeves called for a Sammy Winder rush to the outside. Winder was dropped for a loss of four yards, and Karlis came on to try a 23-yard field goal. He missed, setting the record for shortest field goal miss in a Super Bowl a little more than a quarter after setting the record for the longest. After Simms drove the team to the 47, the Broncos were pinned by a Landeta punt at their own 15. There, the defense piled on during the Broncos' next possession, sacking Elway and recording a safety with just under three minutes to play in the half. Karlis would miss another field goal, this one from 34 yards with 18 seconds to go before the break, leaving the score at 10–9, and leaving the Giants lucky to not be trailing by more.

After their first-half struggles, the third quarter played by the Giants would go down as arguably the most dominant quarter in the history of the Super Bowl. Defensively, coordinator Bill Belichick made the decision to alter the approach of the defensive backs on the Broncos' short routes—rather than playing off the receivers, the Giants would now jump the routes, forcing Elway to stay in the pocket longer and giving the New York pass rush a chance to put some hits on him. In all, not including punts, the Broncos ran just seven plays in the quarter, and Elway dropped back to pass on all seven of them. He completed only two, for a total of 13 yards. He threw four incompletions and was sacked by Leonard Marshall for an 11-yard loss. That left Denver's net third-quarter production at two yards. While Elway, who did not have much help on hand, languished, Simms thrived. He completed all 10 passes he threw in the second half. The Giants' first score was boosted by a gutsy fake punt called by backup quarterback Jeff Rutledge that converted a 4th-and-1 situation and set up a 13-yard touchdown to Mark Bavaro. A field goal by Allegre with 3:56 to play in the quarter made the score 19–10. But the knockout blow came with just under 30 seconds to play in the third. On a 2nd-and-6 play from the Denver 45, the Giants called for a flea-flicker, a play they had practiced for six months but had not used during the season. Simms gave the ball to Joe Morris, and the Denver defense collapsed to stop the run. But Morris flipped the ball back to Simms who found McConkey downfield running toward the left sideline. McConkey caught the pass and raced toward the end zone. "I wanted that touchdown so bad," he said. But he was upended by ex-Giants teammate Mark Haynes at the 1 yard line. McConkey stood up and pointed both hands at the sky. He had not scored, but the implication was clear: The Giants were going to win. Joe Morris finished off the yard McConkey did not get, and the Giants led, 26–10. "I think," Simms said, "it just about ended the game."

It was fitting that, for all the pregame attention given to Elway on one side and the Giants defense on the other, it was Simms who carried the day and was named MVP, putting together a record-breaking statistical line: 22-for-25 passing, 268 yards, three touchdowns, zero interceptions. For so long, even as the Giants rose out of the franchise ashes of the '70s and gained respectability, they were known as the team that could not win the big game. But by the time the 39–20 rout of the Broncos was over, Simms had led them to three big playoff wins by a total score of 105–23, throwing eight touchdowns and no interceptions, completing 66 percent of his passes. Three weeks earlier, in the waning moments of the win over the 49ers, Simms had been sitting on the bench, his head between his knees, waiting for the clock to expire. McConkey was behind him, pointing to him for the Giants Stadium crowd, and raising his arms to incite cheering. Simms had no idea, not until he saw tape of the game later. McConkey made his point. "I've been there enough times when he's gotten booed," he said. Now, three thousand miles away from the Meadowlands, Simms was reveling in his finest hour. "It was as good a game as has ever been played by a quarter-back—anywhere," Parcells said. "That ought to dispel any myths about Phil Simms." It would, mostly. Simms would still play for the Giants, and he would still—in time—be booed by local fans. The Giants would win another NFL championship in Super Bowl XXV four years later, but with Simms injured, the starting honors went to Jeff Hostetler, who went 20-for-32 with 222 yards. Good, but no Phil Simms.

After the game, McConkey reflected on how narrow the opportunity to win a Super Bowl can be. He had been cut by the Giants to start the season, after all, and he was just coming off a game in which he had made the play that even Broncos players admitted was the back-breaker. The satisfaction from the win brought to mind the wrenching disappointment of the losses that had come before. It had been more than a year since the Giants had suffered their humiliating loss to the Bears in the conference semifinals, and for McConkey, the thing that had stood out about that loss was not just the pain of being so close to a Super Bowl but failing when the opportunity came, it was the flight that followed. McConkey had played football at Navy, and was a pilot. During the flight, while he was watching the end of the AFC Championship Game with Byron Hunt near the front of the plane, he had noticed one of the engines had gone out. It was not apparent to most of the team, and the pilots did not let on that anything was wrong, but McConkey knew enough about planes to know the sound of an engine being restarted unsuccessfully. "When we got to New Jersey, all of the crash equipment and vehicles were on the runway with the lights flash-ing, and the rest of the players thought it was a welcoming. I knew what they were there for, and I knew we weren't going to get a welcome after a loss like that. We got down OK. But coach Parcells' message that we might never get another chance came home with us. Chicago is where this season started."

Now it was over. For the first time since 1956, the Giants were champions. For the first time ever, they were Super Bowl champions. When the Mets had won the World Series in October, fans at Shea Stadium stood up and sang, full-throated, "New York, New York." Three months later and a continent away in California, fans were again standing up for a rendition of "New York, New York," again full-throated. "Both of those teams," columnist Jerry Izenberg said, "really infected the town."

46

IN JANUARY OF 1987, METS general manager Frank Cashen wrote letters to each of his players, with a common theme: They don't think you can repeat as champions. "They" would be other players, opposing coaches, the media. Cashen could not, realistically, be certain just what "they" actually thought, but the letters seemed like a good way to start rallying his players and recapturing the us-vs.-them vibe that carried the Mets in 1986. Truth was, Cashen had to have his doubts, too. A team expects a certain amount of tumult in the wake of a championship, but the Mets' post-World Series hangover was perhaps the nastiest in league history. Tim Teufel and Ron Darling got a year of probation for their roles in the Cooter's fight in Houston. Darryl Strawberry, after his Game Six tiff with Davey Johnson and a *New York Post* "Straw Poll" taken three days after the World Series to determine whether fans wanted him traded, found more trouble off the field that winter. He was separated from his wife, Lisa, in January, and she accused him of punching her and breaking her nose after a postseason game the previous October. The Mets let Ray Knight go, which was the right thing, baseball-wise (he only played two more seasons), but the team would miss his leadership. Even squeaky-clean Gary Carter got caught up in controversy, though was not personally implicated in any wrongdoing. He had done ads for a bogus vitamin company that ran an illegal marketing scheme. And there was Dwight Gooden. The missed parade after the World Series, the three years of probation for his run-in with the Tampa cops, the loaded gun his ex-fiancée brought into the airport—it was a disaster for the Mets' young star. "I'm not looking for a bunch of altar boys," Cashen said. "But I've talked to Davey about the team's troubles. If you're a class team, you behave with class. I told the players people would be taking aim at them. You're from New York, that's part of it. This whole thing about arrogance involves New York. But it's there."

For Gooden, the problems were just beginning. Even after his vow to Tom McEwen he would accept drug testing "forever" in his next contract, even after the incident with the police, he had been using cocaine heavily in the offseason, and had not stopped in spring training. In his autobiography, he described that time in his life, when he really became hooked on coke: "I didn't know when to stop. I was the guy from last night who was still wearing a party hat while the maid was vacuuming the living room rug. Everyone else had gone off to work, and I couldn't make it off the couch." The Mets and Gooden worked out a new $1.5 million contract in February, and because of the collective bargaining agreement, any deal to have Gooden drug tested throughout the season would have to be made by a separate letter. Gooden had not backed down on his insistence on drug testing, overtaken by a sense of righteousness that had started with his interview with McEwen in November and a corresponding sense of hubris that told him he could beat any test. "I feel I have to do it, I want it," Gooden told reporters that spring. "Last year, there were a lot of things written like, 'What's wrong with Doc?' And since I'm young and black, they probably wondered if [drug use] was it." The Mets did not want Gooden to get caught, of course. Even with his midseason slump in 1986 and his World Series failings, he was still their ace. Team officials informed him through agent Jim Neader that if he failed a drug test, the results would have to be sent to the commissioner, and based on the punishment Ueberroth had doled out to those involved in the Pittsburgh cocaine scandal, Gooden would be looking at a year's suspension or a stint in rehab. Neader finalized an agreement with the Mets on March 25 that allowed for the team to test him once during spring training and three times at random during the season. To Gooden's shock, the team wasted no time in asking for a urine sample—the request came the next day. He had used cocaine twelve hours before.

The Mets got the results back on March 28. Gooden failed. The next day, Cashen would have to inform Ueberroth and NL president Bart Giamatti. Ueberroth was not surprised—he had been informed by police in Tampa that Gooden had been known to hang out at some of the city's most drug-infested spots, including a place called the Manila Bar & Restaurant in Tampa's Ybor City section. Cashen would have to wait on their discussions before he could tell Gooden, setting himself up for an excruciating forty-eight hours. Having gone four days without word from the team, Gooden thought he was in the clear. But on April 1 Cashen called him into his office and told him the situation. Gooden insisted the test had been wrong. Cashen, stone-faced, told him it was not wrong. Gooden finally broke down and admitted his drug use. Ueberroth offered him a chance to avoid suspension by checking into rehab. Some sympathetic media members framed Gooden's demands to be tested as a cry for help, an acknowledgment he was in trouble. Cashen told reporters, "The sudden fame and fortune he achieved was nice. But we sort of robbed him of his youth." But Gooden still did not think of himself as an addict, did not think he needed help, thought he could stop his cocaine use any time he wanted. He figured a stint at rehab would be a faster way back onto the mound, and he would still be paid. On April 3, Gooden left spring training and was in the front row of a flight from Tampa to New York, where he was met on the tarmac by a van that whisked him to Midtown Manhattan. He checked into the Smithers Alcohol and Treatment Center, surrounded by a phalanx of reporters and cameramen, documenting his public humiliation.

Giants coach Bill Parcells, watching the spectacle on the news, called his wife in to watch. "This is obscene," she said. "You got that right," Parcells said. But within a little more than a year, Parcells would see his own player—Lawrence Taylor, whom he had proudly said had been treated for drug abuse on his own—put through a similar gauntlet. When the NFL endured a strike to start an injury-riddled and miserable 1987 season for the Giants, Taylor had crossed the picket line and alienated teammates. He promised to remake his image in 1988, telling reporters, "I've been thought about around this place as a wild person. I don't mind what people think of me personally. What I do care about is what they think of me when I step into a locker room or when I step on a football field." But even as he was saying that, Taylor had already failed another drug test, and would fail a second one from the league that resulted in a four-game suspension in 1988. In 1989, too, he was arrested on a DUI charge, and would continue to add to a litany of offenses as he transitioned into retirement. Years later, when he saw a documentary about his life, Taylor cried. "To see your life through the eyes of others, I mean, that's a bitch," Taylor said. "That's hard to handle. And I mean, I really apologize to the people who, if I harmed them in any way, especially my kids and stuff. It's very, very humbling."

Gooden was released from Smithers at the end of April 1987, and was back on the mound in early June. But his drug troubles haunted him throughout his career and into his retirement—as late as 2016, Gooden was still battling relapses into cocaine abuse. On the mound, he was never the second coming of Bob Gibson. He went 15–7 even after his late start in 1987, and was an All-Star again in 1988, with an 18–9 record. He won 19 games in 1990, but, at age twenty-five, that would be his final great season. He was 119–46 through that year, and after, as he lost control of both his drug problem and his fastball, he went 75–66. Davey Johnson, looking back, would later say, "The problem with Dwight is he couldn't say no. He was too nice. Evidently, he knew people in Tampa who could get you in trouble. It was like he was the lucky one, and it would be wrong for him not to be their friend, like he wanted to prove to them he wasn't acting like a big shot and turning his back on them."

To which Gooden said, "That's 100 percent true."

47

It was difficult to puff up the ego of Donald Trump beyond its already established limits, but his success in besting the city and Ed Koch with the renovation of the Wollman Rink in late 1986 did just that. For the first time, acting mostly on his own, without the help of Roy Cohn or Stanley Friedman or his football team, Trump had conceived of a major public relations campaign, and pulled it off as an unqualified success. Koch groused that Trump had advantages in getting the rink done so quickly the city did not have—mostly, he did not have to endure the vagaries of the bidding process. Trump began speaking as though he had long been a rock-solid advocate of the virtues of private business over wasteful bureaucracy. He told CBS News, "I really wanted to prove a point. The cities, New York City in particular, but the cities are so wealthy, if we could only save the money that we're wasting." He was hailed for that across New York, and basked in the frigid glow of the rink. One former aide told a Trump biographer, "Wollman Rink was a turning point. After that, Donald started referring to himself in the third person. He'd call me and say, 'What did you think of that story about Trump in the newspaper today? What did you think of the story about Trump on TV?' I'd say to him, 'Hey, Donald, you *are* Trump.'"

Trump knew just what he wanted to do with the public goodwill he had earned. Koch knew, too. For more than a year, Trump had been proposing to block out the sun on the Hudson River. Not literally, perhaps, but close. Since he bought a one-hundred-acre parcel of land on the Upper West Side in late 1984—-the old Penn Central Rail Yards—Trump had been trying to get the city behind a plan to convert the site into a hulking development that would have as its centerpiece a 1,910-foot tower surrounded by seven seventy-six-story buildings and a seventeen-story building dedicated to studio space. There would be thirty acres of park space, and housing available for 14,700 mostly affluent residents. There would be a heliport. He was calling the project Television City, and he intended to recruit a major network to anchor the whole thing. NBC had been his target, because the network's lease at 30 Rockefeller Plaza, with aging studios that had been designed for radio and increasingly high rent, would be up beginning in 1989. When he first introduced the design the previous year, his company put out a press release calling it "the master builder's grandest plan yet," and he was asked why New York might need the tallest building in the world. "We are prone to go forward," was his response, perhaps his grasp at pithy profundity. Architecture critic Paul Goldberger summed up his reasoning more concisely, saying that for Trump, the plan, "makes sense mainly as a symbol—a symbol of New York's eminence, of course, and of his own."

But the plan required an environmental impact study, and that is where the sun became a problem for Trump. Because the buildings were lined up, single file, along the bank of the Hudson River, once noon hit, they would begin casting their shadows back toward the east, over Manhattan. At worst, around 3:00 p.m. on most days, shadows would stretch from the river all the way to Tenth Avenue, from 59th Street up to 77th. That would leave a total of thirty-six city blocks fully in the shade. The park along the river would be a nice concept, but it would be in the shade for most of the day, the study reported, until 3:00 p.m. At 9:00 a.m. on December 21, with the sun at its lowest point of the year, the shadow would stretch all the way across the Hudson and reach New Jersey. Airline pilots expressed their concern that the height of the TV City tower would interfere with flight patterns.

West Side residents feared what the project would do to traffic, and formed a TV City–opposition group called Westpride, buoyed by affluent and influential residents of the neighborhood, including television journalist Bill Moyers, writer Betty Friedan, and historian Robert Caro, who called the project a "phalanx of monstrous skyscrapers looming up against the sky." Paul Gapp, an architecture critic for the *Chicago Tribune*, who had bemoaned the impact of "giantism" in his own city, which housed the Sears Tower, called Trump's proposal "an atrocious, ugly monstrosity, one of the silliest things anyone could inflict on New York or any other city." He told a reporter from the *Wall Street Journal* that the building would be "aesthetically lousy." (Indignant, Trump channeled Roy Cohn and filed a frivolous $500 million lawsuit against Gapp, which was quickly thrown out.) Goldberger told an interviewer, "[Trump] has yet to commission a really serious work of architecture. If he has a style, it is flashiness. It's a malady of the age. Trump just represents it the most."

The city was taking seriously Trump's plan for Television City, even if the entire idea appeared to be a moonshot, much as both the city and state had gotten behind Trump's half-baked Trumpdome scheme in Queens, which by April 1987 was declared "pretty much dead." His success with the Wollman Rink and his ongoing identification with Trump Tower, the most prominent new building of New York's 1980s real estate renaissance, kept up Trump's reputation as an attractive partner for the city. Which, in itself, was strange. By all rights, Trump should have been reviled in New York for how he had handled the building of Trump Tower. He had hired a contractor, the Kaszycki Corporation, to start the project in 1980, and Kaszycki's first act was to bring in two hundred illegal immigrants from Poland who were put to work in twelve-hour shifts, making non-union wages of $4 to $5 per hour demolishing the old Bonwit Teller Building to make way for the Tower. Most of those workers never received their full pay, and a suit was filed by a dissident of the Housewreckers Local 95 union, Harry Diduck, in 1983. (Diduck stuck out the lawsuit through his death in 1993, and Trump settled with the union in 1999.)

Additionally, there were almost certainly Mafia connections involved with that demolition crew. For Trump to have permission, even through a contractor, to use illegal non-union labor, he would need the tacit approval of the heads of the Housewreckers, who were identified in a 1987 government report as members of the Genovese family. The acting head of the Genovese family was Fat Tony Salerno, whose lawyer was Roy Cohn, who was Trump's guru before he contracted AIDS. Two workers died during the demolition. Trump also earned negative headlines when he had two classic *bas relief* sculptures that had adorned the Bonwit Teller Building destroyed after having promised to preserve and donate them to the Metropolitan Museum of Art. He asked a writer who was interviewing him in 1980 whether she thought the destruction of the bas reliefs had hurt his image. She said yes. He shrugged: "I'll never have the goodwill of the Establishment, the tastemakers of New York. Do you think, if I failed, these guys in New York would be unhappy? They would be thrilled!" He welcomed domestic and international criminals as residents in Trump Tower, too—recently deposed Haitian ex-dictator Baby Doc Duvalier, for example, had apartment 54-K, five floors down from Robert Hopkins, who ran a gambling ring and was charged, in 1985, for ordering the murder of a rival.

Trump's strategy for Television City had separate parts that were dependent on each other. First, he had to recruit NBC, getting its brass to make his site the preferred destination once its 30 Rock lease ran up, though there was stiff (and inexpensive) competition coming from sites across the river in New Jersey. Then, he had to get the city behind his audacious design. Finally, he would need a combination of support from both the city and NBC in the form of an acceptable package of tax abatements from the city that would allow him to give the network rents it could handle. He began a public offensive, tying NBC's future to the future of the city, and portraying the loss of NBC to New Jersey as a devastating possibility and part of a trend of corporate exodus. In 1967, New York was home to 139 companies on the Fortune 500. By 1987, it was fifty-three, and had dropped by thirteen in just four years. Trump played up this angle, and fed stories to all the city's major papers. By early 1987, there was momentum for NBC moving to the Upper West Side. In January, the company announced its choices were down to three: moving to the Meadowlands in New Jersey, anchoring TV City, or staying put and renovating its current home. But Trump's project had several problems beyond its environmental impact, the most significant being the size of the tax abatement he was seeking and the guy who would, ultimately, have to approve that abatement, Ed Koch. After the way Trump had delighted in the city's failures in the Wollman Rink saga, Koch was none too keen on giving away a slice of city funds for Trump's mega-project. Besides, the city could not even pin Trump down on what the expected cost of the abatements would be. Trump tried to manipulate and deceive Koch's deputy mayor, Alair Townsend, into quick action—in early May, he gave her what was described as a "panicky phone call" to say NBC was on the verge of a decision and she would need to approve the tax abatement immediately. That wasn't true, and Townsend quickly got a sense of what it was to deal with Trump. She said of him (a quote she later claimed was supposed to have been off the record), "I wouldn't believe Donald Trump if his tongue were notarized."

The Koch administration estimated Trump's abatement would run around $1 billion, a staggering sum for the objective of keeping NBC from moving to New Jersey. Negotiations with Trump cut that number to about $700 million in abatements, with a complicated revenue-sharing package to repay the city over time. The city was close to giving the deal the OK. But there was a piece Koch could not get past. Trump was asking for the tax break to be applied to the entire Television City project, when only a small portion (about a tenth) of the overall project would be dedicated to NBC. He would use what he needed to out of the abatement to lower the network's rents, and put the rest toward his luxury condos. Koch did not see that as a responsible use of city revenue. In late May, Koch announced the city would not grant Trump his abatement, and would focus on an approach that had not borne much fruit to that point: negotiating directly with NBC to come up with a package of tax incentives the company could use anywhere in New York City, whether at their current location, on the Upper West Side, or in some new location altogether. Trump was infuriated and took direct aim at Koch. The two exchanged heated letters, which Koch released to the media—in one, Trump called Koch's refusal to give the abatement "both ludicrous and disgraceful."

The floodgates were open. Koch had always had disdain for Trump, but had kept the relationship cordial. No more. Now, two of the city's most prominent loudmouths and media regulars were in stark conflict. TRUMP VS KOCH – IT'S WAR! read one headline in the *Post*. Trump told reporters, "He is more concerned about appearing to give anything to Donald Trump than he is about losing NBC. The city under Ed Koch is a disaster." Koch, combative as usual, read a quote from Trump only days earlier, when he said of Koch, "A very good man, a man that I have little skirmishes with every once in a while, but I think he is a very good man and a very good mayor." Koch shrugged at that and said, "Will the real Donald Trump please stand up?" When told that Trump had suggested Koch was at fault for companies leaving the city, Koch added, "If Donald Trump is squealing like a stuck pig, I must have done something right. Common sense does not allow me to give away the city's treasury to Donald Trump." Trump responded by calling Koch a "moron," and saying the mayor's only ability was in delivering "Henny Youngman one-liners, but Henny Youngman does them better." In an odd twist, the black weekly *Amsterdam News*, which had been running a front-page weekly column under the headline KOCH MUST RESIGN, dating back to the beginning of the municipal scandals of 1986, handed the space over to guest columnist Trump (who had been sued, with his father, for civil rights violations at their properties in 1973) for a week in May. Trump took the Koch-must-go rhetoric to the media himself, too, telling reporters, "Most of New York does not even have cable television, the homeless are unnecessarily wandering the streets, the schools are a disaster, and . . . after seven years, the city cannot even build a simple skating rink." He labeled the city a "cesspool of corruption," which was a statement slathered in hypocrisy—it was Stanley Friedman, one of Trump's top political button-pushers, who had been the face of the corruption Trump was now decrying. Koch said he considered the TV City abatement an important policy issue, and he did not want to see the whole thing "degenerate into a barnyard kind of contest." But then, Koch also had his most famous, and barnyard-inspired, line of the conflict: "Piggy, piggy, piggy Donald Trump! Greedy, greedy, greedy!" It may have been that Trump started the petty insults with Koch, but an editorial in the *Daily News* reminded readers, "Ever notice how Koch likes to turn what should be sober public policy issues into personality conflicts and name-calling contests?"

The *News* also ran a telephone poll that invited readers to call in and confirm their support of either Koch's position or Trump's position. Trump came out ahead by a whopping nine-to-one margin. *Crain's New York Business* ran a similar poll, and Trump came out on top. Disturbing, too, for Koch was that Rupert Murdoch's always sympathetic *New York Post*, which had been critical to vaulting Koch into office in the 1977 campaign and had drafted him into the 1982 governor's race, was treating the squabble with extra tabloid relish. But it was not Koch who was portrayed as the common New Yorker's choice. It was Trump. That fall, eight months behind the original deadline to announce a decision, NBC finally settled on remaining at Rockefeller Center, taking the city's package of interest-free loans and hundreds of millions of dollars in tax abatements. Neighborhood resistance, especially from well-heeled activists from Westpride, scared off NBC from Trump's project, and would scare off other corporations that might have otherwise gotten involved. Television City was never built, which meant Koch, essentially, won. But at least in a contest of public support, Trump had beaten Koch, handily.

·····

The confrontation with Koch had led to speculation about Trump's future. Koch, of course, was planning on running for reelection for a fourth term, and because Trump had proven so much more popular in the *Daily News* poll, he was a natural possibility to be an outsider challenger to Koch for the mayor's seat in 1989. With the city beleaguered by scandal for all of 1986 and with the political splintering that followed the Howard Beach incident to open 1987, the thinking was Koch still could win the Democratic nomination but the erosion of his support meant he would struggle against a qualified Republican, especially one who was, like Trump, capable of self-funding. Some saw the fight over TV City as a prelude to a mayoral showdown. Andy Logan, in the *New Yorker*, wrote that Trump was asked regularly if he was planning to run for mayor someday. "Although Trump's usual answer is no," she commented, "many of the recent exchanges between the two men sounded much like the verbal brawl one might expect at the height of a bitter political campaign." Despite his denials, Trump did have the look of a political stalwart. He had been recruited by state GOP chairman George Clark, who was desperate for a credible candidate, to run for governor against Mario Cuomo in 1986. Trump turned down that bid. Late in 1987, after an appearance on the *Phil Donahue Show*, he received a card reading, "I did not see the program, but Mrs. Nixon told me that you were great on the Donahue Show. As you can imagine, she is an expert on politics and she predicts that whenever you decide to run for office, you will be a winner!" The card was signed by Richard Nixon.

That would come. In the short term, Trump had just one use for politics, and that was to sell books. More than a year earlier, publishing magnate Si Newhouse noticed something about one of his magazines, *GQ*. When Trump was on the cover, there was an uptick in newsstand sales. Newhouse could not explain it, but he also could not deny with Trump came a popular fascination few celebrities could match. Newhouse, a close friend of Roy Cohn's, spent a year recruiting Trump and finally got him to agree to a book contract when associate publisher Peter Osnos approached him with a thick Russian novel around which he wrapped a black book jacket adorned with a photo of Trump beneath block letters reading: TRUMP. The sight won over Trump, whose only criticism was that the letters be bigger. Trump, oddly, picked *New York* magazine writer Tony Schwartz to be his ghostwriter, shortly after Schwartz had written a cover story for the magazine headlined A DIFFERENT KIND OF DONALD TRUMP STORY, and chronicled his battle with rent-controlled tenants at the Central Park South property he owned. In the article, Trump had come off as arrogant and spiteful ("If I were a regular guy, I couldn't go through this," he said), and the cover photo was an artist's touch-up of a Trump portrait that had him bearing a five-o'clock-shadow and a greasy shine on his chin and forehead. Schwartz was shocked to find that Trump had framed the unflattering cover for his office, and sent Schwartz a thank you note. Schwartz took the book job to write *The Art of the Deal* with Trump, and worked with him for eighteen months to come up with material, which was a struggle. Schwartz would later recall he was "shocked" because "Trump didn't fit any model of human being I'd ever met. He was obsessed with publicity, and he didn't care what you wrote."

As part of his publicity agenda for the book, due out just ahead of Christmas, Trump feigned interest in running for president in 1988. On September 2, Trump ran ads in the *Washington Post*, the *New York Times*, and the *Boston Globe*, pounding President Reagan on the United States's failures in international trade—specifically, he wanted America to give a bill to the countries of Western Europe and Japan for the cost of trying to keep the peace in the Middle East. As Howard Kurtz wrote in the *Post*, "When a prominent private person spends $94,801 to publicize such a message, it raises the age-old question: What's he running for?" Trump insisted he was not running for anything, but kept up the ruse by offering quotes and actions that indicated otherwise. "I believe that if I did run for President," he told the *Times*, "I'd win." He was invited to speak to the Rotary Club in Portsmouth, New Hampshire, in October 1987 by a draft-Trump-for-President group of Republicans, and his speech was well received. Trump was never serious about running, but the national flirtation with the possibility helped carry *The Art of the Deal* to the top of the bestseller list.

It was a welcome boost for his brand, which was at its peak in the days after the book was released, even as his personal life and the empire he had built was eroding, beyond public view. Trump's wealth was far too leveraged for him to fund a presidential campaign on his own, weighed down by a spending spree that came around the time of his battles with Koch: a third money-losing casino in Atlantic City, an ill-advised partnership with Lee Iacocca on a property in West Palm Beach, a $29 million yacht he had bought from the Sultan of Brunei, and an excursion into the airline industry with the Trump Shuttle. Three years later, the *Wall Street Journal* would estimate Trump had personal guarantees on properties and businesses that amounted to $600 million in debt, and *Forbes* magazine would drop his estimated net worth from $1.7 billion in 1989 to $500 million in the course of one year. For the political class in New York, this was why Trump was not considered a real threat to run for mayor or governor or even president—he owed too much to too many banks and too many people, and once the reality of those deals was put up to public scrutiny, his candidacy would collapse. In the summer of 1987, one New York politician discussed a possible mayoral run for Trump with *New York* magazine: "I think Donald Trump is just playing, he won't really run, although it would be fun to watch Koch rip him to shreds in a debate. And, anyway, the campaign wouldn't last beyond the first question: 'Show me your income taxes for the last five years.'" Trump, the magazine pointed out, would be a hypocrite if he did not show his taxes because that would contradict what he had previously said on the topic. Trump "says he believes candidates for public office should make full financial disclosure."

48

THE LETTER WAS DATED JULY 31, 1987, and *Washington Post* reporter Margot Hornblower was surprised to receive it. Days earlier, she had interviewed Ed Koch in his office for a lengthy story about the aftershocks of 1986's Parking Violations Bureau scandal in New York, and the new scandals that had emerged since. Koch felt the interview had not gone well. In his second sentence, Koch wrote, "I know from my point of view, it went from bad to worse. I think you have interviewed me in depth three times that I can recall. Each was bad and it's clear that the chemistry between us is such, that the outcome of any interview is almost preordained." Hornblower was taken aback. *Preordained? Bad chemistry?* A Harvard graduate who had been at the *Post* for thirteen years, Hornblower never thought of chemistry as a prerequisite for interviewing a politician or any subject, for that matter. Shrugging off Koch's strange lament, Hornblower went through his three-page letter. More than a year-and-a-half since Donald Manes had first attempted suicide, Koch was still hung up on protecting his own integrity and offering the usual rationalizations: corruption was not "systemic"; he took responsibility for the scandals but could not have known about them because "there were no milestones to gauge this corruption"; there should be a distinction drawn between those who left the administration because of ties to corruption and those who left "for some other reason involving fitness to serve." At particular issue for Koch was a question whose phrasing he found prejudicial—Hornblower had asked about "dozens" of members of his administration who were found to be corrupt. "Using your description," Koch wrote, "I interpreted 'dozens' to mean 36 (although I suppose you could have intended to mean as little as 24 or as many as 48 or more). Whichever number you choose to quantify the phrase 'corrupt officials,' I believe it will distort the reality of the past eighteen months."

But Koch's interpretation of Hornblower's question showed how desperate he was, even still, to defend his administration. Hornblower had used the word "dozens" to describe the totality of corruption in the city, including those who were not Koch appointees, like judges, contractors, and Democratic party officials. Those numbers were certainly in the dozens. But Koch, combative as always, had interrupted the question and did not listen to its ending. It was remarkable that, coming out of the most difficult year of his professional life, Koch had not changed much. He was still leaning on the same rhetorical crutches to fend off any corruption discussion, and he was still doing so with verve. When the *New York Times*, generally protective of Koch, did a front-page story in March 1987 titled WITH SCANDAL AND RE-ELECTION IN MIND, KOCH MELLOWS STYLE, one columnist wrote the headline caused "reporters at whom he had snapped and snarled that week to wonder what he might have called them if he had not mellowed."

Koch's government had been stifled, and little was getting done despite growing crises in homelessness, crime, and drug abuse. Little had changed politically in the city, either. In Queens, Manes was no longer borough president, but he was replaced by a former aide of his, Clare Shulman. In the Bronx, Stanley Friedman was replaced by close ally George Friedman (no relation) as the party boss, and, same as it ever was, borough president Stanley Simon was indicted on extortion charges and resigned in March 1987. The city was still relying heavily on no-bid contracts without records or details, which accounted for about 40 percent of city deals, or $2 billion worth. State comptroller Ned Regan called such contracts "an invitation to steal." Koch saw his approval poll numbers drop from 67 percent at the outset of 1985 to 55 percent in 1987. His mental and political malaise took on a physical form, too—he was putting on weight, and adding jowls. He had been 182 pounds when he ran for mayor in 1977, but was now over 220. In a rare moment of non-confrontation, Koch confided in *New York* writer Joe Klein: "I worry about my place in history. But you look at the polls and a majority of the people still support me. That's not bad. It's true I have made a lot of enemies, but I've been mayor for 10 years now . . . I find it *amazing* that I'm still as popular as I am."

Even for a mayor who had thrived on conflict, though, Koch was wearing down. Throughout the summer, as Giuliani's office pressed forth with its investigation into Bess Myerson, Koch grew more stressed. He had been a willing participant with reporters in repartee over the municipal scandals, but increasingly, there were signs that the personal life he had been so careful to protect was under siege. There was a column in the *Daily News* from his nemesis, Jimmy Breslin, in June in which Breslin savaged the administration and called out the mayor's assistant and Myerson pal, Herb Rickman, as gay. "Nowhere in the municipal history of this city," Breslin wrote, "has there been anything as evil as the New York of Koch, Bess Myerson and Herb Rickman. . . . It is now obvious that people involved in City Hall have allowed sex lives to directly interfere with the honesty of our government." There was something ominous about that—if Rickman's friendship with Myerson was inappropriate, he could be called on it, but that had nothing to do with his sex life. And Myerson was in a relationship with Capasso. She had not helped him for sex. "The column was a particularly vicious example of what used to be called fag baiting," Koch told Joe Klein. "It is an absolute outrage."

The Breslin column was just a bellwether, though. The more Giuliani's office looked into the Myerson case, the more interested it seemed in the sex lives of those in City Hall, rather than the cut-and-dried (and relatively minor) case that could be made against Myerson for attempting to curry favor with a judge on behalf of her boyfriend. One of the potential witnesses interviewed by Giuliani's people was Larry Kramer, the playwright and gay activist, who had long sought to out Koch as gay because he had felt Koch had not done enough to combat AIDS. Kramer told a story of Richard Nathan, who had been a campaign aide for Koch in 1977, and had met with Kramer in Los Angeles the previous year. There, according to mutual friend and producer/activist David Rothenberg, Nathan had told Kramer he "was the much-rumored secret lover of Mayor Ed Koch." Later, back in New York, Kramer began calling journalists and telling them about Nathan, saying Rothenberg could confirm that he was Koch's lover. When Rothenberg went to his office the day after Kramer's calls, he was met by a half-dozen reporters and feigned ignorance of their questions about Nathan. But he called Nathan that morning, warning him about what would happen if he became the central figure in a story that confirmed the mayor of New York was gay. Rothenberg asked Nathan "if he was out of his mind. 'You could become the Judith Exner of New York politics.'" Nathan, according to Rothenberg, said he had had no idea that Kramer was going to go to the media.

But it wasn't just Kramer. In the summer of 1987, reporters began calling press secretary George Arzt with questions about the mayor's sexuality, many having been allegedly fed stories from an IRS agent named Tony Lombardi, who worked for Giuliani and sought as much information on Koch as he could muster. At first, it was a mystery, several prominent city journalists, out of the blue, contacting the press office to ask about the same Koch rumor. Arzt would eventually put together the reality—that the Southern District's office was giving these stories to reporters hoping there would be enough to go public with the Nathan-Koch relationship. (When stories alleging that his SDNY office had made attempts to smear Koch emerged in 1993, Giuliani called them "baseless" and "disgusting.") Rickman, who agreed to cooperate with the Myerson investigation, began meeting with Lombardi in June, and subsequently, with lawyers from Giuliani's office. Arzt recalled that Rickman came back from questioning in the Myerson investigation one afternoon and said, "Boy, they tell me that the Mayor had better watch out because reporters are calling them about reports about the Mayor's sex life."

"Rickman," Arzt said, "what are you talking about? They're the ones putting it out."

"Oh, no they aren't. They're really nice people."

Exasperated, Arzt remembers thinking, "Herb, you're an idiot."

The investigation into Myerson dragged into the early fall. Myerson, Judge Gabel, and Andy Capasso were eventually acquitted, with Giuliani's office taking heavy criticism for its ham-handed prosecution of Myerson and Gabel—Giuliani had Judge Gabel's daughter tape conversations with her own mother, causing public outrage. But on August 6, six days after he sent his testy letter to Hornblower, Koch was scheduled to attend a *New York Post* forum on AIDS, and that had Koch nervous. The as-yet unreported stories about Nathan were spooking him even more than the actual stories about city corruption had. Koch was nervous about what might happen if an audience member—who knows, maybe Larry Kramer himself—shouted something about Richard Nathan or the rumors that Koch was gay. Koch was seated with his aides on his way to the *Post* forum, and blurted out, "I am not a homosexual. I am not a homosexual." Once he arrived at the forum, and it was clear the audience was focused and attentive, Koch was his usual self. Koch graded himself well, saying he was told "that my presentation, with humor and feistiness coupled with an obvious familiarity with the facts, was well-received."

But back in the car after the *Post* forum and headed to Harlem for another event, Koch did not feel well. He had suffered through the weight of the past year: the Parking Violations Bureau, the string of scandals that followed, the Howard Beach incident, the bitter contretemps with Donald Trump, his disappointment in Myerson and concern about what she might reveal about him. But the rumors about Richard Nathan and what they could mean for him must have been a breaking point. Nathan had told friends Koch was not good to him when their relationship ended. In the 2009 film *Outrage*, the trustee of Nathan's estate said, "Ed had made it impossible for him to work in New York. No instance of homophobia hurt [Nathan] more than the treatment by the man he was in love with." Might Nathan act out of vengeance? Koch was lightheaded. Suddenly, he was struggling to speak clearly. "I think I'm having a stroke," he said. With that, the car turned and sped to Lenox Hill Hospital. Koch had been correct in his diagnosis. The mayor of New York was having a stroke.

As it turned out, Koch had a spasm in an artery in his brain, making his stroke relatively mild. When he was recuperating, his doctors termed it a "tiny, trivial" stroke, to which Koch retorted, "Trivial to you!" Koch took six days of convalescence, and was back on the job, as his doctors recommended. One doctor even declared, "As far as we can tell, he is ostentatiously healthy." But as small as the stroke might have been, it did represent a turning point for Koch, a sort of psychic break from the rolling scandals that had consumed him and his administration. When he returned to the office, he was reinvented, even if slightly. He took up a restrictive diet, cutting far back on salt, sugar, and fats, no easy proposition for a guy who prided himself on his knowledge of food and familiarity with the best cheap restaurants in the city. His beleaguered chef, Mitchel London, said the diet change would be a significant difficulty for both the mayor and for him: "You are talking to someone who is unfamiliar with low-calorie anything." If Koch needed some purification of the body, he also understood he needed a little soul cleansing. Koch took a more religious posture, replacing the sign on his desk with the lyrics of the Catholic hymn "Be Not Afraid," appropriate for a man who had just had a taxing year: "If you pass through raging waters in the sea, you shall not drown. If you walk amid the burning flames, you shall not be harmed." Koch also announced that he would be writing a book with his friend, Cardinal John O'Connor, called *His Eminence and Hizzoner*. Koch appeared on a Channel 13 show called *Open Mind* in which he reflected on his own death, saying he would like O'Connor to officiate his funeral and to have it at Temple Emanu-El. He talked about the difficulty of the past eighteen months, saying, "The trauma was awful. May even have contributed, who knows, to my so-called trivial stroke: the anger, the feelings that I was having. I don't know." He added that he thought his health scare had caused New Yorkers to reassess their feelings on him, and that the stroke had been a "coda" to the city's scandal-ridden year-and-a-half.

But his poll numbers had crashed too hard, his approval rating dropping into the 30s. Koch never fully soothed the racial mistrust after Howard Beach and, the following year, when commenting on Jesse Jackson's chances in the presidential race, Koch said Jews would have to be "crazy" to vote for Jackson because of his views on Israel. It was a senseless attack on Koch's part and crushed any chance he had at repairing his connections with black leaders. Koch would lose the 1989 Democratic primary to Manhattan Borough President David Dinkins, who would face off against Giuliani—Stanley Friedman was right, he really was looking to run for mayor—on the Republican ticket. For those in the administration, there was almost a sense of relief that Koch had lost. His third term had been a grind on everyone. A fourth might have been worse. New York was already weary of Ed Koch's show, a legacy that might not be able to escape his giveaways to the grand plans of builders and the persistence of the third-term municipal scandals. As historian Robert Caro said of Koch in 1987, "The physical transformation of a city changes it for generations, for centuries. I see a city being cemented into place against the sky—a city of monstrous buildings, with a disregard for human scale, human values. Koch is building a big city, not a great one. The Koch administration, I fear, will go down in history surrounded by shadows, the shadow of corruption and the shadows cast by enormous buildings."

Koch worried about his legacy as it became clearer a fourth term would be a longshot. But more than protecting how history would remember him, Koch found that being out of office was a moribund prospect. He had protected his private life so fiercely he hardly had a private life by 1989. There would be no more press conferences. No one would care about his views on foreign policy, his thoughts on the best recipes, his anecdotes about encounters with Mother Teresa or Prince

Charles. He would not be booked on talk shows. If he had a grand pronouncement to make, who would listen?

"Oh, it was terrible," former deputy mayor Stanley Brezenoff said. "I mean, he has a family. There's his brother and sister. And he has his friends who he's known for years, but—when he goes home at night, it's just him. And there are many times when that's a good thing. When you're grateful that you're alone—but there are others I think where it would be really supportive to have somebody there."

49

IT WAS A HOT FRIDAY in August 1987, and it was clear that most who had been sticking around for pretrial proceedings on the unlawful gifts and bribery case to be presented against Rep. Mario Biaggi and former Brooklyn Democratic Party leader Meade Esposito at Brooklyn's Federal District Court would rather be elsewhere. The defense and prosecution, along with Judge Jack Weinstein and gathered reporters, were listening to the tapes that provided the heart of the evidence in response to a defense motion to test the audibility of the recordings. But most of the tapes being played did not reveal much—at least, they did not reveal a conspiracy in which Esposito lavished free vacations on the congressman in exchange for help drumming up federal business for one of Esposito's struggling clients, the bankrupt ship repair company Coastal Dry Dock. Biaggi had a high-profile public relations agent, Morty Matz, working on his behalf, and while the congressman had a big set of problems developing in another case with his ties to a corrupt Bronx defense contractor, Wedtech, Matz had been working the local media into downplaying the charges involving Coastal, saying federal investigators had little to go on and were conducting a malicious prosecution. Prosecutors were keeping their case private and had no opportunity to respond to Matz in the media, an upper hand in public perception for Biaggi and Esposito. In the early stages of the playing of the tapes, there was reason to believe Matz was right. Many of the reporters left before all tapes were played, to get a jump on the weekend. One who stayed, though, was Jerry Capeci of the *New York Daily News*. He was rewarded. One of the last tapes played was the bumbling interchange between Biaggi and Esposito on June 2 of the previous year, just before the wire on Esposito was taken down. That tape tied the whole case together, and showed an attempt by Biaggi to obstruct justice by coordinating his lies with Esposito. Before the playing of the tapes, Capeci had been asking lead prosecutor Ed McDonald about the shakiness of the case. "This case is so weak, maybe you made a mistake?" he had asked McDonald. After hearing the Esposito-Biaggi exchange, Capeci approached McDonald with a knowing smile. "You son of a bitch," he said to McDonald. "You got them."

The charges against Esposito, even if he were found guilty on all counts, came with light sentences—six-figure fines, but only a maximum of two years in jail on one count and five years on another—that did not match the offenses likely committed in his long career as a political hustler and fixer of judges, mayors, governors, and presidents. During one conversation with Biaggi, Esposito could be heard saying he "put 42 judges in Brooklyn," implying he still had the ability to manipulate those judges. McDonald felt that Esposito should be prosecuted on whatever case could be mustered. Esposito was eighty and retired from his post as the Brooklyn party leader, but his behavior had been that of a man who was neither old nor retired. "He was still getting calls from public officials, and ordering them to meet him for lunch the next day," McDonald said. "And they would." The tapes showed that, other than the nuts-and-bolts work of running the Democrats in Brooklyn, Esposito had kept doing much of what he had been doing when he was county leader. He still wielded enormous influence, he still could get powerful figures around the city to meet with him at his beloved Foffe's whenever he needed a favor, he still could line his own pockets. It was Esposito who, ten years earlier, gave Ed Koch his tacit approval as a mayoral candidate in the meatball meeting at his mother's house, vaulting Koch into office. He had not lost his sway. "He was still dealing with Koch," McDonald said. In his opening statement at trial, McDonald called him "an old deal-maker who expected something in return for everything he does."

During the nine days at trial, Biaggi took the stand to defend himself, but Esposito, unlike Stanley Friedman in the PVB case, declined to testify. In fact, he barely paid attention, and frequently dozed off right in the courtroom. That did not mean he did not speak, though. Throughout his presentation of evidence, McDonald heard Esposito's thick, gravelly voice from the defense table, speaking loud enough for prosecutors to hear him, but out of earshot of the jury. "Boring," Esposito would drone. "This is so *fucking* boring." Initially, a puzzled McDonald looked over at the defense table, first at Esposito then at one of his lawyers, Robert Zito, Esposito's grandson, who could do nothing but shrug apologetically. Much like the playing of the tapes, the case presented by McDonald was cryptic in its early stages, though presented some insight on Esposito's view of city politics. Discussing the late 1985 push-and-pull between Donald Manes and Friedman over who would head the City Council (Sam Horwitz made a late run at eventual winner Peter Vallone), Esposito told Biaggi that Friedman "may go along with, uh, with, uh, that guy in Queens, you know, who's a lying bastard. You know that? Donny Manes?" When Biaggi said he knew Manes, Esposito laughed and said, "He never told the truth in his life. Stanley knows it." There was some irony, too, packed into the tapes. At one point, Biaggi told Esposito he had heard that Brooklyn politicians were under surveillance and being wiretapped. "They always have been," Esposito said, as he was being wiretapped.

The case built to those final June 2, 1986 tapes in which the corrupt bargain between Biaggi and Esposito became clear. On September 22, after sixteen hours of deliberation, the jury returned to give its verdict, with Biaggi eagerly seated at the defense table and Esposito calmly chomping on an empty cigarette holder. The first three charges came back not guilty, and McDonald worried. But he got guilty verdicts on the fourth through the seventh charges and could finally sigh, relieved. One juror told reporters after the trial, "The last tape got them." Esposito would proclaim victory when he hit the courthouse stairs, suggesting his innocence on the first counts somehow meant, "I am not corrupt." But McDonald knew better. Returning to his office, one of his colleagues had brought champagne. He even took a congratulatory call from his Southern District antagonist, Rudy Giuliani. Looking back, he was still thankful for that final conversation between Biaggi and Esposito. "I would like to say that my courtroom brilliance dazzled the jury and won a very weak case," McDonald said, "but the fact of the matter is, that one tape, the obstruction tape, laid out the whole case."

The conviction of Esposito, even on relatively light charges, had enormous consequences, politically and symbolically. He had spent fourteen years running the Democrats in Brooklyn, and was the third pillar of support in the outer-borough Democratic machine that had bolstered Ed Koch into the mayor's chair in 1977 and kept him there for another two terms, and profited wildly and illegally under his watch. By the fall of 1987, though, Queens' Manes was dead, the Bronx's Friedman was off to prison, and Brooklyn's Esposito, too, was a convict (he would avoid jail time, but was fined $500,000). The foundation of New York's political system, the Board of Estimate (which comprised the mayor, the comptroller, and the City Council president, with the five borough presidents) was facing a legal attack it would not survive. The Board did not have the ability to pass laws, but it had even more important uses—it approved city contracts and made decisions about land use and water rates—that made it far more powerful than the City Council. It was also found to be an illegal arrangement by the Supreme Court, because it represented a violation of the principle of one person, one vote and gave too much power to less populated outer borough presidents. By the end of the 1980s, the Board of Estimate was dead, and along with it, the authority of outer borough influence peddlers like Esposito, Manes, and Friedman.

"Koch sold out the city to the gangsters," Jimmy Breslin would later say. "You know—the first day when Koch went to Meade Esposito's house and made a deal. They got the Transportation Department and the Parking Violations Bureau and cable and all the rest of it. Koch didn't even know what the hell they were talking about. He didn't care, as long as he could go around and be the Mayor. Before that, nobody let

Esposito and those guys in. I mean, Esposito could make judges and do things like that, but he never had a run like this. And once it gets bad at the top, it gets worse at the bottom.

"It's just part of the general lawlessness of the times. And the greed, yes."

50

By the end of the second full week of October 1987, there was some grim feeling around the American economy. Investors had been riding a five-year bull market that peaked in August, when the Dow Jones index finished at a record 2,722, but the past few weeks had presented what the *New York Times* dubbed an "October Massacre." There were already concerns about inflation, and the Commerce Department released a sobering report showing that the country's trade deficit in August had hit $15.7 billion, an all-time high. The market had a record plunge of 95 points on the fourteenth, a Wednesday, followed by a 57-point drop on Thursday. It had shed 367 points since its high mark, but there was hope Friday would offer a bit of a recovery heading into the weekend. That was quickly dashed—the market set another record on Friday, dropping 108 points. On Wall Street and across the globe, the mood was skittish coming out of the weekend. By 8:00 p.m. in New York on Sunday, the first of the world markets was opening on the other side of the globe. The Nikkei in Japan dropped 2.3 percent—modest but significant. More troubling was Hong Kong, more closely tied to American stocks, where the market fell by 11.1 percent and officials closed trading for the rest of the week. By the time 9:00 a.m. hit on Wall Street, it was mid-afternoon in London, where the *Financial Times*'s index was already in a mid-afternoon swoon, and would close down 10.1 percent. "I keep thinking about the little man with the sign saying The End of The World is Nigh," one London broker said.

In New York, the Dow Jones was down 67 points at the opening bell. By 11:00 a.m., that was 200 points. There was a mid-afternoon rally that cut losses 150, but by 1:00 p.m., the drop was back to 185 points. At just after 1:00, the head of the Securities and Exchange Commission, David Ruder, told reporters he had not discussed a shutdown of the market with anyone else in government, but added, "anything is possible." For traders, the part about not discussing a closing was ignored, and the focus landed on Ruder saying it was possible. That created an added wave of panic, and the market shed another 100 points as big-ticket money managers sought to ensure they could cut their losses before the federal government ordered the market closed. Treasury Secretary James Baker was in Germany at the time, leaving the administration without a spokesman who could take charge of the freefall. Instead, the White House put out a statement saying talks with leading investors "confirm our view that the underlying economy remains sound." All over the next day's newspapers, that statement was repeated for its similarity to what Herbert Hoover had said during the last major stock market drop, which had led to the Great Depression. "The fundamental business of the country," Hoover had said, "that is production and distribution of commodities, is on a sound and prosperous basis." The worst news for stocks came in the final hour of trading. The market—fueled, in part, by automated trades brought on by the introduction of computers into the trading system—was reduced to ashes, losing an additional 200 points. By the time it was over, the market was down 508 points, or 22.6 percent of its value. Americans had lost $500 billion in a single day, and were now at $1 trillion in losses going back to the August market peak. "This is chaos," one investment services executive said. "Every market in the world is in a panic or close to it."

Across the globe, the wartime-font headlines told the story. The *Australian*: BLACK MONDAY CRASH. The *Daily News*: PANIC! The *L.A. Times*: BEDLAM ON WALL ST. The *London Times*: WALL STREET'S BLACKEST HOURS. The *Chicago Sun-Times*: WALL ST. PANIC. The *New York Post*: WALL ST. BLOODBATH. *Time* magazine: THE CRASH. *Le Quotidien* (Paris): LE CRASH. *Newsweek*: AFTER THE CRASH.

Donald Trump claimed to have escaped trouble with the plunging market (which was not entirely true; he had sold some of his market holdings, but not all). He told the *Times*, "Premonition, luck, call it what you want, I had very negative instincts about the stock market, a feeling that things were not going well for the country. So I got out." Ed Koch speculated that the market crash could tank the New York economy, as the financial sector laid off the employees who had been fueling the city's boom in disposable income. During his tenure as mayor, the total number of employees in New York's financial sector had grown from 77,000 to 157,000. "I am concerned for New York City," he said. His reaction to the crash was to freeze fifty-two hundred planned city hires, and delay raises for four thousand managers. For most of New York, though, there may have been some relief in the crash, some sense that the spike in stocks had been a fantasy anyway, foisted on the country by crooks and liars. Now, maybe, people of grit and substance could get back a measure of control over the nonsense that the 1980s had given them: faceless traders making tens of millions by simply pushing around paper; powerful politicians, some of whom had never even appeared on a ballot, ripping off city money by the thousands; a mayor who had been either powerless or unwilling (or both) to stop them, and powerless to cope with the city's big-picture problems, like AIDS and homelessness and crime; real-estate moguls who crowded city blocks with garish superstructures and demanded eight-figure city tax breaks to fund them; Mafia figures who controlled whole swaths of industries—concrete, garments, waste management—in Manhattan and the outer boroughs, dipping their fingers in New York's collective till. The '80s were not over in October 1987, but maybe the crash could, somehow, bring an end to the decade's unsightly underbelly.

On the day of the market crash, the *Times* roamed the city for man-on the-street interviews, and asked one for his thoughts on the crash. Perhaps fittingly, his line of work—a fundraiser for the New York Public Library—could not have been much farther removed from the grime of politics or Wall Street. And he had the hopeful idea that maybe some good can come out of a crash. That idea might not have lasted long, but it is the kind of impulse that can allow people to maintain their goodwill and sanity even after bearing witness to a decade of wanton public rapacity.

"I was walking down the street," the man, Harold Snedkof, said, "and I was wondering whether I would see people jumping out of windows. Then you realize that nothing is different. But maybe all this will make people serious about real problems, like how to cure AIDS. Maybe it will take the excessive greed out of things, for a while."

NOTES ON SOURCES

Part I

1.

The account of the Stanley Friedman and Roy Cohn operation to prevent an adjournment and secure a tax abatement for Donald Trump comes from my interview with former *New York Post* court reporter Hal Davis, as well as from the *New York Times* coverage of the case. The back-and-forth between Ed Koch and Trump is recounted in Koch's book, *Mayor*. The portrait of Friedman, Donald Manes, and Meade Esposito as Democratic power brokers comes from *New York Times* stories from August 3, 1980, and January 27, 1986 (for Friedman and Manes), and Esposito's background comes from my interview with federal prosecutor Ed McDonald, from the testimony of Rep. Mario Biaggi in front of the House Ethics Committee, and from the book, *I, Koch*. The Koch–Jimmy Carter dynamic can be found in an article by Hendrik Hertzberg in the *New Yorker*, in the February 1, 2013 issue, as well as *The Autobiography of Roy Cohn*.

2.

Comments from Bill Conlin and Bill Veeck on the Pittsburgh drug trials can be found in The Sporting News, March 17, 1986 and October 14, 1985 editions, respectively. The account of Bernie Carbo considering using Mafia ties to injure Keith Hernandez was in the May 13, 2010 edition of the *New York Post*. Harry Carson's recollections of his early days with Lawrence Taylor come from my interview with him, as well as his autobiography, *Captain for Life*, and reports in the New York papers. Taylor told of his drug-test dodges in his book, *LT: Over the Edge*. Sources for details on Taylor's problems with crime figures and drugs: *Washington Post*, April 6, 1986; *The Sporting News*, March 3, 1986; *Sports Illustrated*, January 26, 1987.

Background on Dwight Gooden and his dominant 1985 season comes from *Sports Illustrated*, September 2, 1985, feature story, as well as *SI* writer Tom Verducci's 2015 story about Gooden's 1985 season, "The Summer of Doc." Roger Angell's view on Gooden appeared in the *New Yorker* on December 9, 1985. Details of Gooden's boredom at home in Tampa as a young man come from his autobiography, *Doc*.

3.

The meeting between Donald Trump and *Times* writer Ira Berkow was recalled to me by Berkow. Trump's failed dealings with Shula are told in the book *Rozelle: Czar of the NFL*, by Jeff Davis. The story of the USFL lawsuit press conference comes from my interview with Ira Silverman. Details about the unveiling of plans for Trump's domed stadium in Queens come from the *New York Times* and *Trump: The Greatest Show on Earth*, by Wayne Barrett.

4.

The murder of Paul Castellano is recounted from multiple sources, including Selwyn Raab's *Five Families*, *Boss of Bosses* by Andris Kurins and Joe O'Brien, *Underboss* by Peter Maas, and *Gotti: Rise and Fall* by Jerry Capeci and Gene Mustain, as well as my interviews with G. Robert Blakey, Ed McDonald, and Michael Chertoff, and contemporaneous accounts from the *Times*, *Post*, and *Daily News*. The same sources, as well as transcripts from the Mafia Commission trial, were used in recounting dialogue from the various law enforcement bugs. Tom Monaster's recollection of photographing the bodies of Castellano and Tom Bilotti are from his video on StreetSmartVideo.com.

5.

Donald Manes's speech in front of the Queens Borough Hall was detailed in the December 18, 1985, edition of the *New York Daily News*. Manes's "Primaries are for *goyim*" quote is from *New York* magazine, March 31, 1986. Details about the Koch-Manes relationship are from the *New Yorker*, March 31, 1986. The background of Bernie Sandow comes from a January 19, 1986, article in the *Daily News*, as well as *City for Sale*, by Wayne Barrett and Jack Newfield. Accounts of the interaction between Geoffrey Lindenauer and Manes came out during the trial of Stanley Friedman. Ed McDonald's background comes from my interview with McDonald, and details about Meade Esposito's control of judges (April 15, 1988) and his retirement (January 25, 1984) are from the *New York Times*. Conversations between Esposito and Mario Biaggi are recounted in the report on Biaggi's hearing in front of the House Ethics Committee, dated February 18, 1988.

6.

Sources are noted in the text, except for quotes from Raymond Horton of the Citizens Budget Commission, which are from *Time* magazine, November 30, 1987.

Part II

7.

Ed Koch's inauguration details are from the *New York Times* and *Post*, January 2, 1986. Accounts of Koch's relationship with the media are from my interview with former *Post* columnist and Koch press secretary George Arzt, as well as from Joyce Purnick's 1994 interview on file at Columbia University's Rare Book Library, as part of the Edward I. Koch Oral History Project. David Garth's description of Koch comes from the April 11, 1988 issue of *New York* magazine. Rudy Giuliani's thoughts at the Koch inauguration come from the January 5, 1987 issue of the *New Yorker*.

Observations about Donald Manes's deteriorating condition come from Peter Vallone's book, Learning to Govern, and from Matty Troy's interview in the April 11, 1988 issue of New York. The transcript of the dispatcher conversation about Manes comes from the Daily News, on January 15, 1986. Descriptions of Manes's disappearance come from the Times, Daily News, and Post. Purnick's quote about Manes comes from the transcript of her interview with Columbia's Koch Oral History Project. Arzt told me of his memory of his conversation with Mario Biaggi in an interview. Stanley Brezenoff's recollection of Manes's anger over the line of succession at the Parking Violations Bureau is also on file in a transcript at Columbia University's Rare Book Library, as part of the Edward I. Koch Oral History Project. An account from People magazine about Koch and Manes appeared on March 31, 1986. Breslin and Dowd's interaction, as well as Dowd's connection to the Mario Cuomo campaign and his personal fears about retribution, can be found in the Daily News from January 24, 1986 and in *City for Sale*.

8.

The story of the impact of the playoff loss to the Bears on Bill Parcells comes from my interview with writer Jerry Izenberg, as well as Izenberg's book, *No Medals for Trying*, and Parcells's autobiography, *Parcells: Autobiography of the Biggest Giant of Them All*, with Mike Lupica. The account of Taylor's behavior at the end of the game comes from the *Chicago Tribune*, on January 7, 1986. Quotes about the Giants' involvement with drug testing come from the *Village Voice*, February 25, 1986, and the *Daily News*, January 29, 1986. Taylor's stay in detox is told in his book, *LT: Over the Edge*.

9.

John Lindsay's reluctance to go on camera and apologize comes from my interview with Richard Aurelio. Meade Esposito's insistence on keeping Anthony Ameruso in the Koch administration appeared in I, Koch, and the details about Koch convening advisers and hoping to avoid "schmuckism" come from the February 17, 1986 issue of *New York* magazine and the February 25, 1986 *New York Times*. Ed Koch's story about Stanley Friedman's power in the Bronx was told in Koch's book, *Politics*, and the quote about Friedman and Koch was in the March 16, 1986 issue of the *Village Voice*.

10

The account of Hess's interactions with Ed Koch and Mario Cuomo can be found in the books, *Hess: The Last Oil Baron*, by Tina Davis and Jessica Resnick-Ault; *Trump: The Greatest Show on Earth*; *Gang Green* by Gerald Eskenazi; as well as the February 5–7, 1986 issues of the *New York Times*.

A *Washington Post* feature on Roy Cohn from December 22, 1985, featured his quotes about the New York Bar, and details of his interview with Mike Wallace can be found in the March 30, 1986 edition of *60 Minutes*. Two stories from *Vanity Fair*, one by David Lloyd Marcus in August 1987 and the other by Marie Brenner in September 1990, also discussed Cohn's final days. The assertion that Cohn said Trump "pisses ice water" appeared in the April 14, 2017 edition of the *New Yorker*. The two differing accounts of Trump's March 1 Mar-a-Lago party attended by Cohn appear in *Citizen Cohn*, by Nicholas von Hoffman, and in Wayne Barrett's *Trump: The Greatest Show on Earth*.

11.

A full version of the 1986 Inner Circle production can be found at: youtube.com/watch?v=-L7yIlAJYyg.

Accounts of the Robert Morgenthau–Rudy Giuliani conflict can be found in the *New Yorker*, April 28, 1986, as well as the *New York Times*, March 12, 1986. The possible link between Donald Manes and the Mafia is told in the May 6, 1986 issue of *New York*. The details of Manes's suicide come from contemporaneous reports in the *Times*, *Daily News*, and *Post*, as well as *City for Sale*.

Ed Koch's visit to Antun's for the St. Patrick's Day event is detailed in the *New Yorker*, March 31, 1986, and his visit to the Manes funeral comes from the same, as well as the *New York Times* on March 18, 1986, *City for Sale*, and the book *Ed Koch and the Rebuilding of New York City* by Jonathan Soffer. David Garth's sentiments after Manes's suicide appeared in *New York* on March 31, 1986. Details of Stanley Friedman's background and his arraignment are from the *Times* on December 24, 1974, and March 28, 1986, and from the *Washington Post* on March 28, 1986.

12.

Accounts of the Mets' spring training, and of Gooden's struggles there, can be found in the *Village Voice* (April 8, 1986), the *New York Times* (April 7, 1986), *Sports Illustrated* (April 14, 1986), and *The Sporting News* (April 14, 1986), which also has the account of Gooden missing the spring game in Bradenton. Dick Young's column on Gooden is from the April 8, 1986 edition of the *Post*. Frank Cashen's quote about Gooden's inexperience comes from the *New York Times*, April 14, 1986, and the Gooden incident at LaGuardia Airport can be found in the *L.A. Times* (April 17, 1986) and *The Sporting News* (April 28, 1986).

13.

Information on the USFL vs. NFL trial comes from my interview with Mike Janofsky. Harry Usher's quote about the future of the league comes from the *Washington Post*, May 15, 1986, and details about Harvey Myerson's troubles are from *Time* magazine, June 29, 2001, and the book *Shark Tank*, by Kim Isaac Eisler. Accounts of Pete Rozelle on the witness stand are from the *New York Times*, May 18, 1986, as well as the May 20, 1986 issue of the *Washington Post* and the book *Rozelle: Czar of the NFL*. Donald Trump's interview about the small amount of money needed to get into the USFL is from the Associated Press, February 24, 1985.

14.

The fate of Cubs manager Jim Frey is outlined in The Sporting News, April 28, 1986. The quote from the Phillies about the Mets is from *Sports Illustrated*, October 6, 1986.

Part III

15.

The murder of Frank DeCicco was covered in the *New York Times*, *Post*, and *Daily News*, and details here come from the book *Gaspipe*, by Philip Carlo, and *Chin: The Life and Crimes of Mafia Boss Vincent Gigante*, by Larry McShane. Some details are from my interview with Bob Blakey. John Gotti's job with Arc Plumbing, the contract the company had with the city, and the proximity of the company owner to Donald Manes comes from the *Village Voice*, April 8, 1986, *New York* magazine, June 23, 1986, and the *New Yorker*, April 28, 1986.

Details of Rudy Giuliani and Sen. Al D'Amato's undercover drug "sting" come from an interview with former city official Jay Kriegel, as well as the *Daily News* and *New York Times* from July 10–12, 1986. Ed Koch's plans to combat the drug trade can be found in the *Times* and his quote about "T.S." in relation to the seizing of passenger jets are from the *Daily News*, July 6, 1986.

16.

Jimmy Breslin's column about his disappointment in Mel Lebetkin appeared on January 21, 1987. The quote about Breslin being able to "quote Camus or Teilhard de Chardin without losing his stool at Kennedy's" is from the foreword of his book, *The World According to Breslin*. The account of Breslin's day in Queens with Margot Hornblower comes from my interview with Margot Roosevelt, Teddy Roosevelt's great-granddaughter, who had gone by Margot Hornblower when working for the *Post*. Accounts of the three Democratic fundraisers in May 1986 are from the *Times* as well as the July 2, 1986 issue of the *New Yorker*.

Details on Roy Cohn come from my interview with Margot Roosevelt and from the book *Never Enough: Donald Trump and the Pursuit of Success*, by Michael D'Antonio. The feud between Ed Koch and Larry Kramer comes from the *New Yorker*, May 13, 2002, as well as an interview Kramer did with the show *Frontline*, which can be found on PBS. com. The story of the memos between Koch and an aide on AIDS hospice care comes from GayCityNews.com.

17.

Background on the discovery of Donald Trump's letter in the USFL lawsuit trial comes from my interview with Mike Janofsky, and the article he wrote in the *Times* on June 8, 1986. More of the negative publicity for the USFL appeared in *The Sporting News*, on June 23, 1986. The optimism for the USFL's chances of victory from Will McDonough appeared in the *Boston Globe*, June 22, 1986. From Bill Nack, it appeared in the July 7, 1986 *Sports Illustrated*. Janofsky also discussed Trump's testimony, and an account of Trump on the stand also appeared in *Rozelle: Czar of the NFL*.

18.

Background on Mario Biaggi and the relationship between Biaggi and Meade Esposito comes from former Brooklyn US prosecutor Ed McDonald, and the story about Biaggi being forced out of the 1973 race for mayor comes from Roy Cohn, as told to Sidney Zion in Cohn's autobiography. The wording of the Biaggi-Esposito conversation comes from the 1988 House Ethics Report on Biaggi.

19.

Wellington Mara's quote about the relevance of Howard Cosell's testimony in the USFL trial comes from the *New York Times*, June 25, 1986.

Cosell's own review of his testimony comes from *Sports Illustrated*, July 7, 1986. Jerry Izenberg's recollection of Cosell's testimony comes from my interview with him.

20.

Rick Rhoden's background comes from his biography compiled by the Society of American Baseball Research. His quarrel with the Mets appears in the June 7, 1986 issue of the *Pittsburgh Post-Gazette*. A story about the Mets' brawling ways comes from *The Sporting News*, June 9, 1986, and details of the fight against the Dodgers were in the *L.A. Times*, on May 28, 1986. The fight in Cincinnati was detailed in *The Sporting News* on August 11, 1986, and in the *Cincinnati Enquirer*, July 23, 1986. Phil Garner's quote comes from an interview he did with Marty Noble of MLB.com, at mlb.com/news/article/22122490.

For the Mets' trip to Houston, some details come from my interview with Ira Berkow as well as the article he wrote for the *New York Times* on October 11, 1986. The details of the Cooter's incident come largely from the *Houston Chronicle*, July 20–22, 1986, but also from the *Times*, *Daily News*, and *Post* on those dates. For the Cincinnati fight, Ray Knight's struggle with booing in New York comes from the March 26, 1986 *Times*, and the brawl itself is covered in the *Cincinnati Enquirer* on July 23 and 24, 1986, as well as *Sports Illustrated* and *The Sporting News* on August 4, 1986.

21.

Extensive coverage of the Fourth of July weekend in New York City was given by *Time* magazine (July 13, 1986) and *Newsweek* (July 14, 1986), as well as daily coverage from the *Daily News*, *Post*, and *Times* ranging from July 1 through July 7, 1986.

22.

The *Chicago Tribune* reported on Ron Darling's *GQ* interview on August 3, 1986, and *Sports Illustrated* did an in-depth story on the Mets' pitching on August 25, 1986, in which Davey Johnson discussed his experiences as a position player in Baltimore and his relationship to the Orioles' pitching greats. Johnson's ignorance of the book he supposedly authored himself comes from the *Village Voice*, May 20, 1986. George Foster's comments on the Mets' racial attitude are from *The Sporting News*, August 18, 1986, and Knight's defense of Foster is from the August 8, 1986 edition of the *New York Times*.

23.

Accounts from the conclusion of the USFL trial come from my interview with Mike Janofsky; the books *Rozelle: Czar of the NFL* and *Rozelle: A Biography* by Jerry Izenberg; the *Boston Globe* and *New York Times* of July 30 and 31, 1986; and Charley Steiner's quote is from *Vanity Fair*, January 13, 2016.

24.

Harry Carson background information comes from my interview with Carson, and from his book, *Captain for Life*. Teammates' view of Carson comes from the *Washington Post*, January 21, 1987. Carson's quote, "You find out you're human," comes from the *New York Times* from July 27, 1986. Notes from the Giants opener of the 1986 season come from the *Post*, *Times*, *Newsday*, and *Daily News* of September 7–9, 1986. Parcells's showing of the game tape comes from the *Times* on September 15, 1986. Carson described the racist letter he had received after Week 1 in my interview with him, and his quote following the Chargers win is from the *New York Post*, September 15, 1986.

25.

Blakey's description of his background and his involvement in the development of the RICO statute comes from my interview with him. Ed McDonald described Rudy Giuliani's ambition in an interview. The lieutenant's description of Carmine Galante as "pure steel" is from the *New York Times*, February 20, 1977. The details of building a case against the Mafia Commission for the murder of Galante were given to me in my interview with Michael Chertoff, with background coming from contemporaneous accounts (in the *Times, Post,* and *Daily News*) of the Commission trial as well as the books *Five Families* and *Busting the Mob: The United States v. Cosa Nostra,* by James B. Jacobs. The *New York Post* headline (GREED!) appeared on July 13, 1979.

26.

The history of the early days of the New York Mets comes from Jimmy Breslin's book, *Can't Anybody Here Play This Game?* Darryl Strawberry's account of his background is given in his autobiography, *Straw: Finding My Way,* as well as the book, *High and Tight: The Rise and Fall of Dwight Gooden and Darryl Strawberry* by former Mets beat writer Bob Klapisch. Dick Young's column on the booing of Strawberry appeared in the *New York Post* on September 11, 1986. Strawberry's quotes on his frustration with being singled out for booing come from the *New York Times,* September 1, 1986. The accounts of the Mets' clinching of the National League East come from the *New York Post* and *Daily News,* September 18 and 19, 1986.

Mike Scott's development of the split-finger fastball under Roger Craig was described in a *Sports Illustrated* feature from October 20, 1986. The Astros' clinching details are from the *Houston Chronicle,* September 26, 1986.

27.

The relationship between Tom Puccio and Rudy Giuliani is described in Puccio's autobiography, *In the Name of the Law.* Ed McDonald, in an interview, provided additional details, and Michael Chertoff told me about Giuliani choosing to try the Stanley Friedman case rather than the Commission case. The quote from Giuliani's assistant, David Zornow, appeared in the *New York Times* on December 10, 2007, and additional details about the decision to move the case to New Haven, Connecticut, come from *City for Sale.* The lurid details of Donald Manes's sex life also appear in *City for Sale,* and are part of the trial record in the Stanley Friedman case. The description of Giuliani's ambition and his willingness to speak to any group comes from Puccio's book, *In the*

Name of the Law, and the *Washington Post*, June 20, 1986. Ray Kerrison's column describing Puccio's style as a lawyer is from October 1, 1986, in the *New York Post*, and the description of the opening statements of Puccio and Giuliani is from the *New York Times*, October 1, 1986.

28.

Michael Chertoff detailed his strategy in building the Commission case to me in an interview. The view of him from author Scott Turow appeared in the *Harvard Law Bulletin*, Summer 2005 edition. Ed Koch joked about the Concrete Club in the January 12, 1986 edition of the *New York Daily News*. Contemporaneous accounts of the trial come from the *Washington Post*, September 19, 1986; the *L.A. Times*, September 26, 1986; the *New York Times*, September 19 and 20, 1986; and *Time* magazine, September 29, 1986.

29.

The origins of the Astrodome come from Roger Angell's May 14, 1966 article in the *New Yorker*. Both Gene Tenace's description of playing in the Dome and Ray Knight's objection to the lack of respect the Mets got are in the October 8, 1986 edition of the *New York Post*. Umpire Doug Harvey discussing the mind games played around Mike Scott's split-finger appeared in the October 14, 1986 edition of the *Post*. Quotes from Hal Lanier (on pitching Scott in Game Four) and Lenny Dykstra (on his home run) are from the *New York Times*, October 12, 1986. Dave Smith's quote about a death threat from a machine gun appeared in Jerry Izenberg's book, *The Greatest Game Ever Played*. Additional details are taken from *One Pitch Away: The Players' Stories of the 1986 LCS and World Series*, by Mike Sowell.

30.

The accounts of Geoffrey Lindenauer's testimony come from contemporaneous newspaper (the *New York Times*, *Post*, *Daily News*, and *Newsday*) stories taken from the trial transcripts, from Puccio's book, *In the Name of the Law*, and from *City for Sale*. Ed Koch's thoughts on the trial, and his inclusion in some of the evidence, comes from the *Times* and *Post*, October 4 and 10, 1986. The atmosphere around City Hall was described in my interview with George Arzt, then of the *Post*, and the *Times* story on the paralysis of the Koch administration came on October 9, 1986. Felix Rohatyn's quote about the lack of response to corruption from the public appeared in the *Times* on November 16, 1986. Stanley Friedman's testimony is detailed in *In the Name of the Law* and *City for Sale* as well as the *New York Times*, November 12, 1986 edition.

31.

Bob Knepper's background is described in his Society of American Baseball Research biography, an article about him in the September 21, 1981 edition of *Sports Illustrated*, and the *Houston Chronicle* from October 15, 1986. Bob Ojeda discussed the cortisone shots he had had during the 1986 playoffs in an article he wrote for the *Times* magazine on May 26, 2012. Accounts of Game Six come from the *New York Times*, the *Houston Chronicle,* the *Boston Globe*, and the *New York Post* from October 16 and 17, 1986. Additional background comes from my interview with Jerry Izenberg and from his book, *The Greatest Game Ever Played.*

Part V

32.

My interview with Michael Chertoff provided much of the information on Carmine Persico, with additional quotes from the *Washington Post*, September 19, 1986, *Time* magazine, September 29, 1986, and *People*, November 3, 1986. *Five Families* by Selwyn Raab and *Busting the Mob* by James B. Jacobs provided additional details on the trial transcripts and tapes. Ed McDonald described the mundane nature of the Paul Castellano tapes in my interview with him.

33.

The account of the Mets–Red Sox September exhibition can be found in the *Boston Globe*, September 5, 1986, and Dwight Gooden's quote about Roger Clemens is in the New York Times, July 15, 1986. Oil Can Boyd's summer travails are told, from his perspective, in his book *They Call Me Oil Can*, with Mike Shalin. Cashen discussed the Mets' infamous Game Six plane ride in his book *Winning in Both Leagues*, and an account was also in *The Sporting News*, October 27, 1986. Quotes from Dwight Gooden and Wally Backman about the flight come from *High and Tight* by Bob Klapisch. Quotes from Ron Darling on the lackluster fans at Shea Stadium and from Davey Johnson about Ray Knight are from the *New York Post*, October 20, 1986.

34.

Phil Simms's quotes about New York fans are from the September 29, 1986 edition of *Sports Illustrated*, and his quotes about his 1983 injury are from the *New York Times*, October 11, 1983. Harry Carson's quotes about Simms are from *The Sporting News*, January 27, 1987. Simms's insistence on not leaving the Chargers game in Week 2 comes from Jerry Barca's book, *Big Blue Wrecking Crew: Smashmouth Football, a Little Bit of Crazy, and the '86 Super Bowl Champion New York Giants*. Stories from the Giants' Week 4 win over the Saints come from the *Times* and *Post*, September 29, 1986.

35.

Andy Warhol's recollections about Donald and Ivana Trump are recorded in *The Andy Warhol Diaries*. Susan Mulcahy's story about her interaction with Trump comes from her book *My Lips are Sealed: Confessions of a Gossip Columnist*. Bob Sansavere's conversation with "John Barron" comes from my interview with Sansavere, Paul Zimmerman's call to Trump comes from his book, Dr. Z: The Lost Memoirs of an Irreverent Football Writer. The account of Dave Anderson talking with Trump comes from interviews with Anderson and Ira Berkow.

Details about the failed attempts to revamp the Wollman Rink, and the involvement of Arc Plumbing, come from the *Village Voice*, April 8, 1986, and the *New York Times*, June 17, 1986 and November 21, 1986. Ed Koch's thoughts on Trump come from my interview with George Arzt and Koch's book, *Citizen Koch*. Quotes from Henry Stern come from the *New York Times*, November 15 and 21, 1986.

36.

Marty Barrett's thoughts on playing in the World Series come from the *Boston Globe*, October 20, 1986. Keith Hernandez's quote is from *The Sporting News*, October 20, 1986. Oil Can Boyd's press conference quotes are from the *Globe* on October 21, 1986, and Bill Robinson's quotes on Darryl Strawberry were from the *New York Post* on October 22, 1986. Gary Carter's press conference quote is from the *Post* on October 23, 1986. Accounts and quotes about and from Dwight Gooden in Game Five come from the *Times*, October 24, 1986, and the *Post*, October 29, 1986. Lyle Spencer's story on Bill Buckner was in the *Post* on October 24, 1986.

Michael Sergio's landing during Game Six was recounted in *Sports Illustrated*, October 9, 1989. John McNamara's version of what happened in the game appeared on NESN.com, on November 8, 2011. Darryl Strawberry's irritation with Davey Johnson comes from the *New York Post* on October 27, 1986. Frank Cashen's whereabouts during Game Six are told in his book *Winning in Both Leagues*, and Bob Costas's recollections are in the book *I Was There!* compiled by Eric Mirlis. Quotes from Knight are from the *Times*, *Post*, and *Globe*, October 26, 1986.

37.

Stanley Friedman's quote about "the system" is from the *New York Times*, November 12, 1986, and his subsequent quote about Giuliani is from the *Times* on November 9. The *Times* also reported on Judge Knapp's advice to William Schwartz (November 22, 1986), and Giuliani's characterization of Friedman comes from *New York* magazine, April 11, 1988. Accounts of the lawyers' summations come from the *Times* on November

20 and 21, as well as Puccio's book, *In the Name of the Law*, which is also the source for Stanley Friedman's criticism of Giuliani's gloves.

Quotes on the financial scandals of late 1986 come from the *New Yorker* (on Marty Siegel) in the March 11, 1991 issue, and from *New York* magazine (on Giuliani's overzealousness), September 4, 1989.

38.

The account of the Mafia Commission trial comes from my interview with Michael Chertoff, with details added from Selwyn Raab's *Five Families*, and *The Mafia Encyclopedia* by Carl Sifakis. The text of Chertoff's summation can be found in *Busting the Mob*. The quote from Gennaro Angiulo about RICO is from *United States v. Cintolo*, provided by Robert Blakey. His quotes to close the chapter are from our interview.

39.

The story of Ira Berkow's ride with Ron Darling was told to me in my interview with Berkow, and his column about Darling appeared in the *New York Times* on October 27, 1986. Oil Can Boyd's reactions to being pulled from Game Seven appear in his book *They Call Me Oil Can*. Details from the series in general come from Peter Gammons's *Sports Illustrated* article in the April 6, 1987 issue. Stories from the *Post*, *Globe*, and *Times*, as well as video footage of the games, were used to construct the game accounts. Ed Koch's thoughts on the Mets were from an editorial he wrote on October 19, 1986, in the *Times*.

Accounts of the Giants' game against the Redskins on the night of Game Seven come from interviews with Harry Carson and Joe Jacoby, as well as the October 28, 1986 edition of the *New York Post*.

Part VI

40.

Bill Parcells's quote about the 1986 draft is from the *New York Times* on May 1, 1986. Michael Katz's discussion with Parcells is from January

13, 1987, in the *Daily News*. Jerry Izenberg's recollection about Parcells's press conferences come from my interview with him. Pat Hodgson's quotes about Phil Simms are from the *Times*, November 5, 1986, and Bobby Johnson's discussion of his crack addiction are from Jerry Barca's *Big Blue Wrecking Crew*. Quotes on the way the Eagles handled Lawrence Taylor are from the *Philadelphia Inquirer*, October 13 and November 9, 1986. Parcells's discussion of Simms's plight as quarterback of the Giants are from *Sports Illustrated* (December 15, 1986) and *New York* magazine (January 26, 1987). Kenny Hill's quote about Simms is from the *Minneapolis Star-Tribune* on November 17, 1986. The recounting of the Giants' fourth-down play against the Vikings and Simms's quotes on his style come from *New York* magazine, as well as the *Daily News*, January 26, 1987.

41.

Dwight Gooden's interview with the *Tampa Tribune* appeared on November 11, 1986. The fight between Gooden and the Tampa police was detailed in the *Tribune* from December 14 through December 21, with the incident warranting front-page coverage, as well as Bob Klapisch's book, *High and Tight*, and Dwight Gooden's autobiography, *Doc*.

42.

Ed Koch's conversation with Charles Rangel is available in an online video, *Sydenham 2015*, at the LaGuardia and Wagner Archives of the City University of New York. Details on Koch's trouble with the black community come from *New York* magazine, April 11, 1988 (Major Owens's quote), as well as the *Amsterdam News* and the *New Yorker* from February 9, 1987. The meeting between city officials and black leaders was told in the *New York Times* on January 1, 1987. Additional details about Koch's handling of the Howard Beach incident come from my interview with George Arzt, Koch's press secretary.

43.

The golf tournament conversation between Joe Jacoby and Lawrence Taylor is from my interview with Jacoby. Bill Belichick's comments on Taylor are from *Sports Illustrated*, January 26, 1987, and Jacoby's assessment of his bad game against the Giants were from the *Washington Post*, January 8, 1987. Parcells's certainty that the Giants would play the Redskins comes from the *New York Daily News* on January 6, 1987. The Giants' problems with Washington's Dexter Manley, and his odd behavior, are covered in the *Washington Post* and *Daily News* from January 6, 1987.

44.

George Arzt told me about the relationship between Ed Koch and Rudy Giuliani in our interview, and details from Giuliani's exploration of Koch's sex life were included in Wayne Barrett's book, *Rudy! An Investigative Biography of Rudy Giuliani*. Koch maintained his stance on his sexuality until his death, including in the 2013 documentary, *Koch*. Koch's interview on CNN with Howard Kurtz is recounted at www.papermag.com/ed-koch-tells-us-how-were-doin-1425144412.html.

45.

Quotes about Ed Koch's refusal to host a parade for the Giants come from the *New York Daily News* and *Times* on January 12 and 13, 1987. Harry Carson's recollection of the coin toss at Super Bowl XXI was told to me in my interview with him. Notes and quotes about the game come from the *New York Post*, *Daily News*, *Times*, and *Washington Post* from January 25 through January 27, 1987. Jerry Izenberg's quote about the Mets and Giants comes from my interview with him.

46.

Frank Cashen's letters to his players were discussed in *The Sporting News*, March 2, 1987. Gooden's actions at spring training in 1987 come from his autobiography, *Doc*, as well as *High and Tight*, and *The Sporting News*. Bill Parcells's observations on Gooden's arrival at rehab are recounted in his autobiography, *Parcells: Autobiography of the Biggest Giant of Them All*. Lawrence Taylor's quotes come from an article in *Politico*, September 18, 2013. Quotes from Davey Johnson and Dwight Gooden come from *Sports Illustrated*, February 27, 1995.

47.

The beginning of Donald Trump's propensity to refer to himself in the third person comes from Harry Hurt's *Lost Tycoon: The Many Lives of Donald J. Trump*. Details of Trump's original plans for the Lincoln West site come from the *New York Times*, November 19, 1985. Quotes about Trump come from the *New York Times* (September 27, 1987) and *Time* magazine (January 16, 1989). Details of Trump's interaction with the city on behalf of his Television City project come from Wayne Barrett's book, *Trump: The Greatest Show on Earth*. The Trump-Koch feud was detailed in the *New York Times*, May 29, 1987, as well as the *New Yorker*, June 15, 1987. Tony Schwartz told the *New Yorker* about his interaction with Trump when he wrote *The Art of the Deal* in the July 25, 2016 edition. The account of Trump's dabbling in politics come from the *New York Times* and *Washington Post* on September 2, 1987, and his financial fall is outlined in *Vanity Fair*, September 1990. The quote about his tax returns comes from *New York* on July 13, 1987.

48.

Ed Koch's letter to Margot Hornblower (now Roosevelt) was provided to me by her. Ed Koch's 1987 self-reflections come from the *New Yorker*, April 27, 1987 and September 14, 1987, as well as the *Washington Post*, August 26, 1987. David Rothenberg's recollection about Richard Nathan comes from his book *Fortune in My Eyes: A Memoir of Broadway Glamour, Social Justice, and Political Passion*. George Arzt's recollection of his conversation with Herb Rickman comes from my interview with Arzt, and details of Rudy Giuliani's investigation into Koch's sexuality are in Wayne Barrett's *Rudy! An Investigative Biography of Rudy Giuliani*. Koch's reaction to his stroke is told in the *New Yorker*, September 14, 1987. Robert Caro's view on the city under Koch was given in *Time* magazine, November 30, 1987. Stanley Brezenoff's assessment of Koch in retirement was given in his interview with the Edward I. Koch Oral History Project, at Columbia University's Rare Book Library.

49.

The account of the trial of Meade Esposito and Mario Biaggi comes from my interview with Ed McDonald, as well as the *New York Times*, September 1 and 23, 1987. Jimmy Breslin's quote about Koch appeared in *New York* on April 11, 1988.

50.

Stories about the stock market crash of 1987 are from the *New York Times* and *Washington Post*, October 20 and 21, 1987, as well as *Time* magazine, November 2, 1987. The book *Crash: Ten Days in October*, by Avner Arbel and Albert E. Kaff, provided additional details.

Bibliography

Oral History Interviews from Columbia University's Butler Library

Reminiscences of Joyce Purnick, 1994, *Edward I. Koch Administration Oral History Project*, Columbia Center for Oral History Archives, Rare Book & Manuscript Library, Columbia University in the City of New York.

Reminiscences of George Arzt, 1995, *Edward I. Koch Administration Oral History Project*, Columbia Center for Oral History Archives, Rare Book & Manuscript Library, Columbia University in the City of New York.

Reminiscences of Stanley Brezenoff, 1992, *Edward I. Koch Administration Oral History Project*, Columbia Center for Oral History Archives, Rare Book & Manuscript Library, Columbia University in the City of New York.

Books

Arbel, Avner and Albert E. Kaff. *Crash: Ten Days in October.* New York: Longman Financial Services, 1989.

Auletta, Ken. *The Streets Were Paved with Gold.* New York: Random House, 1975.

Barca, Jerry. *Big Blue Wrecking Crew.* New York: St. Martin's Press, 2016.

Barrett, Wayne. *Rudy! An Investigative Biography of Rudolph Giuliani.* New York: Basic Books, 2000.

———. *Trump: The Greatest Show on Earth.* New York: Regan Arts, 2016.

Berkow, Ira. *Giants Among Men: Y.A., L.T., Big Tuna and Other New York Giants Stories.* Chicago: Triumph Books, 2015.

Bonanno, Joseph. *A Man of Honor.* New York: Simon & Schuster, 1983.

Boyd, Dennis and Mike Shalin. *They Call Me Oil Can.* Chicago: Triumph, 2012.

Breslin, Jimmy. *The World According to Breslin.* New York: Open Road Media, 2012.

———. *Can't Anybody Here Play This Game?* New York: Viking Press, 1963.

Browne, Arthur; Collins, Dan; and Goodwin, Michael. *I, Koch: A Decidedly Unauthorized Biography of the Mayor of New York City, Edward I. Koch.* New York: Dodd, Mead & Co., 1985.

Burt, Jim and Hank Gola. *Hard Nose: The Story of the 1986 Giants.* Harcourt Brace Jovanovich, 1987.

Byrne, Jim. *The $1 League.* New York: Prentice Hall, 1986.

Capeci, Jerry and Gene Mustain. *Gotti: Rise and Fall.* New York: Onyx, 1996.

Carlo, Philip. *Gaspipe: Confessions of a Mafia Boss.* New York: William Morrow, 2008.

Carson, Harry. *Captain for Life.* New York: St. Martin's Press, 2011.

Cashen, J. Frank. *Winning in Both Leagues.* Lincoln, Nebraska: University of Nebraska Press, 2014.

D'Antonio, Michael. *Never Enough: Donald Trump and the Pursuit of Success.* New York: Thomas Dunne Books, 2015.

Darling, Ron, and Daniel Paisner. *Game 7, 1986: Failure and Triumph in the Biggest Game of My Life*. New York: St. Martin's, 2016.

Davis, Jeff. *Rozelle, Czar of the NFL*. New York: McGraw-Hill, 2008.

Davis, Tina, and Jessica Resnick-Ault. *Hess: The Last Oil Baron*. Hoboken, New Jersey: John Wiley & Sons, Inc., 2016.

Eisler, Kim Isaac. *Shark Tank: Greed, Politics, and the Collapse of Finley Kumble, One of America's Largest Law Firms*. Washington DC: Beard Books, 1990.

Eskenazi, Gerald. *Gang Green: An Irreverent Look Behind the Scenes at Thirty-Eight (Well, Thirty-Seven) Seasons of New York Jets Football Futility*. New York: Simon & Schuster, 1998.

Fadiman, Mark. *Rebuilding Wall Street*. Eaglewood Cliffs, New Jersey: Prentice Hall, 1992.

Fitch, Robert. *The Assassination of New York*. New York: Verso, 1993.

Franceschini, Remo. *A Matter of Honor: One Cop's Lifelong Pursuit of John Gotti and the Mob*. New York: Simon & Schuster, 1993.

Frankfort, Ellen. *The Voice: Life at the Village Voice*. New York: Morrow, 1976.

Giuliani, Rudolph and Ken Kurson. *Leadership*. New York: Hyperion, 2002.

Gooden, Dwight and Ellis Henican. *Doc: A Memoir by Dwight Gooden*. Boston: Houghton Mifflin Harcourt, 2013.

Gooden, Dwight and Richard Woodley. *Rookie: The Story of my First year in the Major Leagues*. Garden City, New York: Doubleday & Co., 1985.

Hurt, Harry. *Lost Tycoon: The Many Lives of Donald J. Trump*. Brattleboro, Vermont: Echo Point Books, 2016.

Izenberg, Jerry. *Rozelle*. Lincoln, Nebraska: University of Nebraska Press, 2014.

———. *"No Medals for Trying": A Week in the Life of a Pro Football Team*. New York: Macmillan, 1990.

———. *The Greatest Game Ever Played*. New York: Henry Holt & Co., 1987.

Jacobs, James; Parnella, Christopher; & Worthington, Jay. *Busting the Mob: United States v. Cosa Nostra.* New York: New York University Press, 1994.

Klapisch, Bob. *High and Tight: The Rise and Fall of Dwight Gooden and Darryl Strawberry.* New York: Villard, 1996.

Koch, Edward I. *Mayor: An Autobiography.* New York: Simon & Schuster, 1984.

———. *Politics.* New York: Simon & Schuster, 1985.

Koch, Edward I. and Daniel Paisner. *Citizen Koch.* New York: St. Martin's Press, 1992.

———. *I'm Not Done Yet! Keeping at It, Remaining Relevant, and Having the Time of My Life.* New York: William Morrow & Company, 2000.

Maas, Peter. *Underboss: Sammy the Bull Gravano's Story of Life in the Mafia.* New York: HarperCollins, 1997.

Maier, Thomas. *Newhouse: All the Glitter, Power & Glory of America's Richest Media Empire & the Secretive Man Behind It.* Boulder, Colorado: Johnson Books, 1994.

McConkey, Phil; Simms, Phil with Dick Schaap. *Simms to McConkey: Blood, Sweat and Gatorade.* New York: Crown, 1987.

McShane, Larry. *Chin: The Life and Crimes of Mafia Boss Vincent Gigante.* New York: Kensington, 2016.

Mirlis, Eric. *I Was There! Joe Buck, Bob Costas, Jim Nantz and More Relive the Most Exciting Sporting Events of Their Lives.* New York: Sports Publishing, 2016.

Mulcahy, Susan. *My Lips are Sealed: Confessions of a Gossip Columnist.* New York: Doubleday, 1988.

Newfield, Jack and Wayne Barrett. *City for Sale: Ed Koch and the Betrayal of New York.* New York: Harper & Row, 1988.

O'Brien, Joseph and Andris Kurins. *Boss of Bosses: The FBI and Paul Castellano.* New York: Dell Publishing, 1991.

O'Brien, Timothy L. *TrumpNation: The Art of Being The Donald.* New York: Grand Central Publishing, 2005.

O'Donnell, John and James Rutherford. *Trumped! The Inside Story of the Real Donald Trump—His Cunning Rise and Spectacular Fall.* New York: Simon & Schuster, 1991.

Parcells, Bill with Mike Lupica. *Parcells: Autobiography of the Biggest Giant of Them All.* New York: Bonus Books, 1987.

Parcells, Bill and Nunyo Demasio. *Parcells: A Football Life.* New York: Crown Archetype, 2014.

Pearlman, Jeff. *The Bad Guys Won: A Season of Brawling, Boozing, Bimbo Chasing, and Championship Baseball.* New York: HarperCollins, 2004.

Pistone, Joseph and Charles Brandt. *Donnie Brasco: Unfinished Business.* Philadelphia: Running Press, 2008.

Preston, Jennifer. *Queen Bess: An Unauthorized Biography of Bess Myerson.* Chicago: Contemporary Books, 1990.

Puccio, Thomas P. and Dan Collins. *In the Name of the Law: Confessions of a Trial Lawyer.* New York: W.W. Norton & Company, 1995.

Raab, Selwyn. *The Five Families: The Rise, Decline, and Resurgence of America's Most Powerful Mafia Empires.* New York: Thomas Dunne Books, 2005.

Reeths, Paul. *The United States Football League, 1982-86.* Jefferson, North Carolina: McFarland & Company, Inc. 2017.

Rothenberg, David. *Fortune in My Eyes: A Memoir of Broadway Glamour, Social Justice, and Political Passion.* Milwaukee: Applause Theatre & Cinema Books, 2012.

Sherman, Erik. *Kings of Queens: Life Beyond Baseball with the '86 Mets.* New York: Berkley Books, 2016.

Sifakis, Carl. *The Mafia Encyclopedia.* New York: Facts on File, Inc. 1987.

Silverman, Matthew. *One-Year Dynasty: Inside the Rise and Fall of the 1986 Mets, Baseball's Impossible One-and-Done Champions.* Guilford, Connecticut: Roman & Littlefield, 2016.

Sobel, Robert. *Panic on Wall Street: A History of America's Financial Disasters.* Washington DC: Beard Books, 1999.

Soffer, Jonathan. *Ed Koch and the Rebuilding of New York City*. New York: Columbia University Press, 2010.

Sowell, Mike. *One Pitch Away: The Players' Stories of the 1986 LCS and World Series*. South Orange, New Jersey: Summer Game Books, 1995.

Stewart, James B. *Den of Thieves*. New York: Simon & Schuster, 1992.

Strawberry, Darryl and John Strausbaugh. *Straw: Finding My Way*. New York: Ecco, 2009.

Taylor, Lawrence with Steve Serby. *LT: Over the Edge*. New York: HarperCollins, 2003.

Taylor, Lawrence with William Wyatt. *Lawrence Taylor: My Giant Life*. Chicago: Triumph, 2016.

Trump, Donald with Tony Schwartz. *The Art of the Deal*. New York: Random House, 1987.

Trump, Donald J. and Charles Leerhsen. *Trump: Surviving at the Top*. New York: Random House, 1990.

Vallone, Peter F. *Learning to Govern: My Life in New York Politics, from Hell Gate to City Hall*. New York: Chaucer Press, 2005.

Von Hoffman, Nicholas. *Citizen Cohn*. New York: Doubleday, 1988.

Warhol, Andy and Pat Hackett (ed.). *The Andy Warhol Diaries*. New York: Hatchette Book Group, 1989.

Zimmerman, Paul. *Dr. Z: The Lost Memoirs of an Irreverent Football Writer*. Chicago: Triumph Books, 2017.

Zion, Sidney. *The Autobiography of Roy Cohn*. Secaucus, New Jersey: Lyle Stuart, Inc. 1988.

Index